DEATH
OF A
REPUBLIC

DEATH

POLITICS AND POLITICAL THOUGHT
AT ROME 59–44 B.C.

Edited and with an Introduction

by George Lee Haskins
PROFESSOR OF LAW
AT THE UNIVERSITY OF PENNSYLVANIA

OF A ▨▨▨▨▨▨▨▨▨▨▨
REPUBLIC

JOHN DICKINSON
LATE PROFESSOR OF LAW
AT THE UNIVERSITY OF PENNSYLVANIA

The Macmillan Company, New York
Collier-Macmillan Limited, London

© George L. Haskins 1963

First Printing

The Macmillan Company, New York
Collier-Macmillan Canada, Ltd., Toronto, Ontario
DIVISIONS OF THE CROWELL-COLLIER PUBLISHING COMPANY

Printed in the United States of America

Library of Congress catalog card number: 63-9336
DESIGNED BY CHRISTIAN OHSER

13577

Contents

Contents

Preface

It has been said that the history of Rome is, in a certain sense, the history of the world, that, as all roads lead to Rome, so all history ends or begins with Rome. That the late John Dickinson would have agreed with this observation cannot be doubted. At the time of his death in April, 1952, he had been at work for a number of years, first as a member of the Law Faculty at the University of Pennsylvania and later while Vice President-General Counsel of the Pennsylvania Railroad, on a massive history of Roman political thought and institutions. The writing had been substantially completed for the period from the founding of the republic through the age of Augustus and amounted to some three thousand manuscript pages. It is a work of immense scholarship, reflecting Mr. Dickinson's prodigious knowledge and understanding of history, law, and political science. Solidly grounded on original sources, both archaeological and literary, it reveals his detailed knowledge of modern works and special studies not only in English but in Italian, French, and German. Its originality lies in the fresh analysis and new interpretations given to known facts by a man trained in history, law, and jurisprudence, who was almost as much at home in Roman law as in the Anglo-American system.

This great undertaking grew out of Mr. Dickinson's thinking about the basis and relationship of law and political authority, first reflected in a series of articles published in learned journals a number of years ago. Present-day problems in that area, he believed, cannot be investigated to any considerable degree by statistical techniques but require historical analysis accompanied by perceptive observation of recognizable uniformities in the patterns of human behavior. Impressed by how small a portion of the human race has ever known any kind of government in which the voice or interests of the common man had any determining part, he was drawn to a study of those states which had experienced popular government. With but one exception, until modern times, even the history of western Europe is illumined by only intermittent flashes of freedom, and that exception was the Roman republic, which provides an enduring example of stable popular government that lasted over four centuries. Inevitably, as a constitutional lawyer and as a student of politics and political science, Mr. Dickinson became deeply absorbed in the development of the Roman constitution, with the reasons for its success and the causes of its fall. Of particular interest to him was the light that the gradual extinction of constitutional government at Rome sheds upon the conditions that are hospitable to political freedom on the one hand and to absolutism on the other. The antithesis of government by law and government by popular will he saw vividly illustrated in the fall of the republic and recognized its special importance because the issue has been a perennial one in the history of Western political thought. This importance he constantly underscored in his writings and addresses. For example, in an address before the Virginia State Bar Association in 1943, he remarked that Rome was one of the few states in which over a long period of time government has been a help rather than a hindrance to the progress of ordinary civilized living, a steady and dependable source of protection for individual effort and accomplishment rather than a disturbing factor that interrupts, deflects and defeats those efforts and minimizes their results.

Partly for reasons of personal friendship, partly because of my familiarity with and interest in the subject matter of the work, it was Mr. Dickinson's wish that the manuscript be turned over to me for revision and publication after his death. Unfortunately, it has not proven feasible to arrange for publication of more than a small portion of the entire work. With the concurrence of his widow, Mrs. Lula Martin Dickinson, it was decided to publish those chapters which cover the years 59 to 44 B.C., in many ways the most crucial period in the fall of the republic, and which Mr. Dickinson himself regarded as his most significant contribution to Roman history and

political thought because of the evaluation therein of the antithetical
political philosophies of Cicero and Caesar, appearing as Chapters
6 and 7 of this book. Mrs. Dickinson's interest and generous support
has made printing and publication possible.

It is no easy task for an Editor to excerpt a few hundred pages
out of a coherent whole and remake them into a work that will
stand as a unit by itself. The last five of the seven chapters that com-
prise Parts II and III of the book are entirely the work of Mr.
Dickinson, revised only insofar as appeared necessary. At the express request of Mrs. Dickinson, minimal revision has been made
in Chapters 6 and 7. The first two chapters of Parts II and III
are a combination of portions of earlier chapters of his manuscript,
rearranged and recast by the Editor so as to give the work a more
definite beginning. However, they entirely reflect Mr. Dickinson's
own analysis and conclusions. Part I has been written by the Editor
and is designed to provide, first, a necessary introduction through a
summary of Roman political institutions as they had developed up
to the year 59 B.C. and, second, an abbreviated account of the course
of the Roman revolution from the year 133 B.C. Although I assume
responsibility for the authorship of Part I, I believe that Mr. Dickinson would have welcomed its inclusion and agreed with the conclusions therein contained and expressed, particularly since I have
felt free to draw, when appropriate, upon his own conclusions expressed elsewhere in the manuscript.

I am responsible for the title of the book, *Death of a Republic,*
as well as for the divisions into Parts and Chapters, and for the
headings and titles thereof. In the course of revision I have altered
Mr. Dickinson's text as little as possible. The facts, analysis and conclusions are entirely his; sentences and paragraph structure have
been revised or deleted only to the extent necessary for clarity and
cohesion. All footnote references as well as quotations have been
checked and verified. Translations from Greek and Latin authors
are mine or Mr. Dickinson's, except in Chapter 6, where the extensive quotations from Cicero's philosophical works seemed to require the uniformity provided by the conveniently available Loeb
translations of the *De Legibus, De Officiis* and *De Re Publica.* For
permission to use and quote from those translations of these three

works I am indebted to the Harvard University Press. I wish also
to acknowledge the kindness of one law journal and of several publishing houses for permission to quote from works published by
them as follows: the *American Bar Association Journal* for excerpts from an article by Judge John J. Parker appearing in Volume
36 of the *Journal;* the Cambridge University Press for excerpts
from the *Cambridge Ancient History,* Volume IX, and from W. E.
Heitland's *The Roman Republic;* Holt, Rinehart & Winston, Inc. for
excerpts from Tenney Frank's *History of Rome;* the Tweedsmuir
Trustees, A. P. Watt & Son, Houghton Mifflin Co., and Mssrs.
Hodder & Stoughton Ltd., for permission to quote from page 97 of
John Buchan's *Augustus;* W. W. Norton & Co. for excerpts from
the translation of Ortega y Gasset's *Concord and Liberty;* the
University of California Press for excerpts from L. R. Taylor's *Party
Politics in the Age of Caesar.* The American Philological Society has
kindly consented to permit me to quote from L. R. Taylor's *The
Divinity of the Roman Emperor.*

Of those who have read portions of the work before publication
I wish particularly to thank the following: Dr. T. R. S. Broughton,
of the Department of Latin at Bryn Mawr College, for helpful
comments on my introductory Part I; my mother, Mrs. Charles H.
Haskins, for numerous suggestions relating to Parts II and III; Miss
Mary Hutton Warfield, of Bryn Mawr College, for checking sources
and quotations. Such aid and interest have saved me from many
oversights. I wish also to thank John B. Prizer Esq., successor to
Mr. Dickinson as Vice President-General Counsel of the Pennsylvania Railroad, for his continuing interest in the work and for his
constant personal encouragement.

G.L.H.

Philadelphia, September, 1962

List of
Abbreviations

Appian, *Bell. Civ.*	*The Roman History of Appian of Alexandria* (H. White, transl., New York, 1899), Vols. I–II.
Caesar, *Bell. Civ.*	Caesar, *De Bello Civili Commentarii*
Bell. Gall.	Caesar, *De Bello Gallico Commentarii*
Cambridge Ancient History	*The Cambridge Ancient History* (S. A. Cook, F. E. Adcock, M. P. Charlesworth, eds., Cambridge, 1932), Vol. IX.
Cicero, *Att.*	Cicero, *Epistulae ad Atticum.*
Fam.	Cicero, *Epistulae ad Familiares.*
Leg.	Cicero, *De Legibus.*
Off.	Cicero, *De Officiis.*
Q.F.	Cicero, *Epistulae ad Quintum Fratrem.*
Rep.	Cicero, *De Re Publica.*
Ferrero	G. Ferrero, *The Greatness and Decline of Rome* (A. E. Zimmern, transl., New York, 1907), Vols. I–II.
Heitland	W. E. Heitland, *The Roman Republic* (Cambridge, 1923), Vols. I–III.
Long	G. Long, *The Decline of the Roman Republic* (London, 1864–1874), Vols. I–V.
Mommsen	T. Mommsen, *The History of Rome* (W. P. Dickson, transl., New York, 1887), Vols. I–IV.
Plutarch	*Plutarch's Lives* (ed. A. H. Clough, Boston, 1891), Vols. I–V.
Suetonius	Suetonius, *De Vita Caesarum.*

Part ONE

PRELUDE
TO DESTRUCTION

By GEORGE LEE HASKINS

Prelude
to
Destruction

THE history of human government has but little to record of free popular government. Although the Greeks knew democracy for a short span of years, one of the few examples of stable democratic government until modern times is that of Rome at the height of the republican period. Special interest therefore attaches to that era, during which many of the greatest Roman contributions to civilization were made, but the later years of the period are of no less interest because they witnessed the emergence of forces that brought about the gradual erosion and finally the destruction of democratic institutions.

The process of destruction took place during the course of a revolution extending over approximately one hundred years, from 133 B.C. to 31 B.C. The revolution falls into two distinct phases, a first or preparatory phase, from 133 to 79, during which popular excesses and the habit of public disorder became a pronounced feature of the conduct of government, and a second phase, beginning with the abdication of Sulla in 79 and culminating in the Battle of Actium, during which the agonies of the expiring republic filled every land with marching men and carried civil commotion to a pitch that literally tore the world apart. The most crucial years of the second phase of the revolution were those between 59 B.C., when Julius Caesar became consul, and 44 B.C., when he was assassinated.

3

It was in that period that Caesar, more than any one individual, accelerated the course of destruction and brought about the annihilation of republican institutions. The process and the methods by which this result was accomplished afford an instructive case study with respect to the principles upon which democracy and autocracy rest and the circumstances under which they develop and flourish. More importantly, however, the process brings into sharp focus two opposing philosophies of government—constitutionalism and absolutism—which have played a continuing and vital role in the history of Western political thought. In the perennial debate as to whether government should reflect the immediate interests of a ruling class or of an individual, or whether it should reflect abiding principles of law based upon the organic growth of institutions, the opposing ideals of Roman leaders at the end of the republic have continuing significance even in modern times.

That it should have required a hundred years to accomplish the destruction of the republic is a tribute to the toughness of the fiber of its early institutions and the ideals of constitutional government which they embodied; it is also proof of the inherent caution and legalism of the Roman temper, which have left their mark on the thought of succeeding civilizations. The persistence of these ideals and attitudes owes much to the fact that the principal spokesman and champion of republican institutions was Marcus Tullius Cicero, who, through his writings on politics and philosophy, has left an indelible imprint on the subsequent development of political thought.

No adequate understanding of the developments that were initiated by and followed Caesar's consulship in the year 59 is possible without some preliminary account of Roman political institutions as they then existed and of the course that the revolution had taken up to that time. Needless to say, any attempt to describe in short compass the political, social and other institutions of Rome at any given time runs the serious risk of oversimplification and hence of inaccuracy. The social and institutional arrangements of the last century of the republic were the product of innovations and adjustments caused by wars, internal upheavals, the ambitions and opportunities of generals and political leaders, as well as by the impact in Italy of the expanding influence of Rome throughout the Mediterranean world. In the course of over four hundred years, the republican constitution, established upon the expulsion of the kings in 509 B.C., had become, simple though its principles were, an intricate and complex body of technical rules and practices, the accretion of generations of growth and change that reflected a habitual spirit and practice of compromise. Despite their continual modification and obsolescence, ancient institutions had been retained, so that the constitution embodied the gains which had been won by particular groups or leaders of groups and which had become stabilized by custom or express legal enactment rather than by an equilibrium of opposing forces.[1]

Three objectives appear to have actuated the framers of the original republican constitution: the eradication of monarchy without weakening the executive force of government, provision for the more active participation of the citizen body in government, and ensuring that ultimate political power should be in a council of elders known as the senate. Efforts to attain the first objective resulted in assigning the chief authority in the state to two annually elected consuls, who were considered to be the embodiment of kingly power and at the same time the spokesmen of the people in the relationships of the Roman community with gods and men. The early consuls were charged with duties which included the supervision of religious matters bearing on political action, representing the state in its dealings with individuals and other communities, commanding the army, the exercise of criminal and civil jurisdiction, the issuance of edicts and proclamations, the summoning of the senate and assemblies of the people, and the supervision of a variety of administrative matters affecting the welfare of the state.[2]

The extensive, almost regal, powers and responsibilities of the consuls were circumscribed at the outset, and later on as well, and were also subjected to restraints other than those exercised by the people and by the senate. Annual elections were insisted upon to prevent the possibility of an established dynasty, and in time it was specifically provided that reelection could not occur until after an interval of ten years. It also became a settled rule that no one might be consul unless he had held lesser offices in a stipulated sequence known as the *cursus honorum,* with the result that a candidate for the consulship must have attained the age of at least forty-three. As a check upon arbitrary or autocratic power, either consul had the right to enjoin and hence neutralize the acts of his colleague, but neither could enjoin the convoking of the senate. A third limitation was imposed through the periodic creation of further elective magistracies to whom segments of the original consular powers were delegated. Chief among them were the praetors and the quaestors, whose primary duties were, respectively, judicial and financial, and the censors, whose duties included property assessment and supervision of the voting lists. In due course, other consular responsibilities were lodged in additional magistrates, whose functions—frequently duplicative and seldom exactly defined—were expanded or modified, as time went on, to meet the increasing legal, financial and administrative needs of Rome, the Italian peninsula and the provinces. In the first century B.C., all the principal magistracies, including the consulship, were open to men of both plebeian and patrician origin. At that date the consuls were still the chief officers of the state, but the most important of their powers now included the presidency of and the right to convoke the senate and the popular assembly known as the *comitia centuriata,* the right to propose legislation, the power to conduct diplomatic negotiations, and certain extraordinary powers in times of emergency.[3]

Of the later additional magistrates, one in particular, the tribune, requires special comment because of the political importance the office had acquired by the last days of the republic. The tribunes were not magistrates in the strict and original sense of that term, but it has become customary to refer to them as such because by that time their powers so closely resembled those of a magistrate. Moreover, in the contest that developed in those years between the protagonists of republican government and its enemies, the tribunes at times played a more important role than even the consuls. The tribunate had been established very early in the republic for the express purpose of protecting the individual citizen, and particularly the plebeian citizen, from arbitrary action on the part of a magistrate. For this reason it was required by law that a candidate for the office be a member of a plebeian family and that he be elected in the *concilium plebis,* the popular assembly which was regularly presided over by a tribune. At the outset, there seem to have been five tribunes, but in 457 the number was increased to ten. The source of the tribune's power was his right to inflict punishment on a magistrate who took action that he had forbidden; moreover, his person was sacrosanct, and a violation of that immunity was punishable by death without legal process. As a result of this power and this immunity, the tribunes became the chief leaders of the plebeian order in its early struggle with the patricians, and their strength inevitably increased with the growth of the political rights of the plebeian class.[4] However, with the gradual equalization of political rights in those orders, the reason for the office largely disappeared; but their legal powers were not curtailed, so that the tribunate remained a potentially powerful weapon of political action. This was so because well before the first century B.C. the right of the tribune to protect a citizen had been extended in three directions. First, he had acquired the right to thwart any official act of administration through a prohibition directed against a magistrate. Second, from his power to punish a magistrate persisting in a course he had forbidden, the tribune had acquired the further power to prosecute a magistrate for acts and conduct prejudicial to the interests of the state, and he had thus become a public prosecutor in trials of magistrates which were conducted in the *concilium plebis,* over which a tribune presided. Third, he had acquired the right to convoke the senate and to present matters before it for consideration and deliberation. It was the potentiality of the uses and abuses to which these powers might be put that gave the tribunate the overwhelming political importance that it had in the final days of the republic.

The popular or democratic element in the Roman constitution was in the assemblies. Considerable confusion exists in the ancient sources as to the identity and jurisdiction of, and the nomenclature appropriate for, these bodies,[5] but in accordance with the usage and terminology of recent scholarship [6] it may be said that only three had significant institutional importance at the end of the republic —the *comitia centuriata,* the *comitia tributa* and the *concilium plebis.* Although each of these assemblies had certain judicial duties, their chief functions were elective and legislative. The *comitia centuriata* elected the consuls, praetors and censors, the other two the lesser magistrates. Tribunes were always chosen in the *concilium plebis* at elections in which only plebeians could participate. All three assemblies might enact legislation, but by the first century B.C. the *comitia centuriata* was seldom summoned for that purpose,[7] so that the other two had a virtual monopoly of legislation. A principal difference between these latter two assemblies was that a consul or praetor presided over and proposed bills to the *comitia tributa,* whereas the *concilium plebis* met under the presidency of a tribune. From this and other circumstances a further difference appears, namely, that the *comitia tributa* included all citizens, patricians as well as plebeians, whereas the *concilium plebis* was strictly plebeian in its composition.[8] Nevertheless, because of the numerical insignificance of patricians in the last century of the republic, it is not inappropriate to refer to both as the popular or tribal assembly, as is done in the ensuing chapters, since either assembly could enact legislation binding on the whole people. The apparent duplicativeness of function in the assemblies, as in the magistracies, was the consequence of a spirit of legalism which found expression in the typically conservative Roman habit of preserving existing institutions after others had been created as a result of political or other compromises.

The importance and role of the assemblies in the government of Rome cannot be understood without some description of the method of voting. All citizens entitled to vote were assigned to tribes or voting districts, of which there were thirty-five—four urban and thirty-one rural.[9] These arrangements reflected conditions existing in the early days when Rome was a farmer commonwealth and when political power was in the hands of men living within a short distance of the city and assigned to the rural tribes of adjacent districts. As Roman citizenship and territory were extended, new citizens and communities were enrolled in the existing rural tribes, and, as the franchise was enlarged geographically, the voters became widely scattered throughout Italy south of the Po River. The four urban tribes originally consisted of industrial workers in the city, but, although the number assigned to these tribes steadily increased as the urban populace expanded, in principle those tribes still counted for little because they could easily be outvoted by the rural tribes. Members of rural tribes who had moved to or happened to reside in Rome—including senators, wealthy businessmen and small farmers who had given up agricultural life—generally retained their connection with the tribes to which they or their families had originally been assigned, and they continued to vote as members thereof. Membership in a tribe was hereditary, but reassignments for political and other reasons were not uncommon.

In the *comitia centuriata* the tribal vote was so organized as to give principal weight to men of property. Two "centuries" from each of the thirty-five tribes made up a so-called first class of seventy centuries composed of men having property of an approximate value of $2500 or more.[10] Theirs was a weighted vote that counted far more than those of the other four classes of centuries, with the result that the vote of the first class was usually decisive. As long as men of wealth and property tended to be on the side of, and to have close relations with, the nobles and other members of the senatorial class, it was not difficult for the senate to keep the chief magistracies in their own hands and to bar outsiders from the consulship in particular. For the same reason, the senate had an overwhelming influence in the enactment of bills that came before the *comitia centuriata,* as is illustrated by the legislation that brought Cicero back from exile,[11] but the effectiveness of that body was severely curtailed by the fact that considerable effort was required to induce the voters to come to Rome from their homes throughout Italy to attend its meetings.

In the two popular assemblies, the *concilium plebis* and the *comitia tributa,* the voting was not weighted in the same way, and each tribe voted as a unit, regardless of its size. In principle, as stated, the thirty-one votes of the rural tribes gave them a numerical and hence a preponderant advantage over the other four, consisting largely of the urban proletariat; but, again, the distances that most members of the rural tribes had to travel to Rome often impeded the effectiveness of their vote. For election purposes, the tribal assemblies generally met immediately after the *comitia centuriata,* convened usually at the end of July. Such meetings were well attended. However, no bills could be presented in the twenty-four days before the elections, and no vote thereon could be taken until twenty-four days thereafter. By that time, large numbers of the voters of the rural tribes would have returned to their homes in various parts of Italy, and because of the distances they had to travel they were often reluctant to return to Rome between elections unless induced by some personal interest. Consequently, by the first century B.C., the active voters on legislation tended to be the members of the four urban tribes. It was thus frequently advantageous to the sponsors of partisan legislation to introduce it when the latter, consisting largely of the Roman proletariat, constituted the majority of the electorate on hand. Although all tribes had to be represented at meetings of the tribal assemblies, if no member of a rural tribe was present (as not infrequently happened), the presiding officer, generally the tribune, could call upon men of an urban tribe to cast the vote of a rural tribe. Obviously, he would pick those who would vote as he desired, and he thus had an effective means of influencing the fate of a proposed measure. Cicero even refers to a bill that was passed by armed slaves.[12]

The senate began as, and remained throughout the whole republican period, the most vital part of the mechanism of the traditional Roman government. Initially, it had been composed of patricians who were members of the officially recognized clans of prosperous yeoman farmers that constituted the original citizen body, but, at an early date, members of the so-called plebeian class became eligible for admission. By the year 59 B.C., membership in the senate was limited to citizens who had held one of the principal magistracies and who passed automatically into that body at the end of their respective terms of office. At that date, the senate contained approximately six hundred members, many of whom had by then been drawn from the wealthy business class of knights.[13] A senator served for life and received no compensation, so that the position, like that of most of the magistracies, could be held only by a man of means; in fact, certain occupations temporarily or permanently disqualified a citizen for membership.

The officials who could convene and preside over the senate were the consuls, praetors and tribunes. There was no regular time of meeting, and no meeting could take place except at the call of one of them; yet failure to consult the senate on matters on which it customarily gave advice was considered unconstitutional. The presiding officer had substantial constitutional powers. He laid before the group the business to be discussed and then proceeded, following the order of rank, to ask the opinions of individual members. A senator, as he was called upon, would address his colleagues, indicating approval or disapproval of an opinion that had been expressed or of a motion that had been made, or he might address them on a matter entirely alien to the subject under discussion. Because of the procedure of calling on members in order of rank, most senators had no opportunity to speak, so that the controlling voices were those of men of the highest rank, chiefly the ex-consuls who constituted the hereditary nobility. There were no organized parties and no fixed order of business; no minutes were kept, and little use was made of committees. When the discussion was brought to an end, the various proposals were voted upon, and the result, representing the opinion of the majority of the entire group, was set down in writing. The presiding officer could cut off debate when he wished or refuse to put a motion to a vote. More importantly, at any stage in the proceedings, a tribune might interpose his veto on the presiding magistrate and so prevent or nullify senatorial action.

Under these circumstances, it may appear surprising that any business, much less the complex questions that were regularly presented, could be settled in any final and orderly fashion, even at the height of the senate's power. The truth is, however, that there was an extraordinary *esprit de corps* within the senate that resulted in large part from the fact that it was chiefly composed of men of rank and property who had a strong affinity of interest. Nearly all the principal magistrates were elected from the same class through the weighted votes of the centuriate assembly, which the senate largely controlled. Nearly all its members had gone through the *cursus honorum* which prescribed the order in which, and the age at which, office might be held. Hence, as the magistrates passed into the senate at the rate of about twenty a year, they continually strengthened the core of legal and administrative experience within the senatorial order. These magistrates, ruling for a brief annual term, and occupying before and after that term a position in the senate, were bound by every incentive not to antagonize the influential members of their own class, who had been instrumental in bringing about election to office. This was especially true of the consuls and praetors. Until at least the middle of the second century, there was little friction, therefore, between the senate and the magistrates, and there were few occasions for the imposition of the checks, or the use of the safety valves, that law and custom prescribed. Moreover, the rules with respect to the order of speaking, together with an ingrained habit of deference to the opinions of the older men of established reputation and noble extraction, not only meant that the senate exerted a strong influence on the magistrates but provided a leadership within that body that might otherwise have been lacking.

The senate, in theory, was not a legislative body but an advisory council. Hence, a decree of the senate did not stand on the same plane as a law of one of the assemblies, but the senate could prepare a bill and, through a consul, praetor or tribune, cause it to be introduced into one of the assemblies; if it passed, it was binding on the whole people. The senate could also declare a law void if there had been a procedural defect in its enactment. Moreover, it could interpret legislative acts and even extend their application through decrees which were assumed to be valid and approved by the people if no tribune interposed his veto. Hence, despite constitutional theory, the senate in fact participated actively in the legislative process.

Certain types of important business were within the exclusive competence of the senate, notably appropriations of money and the conduct of foreign affairs. In the former sphere, the senate exercised through the power of the purse effective control over numerous aspects of government policy and over generals in the conduct of their campaigns. In the latter sphere, it conducted diplomatic negotiations involving wars and treaties, appointed the provincial governors, reviewed and ratified the acts of conquering generals. In addition, it had power to order the appointment of a dictator and to pass the "last decree," the *senatus consultum ultimum,* whereby it could confer on magistrates extraconstitutional authority in times of grave public danger and emergency.

The sum and substance of Roman constitutional arrangements as they were developed in the first three hundred and fifty years of the republic, and as they still existed at least in form in the first half of the first century, was an elaborate system of checks and balances which depended largely on the existence of a series of veto powers but partly also on the principle of collegiality whereby within the several magistracies one official could neutralize or impede the acts of his fellow. Thus, in theory, the magistrates were dependent on the senate and on the people, the people were dependent on the magistrates and on the senate, and the senate was in turn dependent on the magistrates and on the people.

This is the essence of the frame of government that Polybius described, just before the fatal fissures first became apparent, as "a constitution than which it is impossible to discover a stronger." [14] To that wise Greek statesman there were two causes for its excellence. First, the constitution was not the product of deliberate invention but the result of the slow growth of experience and of time and historical development, so that it was firmly interwoven in the texture of the habits of the community. Second, it was the outstanding example of that "mixed" form of government which Greek political thought had come to regard as essential to hold in check the degenerative tendencies of the simple forms of monarchy, aristocracy and democracy. According to Polybius, each of these forms was represented, respectively, by the consuls, the senate, and the assemblies; but, through the reciprocal checks and balances which existed among the organs representing the principles of these different forms of government, the mixed form, operating in mutual interdependency of all three, exhibited special strength by maintaining an appropriate equilibrium among them.

The existence of these checks and balances helped to keep the Roman constitution in health for a long period, and until the middle of the second century B.C. it functioned well and had enabled Rome to become the foremost power in the civilized world. In principle, the senate and the magistracies were by then open to all, and the assemblies both elected the magistrates and were the ultimate organs for legislation. In practice, however, the administration of government had by then fallen into the hands of the senate. For reasons of self-interest, as stated above, the consuls and other chief magistrates cooperated closely with the senate: they were drawn from its membership and returned to its ranks after their year of office. Since the tribunate was a steppingstone to the magistracies, the tribunes likewise cooperated with the senate, which, in turn, cultivated good relations with them because of their power in the tribal assembly. Like the consuls, therefore, tribunes seldom took the initiative without the concurrence of or instructions from the senate. Moreover the latter body, consisting as it did of ex-magistrates after the Ovinian Law,[15] had a prestige and expertise in administration that peculiarly fitted it for providing continuity and consistency of policy and for settling the difficult and intricate problems of foreign affairs which overshadowed domestic questions during the third and second centuries and in which the general populace took little interest. For these reasons the senate rather than the assemblies ruled Rome, an oligarchy governing in the name of democracy.

The potential weakness in the hegemony of the senate's rule was, of course, its lack of legal power to control the magistrates, the tribunes, and the assemblies. The basis of its rule, in the last analysis, was the respect it commanded. Its constitutional authority was advisory, and its advice might be ignored. The consuls might act independently, or a tribune might cease to be its spokesman and not only interpose a veto but take a hostile stand in the assembly. Opposition to the existing arrangements, or the use of any of the legal checks on official action, could therefore quickly disrupt the functioning of the system that had developed.

At least as early as the middle of the second century B.C., there were increasing signs of dissatisfaction with senatorial government. A number of circumstances had combined to bring this about. Composed though it was of men of both patrician and plebeian descent, the senate had become an oligarchic class, divided within itself into groups that were ranked according to the public offices which had been held. Families whose members had held the consulship formed the most important group within the senate, and these constituted a small and conservative hereditary nobility of patricians and plebeians who directed governmental policy and largely controlled the selection of the principal magistrates who ran for office.[16] Outsiders were excluded from this inner circle, which had a monopoly of office and power and which had become steadily less responsive to new interests pressing for recognition and to new problems demanding solution. Long wars had disrupted agriculture and displaced independent cultivators, the government had lost interest in the development of domestic trade and industry, and the cities now teemed with the unemployed, with aliens and with manumitted slaves. These and other emergent forces were gathering strength and were in the process of transforming radically the Romans' way of life, their habits, attitudes, beliefs and interests, and in the long run they were to have a decisive effect on their institutions. Of the problems engendered by the vast changes that were taking place in the structure of their society most Romans, particularly those in power, seemed hardly aware.

Of the economic changes that took place in the second century few are more striking than the sudden and progressive increase in wealth. The conquests of the Mediterranean world had resulted in huge inpourings of indemnities, tribute levies and other payments from conquered and friendly states. Commanding generals accumulated the spoils of war, and governors amassed fortunes from the administration of new provinces. Much of this new wealth which passed into private hands was invested in Italian land and resulted in commercializing agriculture through the accumulation of great estates that were supervised by overseers and manned by cheap and increasingly available slave labor. Against the competition of the new plantations individual proprietors found it difficult to survive. In large numbers, they drifted away to the city to swell the urban proletariat, so that wealthy landowners rather than small farmers became a progressively dominant force in politics. The state, in turn enriched, was embarking upon an extensive program of public works from which a growing business class reaped enormous profits. The newly created provinces afforded Roman citizens vast opportunities to amass fortunes—for officials through bribery and extortion, for capitalists through privileged foreign investment, and for private citizens through tax collecting let out by state contract.

Among other consequences of war and conquest was an influx of foreigners who brought with them from Greek and Eastern lands the culture of highly developed civilizations. This new learning, together with the new wealth that had come to Rome, stimulated interests, tastes and standards which were not only incompatible with the traditional fabric of Roman life but helped to alter the relations between the governing class and the citizen body. At an earlier time, there had existed no unbridged gulf between the people and their leaders. Despite differences of birth and station, all lived the same kind of simple lives, thought in much the same way, and understood one another because they knew one another. This high degree of social cohesion was one reason why the early compromises between the plebeians and patricians had been brought about without leaving any radical bitterness behind. Now, luxury and sensuality were introduced, and these not only created a widening gap between rich and poor but brought about a breakdown of traditional ideas of morality and behavior. The pursuit of riches led the privileged few to cultivate office for the sake of the financial rewards it could bring and hence contributed to a declining sense of civic responsibility as the craving for personal distinction became more alluring than the performance of public duty. For others, the routine of farm life, with its emphasis on steady habits, gave way to idleness and the perpetual quest for the excitements of urban life.

These changes inevitably produced a new atmosphere which quickly affected politics. The Romans' traditional and instinctive passion for order and regularity, for adherence to established patterns of conduct, and their consequent self-discipline and moderation, were undermined. The changed atmosphere helped to breed an unstable and excitable mob spirit among the people and to pave the way for irresponsible demogoguery as a normal feature of political activity. Efforts of old-fashioned Romans, such as Cato the Censor, to check the tide of change through governmental action were essentially battles against symptoms rather than attempts to cope with the harder and more difficult task of dealing intelligently with causes.

The spirit of exclusiveness which had long characterized the senatorial nobility became intensified. Its members failed to heed the growing importance of the business class of knights drawn from the aristocracies of Italian municipalities, even though both groups had fundamentally the same conservative interest in stable and orderly government. The contemptuous snobbishness with which the knights were treated helped to consolidate them and to drive them into an unreasoning opposition to senatorial policy and created, when the opportunity came, a willingness to support and finance the demogogic agitation which became a source of some of the worst evils of the early part of the first century.

In short, the whole tone and organization of Roman society in the second century B.C. had the effect of dividing the state into powerful selfish groups—senators endeavoring to maintain the exclusiveness of their order, the knights intent upon amassing wealth, and the populace eager for government subsidies, free entertainment and the excitements of urban life. So intent was each group on extending its advantages and opportunities that the way was closing to the kind of intelligent and fruitful compromises that had characterized the struggles between the patrician and plebeian orders in the early years of the republic. Concurrently, the insistence of each group on its own privileges and on attaining objectives incompatible with those of the others led to a jealous and suspicious attitude of antagonism always ready to afford a basis for quarrels. The old balance of adjustments was gone, and the eddies of the political currents were enlarging their circumferences into the whirlpools of political revolution.

These conditions provided the impetus for the hundred years' revolution which, if a date may be set for its beginning, started in 133 B.C. In that year, a newly elected tribune, Tiberius Gracchus, introduced before the tribal assembly a land-distribution bill whose purpose was to alleviate the poverty of a large section of the populace. The proposal aroused immediate and violent opposition among wealthy landowners in the senate, and, as class legislation, it inevitably accentuated the antagonisms between rich and poor. This in itself was a serious matter, but the method by which the bill was enacted into law was even more so from a constitutional standpoint. The senate leaders saw that the bill would probably pass, and they accordingly procured its veto by another tribune, Octavius, who was favorable to their position. Gracchus then demanded that either he or Octavius be deposed, in effect demanding that the voters in the assembly should decide whether or not the tribune's constitutional veto should be exercised. Such a demand was entirely inconsistent with existing constitutional arrangements, which did not contemplate the translation of the assembly's will into action in this way. Essentially, it was a demand that direct popular action, on the model of the Greek democracies, be substituted for the system of checks and balances which had been developed at Rome. Once asserted, as it was when the assembly voted to depose Octavius, the principle was in effect a repudiation of the constitutional limitations on the expression of popular will and put the state at the mercy of any temporary popular majority.

The Roman republic was never thereafter free of the threat of this new principle, which, with the organized alignment of the poor against the rich, was the chief legacy which Tiberius left to his successors. Later in the year, in the course of a riotous campaign for reelection, he was murdered. His violent end had far-reaching consequences. In the first place, it was the first act of political violence, the first instance of resort to extralegal force, in the course of nearly four centuries of the history of the republic. More importantly, it signalized the disappearance of the sanctions on which the constitution had hitherto rested. The spell was broken: the influence of the senate, protected by the sanction of acquiescence, was shattered; it lost the respect of the sovereign voters under the impact of the competitive struggle for political advantage. Within two generations men were saying that the death of Tiberius was the turning point in Roman history, the beginning of the revolution.[17]

The ensuing ten years witnessed increased activity in the assembly in defiance of the policies of the senate, and in 123 another crisis arose. In that year, Gaius Gracchus, the brother of Tiberius, was elected tribune. A man of burning ambition, he immediately set about avenging the death of his brother and weakening still further the supremacy of the senate. For this purpose, he sought to enlist the support of the proletariat and of the business class of knights. He courted the electorate first by reenacting the agrarian law of Tiberius, second, by a law which assured grain to the urban populace at a lower-than-market rate and, third, by a public works program which provided both a new source of income to large numbers of voters and a host of dependent subordinates for himself. The grain law marked a new stage in the history of the proletariat and set the stamp of Gaius on the whole future of Roman history. Subsidization of the price of grain had been resorted to on earlier occasions in times of scarcity, but now an emergency device was turned into a permanent institution which assured not only the political support of the proletariat but its steady growth by providing conditions which would continually attract countryfolk to the city. The state-subsidized urban proletariat thus became a new and powerful force in the government.

To finance the grain subsidy and the public works program for which ready cash was needed, Gaius caused legislation to be enacted for farming out the collection of the entire revenues of Asia by a single contract for a lump sum. This law, the *lex Sempronia de provincia Asiae,* gave a new status and importance to the business class of knights, who derived from it a source of unprecedented profit. At the same time, he made a frontal attack on the morality and honesty of senatorial governors by providing that only knights might serve on juries in the courts which had jurisdiction over cases of extortion. By expressly exempting equestrian jurors from prosecutions for bribery, he guaranteed the knights a free hand in their activities in the provinces, safeguarding them from the interference of senatorial governors. The combined effect of the *lex Sempronia* and the judiciary law was to elevate and consolidate the knights into another powerful order which became a "ruinous political force." [18] Senators and knights now faced each other in open rivalry, with the latter standing ready to buy the electorate and to finance popular agitators, whose stock in trade was opposition to the senate. Demagogues were now able to carry on agitation on an impressive scale, and the senate's leadership in government policy was permanently broken.

Aside from the foregoing consequences of the Gracchan legislation, the rule of the two brothers, whose lives both ended in violence, provided a clear demonstration of an inherent weakness in the kind of one-man government which they, and others after them, succeeded in substituting for the traditional processes of the constitution. Its weakness was that it depended for support on the momentary will of an unstable and selfish electorate. It could lead only to a series of short-lived popular rules, lacking continuity of policy and program, and to the succession of crises which were to become a normal and usual feature of the next half-century of Roman politics.

During the two generations that followed the death of Gaius Gracchus, when the new democracy was revealing the measure of its weakness, Rome became involved in a series of wars which taxed her strength to the utmost. These wars—with Jugurtha, with the Cimbri, with the Italians, with Mithridates, with Sertorius and with the Mediterranean pirates—introduced a military factor into the political problem. In the course of emergencies which the senate found itself unable to handle, the people assumed the right to assign important military commands to particular individuals by direct popular vote. This constitutional innovation, first introduced when Gaius Marius became consul in 108 B.C., was of foremost importance, for it in effect transferred control over the armies to demagogues who could manipulate the popular assembly, and thereby gave them a large new leverage. With the professionalization of the army that took place at about the same time, the ensuing period of the republic's history tended progressively to revolve around the successive efforts of ambitious leaders, supported by their personal armies, to win or hold the favor of the voters. It was Marius who set this pattern of the successful general in politics—a pattern that was later exemplified in the careers of Sulla, Pompey and Caesar and pointed the way toward a permanent military head of the state. It was a pattern that hastened the road to absolutism, for the masters of the legions became the masters of Rome.

During this period, at the beginning of the first century, the excesses of radicals were matched by those of conservatives. Thus, the efforts of Sulla to restore the old Roman constitution were accompanied by mass confiscations and mass murders which, like the blood purges of Marius, helped to destroy in men's minds the ideals and beliefs to which constitutional government is congenial and replaced them with conceptions compatible only with absolutism. The horrors of civil strife bred timidity, apathy and cynicism, and when Sulla's reforms were swept away, little survived but the evil shadow of his methods and his example, and these provided a lesson from which his successors were astute to profit.

The movement of the revolution was in long surges: tensions built up to a crisis, then relaxed, affording a breathing spell in which conditions returned in appearance, though not in fact, to normalcy. Yet two generations after the Gracchi a vast change had come over Roman politics. Not only had the ascendancy of the senate been broken, but election riots were chronic, and bloodshed had become recurrent and common. The constitution itself had undergone little change, but with the abeyance in the senate's ascendancy it no longer functioned as it had. Wealth and the spoils of office had corrupted knights as well as senators, who looked to politics as a source of profit. Such attitudes tended constantly to weaken the senate as an effective ruling body, while at the same time the government was brought into a position of high instability through the rivalries of the contenders for power. The growing urban populace stood always ready to give its vote to whoever would promise them greater subsidies and entertainment. Those who sponsored reforms gave far more attention to enhancing their personal positions than to attempting to satisfy any real need of the people through constructive social and political reforms.

Modern historians, notably Mommsen, have been led to describe the political contests during the last half century of the republic in terms of a struggle between a senatorial and a democratic party. In fact, as the subsequent chapters of this work amply demonstrate, there was not only no popular or democratic party at Rome but no organized party in any modern sense.[19] Opposing the senate were only amorphous groups clustered about "popular" leaders and bound to them by family and clientage ties, marriage alliances and pacts of friendship. Within these groups there was no party line, no well-knit organization or spirit of loyalty, only individual ambitions seeking expression in the attainment of personal power and prestige. Hence there was no struggle between the senate on the one hand and the "people" on the other, but rather a continual series of contests between individuals, nearly all of whom were of noble or senatorial rank. These men, however, came to be divided into two groups. One, the self-styled *optimates,* or "good" men, endeavored, sporadically to be sure, to maintain the senatorial oligarchy and to reestablish the constitution as it had functioned prior to the Gracchi. The other group, characteristically referred to as *populares,* were bent upon measures and programs that would secure for themselves the great financial rewards of officeholding and establish or heighten their personal supremacy. The latter, generally unable to obtain support for their programs within the senate, turned to the tribunes as their lieutenants for managing the assembly and procuring the enactment of the legislation that promoted their aims. The fiercest contests over some supposed "democratic" reform usually turned out to be contests as to whether one or another aristocrat should enjoy the power and emoluments of office.

It is one of the peculiarities of Roman history that the continual democratic agitation from the time of the Gracchi onward never produced among the populace at large any sustained conviction that the high offices of state should be held by men of humble birth. The electorate went on contentedly voting for candidates drawn almost exclusively from the upper classes. Moreover, political power was almost never sought, won or exercised in the interests even of the aristocracy as a group, but nearly always for private individual advantage. A further striking feature of the revolution, particularly in its second phase that began with Sulla's retirement in the year 79, was the willingness of the contenders for power to go to almost any length to attain their ends. Under such conditions, in any age, men of ambition were destined to be ruthless individualists.

It must be emphasized that Roman politics could not have taken the course they did in the first century without the acquiescence of the voters who were the ultimate arbiters in the struggle for office and power. By then, however, the electorate consisted for most practical purposes of the urban voters, and these the politicians had learned to influence and manage by a standardized system of cheap or free food, free entertainment and, above all, outright bribery. When these methods failed, recourse was had to inciting their cupidity through radical proposals for distributions of property or to intimidating them by mob riots or a show of military force. The voters, in other words, had become the tools of the rival aristocratic leaders. Despite the existence in Rome of a certain amount of disinterested public opinion, it had little leverage except in times of special emergency, so that there were seldom any serious issues of principle or policy involved in elections. Moreover, the knights had learned a lesson from the proscriptions of Sulla and were no longer the active force in politics that they had been at the beginning of the century. As a class they were too engrossed in their private business affairs to be interested in promoting the general interests of the state, and most of them were completely lacking in those political virtues of duty, stamina and resolution which were possessed by the best Roman aristocrats. With the middle class thus reduced to political apathy, Roman government by the time of Cicero and Caesar had largely degenerated into an affair between the rival nobles on the one hand and the urban electorate on the other. Because the rural voters were generally unable or unwilling to journey to Rome several times a year and hence did not regularly exercise their voting privileges, the Roman proletariat dominated the assembly. As stated above, if no members of the rural tribes appeared, the tribune might pick men of his own choice to represent them, so that at many meetings of the popular assembly actual tribes gave way to mere skeleton tribes of a few voters recruited within Rome, and not for nothing. Thus the descendants of oriental freedmen, embittered, dispossessed landowners and other malcontents, reenforced by the more turbulent elements of the Roman mob, stood ready to make what they could out of their right to vote.

With an electorate of such a character, it was inevitable that the methods of the "popular" leaders should have entailed not only bribery but the proposal of measures that would appeal to voters of this sort. Hence the recurrent proposals to increase the state subsidized grain dole and to distribute or redistribute Italian lands; hence also the increasing resort to bribery of the urban voters and to mobs or the threat of armed force to keep others from the polls. The ensuing chapters illustrate the extent to which these "popular" measures—whether for the benefit of the proletariat or for the soldiers of the legions—were in no sense genuine democratic reforms but nearly always a part of programs for personal aggrandisement.

As the first century wore on, and Caesar came to power, the contest that emerged is to be viewed less in terms of a conflict between the conservative efforts of members of the senatorial group and the selfish drives for personal supremacy on the part of men such as Crassus and Pompey, than as a basic conflict between rival philosophies of government. The deliberate destruction of republican institutions by Julius Caesar and his substitution of the personal rule of a single man brought into high relief the issue between constitutionalism and absolutism, the age-old question of whether men are to be ruled by law or by arbitrary will. The collision between these opposing conceptions of government, represented respectively by Cicero and Caesar, lends lasting significance to the final years of the Roman republic, for the triumph of will over law necessarily means the end of democracy.[20]

NOTES

PRELUDE TO DESTRUCTION

1. Cf. C. N. Parkinson, *The Evolution of Political Thought* (Boston, 1958), 103.

2. F. F. Abbott, *A History and Description of Roman Political Institutions* (Boston, 1901), 157–158.

3. *Id.* at 175–181.

4. *Id.* at 197–202.

5. See the exhaustive discussion in G. W. Botsford, *The Roman Assemblies* (New York, 1909), 119–138.

6. For example, L. R. Taylor, *The Voting Districts of the Roman Republic* (American Academy in Rome, 1960), 13.

7. Apparently, aside from the regular censorial laws, only one bill—that for Cicero's recall from exile—is known to have been submitted to the *comitia centuriata* between 70 and 50 B.C. L. R. Taylor, *Party Politics in the Age of*

Caesar (Berkeley, Calif., 1961), 59. During the dictatorship of Sulla, however, considerable legislation was enacted in this assembly. Botsford, *supra* note 5 at 236–237.

8. This is the view of Abbott, *supra* note 2 at 260. Among the other circumstances supporting this conclusion is the fact that only plebeians could vote in the election of the tribunes. *Id.* at 247. However, Miss Taylor, *supra* note 7 at 206, states that the only essential difference between these two assemblies in the age of Cicero was that a consul or praetor presided over one and a tribune over the other. Elsewhere, *supra* note 6 at 47 note 1, her statement is more cautious. For further discussion, see T. Mommsen, *Römisches Staatsrecht* (Leipzig, 1887), I, 192–195.

9. The standard discussion of the tribal arrangements is still that of Mommsen, *supra* note 8, at III, 161–198. The recent scholarly work on this subject by L. R. Taylor *supra* note 6, is indispensable.

10. For a conveniently brief statement of the method of voting in this assembly, see Taylor, *supra* note 7 at 56–57.

11. *Infra*, p. 107.

12. *De Legibus*, III, xix, 45.

13. See P. Willens, *Le Sénat et la république romaine* (Louvain, 1878), I, 427 *et seq.*

14. Polybius, VI, 18: "Τοιαύτης δ' οὔσης τῆς ἑκάστου τῶν μερῶν δυνάμεως εἰς τὸ καὶ βλάπτειν καὶ συνεργεῖν ἀλλήλοις, πρὸς πάσας συμβαίνει τὰς περιστάσεις δεόντως ἔχειν τὴν ἁρμογὴν αὐτῶν, ὥστε μὴ οἷόν τ' εἶναι ταύτης εὑρεῖν ἀμείνω πολιτείας σύστασιν."

15. Passed at some date between 339 and 312 B.C.

16. M. Gelzer, *Die Nobilität der römischen Republik* (Berlin, 1912), 22 *et seq.*

17. E.g. Cicero, *De Re Publica*. I, xix, 31.

18. R. Syme, *The Roman Revolution* (Oxford, 1960), 13.

19. See generally, Taylor, *supra* note 7 at 6 *et seq.*

20. Cf. C. H. McIlwain, *Constitutionalism and the Changing World* (New York, 1939), 267.

Part TWO

THE COURSE
OF DESTRUCTION

1

Ambitions
and
Opportunities

I

THE poet Horace, looking back from the vantage point
of the next generation, identified the year 60 B.C., the
consulship of Metellus, as the beginning of the great
civic upheaval which led to the extinction of the Roman republic.[1]
It was the year in which Julius Caesar was elected consul and the
way paved for his official entry upon a program that first accelerated
the disintegration of the institutions of government and finally destroyed them.

Seldom does a single event by itself entirely change the course
of history. A revolution in the Roman governmental system had
been under way since 133 B.C. The land reform program of Tiberius
Gracchus, and the encouragement of the proletariat by his brother,[2]
had helped to destroy senatorial leadership by making the state-
subsidized proletariat the controlling power in government. By set-

ting the Roman republic in divided opposition against itself, they
made possible the military rule of the generals—first Sulla, later
Pompey and finally Caesar. Civil war, blood purges and conspiracies
in high places had contributed to the demoralization of social as well
as political institutions, so that the way was well prepared for the
course upon which Caesar was to embark. That course, however,
was not one that he was able to pursue without resistance. Opposed
to the principle of autocratic power which he sought to establish
were ancient conceptions of republican government which went
back to the early days when Rome was a farmer commonwealth and
which the course of the revolution had by no means yet destroyed.
The principal spokesman for constitutional as opposed to autocratic
government was the great orator and lawyer, Marcus Tullius Cicero,
who, with Caesar, stands out preeminently among those who played
the most conspicuous opposing parts in the drama of Roman political
life in the final age of the republic. Their characters and personalities
were interwoven with almost every significant event of those years,
which were to witness the formulation and elaboration of rival
theories of government and their testing in the political arena. Above
all others, these two men represent contrasting types of forces and
traditions which were to have lasting importance not only at Rome
but in the history of Western politics and thought. For these reasons,
and in an effort to provide new insights into the causes of the death
of the republic, their respective careers and political thinking have
been made the central theme of this volume.

If Caesar's opportunity to destroy the remnants of republican
institutions was marked by his election to the office of consul, that
event was accompanied by one equally important, namely, the formation of an informal political alliance which was to afford an indispensable basis of power. This was the so-called first triumvirate,
a behind-the-scenes arrangement between him and two political figures indispensable to his immediate plans—Gnaeus Pompey and
Marcus Licinius Crassus. Opinions have differed as to whether the
specific event that Horace had in mind in the verses above referred
to was Caesar's election or the formation of the triumvirate, but for
all practical purposes the two events must be considered together.
The election would not have had the significance that it did apart

from the formation of the triumvirate, and the triumvirate would almost certainly not have been formed without Caesar's election. In order to understand the significance of this alliance, which was to dominate the political scene and to guide the events of the ensuing fateful years, it is necessary to consider the character of Caesar's colleagues and the circumstances in which he found himself at the time of his election.

Of the contenders for political power at Rome in the year 60, Pompey was in many ways the strongest. Born of a plebeian family forty-six years before, his success had been extraordinary in spite of this social handicap. His military career from first to last had been unparalleled, for he had commanded legions at an age when his contemporaries were serving in the ranks, and he had been accorded the unprecedented honor of a triumph before he had held any high office of state. Elected consul in 70, he had brought about the repeal of Sulla's constitutional reforms and had become the acknowledged leader of the "popular" party at Rome. In 67 he had gone to the East, and in the course of six years he had become a great military hero, first in the war against King Mithridates, and later in the conquest of the rich kingdoms of the East. His continuous triumphal progress had ended with the annexation of Syria, whereby Rome openly and definitively assumed the leadership of the Eastern Mediterranean world. He had augmented the tributary revenues of the state by 70 percent,[3] and only Egypt remained outside of the orbit of Rome's acknowledged supremacy. At the time of his return to Italy, at the beginning of the year 61, he was unquestionably the most successful Roman of the age.

Pompey was ideally qualified to play the role of a hero in the eyes of the Roman public. He was remembered as strikingly handsome, with the physique of an athlete, and with that statuesque gravity of mien by which Romans were most likely to be impressed. He was not eloquent, but he had a friendly manner and great personal charm, not untinged with dignified aloofness and condescension. His popularity was not impaired by the fact that he was without imagination or a sense of humor and had a slow, laborious mind which almost never perceived the consequences of his own acts. A serene self-assurance evoked confidence, and the inconsistencies of

his political conduct were covered up by his directness and his obvious singleness of purpose in seeking his own advancement. No one
had ever appeared in Roman politics who was at once so young, so
good-looking, so famous and so popular.

When Pompey returned to Italy, he found a new alignment of
political forces which he neither anticipated nor understood, and
in consequence he became entangled in the snares that were set
for his unwary feet by open enemies and professed friends. His leading trait of character had always been overweening vanity—an emotional determination that no one should be so prominent or so important as himself. He did not so much desire power as recognition
of his preeminence, and he fell into the fatal error of aspiring always
to a special position in the state, of wanting to be something he
could not be. Thinking was always difficult for him, particularly
in the face of the torments of his ambition, and he did not have a
sufficiently good mind to perceive the desirability of conforming to
law, if only for the sake of appearances, so that he was "deeply indignant when persons and laws did not bend unconditionally before him." [4] The combination of these two traits of ambition and
essential lawlessness naturally had caused many Romans to fear
Pompey from the very first as a man bent on subverting the constitution. Conservative senators viewed with hostility and alarm his
elevation to unprecedented heights of power, and they were fearful
lest upon his return, tutored by the example of Sulla, the conquering
general would seize the central government of Rome. While he
was in the East, these opponents had not been idle. His absence had
become an important factor in the political situation in the sense
that his ultimate homecoming dominated the thinking of politicians
and gave direction to their maneuvers.

The core of the resistance movement was the conservative part
of the senate, which was available to lend support to any effort that
might create a breach between Pompey and his popular supporters
or assist in building up a rival leadership within the "popular" party.
The beginnings of the resistance to Pompey were more personal than
they were political in their nature. His most openly declared enemy
was Crassus, a "spoilt child of fortune," [5] of mediocre distinction,
who had served with him as consul and become furiously jealous

of him at that time. That jealousy had been fanned into a rage by Pompey's continuing success as a military leader, which far outshone his exploits in the suppression of the slave war, with the result that he determined to build himself up as a rival leader. By birth Crassus was a member of the senatorial class and occupied a strong position with that group. Yet he did not enjoy the confidence of the inner circle of the senate, not only because he was one of the busiest intriguers of the time but also because, as the richest man and greatest moneylender at Rome, he was closely tied to the business class of knights. Although this connection with the knights provided Crassus with an element of support that more than made up for his failure to win the confidence of the conservatives, he was shrewd enough to understand that he could not hope to advance his ambition with a combination that included only the knights and such senators as were beholden to him, but that he required a strong element of popular support. Inept and clumsy as he was in political matters, he seems to have realized that he had none of the personal qualifications to become a popular leader. His name, his great wealth, and his reputation for unfeeling and grasping avarice—all this made it inadvisable for him to make a direct bid for electoral support. He therefore chose a course which rich men have pursued in the politics of every age, namely, that of attaching to himself the support of some popular leader or leaders who would be willing to enter into partnership with him. In carrying out this plan, Crassus made a momentous decision: he decided to build up a popular leader of his own creation, a man on whose loyalty he might for that reason be better able to count. The lieutenant whom he selected for this role was Julius Caesar.

When Caesar first appeared in Roman politics in his early thirties, the role he chose to play was that of a young man of pleasure and fashion with no serious interests beyond the enjoyment of life. He must have been strikingly handsome—tall, slender, lithe and muscular, with the aquiline aristocratic face which the famous British Museum bust shows developed in early middle life into the face of a magnificent human animal, smooth, symmetrical and refined. His high-bred appearance was tempered by a remarkable suavity and charm of manner which never sacrificed his dignity but flattered and complimented those whom he chose to treat as equals.

Caesar's family background and social position might well have presented grave disadvantages to a young man possessed of less self-assurance; but with exceptional skill, and almost imperceptibly, he knew how to turn them into a source of extraordinary prestige. A member of the ancient Julian clan, he was descended from one of the few remaining Roman families of pure patrician blood who were proud to claim a mythical Trojan origin and, in his case, descent from no less an ancestor than Aeneas himself. For some generations, however, Caesar's own branch of the family had been neither prosperous nor prominent, and his father's sister had condescended to become the wife of the famous Marius, victor of the battles with the Cimbri and the Teutons and great hero of the "popular" cause. This connection, which might have ruined another man, Caesar knew how to convert into an asset. He was one of the very few of those aristocratic by birth who had a personal tie with the old democratic hero, and the only one who could claim a direct family relationship with him. This gave the young Caesar a strong emotional hold on the affections not only of middle-class equestrian families which had followed the cause of Marius but of the populace, to whom the memory of the old hero was still dear.

Boldly acknowledging rather than repudiating this tie to Marius, Caesar thereby gained for himself, through one of those peculiar paradoxes which so often determine social status, a kind of enhanced prestige in the eyes of the aristocracy. Not only was it slightly scandalous for a handsome, well-bred young aristocrat to be connected with Marius, but the nobility seem to have taken a kind of secret pride in the fact that the leadership of the Marian party, shattered and harmless, might pass to one of their own class. Caesar was precisely the man to see the possibilities of this anomalous situation and to make the most of it without making too much. At appropriate intervals, and in ways that were bound to attract public notice, he both proclaimed his undying loyalty to the memory of Marius and called attention to the fact that he was now the personal representative of the Marian cause. That was all. For the most part, he was content with the role of a harmless young aristocrat, calm, unhurried and debonair, yet possessed of a kind of steely resolution that occasionally showed itself and kept people from trifling with his dignity.

Such was the outward side of what Caesar gained from his connection with Marius, a side which he kept for public show. However, it is quite certain that a young man having the extraordinary mental qualities which Caesar afterwards displayed must have learned much from a youth spent in the inmost circles of the Marian party, particularly from his own father-in-law, Lucius Cornelius Cinna, the great popular leader who, with considerable truth, has been called the first emperor of Rome. What Caesar owed to Cinna's conversation and example cannot be known; he never emphasized the connection in later life, as he did that with Marius, but it unquestionably afforded him much food for reflection about human nature and the art of government.

In the early period of his life Caesar was more concerned with trying out his hand than in showing it. Under a bland and polished exterior, he concealed effectively his hopes, ambitions and beliefs. He gave no confidences and permitted the world to imagine his purposes or to suppose that he had none. He could be spectacular when he desired, but never until he was ready; his tactics until he was in his thirties were to lend himself to the schemes of others, to take advantage of events and movements which others promoted, and then to wait and see whether they could be made to yield some advantage for the next stage of his own advancement. Meanwhile, he was content to work in the background.

Caesar spent a good part of the decade of the 70's in the East, first in brief military campaigns, later in study. These years were interrupted by a brief sojourn in Rome, where he attempted unsuccessfully to prosecute two senatorial governors for extortion. Nothing about his failure seems to have dismayed him, but it did persuade him to take no active part in politics for the present, and he retraced his steps to the East to study rhetoric under Molo of Rhodes. In 74, he returned to Rome and again took up the life of an idle young aristocrat, bent on assuming the prominence belonging to him by birth and inherited social position.

Doubtless Caesar was then aware that through astute use of his social prestige he could make himself valuable to ambitious political leaders as a go-between in the intrigues that were constantly being carried on among members of the nobility. In fact, he is credited with having been instrumental in bringing Pompey and Crassus together at the time of their election to the consulship in the year 70.[6] Behind the scenes he continued to strengthen his influence by forming and renewing his connections with the lesser leaders and manipulators of elections with whom, as the heir of Marius, he had kept in touch. In no way, however, did he appear as a contender for political honors; now, and for years afterwards, the image that he displayed to the public with great care was merely that of an agent and broker for others, so that he did not become a target of envy or jealousy. Bent on building up goodwill in a quiet way among the nobility and populace alike, he acquired through his winning manners and accommodating disposition a public face that served him well long after he began to manifest quite different intentions. Caesar was so gracious and so friendly, so dignified and perfectly poised, that even those who might be opposed to him did not think ill of him or, indeed, take him very seriously.[7]

Among the ways by which Caesar averted opposition until he was strong enough to overcome it was by working through others and letting them take the brunt of public conflicts. Another was by strengthening his attachments on both sides of the political line that divided the senatorial conservatives from the popular leaders. Caesar's adroitness in thus fortifying his position was conspicuously exhibited by two calculated moves. For the first of these, in the year 68, he chose the occasion of the death of his aunt Julia, the widow of Marius, to deliver in her honor a funeral oration in which he not only eulogized Marius but boldly exhibited to the joy of the populace portrait-images of the old hero, thereby dramatizing his courageous determination to stand forth as a leader of the "popular" cause. Almost at the same time, he advertised his position as a senatorial aristocrat by his marriage to a granddaughter of Sulla, the wealthy and influential Pompeia, no relative of Pompey the general, but the daughter of a conservative aristocrat who had been killed in 88 B.C. by the partisans of Marius. This marriage had the dual advantage of connecting him with several members of the senatorial nobility while at the same time diverting attention from his activities in "popular" politics.

A calculating intelligence, a matchless memory and superb cool-headedness were among the distinguishing characteristics which Caesar exhibited long before he displayed the amazing abilities that enabled him to alter the history of the world. His nature was lacking in those enthusiasms, beliefs, loyalties and inhibitions which interfere with a purely dispassionate calculation of ends and means. Mommsen has praised Caesar for standing "aloof from all idealogy and everything fanciful." [8] The fact is that he stood aloof from convictions and beliefs of every kind, as well as from all principles and standards of moral and political behavior. "Nothing was wrong to him but what was injudicious. He could flatter, cajole, lie, deceive, and rob; nay, he would think it folly not to do so, if to do so were expedient." [9]

Caesar had that kind of aristocratic pride which sets itself above its heritage and above all the traditions from which it has sprung. In him the cynicism with which the age was rife and from which so few escaped took the form of a purely experimental attitude toward every aspect of life. He was ready to try anything for the results it might produce. He had no reluctance to bring obloquy or wrong on men whom he respected if he thought it advantageous to be rid of them, and he never hesitated to abandon a man whom he had used as a tool after he had no further use for him. In consequence, he never had a real friend, but only lieutenants, servants, dependents and satellites. He seems always to have felt that it was more efficient and economical to have competent tools than friends who might prove troublesome. As a result, he attracted those who themselves were seeking success and who for their own selfish reasons contributed the efficient means that he used for his own ends.

Women played a most important part in Caesar's life, but in his relations with them he displayed the same coolness as in his political intrigues. He did not hesitate to use them to further his ambition, yet he never squandered in his love affairs the time or the energies that he needed for more important ends. He was neither a debauchee nor a romantic lover, and he acknowledged in his many mistresses no rights over his heart or conduct. Yet so great was his charm that they continued to accord him their favors even after he had notoriously transferred his affections elsewhere.

Just as Caesar was entirely unhampered by scruples in matters of love, so was he also where money was concerned. He knew that he would need money in great and increasing quantities, and he never scrupled to use it, however obtained. He sold his social and political influence, accepted gifts, and borrowed wherever he could, but he always managed to distribute the proceeds in such a way as to obtain the services of those who looked to him for more, and whose services helped him to obtain more for himself. He had no honesty in his official employments, and, wherever opportunity offered, he extorted through his henchmen and hangers-on enormous bribes.[10] Caesar was, in this respect, much like Talleyrand, taking and receiving bribes under cover, with a show of grave decency and decorum which his opponents were afraid to unmask.

In his concern about public impressions, Caesar exhibited a remarkable astuteness wherein he surpassed almost every other statesman of ancient or modern times, with the possible exception of his nephew Augustus. By an act here, a gesture there, a speech or a casual remark, he touched and retouched the public image of himself without seeming to do so, and he was as great an artist in concealment as in display. By such means he presented himself as a man whom none need fear as a rival, but who possessed capacities that might be of much assistance to others. As the years passed, his success came increasingly from his understanding of how far he could press his associates or resist them without unduly arousing their antagonism.

It must always remain a matter for speculation whether the arrangement between Crassus and Caesar, which was certainly entered into by the year 66, resulted from the initiative of the former or the latter. Caesar's admirers have been at pains to deny or explain away the charge that he sold himself to Crassus. Others have taken the position that he allowed himself to become the instrument of the millionaire under the imperative pressure for money, and was able to "argue down his scruples in the ingenuous irresponsibility of youth." [11] Such explanations arise from a misunderstanding of Caesar's character and of his purpose in making his deal with Crassus.

Caesar was no irresponsible youth; he was almost forty years old and had as cool a head as any man in history. He did not covet money in the spirit of youth for extravagant personal expenditures; he wanted it in vast quantities to advance his own political career. In engaging himself to Crassus, he had this purpose strictly in view, and, as he viewed that engagement, it was likely to work more to his own advantage than to that of his nominal principal. Crassus was to supply the money that Caesar would use not only at elections but in building himself up in the role of a great popular leader. The arrangement would further Crassus' plans by undermining Pompey's position as head of the "popular" party, but it would at the same time clear the way for Caesar's own ultimate assumption of that leadership. Caesar was by no means yet ready to come out into the open as a rival of Pompey; it suited him far better to seem to act as the tool of Crassus while he built himself up at Crassus' expense in ways that could give no offense to anyone. Thus, he immediately turned to his own advantage the office of aedile, to which he was elected for the year 65 as the first fruit of his employment by Crassus. The chief function of the aedile at this time was the exhibition of games and spectacles for the purpose of winning the favor of the populace and thus to lay a foundation for later election to higher offices. Contemporaries recount that the gladiatorial contests, theatrical shows, processions and public feasting which Caesar provided through the use of Crassus' money exceeded in magnificence anything ever before seen.[12] Meanwhile, insofar as public measures were concerned, he was astute to appear only as the agent of Crassus.

In the course of seeking to win popular favor, both Crassus and Caesar undoubtedly recognized that their activities in this direction would strengthen them in the good graces of the senate. Each had the initial advantage of being members of the nobility by birth and connections, whereas Pompey was an outsider. From the viewpoint even of the conservative part of the senate, nothing was more desirable than to split the democratic politicians into two factions, one attached to Pompey and the other following Crassus and Caesar.

Crassus appears to have relied heavily on Caesar to find the ways and develop the measures which would gratify his own personal ambition of self-aggrandizement, and these Caesar seems to have mapped out in two directions. The first scheme he projected was the creation of an opportunity for establishing another "great command," rivaling that which had been accorded Pompey and which would be given to Crassus; the second was to encourage a critical outbreak of disorder in Rome which would require extraordinary measures to suppress it and might lead to the appointment of Crassus for the task. None of the steps by which these two projects were pursued was openly taken; on the contrary, they can be traced only dimly and reconstructed with difficulty through a series of apparently unrelated circumstances. It was never Caesar's way to force results but rather to take advantage of situations created by others and use them in a way that for the time being best suited his own plans.

The project for the creation of a great command for Crassus took the form of a scheme to annex Egypt, which, with its enormous wealth that had been piling up for generations in the coffers of the Ptolemies, would enable Crassus, if entrenched therein, to become a match for Pompey.[13] It was anticipated that the project would have great popular appeal because Egypt produced annually a great export surplus of grain, and if this could be expropriated, or brought under the control of Rome, the populace would directly benefit from a liberalization of the grain dole. Unhappily for Crassus, when the project was proposed to the tribal assembly, it was defeated by the adherents of Pompey and by the voters loyal to the strict senatorial conservatives, so that he and Caesar were obliged to turn their attentions elsewhere.

The opportunity for their second project was found in the ambition of Lucius Sergius Catiline for the consulship. It was anticipated that if they were successful in bringing about his election they would not only have a consul whom they could control, but they would promote their own influence in the underworld of Rome, particularly among the leaders of the clubs and guilds which were becoming so powerful at elections. Catiline had great influence in those groups, and Caesar seems early to have seen the advantage of building up as an ally the kind of bold mob leader that Catiline most certainly was. He was, in addition, a senatorial aristocrat who, despite having been recently involved in a homicidal plot, was able to retain the friendship and political support of a large part of the nobility, while at the same time organizing and leading the dregs of the populace. A dual position of this kind was precisely what Caesar needed by way of an alliance. Although it seems unlikely that either Crassus or Caesar participated in, or sponsored, any of Catiline's schemes, each of them expected an opportunity to fish in troubled waters and to profit from the disorders that those schemes might create. With these advantages, together with the gold of Crassus to help buy the election, Catiline's chances of success were excellent. Sponsored by Crassus and Caesar, he was also welcome to many in the senate as a counterpoise to Pompey.

The story of Catiline's defeat through the oratory of Cicero is a familiar one and has often been told. When the extent of election bribery and of Catiline's conspiracies was brought to light, he was deserted by frightened conservative senators and businessmen alike, who began to fear for the security of their property and even for their lives. Cicero became the man of the hour in Roman politics, the indispensable candidate of those who wanted to preserve orderly government, and he was elected to the consulship for the year 63. Thus came to naught the second scheme of Crassus and Caesar in their bid for power, and neither was to forget that it was Cicero who had helped temporarily to check their ambitions.

Cicero was born in 106 B.C., the same year as Pompey. He was not new to public life and had already held the offices of quaestor and praetor. His election as consul, however, brought him into such political prominence that he became at once the target of opposition not only from Crassus and Caesar but from a substantial portion of the senate as well. His situation was both peculiar and anomalous, and the unusual circumstances to which he owed his election held out an invitation to all forces that were menacing the republic to concentrate against him. Before embarking upon an account of his consulship, which brought these antagonisms into sharp focus, it is appropriate to sketch the character of this man whose political philosophy was to play so important a part in the final age of the republic.

Cicero was a many-sided man. Indeed, history records few who have left their mark on more different facets of civilized life. Yet he owed his position and his opportunity to play the role he did to the accident of a single great artistic gift on which his whole career was founded. He could "speak as no Roman ever spoke, before or after." [14] Cicero made many more valuable contributions to history and to human thought than through his oratory, but it is doubtful whether he would ever have had a chance to make them had he not been first and foremost a supremely great orator. From the time of Demosthenes down to that of the elder Pitt, Cicero affords almost the only instance of a man rising to great place in a great state by eloquence alone. His position is the more extraordinary since he lived in an age and in a society in which the power of public opinion was remarkably feeble and ineffective and in which those who were in a position to determine the direction of events were but little influenced by reason or argument.

In such an age, Cicero's oratory owed its force to the fact that its most important characteristic was not argument at all, but a form of splendid entertainment. It was not the closely reasoned speech of Demosthenes, or of such great English and American orators as Pitt, Fox, Webster and Lincoln. The basis of the hold which Cicero's eloquence had on popular audiences was its theatrical quality; it was the lofty declamation of a great actor, measured, cadenced and sonorous. It moved the people because it thrilled them; it was stimulating and exciting. To our modern taste it often seems inflated, but its supreme effectiveness in its own time has been magnificently summarized by Quintilian, when he said that it was Cicero's sublimity and magnificence, his brilliance and tone of authority, that evoked thunderous applause, and that those who heard him were transported and shouted out because they must and not because they chose, acting like men beside themselves who had lost consciousness of where they were.[15]

Yet if Cicero became a great political figure by virtue of his oratorical gifts, which gave him a hold on the affections of the crowd in the Forum, he also brought to the task of a statesman an unusual intellectual equipment as a student of philosophy and of the political and moral sciences. He had nothing of the creative inventiveness of great original thinkers like Plato and Aristotle, but he had what is perhaps equally or even more valuable, in political science, an almost unrivaled ability to distill from the common notions and aspirations of men an understanding of the ends of human action and the conditions associated with their pursuit. Indeed, he was able by this process, and without any pretense to originality, to lay down the outlines of a philosophy of law and politics that was essentially new and so important that it afforded a guide to men's thinking for two thousand years.

Cicero's philosophical writings, like his oratory, show that he was essentially and primarily an artist; they are the works of a great stylist and man of letters rather than of a technician or professional specialist, and largely on that account they have been generally underrated in recent years. This persistent artistic quality runs through all aspects of Cicero's life and character and has been responsible for a good deal of misunderstanding of his work as a statesman, for his artistic temperament has come between him and a balanced appraisal of his political career.

One reason why it has always been so difficult to make an adequate judgment of Cicero is that we know so much about him. Over eight hundred of his personal letters survive, and they provide a more intimate and vivid acquaintance with the man himself and with the inner workings of his mind than of almost any other individual down to modern times. These letters show him off guard, with all his personal foibles and failings exposed. They reveal his doubts, hesitations and uncertainties, as well as his disappointments, wounded vanities and resentments. It is in these respects that his artist's temperament has done him great disservice. Because he was at heart an artist he wrote frankly and impulsively. He had a spirit full of vivacity and sensitivity, quick to receive and to respond to impressions and therefore mercurial and changeful. These qualities account for the extraordinary charm and liveliness of his letters, but they also account for the charge of inconsistency and instability that is generally made against him. Indeed, the vivacity of his imagination left little room for consistency. One writer has written of his "warm Italian nature, open to every gust of feeling, over which impressions came and went like summer clouds." [16] Accordingly, we catch him at one moment inclining in favor of a policy which he afterwards rejects; we hear him abusing a political leader whom he afterwards decides to support; and we are led to blame him for instability, if not downright insincerity. Most of his critics have condemned his changes of position far more severely than those of politicians who have left behind them no record from which to study the succesive mental steps that led to their decisions.

What is remarkable about Cicero is not that he surrendered as he did to his artistic temperament and impulses but that in spite of these he persevered so courageously in a political course which was bound to be a lonely one and which kept him fundamentally at odds with the great and powerful. He was not by temperament an organizer of discontent or a leader of opposition. He had a cheerful and sociable nature, disposed, as Plutarch says, "to mirth and pleasantry." [17] All his life he hated to quarrel, particularly with people he liked, and he found something to like in most people. In spite of this, he was driven by his oratorical talents and his philosophy, as by an inner compulsion, to take an active part in politics; and in politics it was inevitable that he should find himself in double-fronted opposition to the dominant tendencies and leaders of his time.

Almost alone among his prominent contemporaries Cicero did not covet power. As Ferrero has said, he was "untouched by the two great passions, love of money and love of power, which drive men to face the perils of great social conflicts." [18] He did not want to impose his will on anyone; he wanted only to influence his fellow citizens by reason and discussion and to have them follow him because they believed in him and applauded him. He wanted money not to buy elections or pay soldiers but to live in dignified and scholarly surroundings. His vanity and egotism, which were very great, were not intriguing or designing but carried a thirst for approval and applause because he honestly wished to do the things that in his opinion merited applause. Throughout his career he was nothing of a manipulator or intriguer. He was willing to make political concessions when reasonable and necessary, but he rarely sought to accomplish his ends by bargains and deals. Repeatedly he made and announced with courage and firmness political decisions which not only cost him the favor of those whom it would have been to his advantage to conciliate, but sometimes exposed him to grave danger.

Indeed, in the end, he was to lay down his own life with great calmness and dignity.

The reputation for inconsistency and time-serving that critics have sought to fasten upon Cicero results partly from the fact that his good nature and liking for people prevented him from converting political opposition into personal enmity. In the sphere of personal relations he was always ready to do a good turn, even for political antagonists of whom he strongly disapproved, and he would associate and cooperate with them with a surprising degree of simplicity and even naïveté. Yet he seldom permitted these pleasant personal relations to interfere with his advocacy of his own views when he thought that the latter had any real chance of meeting with a successful hearing, and he was therefore often attacked in his own time as an ingrate toward such personal friends as Caesar.

The principal reason, however, which has caused Cicero to be accused of vacillation and time-serving has been the failure of his critics to understand the contemporary alignment of Roman political forces and the peculiar position in which Cicero stood in relation to them. The loneliness of his position left him no choice but to lend his support now to one side and now to the other in the political contests of the times. During the first part of his career he found himself, as a result of his family background, traditions and connections, together with his hatred of the bloodshed and violence of those years, aligned with leaders who took the so-called popular, or democratic side. Beginning in the year 70, and for some years thereafter, he worked in harmony with those men until their tactics and the direction in which their policies were tending alienated him completely.

Cicero had no tolerance for agitation which was designed to bring more power into the hands of individuals who might profit by the resulting confusion. He was a sincere believer in constitutional government, fundamental justice and elementary morality, without the slightest touch of cynicism in his nature. He ardently desired success and honor in public life, but he desired them on his own terms; and those terms were that power should not be amassed either in his own hands or in those of his friends, but rather that the kind of government and law which he believed would make for the public good should be furthered and promoted. This policy was founded on his faith in the fundamental right-mindedness and amiability of human beings and on their capacity for reason; the basis of his philosophy was that men were born for justice. It was this creed which had made him proclaim openly under Sulla's rule of force that it was "better to live among brute beasts than in such a savage state of things as this."[19]

A man of this kind had no place among the "popular" leaders of Rome at a time when their chief objective was to manipulate elections in ways that would bring them power. Cicero's difficulty was that he wished to be a democrat and a constitutionalist at the same time, whereas the other leaders who appealed to democratic sympathies were primarily interested in using the constitution to acquire power for themselves through making the constitution unworkable. Inevitably, those leaders soon came to distrust and dislike Cicero and to brand him with the stigma of a lukewarm moderate, which has clung to him ever since. The only quarter in which any sympathy existed for lawful and tempered government and for the preservation of the balances of the Roman constitution was among the senatorial conservatives. When he became aware of the machinations of Caesar and Crassus as leaders of the popular party, he felt compelled to side with the aristocracy.

Between Cicero and the aristocracy, however, there was a gulf which events were to prove could never be bridged. Although he was in essential agreement with the conservatives on most questions of political principle during the latter part of his career, he always remained an outsider, a "new man," who had, for all his virtue, "no pedigree, no house, no coate, [n]o ensignes of a family. . . ."[20] Therefore, in spite of his great talents and capacities, the aristocracy would have none of him. Indeed, his talents served to enhance their rancor against him and to inflame their jealousy that so able a man was not of their own class. In fact, to some degree, the senatorial aristocrats appear to have objected to Cicero's constitutionalism because they looked on the Roman constitution as their private property, and they were more willing to see it undermined by one of themselves, like Caesar, than to have it brilliantly and conspicuously defended by an outsider like Cicero. Moreover, as plain, blunt men, they were offended by Cicero's intellectual showiness in much the way that the English aristocrats of the late eighteenth century were offended by the same quality in Edmund Burke.

This unrelenting attitude of the aristocracy toward Cicero, which persisted down to the last months of his life, effectively kept him from ever holding a position of influential leadership on the side of political questions where his convictions lay. At the same time, he had no desire or qualifications to be a mob master on the other side. Thus, for the whole later and more important part of his career, through no fault of his own, but rather because of his good qualities, he was a statesman without a party. It was this fact that necessarily caused his policy to be timid and hesitant. On the rare occasions when an issue arose on which he could make himself the mouthpiece of an aroused public conscience, he did so with great effect and power and thereby made himself an ever-present source of fear to the power politicians then in command of the Roman government who were seeking to control the electorate by force or favors. Cicero knew that he had not the resources to go far in offending these men, and when occasionally he overestimated those resources, it was to his own injury.

Cicero had the misfortune to see with clear vision the meaning of the forces that were at work about him and to assess their strength with an accuracy that was shared by no other contemporary save Julius Caesar. He saw, also, that because he lacked the external advantages of rank and position, as well as the personal qualifications for mob leadership and military preeminence, he had no recourse but to throw his influence, such as it was, and his powers of advocacy, for or against the aristocratic contenders who held the center of the political stage. This was no easy task, for the military men as a group disliked Cicero as incurably civilian, and they resented what they looked on as his interference in their personal concerns. Because he did not fit into their pattern they never knew when he would throw that pattern into confusion.

As a result of this situation, Cicero's influence on the course of Roman affairs was necessarily sporadic and casual, and the apparent inconsistencies of his positions therefore caused him to be accused of being a trimmer and a turncoat. In fact, however, he revealed in at least one respect a remarkable consistency, if the key is sought in the right place. This was his persistent refusal to be separated from Pompey. Cicero had served on the staff of Pompey's father in the Italian war, and at first he undoubtedly entertained a high regard for the young hero's abilities, patriotism and political principles; yet even when he began to perceive that his idol had feet of clay, he recognized the importance to his own position of masking his political operations under the protection of an alliance with a great military figure. At an early date he saw that the conditions of Pompey's political preeminence were essentially like his own. He understood, before most others did, that Pompey was no revolutionist and was chiefly kept from being a conservative by the persistent dislike and opposition of the senate. In this respect Pompey occupied exactly the same ground as Cicero. It was only when the senate failed Pompey that Cicero had to fail the senate, because, separated from Pompey, the senate would not follow Cicero as a leader. Thus, over a period of twenty years, in spite of coldness, rebuffs and the most cruel ingratitude, there was only a single important instance in which Cicero allowed himself to be found opposed to Pompey, and that was on the occasion of the trial of Milo in 52 B.C., when the claims of personal gratitude were too strong to leave him a choice. Cicero's relation to Pompey affords the best evidence of his political acumen and the most convincing answer to the charge that he was blinded by egotism. So far from being blinded by egotism, Cicero's understanding of the political situation made him recognize that his own political position lacked independent foundation and that he could stay in politics only with the support of a leader like Pompey. Even this was in the end denied him, when Pompey's alliance with Caesar drove Cicero out of public life at the height of his powers.

It was well for Cicero's later fame that he was thus driven from public life, for it was during those years that he turned his hand to that great series of essays and treatises which made him the schoolmaster of Europe for eighteen centuries, and caused Byron to speak of him as "Rome's least-mortal mind." [21] Through his writings he rapidly achieved, even in his own lifetime, a position of unrivaled supremacy in the field of literature such as he was never able to win in politics. The influence of these works throughout succeeding ages on the minds of men has been more steady, continuous and widespread than that of almost any other writer, for Cicero wrote not for the student, but for men of the world and of affairs. That influence can be traced in the conversion of the Roman world to Christianity, in the mediaeval struggle for law, in the Renaissance, in the Reformation, and in the "Enlightenment" of the eighteenth century. Some of the reasons for this vast influence have been suggested by Mr. Cruttwell:

> In all these works there reigns a magnificence of language and a calm grandeur of tone well befitting the literary representative of the "assembly of kings" [the Roman Senate]. Nowhere perhaps in all literature can be found compositions in which so many sources of permanent attraction meet; dignity, sweetness, an inexpressible and majestic eloquence, drawing the reader along until he seems lost in a sea of grand language and lofty thoughts, and at the same time a sympathetic human feeling, a genial desire to persuade, a patient perseverance in illustration, an inimitable clearness of expression; admirable qualities, whose harmonious combination is perhaps incompatible with the profoundest philosophic wisdom, but which have raised Cicero to take the lead among those great popular teachers who have expressed, and by expressing furthered, the growing enlightenment of mankind.[22]

Although it is by these works and their influence that Cicero's place in history is to be determined, rather than by his career as a politician or as a constitutional statesman, his writings and his political activities are not separate but complement each other. His statesmanship supplies a living commentary on his formulations of political and moral principles.

Cicero's consulship in the year 63 was not only one of the stormiest in Roman history, but it brought to the fore the opposition of policies for which he and Caesar respectively stood. The political battles which he had to fight during his year of office were in the beginning against Caesar, and, in the second half of his consulate, against a second conspiracy of Catiline. He checked them both, but in so doing he made enemies and created a political situation that in the end destroyed his chances for continued leadership.

Caesar and Crassus had apparently decided to go forward with their plans which had as their objective the weakening of Pompey. They both still hoped that an extraordinary military command could be secured for Crassus and that at the same time Caesar would fall heir to the popular leadership at Rome. The program for attaining these results was left to the ingenuity of Caesar, who, with his usual astuteness, saw that a new factor had entered the problem with the elevation of Cicero. Since Cicero was looked on as Pompey's man, it would be possible to strike at Pompey through Cicero, who was in the difficult position of owing his election in part to conservatives who would accuse him of ingratitude and who would destroy him if he went squarely against them on any fundamental issue. If it could also be made to appear that Cicero had deserted the "populars" and gone over to the senate, not only would he lose his own standing as a "popular" leader, but he would seriously impair Pompey's position with the "populars" as well. Caesar accordingly undertook to drive Cicero out of the "popular" party by making it impossible for him to remain in it.

For this purpose there was devised a highly ingenious plan which was intended at the same time to advance the projects of Crassus. The central feature of the plan was a piece of radical legislation which would be stamped with a conspicuous "popular" character and afford a rallying point for democratic agitation and excitement. Such a measure was bound to elicit the opposition of the conservatives and was meant to do so. At the same time there would be wrapped up in the proposal, in a manner not too obvious, provisions which, if adopted, would provide for Crassus the command that he wanted. It was anticipated that a proposal of this kind would put Cicero in an impossible position. If, for the sake of being a "popular," he went along with it, he would deliver himself into the hands of Crassus and Caesar and at the same time would incur the hostility not only of the senate but of Pompey, at whose expense the proposal favored Crassus. If, on the other hand, Cicero opposed a measure framed on such a "popular" model, he would expose himself, and Pompey with him, to the charge of having deserted to the side of the senate and abandoned the "popular" cause.

This scheme was woven into an ambitious and complicated legislative proposal which was ready for submission to the voters at the very outset of Cicero's consulate. The nominal sponsor of the bill was an obscure and unimportant tribune named Rullus, for Caesar and Crassus wished to assume no responsibility and kept discreetly in the background. In form, the bill was an agrarian law of the kind which had not been agitated for half a century, but had once proved an infallible means for touching off a popular explosion. The new bill differed from previous proposals of the same kind in the vastness of its scope and the liberality of its provisions. It not only proposed to make available for free distribution to poor Romans all the remaining public land in Italy, but it provided for the acquisition by purchase of all the additional land that might be needed to carry out its purpose. By providing for the purchase of the lands to be distributed, the issue of confiscation was avoided, but the resulting cost to the state would obviously be enormous. To meet this cost, the bill provided that the money should be raised by selling all the domains and other property which Rome had acquired abroad since the year 88—a provision which was plainly directed primarily at the estates and treasures recently acquired by Pompey and to snatch from his hands the fruits of victories in the East.

To convert this vast accumulation of miscellaneous assets into a fund that could be used for the purchase of Italian land presented an administrative task of unprecedented magnitude. The bill proposed to entrust the task to a commission of ten "decemvirs," vested with very broad powers and assisted by a small army of secretaries, clerks, criers, auctioneers, surveyors and assessors.[23] The decemvirs were authorized to travel everywhere and decide finally and conclusively what was or was not the public property of the Roman people. Such property they were empowered to sell at whatever places and for whatever prices they pleased. The cash accruing from these sales they were to be free to expend in the purchase of land anywhere in Italy at their discretion. The bill was discreetly silent on the subject of Egypt, but the power of the decemvirs to determine what property belonged to the Roman people was phrased with sufficient breadth to enable them to decree the annexation of Egypt if they chose. If the bill were enacted, the roving tribunal of decemvirs could follow Pompey into his very camp and take over the administration of the new lands that he had acquired before he had a chance to organize or even pacify them. In effect, the proposed measure transferred from the commander-in-chief to the commission the task of organizing the Eastern boundaries and provinces of the empire.

Cicero had no choice but to meet head-on the challenge presented by the proposal of Rullus. Not only was this necessary for the protection of Pompey; it was necessary also to check at the outset the renewal of a dangerous kind of legislation which in this instance threatened to throw Italian property rights into confusion and, what was even more serious, to disrupt the Roman settlement of the East. To meet the challenge he adopted a strategy that took his opponents off guard. On the very first day of his consulship he went into the senate and announced that he would oppose the law of Rullus. A few days afterwards, on his own initiative, he called a mass meeting in the Forum and denounced the measure before the people in a speech of such great power and skill that its proponents quietly abandoned it, and it was not heard of again.

Cicero's achievement in defeating the land bill of Rullus represents the greatest triumph of his oratorical career. That a proposal which had been ingeniously drafted to appeal to the passions and appetites of the voters could be annihilated by a sheer display of eloquence was a new experience in the politics of the time, and this feat undoubtedly helped to convince the shrewder manipulators of public action that henceforth they would have to rely on practices with which mere eloquence was powerless to deal. Cicero's speech, like most successful political harangues, was not primarily an appeal to reason, for he was a master of forensic psychology and understood that he could meet an appeal to one set of passions and prejudices only by arousing and playing upon others. From this standpoint the speech against Rullus is more worthy of study than almost any other of Cicero's orations.

The defeat of the agrarian law was undoubtedly felt by Caesar as a severe blow to his prestige. In the undeclared duel that was developing between himself and Cicero, he had lost the first round and he could not afford to lose again. The method which he chose to rehabilitate his public position was as remarkable as it is difficult from our modern point of view to understand. Caesar decided to win for himself the great office of high pontiff, which stood at the head of the Roman religion. The then incumbent was on his deathbed, and Caesar determined to be his successor as chief priest of Rome.

That such an ambition was conceivable on the part of a man like Caesar tells a good deal about Caesar and about Rome and the Roman religion at that time. Caesar was a complete free-thinker, a libertine in life and philosophy, and entirely devoid of piety and reverence. He was at the same time a mere youth compared with the grave leaders who had customarily held the office, and his life was marked more than most men's by what are commonly considered the indiscretions and follies of youth. That such a man of the world and of fashion should aspire to the most sacred and important religious office in the state reveals a remarkable lack of inhibitions on Caesar's part and affords an extreme instance of the detachment of his political planning. At the same time, the fact that the Roman people should have been willing to accept a man like Caesar for the office he coveted indicates in part the success with which he had been able to mask his private character and in part the absence of any deep religious feeling from the official cult of the Roman state. In the eyes of the populace, the chief-priesthood was apparently by now merely another political office, albeit an exceptionally grave and dignified one.

To attain his object, Caesar had first to undo one of the few remaining pieces of Sulla's legislation, which had restored the ancient method of selecting the chief pontiff by the votes of the other members of the pontifical college. Since this method would almost certainly bar the choice of Caesar, he proposed to revert to the practice, introduced during the period of the Gracchi, whereby the pontiff was elected by popular vote. A bill for this purpose was introduced by a tribune named Titus Labienus who, on this occasion, appears for the first time in the role he was to play for a dozen years as Caesar's most trusted lieutenant in peace and war. The law of Labienus seems to have passed without difficulty, and preparations for the electoral campaign commenced.

The two leading candidates were men of the type from which high pontiffs were usually chosen, prominent, elderly aristocrats who had held a long list of high offices. These were Quintus Lutatius

Catulus, at that time leader of the senate, and the respected general, Servilius Isauricus. Because Caesar had as yet held no high office he was hardly taken seriously by his competitors until it became apparent that a good deal of money was being spent on his behalf. With Catulus and Isauricus both in the field, the aristocratic vote was divided, and the use of money told in Caesar's behalf. When the day of election came, he carried off the prize and was satisfactorily rehabilitated as a master hand at political management. In this episode Cicero took no part; indeed, he could have taken no part without exposing himself to criticism for serious impropriety. Religious offices were considered so peculiarly the exclusive preserve of the high aristocracy that for an outsider to meddle in their disposition would have seemed an impertinence to the senators whose support as consul he could not dispense with. He therefore had to stand aside while his opponent reestablished his position.

There can be little doubt that Caesar's election as high pontiff was one of the shrewdest moves of his entire political career. It immediately lifted him in prestige and distinction above the heads of many men who had already held high office, while he himself had as yet not even contended for any. Moreover, the new office gave colorable support to the reputation he wished to have of standing apart and above the political battle, for it vested his acts and words with an authority more respectable than that of an ordinary officeholder. Naturally Caesar used these advantages to the full. Hitherto his political activities had been conducted from behind the scenes and ostensibly in the interest of others. Now he was ready to launch a political career of his own, and he would be able to do so from the vantage point of the most venerable and dignified post in the state.

Caesar's next political move suggests that he already suspected, if he was not actually aware of, what might soon be looked for from Catiline, who was formulating a new plot against the government. If this were to eventuate, and the matter and the affair became serious, the government would need to resort to martial law under the protection of a *senatus consultum ultimum,* or "last decree" of the senate. It was Caesar's purpose to prevent this, and thereby render more difficult, if not impossible, the task of suppressing the conspiracy. If this was not what Caesar intended, there seems no way of understanding the legal proceeding which was now commenced under his auspices in order to obtain a judicial decision that the senate's "last decree" was invalid to protect those who acted in reliance on it. The case took the form of a prosecution of an aged and inconspicuous senator named Rabirius, who had participated in putting down the sedition of Saturninus and Glaucia nearly forty years before and who was said to have been the person responsible for Saturninus's death. Since a *senatus consultum ultimum* was in force at the time, Rabirius's act would not constitute a crime if the senate's decree were legally effective. Thus the purpose of the case could only have been to test this point.

Caesar's close connection with this prosecution is proved by the fact that it was initiated by his henchman Labienus and brought before a special court of two men of whom Caesar and one of his cousins were the members. As might have been expected, these judges found the defendant guilty, and he appealed from their decision to the centuriate assembly, the *comitia centuriata*. At this stage Cicero entered the case as counsel for the defendant.[24] It was clearly of the utmost importance for Cicero, as a consul in office, to preserve the government's power to take effective action against conspirators and rebels. If the senate's last decree were held invalid, there would be no way of imposing forceful restraint or punishment on Roman citizens for any reason save after a formal trial before one of the assemblies, and such trials never resulted in a sentence more severe than exile. Accordingly, there would be no effective means of checking a plot or rebellion by Roman citizens until after it reached the stage where hostile armies met on the field of battle, since up to that time there would be no lawful way of imposing the death sentence on the plotters. With the sinister figure of Catiline known to be at work in the background, the seriousness of such impotence on the part of the government was clear.

With characteristic forensic astuteness, Cicero did not attempt to argue constitutional law to the voters but sought instead to bring out the inconsistency of punishing Rabirius as a criminal because he had punished the crime of one who attacked the state. He first pointed out that it was none other than Marius himself, the great democratic leader, under whose command as consul Rabirius had acted, and if Rabirius had committed a crime, then, argued Cicero, so had Marius. Cicero then appealed, as he had done in opposing the agrarian law, to the true interests of the state, and warned that the way to promote the welfare of the Roman people was the way of tranquillity and good order, not the way of conspiracy and revolution. At about this point, his speech was interrupted by a disorderly tumult in the crowd, which turned into rioting, so that the assembly had to be adjourned hastily before a vote could be taken. Apparently those who in the past had been borne down by Cicero's eloquence had decided this time to take no chances and had, therefore, organized the kind of argument which mere eloquence could not overcome. Thus, once again, the orderly deliberative processes of government were defeated and rendered ineffective, as in the times before Sulla and Marius, and meanwhile the indecisive result of the trial was, from Caesar's standpoint, almost as helpful as if Rabirius had actually been condemned. Caesar had gained his main point. The Roman voters had failed to sustain the legality of the senate's "last decree." With the question of legality remaining in doubt, the power of the government to deal with a conspiracy was seriously impaired.

This was no small victory for Caesar. By it he accomplished four objectives. He had presented himself as champion and defender of the strict constitutional rights of Roman citizens even when they were conspirators against the life of the republic; he had shown himself at the same time the protector of the mob element in politics which was ready to engage in tumults and seditions; he had helped to keep the door open for the kind of disorder in the state which would enable ambitious men to advance to greater power; and he had further established himself as an outstanding leader of the more radical wing of the "popular" politicians of Rome. This achieved, he then sought to safeguard himself in the opposite direction by another step quite characteristic of his political strategy. Although he had tried only a few months earlier to cut the ground from under Pompey by the proposal of Rullus, he now sought to make himself rather than Cicero appear in the public eye as Pompey's friend by having Labienus introduce and obtain the passage of a law flattering to Pompey's vanity because it authorized the conqueror of the East to wear a crown of bay leaves when attending the circus or the theater.[25]

The second half of Cicero's consulship was occupied with one of the great episodes of Roman history—the second and final conspiracy of Catiline, which Cicero brought to light and put down. The dramatic story of the discovery of this plot to overthrow the government has often been told and is well known from the famous orations against Catiline.[26] Its significance from the standpoint of the theme of this book lies partly in the light that it sheds on Cicero's capacities as a statesman and man of action and partly in the ultimate effect it was to have on his career. Despite the plea of Caesar that the self-confessed conspirators should be treated leniently,[27] the senate, egged on by Marcus Cato,[28] voted in favor of the death penalty, and Cicero ordered them strangled with a cord.[29] Within only a few years, he was forced to pay bitterly for his action, for which he was driven into exile and obliged to hear himself denounced as a tyrant, a destroyer of the constitution, and a lawless shedder of human blood. Even after nineteen centuries, the question is still debated whether his act was that of a bold and public-spirited magistrate, using legitimate powers with vigor and discretion, or whether it was a judicial murder, an act of brutal tyranny, perpetrated without legal warrant by a timid and self-seeking partisan.[30]

The issue was simply whether men caught red-handed in aiding a hostile army and proved guilty by their own signatures and confessions might be punished as enemies under the laws of war when the state had been placed under martial law. With the counsel of the senate, his constitutional advisers, Cicero concluded that they might be. The argument on the other side requires two assumptions: first, that the senate, which had earlier passed its "last decree" to deal with the emergency, had no constitutional power to do so and that, therefore, a state of martial law did not exist; second, that irrespective of validly declared martial law, a citizen in correspondence with an armed enemy and engaged in a plan to bring that enemy within the gates was, nevertheless, under Roman law, immune from the death sentence and indeed from any punishment, except by the vote of a popular mass meeting. To accept the first of these assumptions is simply to accept the view of the Roman constitution which Caesar had caused to be put forward at the trial of Rabirius. That view would have the absurd result of leaving the community without any lawful power to protect itself against internal force and violence. For centuries the senate had enjoyed and exercised such a power in its admitted right to appoint a dictator. Since the senate had that right, it is difficult to understand why that body did not have the lesser right to vest the consuls with some of the powers that a dictator could have exercised, and this is all that the "last decree" purported to do. In the face of this argument, there is no ground for modern scholars to assume as they have that the senate's power to pass its last decree was so clearly invalid as to convict Cicero of judicial murder. Moreover, if the senate's decree was valid, there is no reason to assume that it left a consul powerless to deal with the conspirators because they were not themselves actually in arms but only aiding and abetting an armed enemy. Martial law reaches to the one case as well as to the other.

It is to be noted that in the debate in the senate not even Caesar urged that the conspirators were immune from punishment. All that he objected to was the death sentence. However, if martial law could properly be regarded as in effect, then the death sentence was not inappropriate; whereas if it were not validly in effect, then no form of punishment was proper, not even the mitigated sentence which Caesar himself proposed, without a trial before some regularly constituted court, and the senate was not such a court. This raises the further question as to whether the senate had any right to act in the matter at all, and it has been made an additional ground of criticism against Cicero that he consulted the senate and sought its opinion. Forsythe says that by referring the question to the senate he abdicated his constitutional responsibility;[31] in Mommsen's final judgment, this seems to have been Cicero's chief offense, since, if the "last decree" conferred power to act, as Mommsen in the end admitted that it did, the power was conferred on the consul and not on the senate.[32] It is therefore said that Cicero showed timidity in taking counsel of the senate and in conforming to its opinion. These contentions overlook the relations between the consul and the senate under the traditional Roman constitution, under which the senate was the consul's advisory body for all purposes, standing in the same relation to him as a "family-council" to the head of a family. He was expected to consult it on important occasions and with respect to his own proposed course in important matters. This is all that Cicero did in seeking the opinion of the senate on the matter of punishment. The senate had no powers as a court, and he was not asking it to sit as a court; he was soliciting the counsel of his constitutional advisers as to how to exercise the powers with which he had been vested.

Not only has Cicero been charged by modern historians with arbitrary and tyrannical conduct in executing the Catilinarian prisoners, but he has also been blamed for playing turncoat against his party and deserting to the side of the aristocrats because he failed to follow the lead of Caesar. This charge rests on two misconceptions. It assumes in the first place that the so-called "popular" party at Rome was a well-defined and articulate organization with a policy and program such as political parties are supposed to have in modern parliamentary democracies. If a member of such a party adopts a course at variance with that laid down by the party leadership, as the Liberal Unionists in Britain did in 1886 or as Winston Churchill has done on several occasions during his career, there is a basis for the charge of leaving one's party, although the desertion may be susceptible of justification. At Rome, however, in the age of Cicero, the basic conditions did not exist which would support such a charge. There was no "popular" party in the sense of an articulate organization like a modern political party, with a leadership responsible for dictating party policy. There was only an unorganized group of politicians, great and small, who generally found it to their advantage to oppose whatever a majority of the senate desired. That there was no well-knit organization or spirit of loyalty to the "party" is evident, for example, from the way in which Caesar and Crassus, who professed to be "popular" leaders, had sought with senatorial assistance to undercut Pompey, another "popular" leader, in the manner already described. If Caesar thus showed no loyalty to Pompey, certainly there is no basis for charging Cicero, who had always followed Pompey rather than Caesar, for not adopting Caesar's view as to the proper method of disposing of the Catilinarian prisoners. There was no "party line" in these matters, and Cicero cannot be criticized as a turncoat because he did not choose to subordinate his own judgment to Caesar's.

A second mistaken assumption which underlies the charge that Cicero became a turncoat against the popular party when he executed the associates of Catiline is the assumption that Catiline's conspiracy was a "popular" movement. It must be pointed out that the "poor" for whose benefit the conspiracy was supposedly conceived were not the honest and industrious working class of Rome, or even the urban proletariat, but ruined aristocrats who had squandered or gambled away their fortunes and wished to become rich again by appropriating the fortunes of others. The only sense in which Catiline's conspiracy can be conceived as promoting democracy or the interest of the people is that it aimed at overthrowing the existing government and introducing a period of anarchy, out of which conceivably a more democratic government might have emerged. It is apparent that Cicero, who had lived through the times of Marius, Cinna, and Sulla, had no confidence in the kind of "democracy" that emerges from anarchy and terrorism. If he was not that kind of a democrat, is it correct to say that he was a traitor to democracy, or was no democrat at all? The question concerning Cicero's conduct in this respect is essentially the same that arises concerning Burke's attitude toward the French Revolution, and to assume in either case that there was an abandonment or betrayal of previous principles is to ignore the possibility that there may be more than one conception of popular government. To accuse Cicero of being untrue to popular principles is to assume that Caesar was necessarily and always the exponent of those principles.

That Cicero, with his characteristic intuition of the forces at work in Roman politics, foresaw the charges that would be brought against him is shown by the repeated efforts which he made to defend himself against them in advance throughout his Catilinarian speeches. He recognized that not only his future influence and political standing at Rome were at stake but also his position before the bar of history—his fame and reputation which, like all Romans, he regarded as the incentive and chief reward of the hazards of a public career. To this perception rather than mere vanity is almost certainly to be ascribed his constant emphasis throughout the re-

mainder of his life on the magnitude and value of his accomplishment in having saved the republic—an emphasis that from our
modern point of view seems offensively immodest and tiresome. But
Cicero knew his public: indeed, no one was better attuned to its
qualities. He obviously felt that the best way, and indeed the only
way, to imprint permanently on the public mind the principles for
which he stood and the nature of his service to the state was to talk
and to write continually about them. If, in so doing, he seems ob-
jectionably self-laudatory, may it not be partly because unconsciously
we hold Cicero to a higher standard than others, like Caesar and
Pompey, who were doing the same thing, and partly because as a
man of peace he may have felt it necessary to raise his voice more
stridently to overcome the din of arms?

As Cicero neared the end of his consulship and looked to the
years ahead, he well knew that henceforth he would have to reckon
more than ever with the great and growing influence of Caesar, and
that he would have against him the entire group of "popular" politicians who looked increasingly to Caesar for leadership. Yet, if he
clearly understood the movement of political forces in the large, he
was not enough of a student of individual psychology to understand
that he had raised against himself another, and, for the time being, a
more powerful enemy. It came to him with a shock that he had won
the ill will of Pompey.

II

The year 62 found Caesar preparing to turn to his personal advantage the anticipated return of the victorious Pompey from the
East. Caesar astutely recognized that all hope was now gone of
building up Crassus, or anyone else at this time, as a rival of Pompey. Not only would it be folly to attempt to oppose the triumphant
leader, who was on the eve of returning to Rome with greater glory
and prestige than any Roman had ever done before, but it would be
politically foolish not to join forces with him and to profit from his
influence. If Crassus objected, his view seems to have carried little
weight, for Caesar was not afraid at this point to show his independence. Accordingly, he set about making himself appear as

Pompey's friend and supporter and indicating that the votes he controlled could be put at Pompey's service. The latter apparently regarded these indications of support as both natural and appropriate, without any consciousness of their inconsistency with much that had transpired during his absence. Upon his return he would need legislation of two sorts: legislation to provide the liberal bounties which his soldiers would expect of him, and legislation ratifying his treaties and other diplomatic engagements with the rulers of the East, as well as ratifying his official decisions respecting the organization of his conquests. The former required the support of the politicians who influenced the popular assemblies, the latter the senate. It was for the veterans' legislation that he was happy to have an alliance with Caesar.

Pompey's ineptness in Roman politics displayed itself immediately upon his return in January of the year 61. Relying on the enormous prestige he had acquired by his stupendous victories in the East, he hoped to remain the first citizen of Rome, deferred to and admired by all. What he appears to have desired was something like the position that Pericles once held at Athens. The difference was, of course, that in the Athens of Pericles there had been no senate, jealous of its position and prerogatives; moreover, the mass of the Athenians had not been organized and dragooned, as the Romans now were, into disciplined voting bands at the beck and call of professional manipulators. At Rome a statesman could obtain and exert great influence only by constantly playing a shrewd and wary game of maneuver and intrigue, and by constantly forming and re-forming alliances. Pompey seems to have had no sense of this; instead, he cherished the naïve notion that he could maintain his eminence by standing on friendly terms with all the different cliques and groups in Roman politics and without allying himself with any of them. He appears to have thought that he could win and hold them all with a smile.

Such at any rate was the course he pursued after his return to Rome. Cicero reported that his first speech was so insipid that it pleased nobody.[33] Under the conditions of Roman politics, this was not the way to make friends or exercise power, and Cicero pointedly remarked that Pompey's stock was going down.[34] His neutral position rapidly became more and more uncomfortable, and it was soon put to a severe test by the outbreak of the dramatic scandal which has become famous as the "affair of Clodius," which, though not intrinsically important, had far-reaching consequences.

Publius Clodius was in many ways a second Catiline, a reckless, bold and unprincipled member of the aristocracy who was at the same time a master mob leader of the Roman underworld. He chose the occasion of the celebration in Caesar's house of the solemn rites of Bona Dea, from which all males were rigorously excluded, to smuggle himself into the house, disguised in female clothes, for the ostensible purpose of an assignation with Caesar's wife. This was precisely the kind of dare-devil exploit, combining lust with sacrilege, which would quicken the jaded appetites of a fashionable young Roman of the period. His presence was discovered by Caesar's mother, who gave the alarm, and Clodius was barely able to make his escape. The incident created a great uproar, particularly among the senatorial conservatives, who determined to make an example of him. Caesar himself took the affair coolly and made the best of it, for he was farsighted enough to perceive that it would give him an excellent chance to fish profitably in troubled waters. Although he promptly divorced his erring spouse with the famous remark that "Caesar's wife must be above suspicion," he made no move to proceed against the adulterer and was soon found in the position of actively protecting him. Caesar recognized that any controversy of which Clodius was the center would not only be certain to inflame the breach between the senate and the mob but would also inevitably split the senate. For this reason, he prepared to back Clodius enthusiastically. In so doing he could expect to accomplish three objectives. First, he would attach to himself a bold and unscrupulous agitator who, as Appian says, was a great favorite with the people,[35] and who would be useful to him in future election contests. Second, he would reestablish his alliance with Crassus, who had taken Clodius under his patronage and was supporting him unreservedly. Finally, he would be able to force Pompey's hand and demonstrate his political impotence. All three of these objectives Caesar was able to achieve.

Pompey, as Caesar intended, was thrown into a dilemma. If

he opposed Clodius, he would antagonize his new ally, Caesar; if he supported Clodius, he would alienate the senate, whose votes he needed for the confirmation of his official acts in the East; if he took neither side, he would expose his impotence and incur the ill will of everyone. In this situation he decided to play a double game, from which in the end he derived no advantage. He wooed the senate assiduously, took every occasion to defer to it, and spoke no word for Clodius; but a tribune whom he controlled, one Fufius, was among the most active of Clodius's supporters, and Pompey's ally in the consulship, Pupius Piso, did everything that he could behind the scenes to protect Clodius. This double dealing of Pompey drew from Cicero an expression of disgust in one of his letters: "there is no candor in him . . . ," he wrote, "nothing straightforward or direct or highminded." [36]

Hot debates in the senate and wild tumults in the assembly accompanied the efforts of the senatorial conservatives, led by Cato, to vindicate religion and morality in the trial of Clodius. Ultimately, he was acquitted by a jury suborned with the gold of Crassus. Cicero, who had not assumed the lead in the prosecution, took the gravest view of its failure. He saw in it a fatal blow to the prestige of the senate and a fatal encouragement to gang politics and mob rule. The constitution, he wrote, "has slipped from our hands by this one verdict." [37] "The republic received a crushing blow when this jury was corrupted and debauched." [38]

Cicero has sometimes been charged with never espousing a cause unless it was already victorious. The unfairness of this criticism is nowhere better shown than by the course he pursued after the acquittal. Clodius and his supporters were in the ascendant, and to defy them was to oppose head-on the forces which were assuming the dominant direction of Roman politics. There was no need for Cicero to do this, yet he went out of his way to do it, to his own great hurt, as events were to prove. In May of 61 he delivered a powerful speech in the senate in which, as he says in one of his letters, "I revived the fainting spirits of the supporters of the constitution. . . . By my denunciations and invectives against those corrupt jurors, I left none of the favorers and supporters of that victory with anything to say for themselves." [39] He defied Clodius to his face, and by attacking the consul Piso was responsible for depriving him of the appointment to the province of Syria, which had been promised him. This speech was an act of independence and defiance which Clodius and Caesar neither forgot nor forgave.

For the time being, however, Caesar and Crassus were content to let Cicero fulminate, for the game they were stalking was not Cicero but Pompey. Already they had succeeded in reducing him to impotence, even though he did not yet know it. The awakening would come later, and they could afford to wait. What had happened was that Pompey had in effect surrendered his leadership of the "popular" party. By committing his lieutenants Fufius and Piso to the cause of Clodius, he had notified the lesser politicians not to look to him to take an independent line; he had signaled to them in language which they understood that he was willing to follow the lead of Caesar. This was all they needed to know in order to transfer their allegiance.

In these circumstances, Caesar turned his attention to business of his own. For the year 61, following his term as praetor, he was assigned the governorship of Spain, and he was at last able to set out for that province. As propraetor, or governor, he had two objectives. The first and most important was to accumulate enough money to pay off his debts, for by now he owed Crassus an amount that is said to have equalled roughly a million dollars.[40] The second objective was to season himself as a soldier and school himself in the arts of command and strategy. The year in the peninsula proved highly successful from his standpoint. He was of material aid to the merchants and financiers of Spain, and his military campaigns, which opened up new territories to the traders who were his friends, yielded him enormous profits. Of equal importance was the fact that the campaigns afforded him an opportunity to make his debut as a military commander, for so far his military experience had been of the scantiest. With his cool and sure assessment of the Roman political scene, he seems to have reached the conclusion that military power was indispensable to the attainment of the position he desired for himself in Roman politics. He therefore proceeded, with his indomitable will, to turn himself into a soldier and a general in the wild highlands of the Asturias. In this training school was formed the future conqueror of Gaul.

Caesar's year in Spain can hardly be regarded otherwise than as one of conscious and deliberate preparation. If he had been a politician of a different and more ordinary cast of character, this would not be a necessary conclusion; more would certainly have to be attributed to chance and the impersonal course of events. However, everything that is known of Caesar's mind and methods, and all that can be pieced together of his career up to this point, as well as in its subsequent stages, create the impression that whatever he did was for a purpose and in pursuance of a carefully devised plan. In this respect he is almost unique among the great political figures of history. It is therefore not surprising that as the situation with which he had to deal changed and developed before him, in part as a result of his own maneuvers, he was always ready to adapt himself to the change and to alter his tactics, and almost his personality, to take advantage of it. Some historians, therefore, find difficulty in understanding Caesar because to do so appears to require the assumption of changes in character so great as to go beyond psychological probabilities. The difficulty is removed if it is recognized that there was no change in Caesar's character, but only a complete readiness to adopt radical alterations in tactics in response to the dictates of an amazingly bold, clearheaded and inventive intelligence which recognized that the opportunity had now come to assume a guiding and directing post in the Roman state. The remarkable thing about Caesar was that he never pressed beyond the possibilities of an existing situation. He was always willing to wait until the situation was ripe for the next move; but, when the time came, he was ready to take whatever next step was needed, however bold, to consolidate his past gains and put himself in a position for a new series of moves.

Such a turning point had now arrived. After Caesar's departure for Spain, Pompey continued to exhibit his political ineptness by failing to take advantage of Caesar's absence to reestablish his position. It was clearly the part of wisdom for the senate and for him to draw together. Pompey needed the senate if he were not to become a mere dependent of Caesar, and the senate needed Pompey if it were to maintain a counterpoise against Crassus and Caesar. No real issue of principle separated them, and indeed Pompey wished nothing more than to stand well, and cooperate, with it. Cicero did all he could during the twelve critical months between the summer of 61 and the summer of 60 to bring about this *rapprochement* and thus realize his own cherished dream of a "concord of the two orders," which he believed would preserve constitutional government.[41] However, Pompey's political obtuseness was such that he was constantly doing things that nettled, or aroused the suspicions of, the senate, and in the end these efforts were to prove fruitless. By assuming a take-it-or-leave-it attitude over the ratification of his treaties and diplomatic acts in the East, rather than permitting them to be discussed and judged on an individual basis, he brought the matter to an impasse, and nothing was accomplished except a widening of the rift between himself and the senate. When his bill for distributing land to veterans made its appearance, it was found not to be limited to veterans but to contain many of the objectionable features of the measure of Rullus which had been defeated three years before. Cicero felt obliged to risk an open breach with Pompey by publicly opposing much of the bill and offering drastic amendments.[42] Even with the objectionable features excised, the senate would have none of the land law on any terms, however moderate.

By this time, Pompey was exasperated beyond measure as a result of his failure to get done what he wanted through the ordinary processes of constitutional government. Through Caesar's astuteness, and his own ineptness, he had been reduced to a position of political impotence, isolated from leadership in the "popular" party on the one hand and from the senate on the other. Nevertheless, he still had large reserves of influence of which he was hardly aware and which he certainly did not know how to use. With his thirst for eminence and his urgency to attain his immediate ends, he was ready to accept the guidance and invisible mastery of anyone on whom he could lean and who would promise to help him out of his troubles. Caesar, with his remarkable understanding of individual psychology, perceived this and saw that he could take advantage of Pompey's character and position, for, if Pompey now needed Caesar, Caesar still needed Pompey. Pompey was still a towering, overshadowing figure in the Roman world. What was done under his auspices and nominally under his leadership would be accepted in a way that it would not be apart from that leadership and under those auspices. One of Caesar's characteristic qualities was that he had no more illusions about himself than he had about anything else. He knew that he did not yet stand on a level with Pompey and that there was still much for him to do before he could rival Pompey. Meanwhile, the only way by which he could make that further progress was with Pompey's help.

Caesar recognized, however, that while he must for an interval operate in appearance as a second to Pompey, the time had come for him to put himself at least in the same category with Pompey. For this reason he decided that he must become what he had never yet been, an outstanding military figure. Hence the military emphasis which he gave to his Spanish governorship and the novel military training through which he put himself at an age when most Romans were content to retire to civil life. He also determined to rid himself from debt and free himself from his long dependence on Crassus. Hence his connection with the Spanish financiers and his preparations to build up a private fortune of his own. With these foundations laid, he could return to Rome and become consul, with the further prospect of moving to a career that would make it possible for Romans to think of him in the same breath with Pompey.

It was during his Spanish year that Caesar first began to exhibit outward evidences of his great ambition. Cicero had sensed it long before, but hitherto it had not been Caesar's intention to reveal it. Now it was time to do so. With his profound understanding of public psychology, he perceived that he would never reach the position that he coveted in the state unless men began to think of him in connection with it, unless they became used to the idea and were willing to accept it. It is therefore not without significance that two well-known incidents are assigned by tradition to Caesar's year in Spain. The timing of these incidents might have no special meaning in the case of another man, but almost certainly it has a definite meaning in the case of Caesar. The two incidents are related together in Plutarch's *Life*. As he was passing through a small village with but few inhabitants, and those wretchedly poor, Caesar said seriously to his companions, "I had rather be the first man among these fellows, than the second man in Rome." "It is said that another time, . . . after reading some part of the history of Alexander, he sat a great while very thoughtful, and at last burst out into tears. . . . 'Do you think,' said he, 'I have not just cause to weep, when I consider that Alexander at my age had conquered so many nations, and I have all this time done nothing that is memorable?' "[43] If reports of these trivial and seemingly casual remarks were carried back to Rome, as they were certain to be, talk would commence which in time would accustom Romans to the thought that Caesar might one day become at least as great as Pompey. Of course, in the meanwhile, he must show that he was able to measure up to such an ambition. For this the first step was the consulship, and the next another provincial command in which he could prove dramatically his prowess as a conqueror.

With the consulship as the immediate goal, Caesar hurried back from Spain to claim it toward the middle of the year 60 without awaiting the arrival of his successor. He wished very earnestly for a triumph, but the interval before the election was brief and, by established custom, no general could enter the city to canvass for votes while his army was still without the walls. Occasionally the custom had been relaxed, as in the case of Pompey before the election of the year 71, and Caesar, who apparently did not wish to disband his troops, applied to the senate to relax it now in his favor. When his application was defeated by a filibuster on the part of Cato, he decided without hesitation to forego a triumph. The consulate was something he could not afford to lose.

The situation at this turning point in Roman destiny can be summed up in the words of an exceptionally understanding student:

. . . We seem to be contemplating the plot of a well contrived tragedy. We have before us Pompeius, who after having done his part towards shaking the fabric of the State, now at the summit of his greatness, returns to Rome but only to see the last rays of his fortune extinguished;

Caesar, conscious of his powers and of his superior influence, watching the moment which was to give full scope for their display; the State itself scarcely escaped from the ruin with which Catilina had threatened it, governed by men who were, with few exceptions, incapable and selfish voluptuaries; the people for the most part a lawless and undisciplined rabble, at the service of any one who would flatter and court them by supplying their wants, or gratifying their love of pleasure.[44]

III

Against this background of characters and events, of ambitions and opportunities, the significance and importance of the formation of the first triumvirate can be appreciated. The problem of when the alliance was in fact formed is not clearly answered by the ancient authorities. However, it seems practically certain that Pompey and Caesar must have come to terms either before or immediately after Caesar's return from Spain. Not only is this consistent with the growing approach between the two, which had been making itself felt during the previous eighteen months, but it seems proved by the fact that at this election Pompey is known to have had no personal candidate of his own, as he had had at each of the two preceding elections. Pompey was therefore almost certainly backing Caesar.

It is almost equally certain that this was not true of Crassus. It is reported that with the money Caesar brought back from Spain he paid off his debt to Crassus and cleared himself of obligations to him. It is also reported that he turned to another rich man, one Lucceius, a friend of Pompey, to finance the bribery which would be needed at the election, and that he made a deal to support Lucceius for the other consulship.[45] These reports seem to indicate that for the time being Crassus was not playing a leading part in the preelection negotiations, and this is borne out by the statement of Caesar's confidant, Publius Cornelius Balbus, some time after election, that at that time Caesar was looking forward to the possibility of coming to terms with Crassus in the future.[46] However, at the same time he succeeded adroitly in breaking down the old hostility between Pompey and Crassus, but the reconciliation was kept secret.[47] It seems probable that until that reconciliation had been effected and until Caesar's alliance with Pompey had been confirmed by the consular election, Crassus was unwilling to listen to Caesar's overtures and join the victorious side.

The loser in the course of these arrangements was Lucceius. When Caesar's new source of financial aid became known to the aristocrats, they decided to fight money with money in the interest of their own candidate Bibulus, Cato's son-in-law. The aristocracy, according to Suetonius, were fearful as to how far Caesar might carry matters in the consulate with a colleague disposed to concur in and second his measures, and they advised Bibulus to promise the voters as much as Lucceius. Most of them contributed toward the expense, and Cato himself admitted that bribery under such circumstances was for the public good.[48] As a result, when the votes were counted, Bibulus and Caesar were the successful candidates, and Lucceius got nothing for his outlay. At the same time, the presence of Bibulus, a rigid and extreme conservative, as Caesar's colleague, with a constitutional right to veto his every act, made it more vital than ever for Caesar to look for allies in all possible directions, and this undoubtedly explains why he turned again to the wealthy and still influential Crassus.

As earlier stated, the triumvirate of Pompey, Caesar and Crassus was a purely informal and behind-the-scenes working arrangement among three powerful politicians, something like the "rings" or "juntos" which were familiar features in American city government at the end of the nineteenth century. It had no basis in law and no recognized official character such as belonged to the so-called second triumvirate of the year 43. Its purpose, as Suetonius says, was not only to make sure "that nothing should be transacted in the government which was displeasing to any of the three," [49] but, more importantly, to advance the personal ends that each of the three desired. Caesar, as consul, was to obtain for Pompey the confirmation of his official acts and treaties in the East, as well as the enactment of a land law for the benefit of his veterans. For Crassus he was to obtain a revision of the lucrative contract of the Asian tax farmers. In return, Pompey and Crassus were to aid Caesar in obtaining a provincial assignment which would carry with it the command of an army and enable him to emerge in the role of a successful military figure. Naturally these terms were not made public, then or later; even the existence of the alliance was known only to insiders until it was disclosed by its operations.

The loose, informal character of the arrangement at its inception is illustrated by the fact that in his search for allies between the election and the end of the year Caesar even made overtures to Cicero.[50] Cicero's prominence in public life, together with his known partiality for Pompey, could prove advantageous to all the triumvirs, and his eloquence in the Forum and the senate would be an incomparable asset to have on their side. Cicero was exceedingly flattered by the proposal [51] and toyed with it for a time. He liked Caesar personally, and not long before he had written of the possibility of an alliance with him and expressed the hope of "making a better citizen of him," as well as of bringing over Pompey to a more "constitutional" position.[52] For a moment Caesar's offer seemed to afford an opening for realizing these hopes, but Cicero's innate common sense made him in the end decline. He was sure that Caesar would propose measures which he could not conscientiously support; he knew from recent experience how little Pompey valued his advice, and he accordingly concluded that he could not accept the offer and at the same time remain true to his principles. His refusal served notice on the triumvirs not only that they could not count on his aid but that he was to be regarded as a potentially dangerous opponent.

2

Fateful Year

CAESAR took office as consul on January first of the year 59, and within sixty days it was plain that a new force had entered Roman history. From the outset he took over the management of governmental affairs with a boldness, vigor and efficiency that made conservative Romans gasp. His watchword was "thorough," and he made it plain that he would brush aside all obstacles that might be interposed against his will. The result of this policy was a continuous display of ruthlessness in government such as Rome had never before submitted to except in periods of violent revolution. By the end of his year of office, Caesar had completely disrupted the normal operation of the republican government and had delivered blows to the senate and the assemblies from which they never recovered. Most of his actions were carried out in the name, and in the supposed interest, of Pompey and Crassus, who followed with a kind of breathless and surprised assent in the wake of their dynamic coadjutor.

The traditional picture of Caesar as a great democrat has taken so strong a hold on historians that his consulate has not infrequently been represented as a period marked by important and constructive

73

democratic reforms. In fact, however, his legislative accomplishments, with one exception later to be mentioned, had no reference to either democracy or reform, but were exclusively concerned with the objectives in which each of the triumvirs had a direct and selfish interest.

Caesar initiated his program in a spirit of studied and probably sincere moderation, doubtless with the conviction that moderation, if it proved effective, would be the cheapest and least wasteful method of accomplishing his ends, but with full determination to abandon that policy the moment he was satisfied it would not produce the results at which he aimed. The measure which the triumvirs selected to put at the head of their program was the land bill for Pompey's veterans. That measure seems to have been drafted with care to avoid as many objections as possible and to meet the principal criticisms which Cicero had directed against the bill of the preceding year. As now presented, the proposal expressly avoided tampering with the public domain land in Campania and provided for the purchase of other land at its assessed valuation by the use of the revenues from the new provinces in the East. Since Caesar, as consul, expected to sponsor the bill before the assembly, he followed the usual practice of submitting it for preliminary consideration to the senate as his constitutional body of advisers. Here the trouble began. Cicero was evidently prepared to accept the bill,[1] but the conservatives were adamant in their determination to oppose on principle a land bill of any kind. They accordingly resorted to adjournments and obstruction through endlessly protracted discussion. In this filibuster Cato, the ferocious and upright defender of his class, was the chief participant, and, although he advanced no specific objections to the bill, he talked against it on general grounds for hour after hour. Caesar, with his vivid sense of drama, saw at once that here was an opportunity to inaugurate his new policy of "thorough" in a spectacular way. As presiding officer of the senate, he called on the ushers to seize Cato while he was speaking and carry him out of the senate chamber, kicking and resisting, to prison.

The psychological effect of this extraordinary act can hardly be apprehended. It was like the attempt of Charles the First to arrest the Five Members, or like Pride's purge of the House of Commons. That a Roman senator, while addressing his colleagues on the floor, should be seized by the arm of the executive power and carried off to prison was an affront to the dignity of the senate which it was almost impossible for a constitutionally minded Roman to conceive. That the senator so seized should be Cato, the revered and incorruptible champion of the constitution and the republic, made the act still more unbelievable. The senators rose from their benches and trooped out after Cato, whereupon Caesar ordered him released. Then he adjourned the senate in a speech of cold resolution in which he told them that he would not afterwards trouble to consult them about his measures but would deal directly with the people. From this moment, Roman conservatives, distrustful as they had been of Caesar before, regarded him with a deadly hate that was never afterwards extinguished.

Caesar meant what he said. The senate met but seldom during the ensuing months and was practically a nullity in the government. It could convene at the call of a consul, and since one consul could veto any act of the other, Caesar's colleague, Marcus Calpurnius Bibulus, was helpless to bring the senate into action and had to content himself with convening it informally at his house. For the Roman government to proceed without the senate was almost like the modern government of England proceeding without the House of Commons. For hundreds of years the senate had been the working part of the Roman constitution, almost continuously in session and engaged not only in the consideration of major questions of policy but in the day-to-day administration of the details of finance and foreign affairs. Even in periods of democratic agitation its activities had not ceased. In recent years, and more particularly since the overthrow of Catiline, its prestige and importance had, to outward appearances, been greater than ever. For Caesar now to exclude it from participation in the government was a revolutionary act of the first magnitude. It was an act which made the conservatives feel, as Caesar doubtless intended them to, that he and his partners in the triumvirate were the masters of Rome.

Caesar's practical suppression of the senate stunned and surprised Cicero, who had more than merely a constitutionalist's reverence for the august body of which he felt himself to be the most distinguished member. Now that the senate no longer met, there was nothing for him to do at Rome. "I am not allowed to play the statesman," he complained to his friend Atticus.[2] "I am forced to quit the ship, not having cast aside the tiller, but having had it wrenched out of my hands." [3] He therefore withdrew to his villa at Anzio and commenced preparations for composing an extended literary work. "Now," he writes, "that I have found how empty are all those things I once thought so splendid, I am thinking of doing business exclusively with the Muses." [4] Meanwhile, he could not refrain from expressing his disgust with the triumvirs, whom he called tyrants, and asked, "If the power of the senate was disliked, what do you think will be the case when it has passed, not to the people, but to those three unscrupulous men?" [5]

With a courage for which he is not generally given credit, Cicero had not hesitated to state these views publicly before leaving Rome. In arguing a jury case before his departure, he spoke out in open criticism against the existing state of public affairs.[6] This speech had an important sequel, not only for Cicero but for Rome. It was delivered in the morning, and in the afternoon of the same day, at a secret ceremony in which Caesar and Pompey both participated, Clodius exchanged his patrician for plebeian status and thus became eligible for election as a tribune. In the light of what followed, this apparently trivial private incident fits into place in Caesar's farsighted policy of calculated risks.

Having disposed of the senate, Caesar was faced with the necessity of accomplishing his purposes through the assembly, and once again he was in a position where he could not afford to lose. In the rough-and-tumble of popular voting, it was evident from the experience of recent years that about as many electors, influenced by bribery, friendship or the relation of clienthood, could be induced to follow the conservatives as could be bribed or dragooned by the "popular" leaders. Furthermore, the position of Caesar's colleague Bibulus, possessed of the constitutional prerogatives vested in the consular office, was a grave threat to Caesar's power over the assembly. Bibulus could not only veto Caesar's acts, but, through his right to consult the wishes of the gods through taking the auspices,[7] he was in a position to prorogue or adjourn an assembly or prevent it from convening. Caesar saw that the only certain way to guard against these inconveniences was by resort to force. That, however, was a game at which two could play, and in the recent history of increasing disorder at the polls, force had favored the conservatives about as often as their opponents.

With this prospect before him, Caesar, in his usual cool and clearheaded way, recognized that it was necessary for him to make sure that in a trial of strength the greater force would always be on his side. Accordingly, with his passion for efficiency and thoroughness, he set about making preparations to ensure that result. For this purpose the most likely and promising instrument was Clodius, who seems already to have gone far in reorganizing and disciplining the ward clubs or guilds, which still remained a power in underground politics.

Clodius was precisely the man to organize the force that Caesar needed to make sure of his control of the assembly, but he had a price for his services. He wanted to be tribune, and he wanted the office for one special and particular purpose above others: the opportunity to prosecute and punish Cicero. Ever since his trial for sacrilege, when Cicero had testified against him and denounced him so vehemently in the senate, Clodius had cherished a passion for revenge that had become an obsession. Caesar had been delaying the ceremony of plebeian adoption prerequisite to Clodius's eligibility for the tribunate, doubtless to see whether Cicero was prepared to adopt an accommodating attitude toward the triumvirs; if he did so, his aid would be far too valuable to turn Clodius loose upon him. Pompey also demurred because he placed a sufficient value on Cicero's support to be unwilling to sacrifice him. Cicero's jury speech criticizing the triumvirs on the day of his departure for Anzio tipped the scale in Clodius's favor. If, as it now seemed, he intended to make himself troublesome, it would be well to let Clodius deal with him. Furthermore, Caesar's need of Clodius's help with the assembly was becoming imperative and immediate. Accordingly, Clodius was paid the price he asked and, by a hurried ceremony, which seems to have been deficient in some of the essential legal formalities, the way was opened for him to become a tribune at the next election.

The effect on Cicero was thus delayed until the following year, but the effect on the control of the Roman assembly was immediate.

Caesar made good his threat to bring his measures directly before the people. Almost immediately he brought in a new land bill which, by all accounts, was in many respects a much more extreme measure than the bill he had previously presented to the senate. The proposed land distribution was not restricted to veterans but was extended to poor citizens. At some time during the progress of the bill it was also extended to include the Campanian public lands. These were to be distributed in ten-acre lots to poor Romans having three children each. The proposal was unsound, and futile as well, since it would displace competent cultivators who paid a substantial rent to the state with inexperienced proletarians who paid no rent and who would be unable to make a living in an occupation to which they were not accustomed. In fact, after the bill became law, not enough proletarians applied for land to exhaust the quantity made available, and the remainder seems to have been left unoccupied for years.[8]

It is difficult not to believe that Caesar deliberately advanced this proposal to enrage the conservatives, and, if this was his object, he succeeded in doing so. Bibulus addressed a meeting of the people and announced that he would veto the submission of the bill, and it was known that several tribunes were prepared to do likewise.[9] At this point, Caesar committed Pompey and Crassus to responsibility for his further course by calling on them to come forward and say to the people whether they were satisfied with his bill. They answered that they were. He then asked Pompey whether, if armed violence were employed, he would aid the supporters of the bill. Pompey replied, "If anyone dares to draw a sword, I will take up my shield." [10] "Such an utterance from a private citizen in a public meeting was unprecedented, indeed inexcusable. But it served its purpose. None dared offer serious opposition in arms to the chief around whom his veterans would rally." [11]

Having thus struck terror into the opposition in advance, Caesar went promptly into action. When the day for voting came, Bibulus, bent on exercising his veto, appeared in the Forum as Caesar was addressing the crowd from the platform in front of the temple of

Castor and Pollux. When Bibulus attempted to mount the platform he was attacked by Caesar's ruffians and thrown down the steps,[12] while men with daggers broke his consular insignia and wounded some of the tribunes who stood around him. To add insult to injury, someone poured a pot of ordure over his head. His friends carried him, against his will, out of the crowd and into the nearby temple of Jupiter Stator. At this point, Cato forced his way into the crowd and began to make a speech, but he, too, was lifted up and carried out by Caesar's partisans. He went around secretly by another street and again mounted the rostrum, but was again lifted up and thrown out. After this exhibition Caesar carried his law.[13]

By these proceedings Caesar announced his short and summary way of dealing with the assembly as clearly and definitely as he had previously announced his short and summary way of dealing with the senate. He made it clear that he intended to get his measures adopted and that, if necessary, he intended to employ force to do so. Bibulus took his experience so seriously and was in such fear for his life that he retired to his house and did not leave it during the remainder of his term of office. From this place of safety he issued statements and edicts, pronounced vetoes, took the auspices, and forbade assemblies with persistent, if ineffectual, futility. Although as consul Caesar was entitled to propose measures directly to the people, his colleague had an absolute right to forbid him; yet Caesar persistently ignored all prohibitions.

The plain fact is that although Caesar could on occasion insist with studied nicety on constitutional principles, he was really interested in government only as an instrument for getting done the things that he wanted, and what he now wanted was to carry out the program embodied in the bargain with the two other triumvirs. He had by now trimmed down the governmental processes to the point where he could employ them promptly and efficiently to this end. He had eliminated the senate and his colleague in the consulship, and he had reduced the assembly to a submissive and acquiescent ratifying agency. He had already accomplished one of his objectives, the enactment of Pompey's land law. He now proceeded to carry out the rest of the triumvirs' program by the same methods and in the same way.

It is to be noted that the remaining measures which made up the triumvirs' program—the ratification of Pompey's official acts, the revision of the Asian tax contract, and the assignment of a proconsular military command to Caesar—were all of a kind which, under the traditional constitution, fell properly within the exclusive competence of the senate and not of the assembly. Although it was no longer uncommon for extraordinary military commands to be conferred by direct popular vote, until now no such vote had superseded or interfered with the allotment of proconsular assignments by the senate. Caesar proceeded to disregard these constitutional obstacles and carried all three measures by vote of the assembly. It was no longer necessary for him to use force; the knowledge that he would do so, if thwarted, was sufficient.

Caesar's proconsular command was conferred by the Vatinian law, a plebiscite sponsored by a tribune named Vatinius, who was one of his henchmen. The command was so curiously circumscribed as to require comment. In the light of subsequent events, there can hardly be much doubt that Caesar, with his exceptional foresight and habit of planning for the future, had already set his eyes on Transalpine Gaul, beyond the Alps, as the theater for the next act of his career. In the preceding year, an imminent outpouring of the Swiss from their mountain valleys had heralded a great movement of peoples. At about the same time, the German chieftain, Ariovistus, had brought his barbarian hordes across the Rhine. These developments portended war, which meant an opportunity for winning the military renown which was the next item on Caesar's personal program. The only other quarter of the world that could compete with Gaul in this respect was Egypt, which was again in the throes of internal disorder; but Egypt did not offer so promising a field of activity, and, besides, Caesar had other designs on that kingdom, as was soon to appear. He therefore directed his designs toward Gaul but was hesitant for the time being about bringing them clearly into the open. Accordingly, the command which the plebiscite of Vatinius conferred on him was only over the region of Lombardy, known as Cisalpine Gaul, and over Illyricum on the Adriatic, both peaceful provinces where no war was in prospect. Yet, oddly enough, Caesar was empowered to recruit and command an army of three legions comprising a total of roughly 18,000 men.[14] The appointment was also peculiar and unprecedented in that it was for a fixed term of five years, commencing on the first of March of the current year, and so was to run in part concurrently with his consulship.

The most likely reason for Caesar's hesitancy and apparent modesty in the matter of the provincial command was his delicate sense of Pompey's frame of mind. With exceptional understanding and tact, Caesar recognized that he must treat the sensitivities of that great egotist with the utmost deference and circumspection. Pompey was far from satisfied or happy with his current position. Although Caesar had obtained for him what he had so long desired, confirmation of his official acts and bounties for his veterans, these had not been achieved as Pompey would have preferred. Not only had he been involved in disagreeable public contentions, but he had been exposed to criticism and unpopularity. Most of all, he was depressed and irritated by the bad light in which he had been made to appear in the eyes of the members of the senate, with whom he wished to stand well socially and personally, whatever political differences he might have with them. Although it was Caesar who had done the things that offended the senate, he had acted in such a way as to strengthen the impression that he was only acting for Pompey and as Pompey's instrument, and thus Pompey had the chief share of the blame and resentment. This nettled him, and Caesar perceived that if he were to go on acting under the protection of Pompey's great name, as he intended to do, he must assuage the hero's wounded vanity and above all not seem too forward or expansive in designs which concerned himself. This shrewd calculation almost certainly accounts for the somewhat devious course Caesar pursued in the next stages of the development of his personal program. It accounts first of all for the modesty of the initial steps that he took toward obtaining a provincial command. It accounts also for the care with which he spread the impression that he had now obtained all he wanted, that he cherished no further personal ambitions [15] and that all he was doing was for others, chiefly for Pompey. In this way Pompey's sensitiveness would be to some extent assuaged. Yet Caesar saw that he must make further offerings on the altar of the great man's self-complacency, in order to bind Pompey's interests still more closely to his own and ensure the continuance of their cooperation. This he proceeded to do in two very tangible ways.

First he found an effective way of appealing to Pompey's cupidity. Egypt was in a state of internal commotion, and the king, Ptolemy Auletes, known as "the flute-player," and better still as the father of Cleopatra, was applying for Roman support to save his throne. While in the East, Pompey had refused to recognize him and was still reluctant to do so, but Caesar undertook to act as intermediary and to show how the matter could be turned to their mutual advantage. Negotiations were opened, and in the end, Suetonius tells us, Caesar "squeezed out of Ptolemy nearly six thousand talents [roughly the equivalent of $7,000,000] in the name of himself and Pompey." [16] To raise this great sum the king had to borrow from Roman knights, whose interests thus became more closely bound to those of Pompey and Caesar. Again, ignoring the senate in this important foreign transaction, Caesar then completed the bargain by carrying a law by popular vote which recognized the "flute-player" as lawful sovereign of Egypt and which declared him entitled to protection as a friend and ally of the Roman people. [17]

A transient business transaction of this kind was not, however, enough, as Caesar perceived, permanently to bind Pompey to him and allay his jealousy of his personal advancement. A closer bond was needed, and for this other means were at hand. By his first wife, Caesar had a daughter Julia, now a girl of nineteen or twenty and completely devoted to her father. Pompey was wifeless, and Caesar accordingly arranged a match between the two. Pompey, now in his late forties, became completely enamored of his girl-wife. Naturally sensual by disposition, he gave himself up to the pleasures of conjugal life and delighted in whatever might please his young bride. As Plutarch says, he let his fondness for her seduce him into effeminate habits. Not only did he give "all his time to her" but "passed his days in her company in country-houses and gardens, paying no heed to what was going on in the forum." [18] More importantly, because he feared the frowns and tears of Julia, he was brought under an influence which would work ceaselessly upon him in Caesar's favor. Thus the marriage of Julia introduced an element of permanence into Caesar's alliance with Pompey and made it possible for Caesar to presume on Pompey's support as he had not been able to do before.

Notwithstanding the elimination of opposition from Pompey, Caesar's innate caution was such that he was anxious to strengthen his position in still other quarters. He decided that the time had come when he could fairly hope for a breach in the almost solid opposition with which up to now he had been confronted by the senate. So successful had the triumvirs been in carrying through their program, and so completely were they in control over the government, that, as always happens in such cases, many in the senate began to feel that further resistance was hopeless and that it would be advantageous to adapt themselves to the new state of affairs. Crassus had always controlled a considerable number of senators, and others were so closely involved in financial dealings with the knights that they were inevitably influenced by the support which the latter were giving to the triumvirs. Even among the conservative aristocrats there were several who began to think of their own future and of the chances for advancement and profit which would not materialize if they continued to oppose what promised to become a permanent regime. It was these wavering aristocrats that Caesar set out to win, and again he employed the device of a marriage alliance.

Among the highly respectable and socially prominent aristocrats, one was Lucius Calpurnius Piso, a man of no great importance and no very firm political principles. Piso had a daughter Calpurnia, of marriageable age, and Caesar had been without a wife since his divorce of Pompeia three years before. Caesar accordingly contracted a marriage with Calpurnia and let it be known that he favored his new father-in-law for one of the consulships of the ensuing year. There is no doubt that this step accomplished what Caesar sought. It was a sign held out to conservative senators that, if they would consult their interests and not continue in opposition, there would be much for them to gain as individuals at the hands of the triumvirs. Such an invitation was bound to exert a powerful influence on a body composed of such members as made up the Roman senate at that time.

With the opposition thus divided and with the support of Pompey assured, Caesar moved forward a further step in rounding out his ambitions. He let it be known that, in addition to the provinces conferred on him by the law of Vatinius, he desired or would be willing to accept an additional command over Transalpine Gaul, the Provence of modern times, including not only the Roman province of Narbonne but also *Gallia comata* or "wild Gaul," the unconquered country of the free Celtic tribes which included most of modern France. He so managed matters that this new and greater command would come to him not from the people, but from the senate. Reportedly, it was represented to the senate that if they did not confer the appointment, the people would certainly do so, and that the senate ought not to lose the opportunity now afforded of rehabilitating its position by Caesar's willingness to receive his proconsular appointment at its hands. Accordingly, Crassus strongly urged the senate to take the proposed action, and Pompey is said to have done likewise. The matter was treated as a proper occasion for gratitude on the senate's part because Caesar was at last willing to recognize its prerogatives. It is not known how many senators were present when the vote was taken, or whether Cato was there; certainly Bibulus was not. Thus Caesar found himself at last in possession of his coveted military command without substantial opposition and with at least the appearance of the almost unanimous approval of all elements in the state.

Only one more matter remained for the triumvirs to arrange. This was to prolong their control over the government into the future, or at least into the following year. The obvious way of doing so was to bring about the election of consuls whom they could control. Caesar had already selected his new father-in-law, Piso, as his own nominee; Pompey chose his long-time retainer Gabinius, who as tribune had sponsored his original appointment to the command against the pirates. No other candidates presented themselves against these hand-picked nominees, since opposition seemed not only hopeless but dangerous, and they were duly elected. Neither of them cared to assume a position of leadership, and this, of course, was what Caesar and Pompey wished. Pompey, who intended to remain in Rome, doubtless expected to exercise the controlling force in the government while Caesar was absent in Gaul, but Caesar had other plans which centered on the forthcoming election of Clodius as one of the tribunes. That event was to be the key to the important political events of the following year.

The frequently repeated assertion that Caesar during his consulate was a reformer who sought to introduce efficiency and equity into the operation of government [19] rests on the supposition that he sponsored and obtained the enactment of a number of so-called "Julian laws" for these purposes. No historian of Caesar's time describes the nature or content of these supposed laws, with one exception.[20] One of these Julian laws (the lex Fufia) was an act which provided that in trials for extortion and political offenses the jury should vote separately by the classes of which it was composed and that the vote of each class should be published.[21] The obvious and only intelligible purpose of this enactment was to make the senators and others on a jury think twice before acquitting a defendant whom the knights, as chief moneylenders in the provinces, wished to punish. It was thus a political measure in the interest of the knights and their patron Crassus. Another "Julian law" was a codification of existing legislation which dealt with provincial extortion, and which seems to have outlawed expressly, and in much strengthened form, a wide variety of extortionate practices. Just and desirable as these provisions were in themselves, there is room for doubt as to how sincerely Caesar intended them for honest reforms. In any event, he was hardly in his own province before he proceeded to violate them,[22] and, excellent as the measure appeared, it seems to have been mainly intended as only another club to hold over the heads of refractory senatorial governors, another stick with which to beat the senate.

What distinguishes Caesar's consulate is not a record or spirit or reform, but a pervading sense of tension and suppressed conflict. The atmosphere was charged with a sense of fear, resentment, uneasy apprehension and the paralysis of willpower under which opposition wilts. Men were kept in doubt and uncertainty by anxiety as to what would happen next—at one moment cajoled by prospects of advantages, at another alarmed by the specter of nameless dread. These are characteristic marks of the peaceful founding of an absolutism, incidents of the softening-up process which by unperceived gradations shapes community thinking into passive obedience. It was an atmosphere in which men at first struggle and protest aimlessly, then settle into a psychology of helplessness; with nothing tangible on which to focus opposition, they become divided, dispersed, and in the end succumb.

Some feeling of the atmosphere is exhibited in the confidential letters of Cicero written during the spring and summer of the year 59. "We have everything to fear," he writes; "avowedly a despotism is being prepared for us." [23] "We have so completely lost the constitution that . . . a young man . . . scarcely got off with his life because, when he determined to prosecute Gabinius for bribery, . . . he mounted the rostra and, as a private citizen, called Pompey a dictator. Nothing could have been closer than his assassination." [24] For a time there seemed to be an upsurge of discontent and protest throughout the city, expressing itself in demonstrations in the theater and in the gathering of mobs to applaud the edicts of Bibulus. The sullen, angry tone of the demonstrations alarmed Cicero more than the tyranny of the triumvirs. "The republic," he writes, "is in a worse state than when you went away because then the despotism which was oppressing us seemed to be popular with the multitude, . . . but now it has become suddenly so hated by everyone that I tremble to think what will be the end of it. . . . Then they were employing such slow poisons that it seemed as though our end might be painless. Now I fear that they have been inflamed by the hisses of the crowd. . . ." [25] In this mood Cicero brought himself to think that to resist might be even worse than to acquiesce until the storm should blow over.[26] "For myself, . . . I have so completely lost all nerve that I even prefer the ease in which I now languish to a struggle in arms no matter how great the chance of success." [27] At times he rouses himself to a more resolute mood: "We are bound fast on every side, and are making no difficulty any longer as to being slaves, but fear death and exile as though they were greater evils, though they are in fact much smaller ones." [28] But again he is overcome by a feeling of helplessness: "We cannot think resistance possible without a general slaughter, nor can we see what the end of concession is to be except ruin." [29]

Meanwhile, Caesar had taken the growing discontents in hand

in a characteristic way. When the knights demonstrated against the regime, he let them know that unless they behaved themselves he would deprive them of their highly prized front seats in the theater; and when the populace hissed, he notified them that if they hissed the wrong men, he would cut off the distributions of grain.[30]

During these months the triumvirs were playing a cat-and-mouse game with Cicero by holding Clodius over his head. The latter was constantly letting it be known that he was only waiting for the commencement of his tribunate to take vengeance on the orator. Cicero tried to pretend to himself that these threats did not disturb him, but the frequency with which he mentions them belies his assumed indifference.[31] Pompey kept assuring him that he was in no danger. "He swears it; he even adds that he will himself be slain sooner than I injured." [32] A few weeks later he repeats the assurance, coupled with doubt. "Pompey asserts that [Clodius] will do nothing against me. It is risky for me to believe that. . . ." [33] Later Pompey told Cicero that he had talked with Clodius and that the latter had promised to do nothing contrary to Pompey's wishes. "However," writes Cicero, "since then he has not ceased to speak against me with the greatest acrimony. . . ." [34] Again, he tells his brother, "Pompey makes all sorts of promises and Caesar too; but I do not trust them enough to feel that I can afford to neglect making preparations." [35]

It would seem that through these months the two triumvirs were pursuing a double-faced policy toward Cicero because they had not yet quite made up their minds how to deal with him. On the one hand, they did nothing, or nothing effective, to stop the threats of Clodius; on the other, they had clearly not yet given up hope of winning Cicero for an ally. Caesar accordingly baited the hook for him with offers meant to be attractive.[36] First, it was intimated that Cicero might be named one of the land commissioners under Caesar's agrarian law; later, a definite offer was made when a vacancy on the commission occurred.[37] Then Caesar invited him to become one of his lieutenant generals in his forthcoming Gallic campaign.[38] Finally he was offered an "honorary legation," or ambassadorship-at-large, which would enable him to leave Italy and travel for a year at public expense.

That Cicero toyed with these offers is not surprising in view of the fact that Cato himself, the uncompromising and incorruptible, actually accepted an appointment of a comparable character in the following year. There was far more reason for Cicero to do so than for Cato, since Cicero had the sword of Clodius's vengeance hanging over his head. Any appointment of the kind which was dangled before him would give him protection by vesting him with an official status and removing him from Rome. As he weighed and balanced the opposing considerations, he reflected with some bitterness on the slight hope he had of receiving support from the conservatives who, like himself, were interested in preserving constitutional government.[39] This, however, was but a passing mood; when he searched his conscience, he reached a different conclusion, that he would not let it be said that he had accepted a bribe to change his principles. "What would . . . history say of me six hundred years hence? These things I am much more afraid of than of the idle talk of today." [40] In this mood Cicero came out of his retirement and in a notable jury speech flung down a challenge to Caesar.

The occasion was a prosecution, apparently initiated by Caesar, brought against one Flaccus, who had been governor of Asia and had been like other such governors criticized for alleged acts of extortion. The criticism was probably justified, but there seems to have been another and different motive for the prosecution and for bringing it at just this time. Flaccus had been one of the praetors during Cicero's consulate and had actively aided him against Catiline. In fact, he had been at the head of the party which arrested the Gallic allies of the conspirators as they were leaving Rome.[41] There was a general understanding that Flaccus was being prosecuted rather for the part he had taken against Catiline than for the extortionate acts which were nominally the basis of the charge. Cicero, who appeared for the defense, thus had a strong personal motive for doing so. If punishment was to be meted out for having thwarted Catiline, it was clear that Cicero's own turn would soon come when Clodius took office as tribune. Thus, as in the case of Rabirius four years earlier, the prosecution of Flaccus was really a sort of trial run to determine the possibilities of securing a verdict that would later serve as a precedent in an action against Cicero. Of this Cicero was fully aware and openly based the defense of his client on that ground. He put all his power into his speech to the jury, which remains one of his masterpieces of effective forensic eloquence.

> In this case [he told them], you are called on to decide not concerning the Lydians or Mysians or Phrygians who . . . have appeared before you, but concerning your own republic, your own constitution, the common safety, the hope of all good men, if there be any such now remaining. . . . Every other refuge of good men, every other stronghold of innocent men, every other bulwark . . . of the republic and the law has failed. . . . Accordingly, unless we can maintain in this place, before you, and through you as judges, I will not say the authority of the laws, which is lost, but our safety, which hangs on a last and slender hope, we have no place in which we can take refuge. It is therefore most essential that you shall see what is the real object of this proceeding, what is really at stake here and what is the other case, of which the foundations are being laid here in the present prosecution.[42]

> Not only are these certain individuals who are laboring for many other things, and in particular are endeavoring to cause your way of thinking, your decisions and your opinions to appear in a most unfavorable and odious light to every respectable citizen. . . . They do not think that the republic has been sufficiently overturned unless they punish in the same way citizens who have deserved well of the republic. . . . Already I am being mentioned by informers, crimes are being fabricated against me, dangers are being prepared for me. If they did these things through others, if they incited a mob of ignorant citizens in the name of the people, I could endure it with greater equanimity; what can never be endured, however, is that they should think that, by means of Roman senators and knights, who did all these things as chief actors and prime movers in defense of the public safety . . . can be deprived of their fortunes and expelled from the city.[43]

The jury, consisting of men who were instinctively friends of law and order, were convinced by Cicero's appeal, and Flaccus was acquitted. It was a notable victory snatched from under the very noses of the triumvirs, and Cicero's hope of success in his coming contest with Clodius was proportionately increased. "It is amazing," he writes, "how people are making professions, offers of service and promises. Indeed, I have the highest hopes, but my spirits are even higher. . . . If Clodius sets a day for proceedings, the whole of Italy will rush to my support. . . . My old group of constitutionalists is warm in its zeal and attachment to me. If there are any who formerly were somewhat hostile or comparatively lukewarm, they are now uniting themselves with the constitutionalists from hatred of these despots." [44]

Meanwhile the triumvirs, keeping up their war of nerves which was steadily undermining Roman morale and all spirit of resistance, resorted to a familiar device, the alleged discovery of a vague and ominous plot involving prominent names. It was to this that Cicero referred in his speech when he said that he was being mentioned by informers and that accusations were being invented against him. [45] One Lucius Vettius, who had acted as a spy for the government on the Catilinarian conspirators, let it be known that he had been approached with a proposal to assassinate Pompey. On being interrogated, he testified that the secretary of Bibulus had sent him a dagger. Caesar brought Vettius before an assembly of the people, where he gave further testimony implicating not only young Marcus Brutus, Lucullus, and Domitius Aheonobarbus, all members of Cato's coterie, but Cicero and his son-in-law. "The opinion is generally held," writes Cicero, "that the whole affair has been trumped up. . . ." [46] Vettius was remanded to prison, where he was either murdered or committed suicide, and the incident was thus conveniently closed and the opportunity removed of testing the truth of the accusations. The episode was useful both in casting an ugly suspicion on the opponents of the triumvirs and as a means of serving notice on prudent men that opposition was likely to involve them in grave charges which they might have difficulty in disproving.

This sorry business hardly added to the triumvirs' prestige, and Cicero's successful defense of Flaccus rekindled for a moment the spirit of resistance. Nothing, however, disturbed the resolute progress of Caesar toward his goal. Although he had profound respect for public opinion as a factor to be reckoned with, he also had a serene confidence that he possessed the surest means of having public opinion on his side, namely force and fear. He had already been recruiting the army which had been voted to him with his province, and in the last months of the year he kept it encamped outside the walls of Rome. He ended his consulship as he had begun it, like the crack of a whip. When certain of the praetors for the ensuing year ventured to challenge the constitutionality of his acts, as they had a legal right to do, he coolly invited the senate to pass on the question impartially while his legions looked on.[47]

So great is the charm which the figure and personality of Caesar have exerted on historians of all ages, and particularly of the nineteenth century, that his epoch-making consulate has quite generally been judged in a favorable light. Thus, a well-known Oxford scholar of the last generation commented on it as follows:

. . . Caesar, during his term of power, had done what no one else could do. The Senate had failed to perform the most pressing duties of government; he carried them through successfully, without violence and without more hurt to a constitution which could not work than might be expected sooner or later to befall it. He did his best to avoid any violence, and by a union of political leaders and interests to make the clumsy Republic into a working constitution; and in these efforts he even once or twice allowed conciliation to get the better of political principle. Work had to be done; there was but a year to do it in; obstruction and opposition confronted him at every turn; yet that work *was* done, and done on the whole by the hand of a real statesman, true to the principles of a great party.[48]

This judgment, which can hardly be said to square fully with all the facts, combines something of the philosophy of Thomas Carlyle [49] with something of the spirit of twentieth century pragmatism. It is a judgment which rests on an implicit premise that was openly expressed by Caesar's great admirer Mommsen in the following words:

. . The political movement tended thoroughly towards the goal of despotism; the only point still in dispute was whether the close circle of families of rank . . . or a monarch was to be the despot . . . the fundamental principle of a free commonwealth—that the contending powers should reciprocally confine themselves to indirect coercion— had become effete in the eyes of all parties alike, and on both sides the fight for power began to be carried on first by the bludgeon, and soon by the sword. . . . Beyond doubt it was the better for the interests of

Rome, the more quickly and thoroughly a despot set aside all remnants
of the ancient free constitution, and invented new forms and expressions for the moderate measure of human prosperity for which absolutism leaves room; the intrinsic advantage, which belongs to monarchy
under the given circumstances as compared with any oligarchy, lay
mainly in the very circumstance that such a despotism, energetic in pull-
ing down and energetic in building up, could never be exercised by a
collegiate board. But such calm considerations do not mould history; it
is not reason, it is passion alone, that builds the future.[50]

This pessimistic and fatalistic outlook of a nineteenth century
German, with its characteristically mystical emphasis on passion and
power, will be found to underlie most of the favorable judgments
on Caesar's consulate, as on his subsequent career. Mommsen shows
profound insight in one remark in the foregoing passage—the observation that the reason the Roman republican constitution would
no longer work was because the contending powers would no longer
confine themselves to what he calls "indirect coercion," that is, the
coercion of the ballot box and the debates of the senate and the
Forum, but carried on their fight for supremacy first by the bludgeon
and afterwards by the sword. For the use of such means no one was
more responsible than Caesar. Indeed, one of the most noteworthy
features of his consulship was that Caesar was the first Roman since
his father-in-law, Cinna, who had the courage, or the insolence, to
disregard the forms of the constitution and use whatever methods
of direct action were needed to overcome and suppress those elements
in the state that disagreed with him, irrespective of their legal rights.
Thus Caesar himself was mainly responsible for the condition on
which Mommsen relies to justify his conduct, and he continued to
foster it in the months following the end of his consulship.

3

Declining
Resistance

I

At the close of his year of office, Caesar did not leave Rome but stayed on in the city, while his army waited outside the gates. This was part of his plan for exercising control over the government of his successors. Hitherto, the Roman constitution was enough of a reality so that no one had been able to give direction to, or establish a continuous policy for, the succession of annually elected consuls. In general, when men went out of office they went out of power. Caesar's triumvirate, however, smashed this safeguard that protected the operation of the republican system by seeing to it that the consuls for the year 58 were of their own selection.[1] For Caesar, however, it was not enough that Gabinius and Piso were to be the chief magistrates. He had other designs which he planned to further, through a proposal in which his two associates evidently concurred, to the effect that Clodius as tribune, and not the consuls or Pompey, should really hold the central position in the government of Rome during the ensuing year.

93

From the point of view of all three triumvirs, there was some reason for this plan. It was of no particular concern to them that Clodius was a disreputable character, motivated by personal ambition and the slave of his passions and caprices. What they needed was someone who could be depended on to control and dominate the assemblies and use them for furthering the triumvirs' purposes. Clodius had already shown his superb capacities in this direction during Caesar's consulship, and it was therefore logical that he should continue it. However, Caesar appears to have had a more private object. He did not completely trust Pompey. Although in consequence of the marriage of Julia he no longer doubted his partner's loyalty, he nevertheless had some reason to be apprehensive that Pompey would not be sufficiently firm in giving to the government the direction and force that Caesar felt necessary. For what he deemed to be the requisite leadership a more positive character was needed, and Clodius met the requirements. Clodius could be relied on to move vigorously along the lines of Caesar's policy, and Pompey would have no alternative but to follow.

In the formulation of this plan, another factor almost certainly entered Caesar's calculations. Throughout his career he was wedded to the strategy of playing on the divisions between others, his associates no less than his opponents. It was inevitable that a point would some day be reached when Pompey would no longer tamely submit to the domineering spirit of Clodius. When that time arrived, Pompey would turn for advice and help to Caesar. Thus Caesar would keep a firmer hold on Pompey than he could otherwise do, and he could also keep a hold on Clodius, who would naturally wish to enjoy his continued support over the protests of Pompey. In this way, Caesar could play the two against each other, and in the process the prestige and preeminence of Pompey would inevitably be slowly whittled away. In any event, this is what happened, and there is no reason to suppose that Caesar with his uncanny foresight did not intend that it should.

The first step in building up a dominant position for Clodius was to be certain that Gabinius and Piso would be willing to accept positions that were both novel and humiliating for consuls. Greedy as they were for money, their acquiescence was secured without difficulty. Since the proconsular assignments allotted to them were not sufficiently lucrative to gratify their expectations, it was arranged that Clodius, as tribune, should carry through the tribal assembly a law overriding the senatorial allotments and appointing Piso to the rich province of Macedonia and Gabinius to the even richer province of Syria. In order further to ensure Piso's complacency, he was apparently voted an "outfit," or expense money, amounting to the equivalent of nearly a million dollars.[2] After this, the mouths of the two consuls were closed, and they followed where Clodius led. The latter, however, was unwilling to trust them, and he further ensured their loyalty to him by withholding the enactment of their proconsular assignments until his other principal measures were carried.[3]

With the consuls thus reduced to nullities, Clodius came forward with and secured the enactment of a legislative program of the popular type which had become familiar at Rome and which was designed primarily to consolidate and enhance the power of the politician who promoted it. The two principal elements of this program were a new grain law and a law legalizing the guilds or ward clubs which Clodius had so effectively revived and reorganized. The grain law carried to its final and logical extreme the principle first introduced by Gaius Gracchus by providing that henceforth grain should be distributed to the populace *gratis*. Hitherto, a small payment had always been exacted, although far less than the market price; now there was to be no payment at all, and the distribution was to be free.[4] Inevitably, this measure attracted to Rome from all parts of Italy the lazy and the indolent, while at the same time it caused men to relinquish agricultural pursuits for the allowances given in the city.[5] The new law thus produced widespread economic repercussions in that masters hastened to get rid of unprofitable slaves by emancipating them and throwing them on the bounty of the state. Meanwhile, the number of recipients of the grain dole began to grow, and after a dozen years it reached the enormous total of 320,000, when Caesar, then firmly entrenched in power, drastically curtailed the liberality of the distributions.[6] Cicero's statement that the law of Clodius consumed a fifth part of the entire revenue of the state seems entirely credible.[7] There seems good reason to believe that Caesar regarded the measure with satisfaction because the depletion of the treasury might well prove advantageous to him should he find himself at a later time in open conflict with the government.

The second item in Clodius's "democratic" program, the law removing the ban against the popular ward clubs, or guilds, was related to the grain law in that it provided the machinery of force whereby Clodius was enabled to rule the assemblies. These new associations of citizens, depending in large measure on the allowance of grain provided at government expense, in fact constituted an electoral army recruited from among the poor and the needy of the Roman voters. Since Clodius was careful to keep in his own hands the selection of the recipients of the grain dole through a henchman who also headed up the organization of the clubs, the distribution of grain was made an adjunct to the recruitment of a popular mob which was entirely at his service.

The measures of Clodius seem to have been adopted without opposition. In view of the position he occupied, and of the resources at his command, it is hard to see how opposition could have had any chance of success. Within the walls there was no effective force to oppose his organized mob, and his supremacy was reinforced by the ever-present sense of Caesar's army outside the walls.

With the adoption of these laws the grip of Clodius had tightened more firmly than ever on the government. Chief among his objectives was the obliteration of Cicero as a factor in future politics. Caesar also had apparently come to feel that it was no less necessary to destroy, if possible, the position and influence of Cato, although in a different way. Numerous bits of evidence point to the fact that from the moment of the expiration of his consulship Caesar was almost abnormally fearful that a prosecution might be brought against him for his unconstitutional conduct in office.[8] Furthermore, if a prosecution should be brought against Clodius on that ground, the effect would redound to Caesar's disadvantage. No one was more likely to instigate such prosecutions, or more likely to succeed if he did so, than Cato,[9] and accordingly a way had to be found to prevent him from so doing. Caesar and Clodius now found such a way.

The additional burdens on the state budget imposed by the new grain law of Clodius offered an excuse which, on the theory prevalent among Roman "popular" politicians, would justify some act in the field of foreign policy that would increase the revenue. An opportunity for taking such action was now presented. The King of Cyprus, whose claim to the throne was in dispute, had failed to offer a bribe to the triumvirs. It was accordingly determined that Clodius would introduce a bill to displace him and to annex Cyprus as a Roman province. The act was passed, and Cato was named to set in order the affairs of the new province. This put Cato in a difficult position. "He could not on his own principles decline a duty laid upon him by the state. To refuse to recognize the authority of the assembly packed and controlled by Clodius meant abdication of his position as a republican statesman. The assembly might be no true exponent of the will of the Roman people, but at present there was no other. At all events Clodius forced Cato to go, sorely against his will." [10]

By forcing the Cyprian appointment on Cato, Clodius entrapped and incapacitated him in the way that he and Caesar desired. By accepting appointment at the hands of Clodius, and by proceeding to exercise authority under that appointment, Cato felt that he was thereafter estopped from questioning the legality or constitutionality of the power under which he had himself acted. The value that he set on consistency was so great that his mouth was permanently closed on the point which chiefly mattered to Clodius and Caesar, and the basis of their fear of a prosecution was thus largely removed.

The most dramatic and spectacular event of Clodius's year of office was his persecution of Cicero. In the long run this was not to prove of any major political significance; it was a passing incident which missed fire, but it sheds revealing light on the tactics, calculations and methods of the leaders at this time. Clodius was, of course, animated by his fierce desire for revenge, but Caesar's designs went deeper. It is a tribute to Cicero's great abilities and personal force that Caesar regarded him as important enough to be the object of this attack. Although he was the leader of no party or coterie, the captain of no organization, the hero of no army of veterans, he was looked on with suspicion and jealousy by most of the powerful groups and leaders in the state. It was Cicero's power of persuasion that Caesar especially feared—his ability to make men forget for a moment the personal interests that divided them and surrender to the promptings of deeper and more permanent loyalties.

Caesar's strategy suggests that he almost certainly wished to keep Clodius and Pompey, Pompey and Crassus, the senate and the knights, at cross-purposes. He was aware that Cicero had never given up the idea of bringing Pompey and the knights and senate together, and he rightly calculated that amid the crosscurrents of the times a moment might conceivably come when by the power of his eloquence the orator might accomplish this great hope. Nothing could be more disturbing to Caesar's plans, and, in order effectually to guard against the possibility, he determined that Cicero must be removed from politics and his influence destroyed. Accordingly he gave full support from behind the scenes to the proceedings of Clodius.

The story of those proceedings has become so involved with the desire that historians have had to throw light on some phase of Cicero's character, and especially to criticize his vacillation or condemn his supposed weakness or cowardice, that in the usual accounts of this dramatic incident the facts have generally been relegated to a subordinate place. The story itself is plain and straightforward. Cicero seems all along to have anticipated that Clodius would initiate judicial proceedings, which, in the normal course, would be heard by one of the regular jury courts. In such a trial, Cicero would have as his judges senators and knights, or at least men of the higher property classes drawn from the Italian countryside, as well as from Rome, and he would be able to bring to his aid the matchless powers of persuasion which he had so successfully displayed in the recent trial of Flaccus. It was for a contest of this kind that he was preparing himself, one in which he believed that his chances of success were great. Clodius therefore took him completely by surprise and disarranged all his calculations when, instead of instituting a judicial proceeding, he brought a legislative proposal before the subservient tribal assembly that was completely under his control. The bill did not specifically name Cicero but was couched in general terms and provided that, if any man had put to death a Roman citizen who had not been condemned in a judicial trial, he should be laid under the interdict of "fire and water," that is, outlawed and banished from Roman territory.[11] Although the act could not be applied to Cicero's case without giving it *ex post facto* effect, the conditions were such that that effect would almost certainly be given to it by any jury called upon to apply it. Cicero's case would thus be prejudged, and he would be deprived of the possibility of setting up a successful legal defense.

Reviewing his conduct at a later time, Cicero blamed himself for not awaiting the event and then taking the position that a law of this kind could not be applied to him.[12] At the moment, however, recognizing the seriousness of the measure and the importance of resisting it, he resorted to all means in his power to prevent the passage of the proposed law despite the small hope of success. According to traditional Roman practice, he laid aside his senatorial garb and went about in sackcloth and ashes, soliciting the votes of the people, in a spirit of humility of which he never afterwards ceased to be ashamed. He organized his supporters among the knights, of whom large numbers changed their dress as a sign of sympathy and went about with him to join in his entreaties. A body of knights sent a deputation to petition the senate, which was then meeting in the Temple of Concord, but the consuls refused to let them into the building. When some of Cicero's friends attempted to address a popular mass meeting, they were so roughly handled by Clodius's gangsters that one of them was killed.[13] An approach was then made on Cicero's behalf to the consul Piso, who made the admission that he and his colleague were so deeply obligated to Clodius that they could not afford to oppose him. Thereupon, Clodius called a mass meeting of the people at which he presented the consuls to express their views. He asked Piso what he thought of Cicero's consulship, and Piso replied that "he did not approve its cruelty."[14] The same question was put to Gabinius, who not only gave substantially the same answer, but in addition abused the knights for intervening in Cicero's behalf. Meanwhile, the senate passed a resolution that its members should put on mourning garb as a sign of their grief and indignation, whereupon the consuls by an edict that was unprecedented in Roman history forbade the senators to comply with their own resolve.[15]

Clodius now played his trump card. He convoked an assembly outside the walls so that Caesar could address it. Caesar made a characteristic speech of studied and dignified moderation in which he expressed his devotion to the constitution and his disapproval of all unlawful conduct. He said that everybody knew his opinion of the execution of Catiline's accomplices, and he again condemned the illegality of the proceedings taken against Lentulus and his associates. After such a speech from such a source, Cicero's only remaining recourse was to secure, if possible, the aid of Pompey. Accordingly, a deputation of senators waited upon Pompey and entreated him not to desert Cicero and the interests of the republic. Pompey referred them to the consuls, saying that if the republic was threatened it was their responsibility to act. In accordance with this suggestion, the consuls were again approached. Piso replied that it was in Cicero's power to save the republic a second time by bowing before the storm and that neither he, nor his fellow consul, nor Piso's son-in-law, Caesar, would desert Clodius, a tribune of the people.[16] Cicero made a final effort to see Pompey personally by following him to his villa in the Alban hills; but Pompey did not wait for him, and as Cicero came in at the front door, Pompey slipped out by the back.[17]

In this whole episode there is nothing to Cicero's discredit, and nothing that can justly be condemned as abject or cowardly in his behavior. He followed the usual and accepted methods of making a legitimate appeal to the constituted authorities and to Pompey, to whom he had every right to appeal. It was now apparent, however, that his appeals were destined to be in vain. No leader in any position to help him would oppose the determination of Clodius to carry his law. The time had therefore come when Cicero had to make his decision: should he remain at Rome and incur the consequences, or should he remove himself and thereby remove from the issue the explosiveness that threatened to bring on a crisis? It is evident that he considered this question long and carefully, and took the advice of such close friends as Atticus and Cato. Almost unanimously they advised him to leave Rome, and on March 28 he left for the estate of a friend in Bruttium in southern Italy.[18]

It is mainly Cicero's own subsequent criticism of his own conduct, preserved in his correspondence, that has afforded the basis of the charges which historians have ever since leveled against him. Looking back on his decision in the wretched hours of his exile, a man as intensely addicted to introspection and self-criticism as Cicero could not help feeling that in yielding to circumstances he had made a mistake and been untrue to himself.[19] The lamentations, repinings and recriminations with which he filled his letters inevitably excite in modern eyes a certain feeling of contempt. Yet it should be remembered that the very sensitiveness of temperament and power of imagination which made him a great orator also made him the victim of the feelings he was able effectively to evoke in others. Moreover, at the time he made his decision, reflection must have shown him that by risking his life or losing it he could do little or no good to the republic. It was rather his own reputation for courage and consistency at the bar of history that he was afterwards concerned about in the loneliness of his exile. From this standpoint, he feared that, as the nemesis of Catiline, he had lost the chance to stand out again in dramatic defiance against the destroyers of the republic and had shown himself as something less than he wished to be. Yet, a few months later, when he had returned to Rome and to public life, he saw the force of the practical considerations that had induced him to go, and he stated them simply and frankly in a public speech.[20] Clodius, he said, was crying out in all the assemblies that the things he was doing were done with the approval of Pompey and Crassus and Caesar:

These three men he said he would use as his advisers in all his measures and his helpers in carrying them out. One of them, he said, had a very large army in Italy; the other two, who were then private citizens, could, if they wished, easily get together and command an army, and he said that they would do so. And he threatened me not with a judgment of the people, or with any contest, debate or discussion of our controversy, but with violence, arms, armies, generals and camps. What then? . . . It was not his speech, but the silence of those men to whom his infamous speech pointed that influenced me—men who, although they remained silent for other reasons, yet . . . seemed to confess by not denying. . . . When I saw this . . . and that the senate, without which the state could not stand, was entirely abolished, that the consuls . . . had through their own efforts brought an end to the policy of the state, that those men who had the greatest influence were falsely held up in every assembly . . . as people who approved of my ruin . . . when I saw all this, what was I to do? [21]

Cicero further explained that no resistance to Clodius was possible save by resort to force in the Forum, and that even if this should prove successful, and Clodius killed, the next step would have been civil war. He was too clearheaded not to recognize which side was bound to win in such a war and to see that the outcome would immediately seal the fate of the constitution. Neither the time nor the circumstances were appropriate for such a test; indeed, if ultimately any vestiges of the constitution were to be saved, such a test was in fact the one thing most to be avoided at this particular juncture. Hence his decision not to make an issue of his banishment was as reasonable as it was wise from a public point of view. What is unfortunate about the whole episode is that Cicero's nervous sensibilities and wounded spirit during the months of his exile led him to commit to words moods of doubt and regret which have placed in a false light a decision that was undoubtedly sound when it was made.

The man whose course throughout these proceedings was thoroughly improvident and impolitic from his own standpoint was Pompey. By deserting Cicero, Pompey built up in the hands of Clodius a power that could be used against himself by the irresponsible tribune, and at the same time he surrendered the opportunity with which he was presented of strengthening his position with Caesar. Not only would Cicero have been a valuable ally for Pompey in holding his own with Caesar, but by taking Cicero's side at this time Pompey could have consolidated for himself powerful support among the senators and the knights and thus have made Caesar more respectful of his interests. These advantages Pompey threw away and, from fear of coming to an issue with Caesar, permitted Clodius instead of himself to fall heir to Caesar's influence and to assume the position of Caesar's agent at Rome.

During the year 58, Caesar lingered on in the city from week to week and month to month until it was clear that Cicero was beaten. In fact, he did not leave for Gaul until almost the day when the orator went into exile. By this delay he nearly missed the first great military opportunity of his life, and he was saved from the results of his miscalculation only by extraordinary promptness of action and by sheer good luck.

After Caesar left, Clodius took over the conduct of the government on his own account and proceeded to use his position without restraint or control. At first he addressed himself to completing his vengeance against Cicero. For this purpose he apparently abandoned his original bill and instead carried through the assembly a law directed against the orator by name, declaring that he was already an outlaw, forbidding him to come within four hundred miles of Rome and confiscating all his property.[22] With this law as his authority, Clodius proceeded to pull down Cicero's house on the Palatine and consecrate the ground to the Goddess of Liberty, so that it might not afterwards be built upon.[23] He took the same course with respect to Cicero's country house at Tusculum and then began to harass Terentia, Cicero's wife, with legal proceedings to make her disclose and surrender any property of her husband that she might be withholding.

Clodius then turned to the employment of his unchallenged power in ways that promised to bring him direct personal gain. Among his first endeavors was the sale of the office of high priest of Cybele at the mother temple in Pessinus to a wealthy Galatian named Brogitarus,[24] and so satisfactory was the deal to both parties that Clodius proceeded also to sell him a right to share the kingship of Galatia with Deiotarus,[25] an ally of Rome and a friend and protégé of Pompey. By this step Clodius offered an open challenge to Pompey, and he soon followed it with another act of even bolder defiance. Pompey had brought to Rome as a hostage the son of the Armenian king, young Tigranes, who, tired of his captivity, managed to persuade Clodius to set him free. An escape was arranged, but in the course thereof a fight occurred between the thugs of Clodius and the public officers who were seeking to reclaim the fugitive. In the course of the fight a friend and retainer of Pompey was slain. Pompey was doubly outraged, by the disregard of his diplomatic arrangements and by the death of his friend.

These two incidents, and possibly others of a similar nature of which there is no record, weighed more impressively with Pompey than Cicero's banishment and at last determined him to break with Clodius. He saw that the only way of combating the tribune was to build up a mob to oppose the one Clodius commanded, and this he commissioned his henchman, the consul Gabinius, to do from among his numerous clients, tenants and veterans scattered throughout the Italian countryside. Soon there were reports of riots and street fights between the mob commanded by the consul and that commanded by the tribune. In one encounter Gabinius' insignia of office were broken, and the personal bitterness between Gabinius and Clodius began to pass all bounds. Even ceremonies of religion were resorted to by the two opposing factions. For example, Clodius consecrated the property of Gabinius to the gods, while another tribune, friendly to Pompey, repaid Clodius by consecrating his property in the same way.[26] In these broils Pompey could not avoid becoming personally involved. Gabinius warned him that he was in danger of his life from the henchmen of Clodius, and he accordingly shut himself up in his house while emissaries of Clodius besieged his doors. At last he escaped and seems to have spent some months with his wife in Campania. There is hardly any period in his life when Pompey cut so sorry a figure.

The resistance to Clodius, which was organized and begun by Gabinius, seems to have had one salutary effect—it showed that resistance was possible and thus encouraged others to join in it. Conservative senators and knights who feared anarchy began to recover courage and support the resistance movement. We hear of gangs and mobs being formed on the conservative side, one of them led by a new figure who came on the scene at this time, T. Annius Milo. Milo was a swordsman and mob master, but he seems to have been inspired by an honest desire to use his sword in the interest of orderly government. He was an efficient organizer as well as a resolute fighter, and within a few months his gang, recruited largely from slave gladiators, seems to have been well on the way to becoming an effective match for the mob of Clodius. Now that Clodius no longer had Caesar's army at his back, the tide was beginning to turn.

The clearest indication of the change appeared with the results of the summer elections. The two consuls who were chosen were both conservatives, and one, Publius Cornelius Lentulus Spinther, a friend of Cicero's, was a man of outstanding ability and energy. Moreover, eight of the ten tribunes who were elected were friendly to the conservative interest. Plainly Clodius had gone too far. He had aroused and solidified such a mass of opposition that for the time being his tactics of force were no longer able effectively to withstand it. The elections to the consulate and other senatorial offices were held in the centuriate assembly, where the votes of the wealthier classes were controlling and were likely to be attended by many substantial electors from the country who were doubtless encouraged by the new turn of events to come into Rome in greater numbers than usual. Furthermore, the assembly always met outside the city on the Field of Mars, whose open spaces were far less favorable to mob domination than the cramped quarters of the Forum. The remarkable thing is that Clodius also lost out in the election of tribunes, in the course of which there was no rioting or street fighting. Something must have happened to cause him to lose his nerve at this juncture. He was at best an unstable character with no fixity of purpose, and his quarrel with Pompey may for the time being have unbalanced him. Once the guiding hand of Caesar was removed, he seems to have lost his sense of direction and started to go to pieces.

The results of the election, following upon his experience with Clodius, seem to have given a new turn to Pompey's thoughts. In the absence of Caesar, the senatorial party had displayed amazing vitality and unexpected powers of recuperation, as the result at the polls indicated. It was at this point that Pompey wished for Cicero. He knew that he himself was highly unpopular with the senators, who blamed him for the acts of Caesar. Cicero, however, had become for the moment a hero and rallying point for them, for his exile at the hands of Clodius was an insult to their order, so that a strong party among them clamored for his recall. If Cicero could be brought back, the orator might be able to rally the senate to Pompey's support. As early as June, some of Cicero's friends had already solicited Pompey's help, but he had put them off until after the elections, doubtless wishing to see how the voting would go. When the results were known, he no longer hesitated and wrote to Caesar, not wishing to offend his partner by acting without the latter's consent.[27]

Caesar apparently made no satisfactory reply. He could not have felt as complacent as Pompey did about the revival of senatorial strength, which threatened a major setback for his plans by demonstrating that neither Pompey nor Clodius was strong enough to keep control of the city. He does not yet seem to have decided to abandon Clodius, for he did not believe that the tribune had lost his grip. Consequently, he temporized, and Pompey no less than the friends of Cicero were left in uncertainty. What happened in the ensuing months there is no way of knowing. Caesar seems to have realized finally that he could no longer rely on Clodius and that he must yield in the end to Pompey's wishes, even at the risk of facilitating a possible reconciliation between Pompey and the senate. That danger he would deal with when it arose, but in the meantime he decided to preserve a discreet silence, even after the newly elected tribunes announced at the end of October that they intended to sponsor a bill for Cicero's recall.[28] One of these tribunes, Publius Sestius, a friend and strong supporter of Cicero, went all the way to Gaul to interview Caesar in his camp, but he was unsuccessful in discovering his attitude and came home no wiser than he went.[29] Plainly if Cicero was to be recalled, it was not to be with Caesar's public approval.

When the new consuls came into office at the beginning of the year 57, their first act was to lay before the senate a resolution authorizing one of the tribunes to propose a bill to the people for Cicero's return. Some time was taken in settling the form of the bill, and when it was ready for presentation at the end of January, Clodius had again recruited his strength.[30] When the tribal assembly was convened and an effort made to present the bill, the supporters of Cicero were taken by surprise. The mob of Clodius assaulted the tribunes, drove the speakers from the rostrum and killed many of their supporters, whose bodies were flung into the river. It was the bloodiest riot in years. From then on, for months, no legislative business could be transacted. Every time an attempt was made to convene an assembly, a riot occurred. In one of these, Sestius was nearly killed. The mob of Milo was brought into play, and Sestius raised a mob of his own, while on the other side Appius, the brother of Clodius, organized a gang of gladiators which attacked temples and private houses. All government was at a standstill, and the city was at the mercy of what seemed to be equally balanced forces of disorder.

Gradually, however, as the months passed, the forces of Milo and Sestius gained ground over their opponents, and, as this became apparent, Pompey, who in the interval had discreetly kept away from Rome, began to assert himself again. It now appeared that Clodius would in the end be worsted, and in that event Cicero's recall would be assured. Pompey did not wish to lose the chief credit for the recall and began to make vigorous exertions in Cicero's behalf. The latter's supporters seem to have decided to take no more chances with the tribal assembly, which could so easily be disturbed by rioting, but to present their proposal to the *comitia centuriata*. If a meeting of this body were convoked in August, near the time of the games when many countrymen were usually in Rome, a large attendance of substantial Italian voters favorable to Cicero could be assured.[31] Accordingly, the senate passed a resolution formally convening a meeting of the centuriate assembly at that time and instructing the consul Lentulus to bring before it the proposal for Cicero's recall. Another resolution called on all good citizens in Italy to be sure to attend the session, and Pompey visited several towns outside Rome in person to make speeches in Cicero's behalf. The occasion is described by Long as follows:

The people met to vote upon Cicero's restoration on the fourth of August. There were voters from all parts of Italy; the shops in Rome were closed; . . . even the Italian towns were closed. The voting was in the Campus Martius, and never had it been seen so crowded. Lentulus proposed the bill to the Comitia Centuriata. Cicero's friends distributed the ballots and looked carefully after the voters. If Clodius intended to make any opposition, he was kept in check by Milo and his band. Indeed to this bold tribune Cicero appears to have been principally indebted for his restoration; and that which was accomplished quietly in legal form had been made possible by Milo's armed force. The popular vote confirmed the bill, and on the fourth of August [57 B.C.] Cicero ceased to be an exile.[32]

Cicero was already at the port of Dyrrhacium (Durazzo) in Illyria, waiting to cross to Italy the moment it would be lawful for him to do so. Upon his arrival at Brindisi, apparently the whole population of the town turned out to greet him, and from then on his journey to Rome was like a triumphal progress, lasting almost a month. All the way he was greeted by crowds and welcomed by deputations. When he reached the gates of Rome he found the streets and the steps of the temples occupied by great throngs, through which he passed on his way to the Capitol to offer thanks for his safe return.[33] After sixteen months of banishment, which had been for him a period of incredible misery, filled with regrets for the past and forebodings for the future, the rejoicings at Rome were a fitting end to his triumphant return. Everyone but Clodius and his henchmen seemed to be on hand to welcome him.

With the plaudits of Rome in his ears, Cicero might well believe for this moment, in the year 57, that he had recovered the position of leadership which he had held during his consulship and that he might look forward hopefully to influencing with renewed effectiveness the course of Roman government and the future policies of the republic. That these hopes were futile and destined to early and complete disappointment, and that the republic was never again to be what it had been before, had already been determined during Cicero's exile by Caesar's momentous achievements in Gaul.

II

Cicero's return to Rome, and the warmth of his reception in the city, nevertheless fortified more strongly than ever his favorite idea that the balance of power in the republic must be redressed by bringing the senate and Pompey together. In the light of their cooperation in securing his recall, the time seemed ripe for such an alliance. Pompey was obviously jealous of the successes Caesar was winning in Gaul, and he was anxious for some new honor or appointment which would keep his position and prestige more on a parity with his partner's. An opportunity to gratify that wish was now at hand. Apparently the greatly increased requirements of grain resulting from the grain law of Clodius had brought about an ominous shortage,[34] and it was imperative to set up an organization that would ensure a steady flow of grain from the provinces. Here was an occasion to recognize and make use of the abilities of Pompey in a way that was likely to win him the favor of the masses. Accordingly, Cicero's first public act, only three days after his return, was to propose in the senate that the consuls should submit a measure to the people conferring on Pompey the management of the grain supply.[35] A law was duly presented which vested Pompey for five years with supreme authority throughout the Roman world over all matters connected with the supply of grain and authorized him, in accordance with his request, to appoint fifteen deputies through whom he would exercise his functions.

At this point, the fatal divisions and crosscurrents among the different groups of the Roman governing class began once again to make their appearance, and ill feelings and jealousies were engendered which commenced to dissolve the alliance for which Cicero so much hoped, even before it had been formed. The strict conservatives in the senate, men who would have followed Cato if he had been in Rome and not in Cyprus at this time, commenced to murmur that too much power was being conferred on Pompey, whom they still regarded as the chief enemy of the constitution. Meanwhile, another clique, which fawned on Pompey, tried to persuade him that the powers conferred on him in the proposed law were too limited, and they brought about through one of the tribunes the introduction of a rival measure which would give him complete control over the revenues, a fleet, and an army, as well as a proconsular *imperium* superior to that of the provincial governors—in short, many of the powers which a generation later, in the hands of Augustus, were combined to form the prerogatives of an emperor. Pompey publicly professed himself satisfied with the consular bill, but the attitude of his friends created the suspicion that he really would have preferred the broader measure. It was the more limited measure, however, that passed, and Pompey energetically set about his new task.

Unfortunately, at this stage, mutual suspicions began to be felt by Pompey and Cicero. Cicero was not quite sure that Pompey did not hold against him the fact that he had not advocated the bill which conferred the broader powers, whereas Pompey was determined, as always, not to let his course be influenced by the advice of a mere civilian and man of words. Cicero had long ceased to have any illusions about Pompey, but he believed that, in spite of Pompey's shortcomings, it was necessary to build up and maintain his influence because he was convinced that Pompey did not possess the destructive ambitions of Caesar to rule by force. It also seems clear that Cicero was convinced that the prevalent forces of confusion and disintegration could be resisted only by rallying around a leader who had the kind of position and prestige that Pompey still had. If this objective could be achieved, it might be possible to drive a wedge between Pompey and Caesar, and, by balancing the two against each other, prevent either from overwhelming the constitution. This strategy and hope seem to have directed Cicero's course during the next few months and to have led him to persist in his efforts to hold Pompey and the senate together, although by so doing he was rapidly losing the confidence of both.

In these last months of the year 57, while Pompey and the senate were steadily drifting apart, Clodius was active in attempting to widen that breach. Earlier he had attempted, by his usual tactics of intimidation and rioting, to break up the assembly which had been convened to pass upon Pompey's grain-commissionership, and he had apparently afterwards tried to intimidate the senate. When these efforts failed, he set up the cry that the senate, in supporting novel and unusual powers for Pompey, was again allowing itself to be led into unconstitutional paths by Cicero, who had been banished as the destroyer of the constitution and whose return now portended its downfall.[36] No exceptional powers, he urged, should be created and nothing done out of the regular constitutional course. Strange as these arguments may seem from the mouth of Clodius, they struck a responsive chord in the many conservatives who were always

ready to be suspicious of Pompey. Even more effective must have
been the taunt of Clodius that the senate had permitted the wool to
be pulled over its eyes for Pompey's sake by an upstart like Cicero.
All the old caste feeling of the aristocrats was thus aroused, and,
as between themselves and Pompey, the aristocrats were ready to
remember that Clodius was after all one of their own number.
Accordingly, when Clodius touched the chord of class feeling, he
not only evoked against Pompey a ready response on the part of
many conservative senators, but even made them willing to give
their support to the mob master. With singular shortsightedness,
they seem to have believed that Clodius was now playing their game
and that they could make use of him.

A clear picture of these developments is portrayed in the speech
De Domo Sua which Cicero made at the end of September to bring
about the restitution of his property.[37] That speech, however, is
also of interest and importance for another reason: it contains the
fullest exposition of the Roman doctrine, which was to become so
influential nineteen centuries later in America, that an unconstitutional law is no law and is, therefore, to be given no effect in subsequent proceedings. This doctrine had been stated by Cicero in an
earlier speech in which he had referred to the fact that the statute
involved in the case he was arguing contained a clause to the effect
that by the statute nothing should be considered as enacted which
it would not be in conformity with fundamental justice (*jus*) to
enact.[38] He had accordingly urged that whatever was enacted by
the people was not necessarily law unless it accorded with the basic
and fundamental principles of right embodied in the constitution.
He now elaborated this argument to show that the law which Clodius
had carried against him was unconstitutional and hence void for
four reasons. First, Clodius had not been transferred in good faith
and by proper ritual into the plebeian order, and therefore he was
never lawfully a tribune; [39] second, it was void because it was a
privilegium, or law directed against a particular individual, and such
laws were on grounds of sound public policy expressly prohibited
by the Twelve Tables; [40] third, it was carried by violence and intimidation; [41] fourth, it purported to pass sentence on a Roman citizen
without a judicial trial.[42] In ringing words, he stated that there were

established principles of right "which neither the power of time, nor the authority of magistrates, nor the decisions of judges, nor the sovereign power of the whole people of Rome, which in other matters is most absolute, can impair." [43] This argument still stands in the current of one of the most continuous and persistent lines of evolution in the history of Western political and legal thought.

The verdict restoring Cicero's property was the signal for a new outbreak by Clodius. When Cicero's workmen commenced to rebuild his house, the bands of Clodius drove them away, demolished the work, and set upon Cicero with stones and clubs.[44] Since at this time Clodius held no public office, he was amenable to prosecution, but his friends among the aristocrats resorted to vetoes and other obstructive tactics which effectively blocked the efforts of Milo and Sestius to start judicial proceedings. Meanwhile, Clodius sought to clothe himself with immunity by having himself elected an aedile. Although his enemies succeeded in having the election postponed long after the regular date, in order, if possible, to get the prosecution under way, Clodius was finally elected through the aid of his aristocratic supporters. He thus began the new year in a position of official vantage from which to harass both Pompey and Cicero with strong senatorial support.

A new occasion for difference had arisen in the meanwhile between Pompey and the senate. It will be recalled that during Caesar's consulship Ptolemy Auletes, the "flute-player," had paid an enormous bribe to be recognized as a friend and ally of the Roman people.[45] At about the time of Cicero's return, the senate was called on to make good this commitment. The disorders in Egypt had reached a point where Ptolemy had been compelled to flee the country and to appeal to Rome, as his ally, to restore him. The senate was thus in a difficult predicament. It was not at all clear what amount of force the restoration of Ptolemy might require, and it was conceivable that a major war might be necessary. This possibility was eagerly seized upon by the satellites and flatterers of Pompey as an occasion for a new proposal that he be given a fleet and an army for the reduction of Egypt. Such a proposal confirmed conservative senators more strongly than ever in their view that Ptolemy's appeal should go unheeded and that no action at all should be taken. A compromise suggestion, supported by Cicero, was that Ptolemy's restoration should be left to the newly appointed governor of Cilicia, the retiring consul Lentulus Spinther. It was obvious that the senate would never give the appointment to Pompey, and further efforts to promote his command would only add to the bitterness between them. Cicero's own position was thus embarrassing in the extreme: he did not wish to offend Pompey, but he was even more anxious that Pompey should not needlessly offend the senate. Meanwhile, Pompey declined to make clear his political position. In vain Cicero sought to draw him out and was met with only hints and evasions. In the course of a long conversation, Pompey said he was by no means satisfied with his position; he did not care for Syria and thought nothing of Spain—"so he said." [46] As for the Egyptian project, wrote Cicero, "when I hear his own utterances I acquit him of ambition and greed, but when I see his intimates of all classes, I perceive clearly what must now be obvious to everybody, that the whole matter [of Ptolemy's restoration] was long ago betrayed by certain men. . . ." [47]

The moderate senators who were willing to go a certain distance toward placating Pompey thought that he ought to be satisfied with the wide powers which had already been given him as a grain commissioner and should not ask for more. Cicero felt that, if there were to be any hope of an accommodation between Pompey and the senate, the views of these senators must be respected. He therefore devoted himself to obtaining Pompey's consent, if possible, to leave the Egyptian affair in the hands of Spinther; but, in view of Pompey's peculiar temperament, which he knew only too well, he could not feel at all assured that he had made any progress in this direction. [48] Thus, by a perverse kind of revolution in the course of events, the part which Egypt was now playing in Roman politics was exactly the reverse of that which it had been eight years before. Then, Caesar and Crassus had pushed a proposal for an expedition to Egypt to counterbalance Pompey's military successes in the East; now, Pompey was toying with the idea of an Egyptian command to counterbalance Caesar's victories in Gaul. The earlier attempt had failed, even though it commanded very considerable senatorial support; the present effort had no chance of success, partly because of Pompey's indecision and vacillation, but chiefly because of the senate's practically unanimous opposition. The new proposal weakened Pompey's position still further by increasing the suspicion with which he was regarded by the senate, and also by supplying a new occasion for Clodius to attack him.

After Clodius entered on his aedileship in 56 B.C., he renewed his onslaughts against Pompey with redoubled vigor. Gathering his claque of gangsters in the Forum, he put the question, "Who created a grain shortage and tried to starve the common people to death?" "Pompey," was the resounding answer. "Who wants to be sent to Egypt?" "Pompey," yelled the mob. The situation was not improved by the fact that Clodius was suspected at this time of acting with the connivance of Caesar, while it was a matter of public knowledge that he was obtaining support from both Crassus and Bibulus, the confidant of Cato. Such was the extent to which lines of party cooperation had become confused and inverted by personal rivalries and class antagonisms. In irritation and despair, Pompey had a confidential talk with Cicero, to whom he communicated his fears, which Cicero reported to his brother. "Pompey," he wrote, "understands what is going on, and he lets me know about the plots that are being formed against his life, that Cato has the support of Crassus, that money is being supplied to Clodius, that both are being backed by Crassus and Curio, as well as by Bibulus and the rest of his disparagers, that he himself must take extraordinary precautions to prevent being overpowered—all this at a time when the people are almost wholly alienated, the aristocracy hostile, the senate unfairly in opposition, and the younger generation corrupt." [49] Pompey even told Cicero that he was on the point of concluding that force must be met with force and was thinking of calling in his veterans and clients from the country.

The mounting tide of excitement was whipped to further heights by Clodius through an appeal to superstition. Prodigies and portents were said to have occurred on so ominous a scale that these happenings were referred to the official soothsayers for an opinion, and the latter replied that, because solemn rites had been omitted, sacred places profaned, and good faith and oaths had been disregarded, the prodigies had been sent as warnings by the gods lest the Romans bring misfortune on themselves and their city by persisting in their disorderly proceedings and dissensions. Clodius seized on this answer to set up a cry that the gods were angry because Cicero's house, which had been consecrated as a holy place, had now been restored to profane uses.

Cicero took advantage of this charge to extend the debate to broader and more fundamental issues which he apparently felt should be brought out into the open without further delay and squarely faced.[50] After arguing that his house had never been validly consecrated, and that if there were any question of sacrilege it was not necessary to look farther than Clodius, he went on to inquire as to the nature and cause of the dissensions which the religious authorities deplored. These dissensions, he asserted, were those within the senatorial class itself which had led many conservatives who should know better to give aid and support to a demagogue like Clodius. "When the immortal gods warn us of discords . . . they point to dissensions between illustrious citizens who have deserved well of the republic." [51]

Let there at some time be an end of discord, let us at last find rest from our long dissensions. But this pestilential agitator will not have it so . . . he sells himself sometimes to one side and then to another. . . . Is it possible that good men could have cherished in their bosoms this poisonous and deadly viper? With what bait were they deceived? We wish, they say, that there should be some one to speak out against Pompey. . . . Does Clodius injure Pompey by his abuse? I hope that great man, to whom I personally owe so much for my safety, will accept what I say in the spirit in which it is meant. . . . I protest that that fellow seemed to be detracting from Pompey's high dignity only when he was extolling him with extravagant praises.[52]

This was plain speech from Cicero, aimed at both the conservatives and at Pompey. He did not hesitate to point the moral in express words. Stating that hatred existed, burned into the souls of men of the highest position, he concluded that dissensions between men of power usually terminated either in universal destruction or in the rule of one man.[53] Cicero then went on to give his opinion that such a state of affairs had almost been reached:

This republic of ours was once so firm and vigorous that it could withstand the indifference of the senate and even the assaults of disloyal citizens. Now it cannot. . . . The authority of the chief men has sunk to nothing; the concord between the different orders is torn asunder; the integrity of the courts is destroyed; the votes are divided and in the power of a few; the courage of virtuous citizens will soon cease to be responsive to the command of our order; henceforth you will look in vain for a citizen willing to expose himself to unpopularity for the welfare of his country. For this reason, the present state of affairs, such as it is, we can preserve by no other means than through concord. . . . If we are to be any worse off than we now are, there is but one step lower, death or slavery.[54]

Shortly after Cicero made this speech, he found another occasion to drive home the same lesson in a more affirmative way and to make a last appeal for the kind of government he believed essential to save the republic. A prosecution had been instituted against Publius Sestius, his friend and supporter, for alleged breaches of the peace committed during his term as tribune in opposing the gangs and mobs of Clodius.[55] The attack was in reality aimed at Cicero, who undertook the defense. His speech at this trial, the *Pro Sestio*, is not only one of his masterful forensic efforts but is of great importance in revealing more of his political philosophy than he was accustomed to show in his oratorical performances. After recounting the story of Clodius's rise and how he had fastened the reign of force upon the public assemblies, ruling them by violence and intimidation, Cicero entered into a discussion of the basic issue of force versus law in civil society. The chief difference, he said, between civilized and uncivilized life lies in the fact that law is the ruling principle of the one and violence of the other. If a state does not choose to be ruled by law, then there is no alternative but recourse to violence.[56]

Cicero then charged that the present plight of the Roman state could be traced back fundamentally to the presence of two classes or parties among the citizens. One of these was the "populars," the sole aim of whose leaders was to do and say whatever they thought would be agreeable to the multitude.[57] As to these, he said, it should be remembered that "not all those men are really friends of the people who are believed to be so."[58] On the other side, stood the "optimates," or good men. This party was not limited to conservative senators and their clients and followers, as was sometimes supposed, but consisted of all good citizens everywhere who intelligently consulted their own best interests and those of the republic. Their object was to ensure that Roman citizens individually and collectively should enjoy *otium cum dignitate*—personal security and self-respect. The only way in which this object could be attained was to uphold and strengthen the long established and organic institutions of the commonwealth—its "religious observances, the auspices, the constitutional powers of the magistrates, the authority of the senate, ancestral customs, the legal system, the jurisdiction of the courts, respect for good faith, the welfare of the provinces and allies, the glory of the empire, the good management of the army and treasury." [59]

These things, said Cicero, cannot be destroyed or undermined without impairing the individual and collective security and self-respect of Roman citizens, of which they are the foundations. Yet the leaders of the so-called "populars" had not hesitated to impair them. "For in so great a number of citizens there is always a large body of those who . . . are anxious for changes and revolutions in the state, or who . . . feed on the discords and seditions of the citizens. . . . And when these men have found accomplices to be instigators, leaders and promoters for their vicious purposes, great upheavals are stirred up in the state, so that those who are responsible for holding the helm of state must keep watch and strive with all their skill and diligence to preserve those things which I have called the foundations of the republic, and so keep the ship of state in its true course toward the haven of security and self-respect." [60]

Cicero pointed out that the task of defenders of the constitution is always harder than that of its assailants. The latter have the advantage of initiative and movement; the former, as defenders of things as they are, occupy a negative position and cannot act until they are at last aroused by necessity itself, when it may be too late.[61] At the present juncture, he argued, the task of defense should really be easier than in many of the past crises of the Roman constitution because formerly the populace was spontaneously active in pursuit of desires or whims which were at variance with constitutional stability,[62] whereas "at present there is no subject on which the people need disagree with its chosen magistrates, and with the senatorial class; they do not demand anything, nor are they eager for revolution." [63] What then is the source of the continuing public commotions? They are artificially stimulated and concocted and whipped up by bribery, violence and mob organization to further the ends of ambitious and seditious men who cannot find any issue on which to make a real appeal to the people. In support of this contention, Cicero went on to refer to assemblies packed with armed gangsters or consisting of an insignificant number of hired voters, while the great mass of citizens absented themselves from fear of violence.[64] Do the turbulence of such assemblies and their revolutionary acts show any real desire for revolution on the part of the Roman people? "No," answered Cicero. "At present, unless I am mistaken, the republic is in this condition, that if you take away the efforts of these gang hirers, everybody appears likely to hold the same opinion with regard to the republic." [65] The existence of this unanimity he sought to exhibit by reference to recent events, particularly in connection with his own recall from exile.

The speech in defense of Sestius is really a plea, at once reasoned and passionate, for the unanimity of good citizens of all classes, which Cicero, with the advocate's artifice, asserted he saw already existing around him. His assertion seems to have been justified in that there is no evidence of the existence at this time of any widespread discontent or demand for reform on the part of the Roman electorate, or even of the urban populace. Yet instead of the unanimity which Cicero hoped for, there was apathy and indifference which enabled the demagogues to control the assemblies through organized or terrorized minorities. In effect, the majority of electors did not care enough for the preservation of constitutional government to risk their skins in a contest with the mobs, and constitutional government was accordingly going by default. No one was better aware of the existence of this public apathy than the mob masters themselves, who conducted their operations in reliance on it. Cicero's real purpose in his plea for Sestius was to try to dispel that apathy, but that was a greater task than the oratory of a single man, even though that man was Cicero, could accomplish. All that Cicero succeeded in doing was to win his case and save Sestius, and at the same

time again to convince the ruling powers, as he had done at the trial
of Flaccus, how disturbing and dangerous he could be to their plans.

The real force behind the rule of the mobs at Rome, although
now very much in the background, was Caesar, and of this ultimate
fact Cicero, with infinite tact and caution, let it be seen that he was
not unaware. There is a passage in the speech for Sestius where for
a moment, but only for a moment, he drew back the curtain, and
then quickly let it drop. "I hope," he said, referring to Caesar at the
time of Clodius's tribuneship, "that there will never again be just
cause for a general encamped at the gates to allow the terror he
inspires to be falsely thrown in opposition against us." [66] It was
impossible to keep Caesar out of the case of Sestius, for he had clearly
shown his hand, albeit by indirection. One of the chief witnesses
who came forward against Sestius was Vatinius, the tribune whose
services Caesar had used during his consulship and who was publicly
regarded as Caesar's mouthpiece.[67] In conducting the defense, Cicero
had to cross-examine Vatinius, and, under the practice prevailing
in the Roman courts, made a speech propounding and explaining
his questions. In this speech, which was designed to impeach the
credibility of the witness, Cicero could not ignore the shadow of
Caesar standing behind Vatinius. He chose to deal with Caesar now
as he had dealt with Sulla a quarter of a century before, when he
had had to attack the dictator's henchman Chrysogonus, by studi-
ously and almost insultingly absolving and excusing the principal
for the acts of the agent.[68]

Caesar had now been away from Rome almost two years. Just
as Pompey, during his absence in the East, had remained a domi-
nating figure in Roman politics, Caesar, during his absence in Gaul,
also exerted an influence on Roman politics, but in a different way.
His alliance with Pompey effectively prevented the formation of
any combination against him, for only Pompey could have become
the center of such a combination, and this Pompey had steadfastly
declined to do. Meanwhile, in Pompey's broils with the senate,
Caesar's henchmen—men such as Clodius and Vatinius—had taken
the senate's side and thus contributed to widening the breach between
Pompey and that body. Thus, in effect, Caesar had a hand in both
the contending groups at Rome and helped to prevent them from

uniting, while playing them off against each other. In this process he kept himself in the background; and, although he was undoubtedly in constant personal touch with many of the leading figures at Rome, his name was seldom directly involved in the actual political contests that were going on. Instead, he succeeded in having himself brought to public notice only in connection with the series of splendid military successes that he was winning in his Gallic wars. Thus he was able to maintain in the public eye the position which he always affected of being above the battle of petty partisan conflicts.[69]

Sometime during the winter of 57–56 the meaning of this situation seems at last to have dawned on some of the conservatives at Rome, as it had long before dawned on Cicero, namely, that the confusion and futility of the political scene resulted from the fact that the conservatives were wasting their ammunition on Pompey. By so doing, they were lending aid and comfort to Clodius and other mob masters who had come close to completing the destruction of the constitution. The real target of their attack should accordingly have been the mob masters who were tools not of Pompey but of Caesar. Of course, before turning against the gang leaders, it would have been the part of sound and prudent strategy for the conservatives to placate Pompey and bring him over to their side, as Cicero had been trying to persuade them to do; but, since that effort now seemed in vain, there was one other alternative which, while involving great risks, offered at least a possible chance of success. This was for the senate to hazard a direct breach with Caesar. The risk involved, as the outcome showed, was that such a move might cause Caesar to buy back Pompey's support and thus bring the two once more together instead of keeping them apart. On the other hand, there was the bare possibility that Pompey was already so far alienated from Caesar, and had come at last to see his ultimate designs with sufficient clearness, that if the senate struck first he would be willing to follow up the opening and definitely break with his untrustworthy partner. At all events, Cicero seems to have thought it worthwhile to take the chance. Perhaps he took his cue from the conversation mentioned above in which Pompey acknowledged the hostility of Caesar's friends and seemed ready to strike out on a line of his own.[70] If he could be trusted to do this, the plan might succeed. Accordingly, on

April 5, of the year 56, three weeks after the acquittal of Sestius, Cicero made a bold move.

He chose an issue on which senatorial sentiment had already been probed. Early in the previous December, one of the new tribunes had raised in the senate the question of Caesar's Campanian land law, passed two years before.[71] Apparently the tribune pointed out that since the state had been deprived of its revenue from the Campanian lands and that these were not being taken up by settlers under the proposed scheme of distribution, the question should be reopened for consideration, in view of the heavy drain on the treasury for purchases of grain. In the course of his speech he apparently made some sharp thrusts at Caesar. The proposal took the senate by surprise and was met with profound silence. Then one of the consuls-elect stated that such a matter ought not to be debated in the absence of Pompey, and it was allowed to drop.[72] Nothing more was heard of it during the ensuing months, when attention was centered on the duel between Pompey and Clodius, but it must have been the subject of a good many private conversations and thus have entered into Cicero's calculations.

On the fifth of April the senate was considering a large appropriation for Pompey to expend in purchasing grain, and the matter of the revenues was naturally raised. It was then that Cicero came forward with a motion. He proposed that the question of the Campanian lands should be reopened and should be referred for consideration to a full meeting of the senate on May 15th. The debate was vehement, he says, and the senators made almost as much noise as a public meeting because they were exasperated by the shortness of money and the high price of grain.[73] The proposal was carried by the votes of many whom Cicero had not expected to support it.[74] This was a telling victory, an attack on the enemy in the very heart of his position.[75] Caesar's prestige was deeply involved, for no measure of his consulate had been more definitely identified with his policy than the Campanian land law. That Cicero had been able in this unexpected way to open a door for the repeal of that law was new proof of how dangerous he could make himself to Caesar's plans. What was worse from Caesar's point of view, and what gave Cicero added assurance and encouragement, was that Pompey not only did not oppose the proposal but gave no sign to Cicero that he was annoyed by it.[76]

When the news of Cicero's successful stroke reached Caesar, he knew, with his unerring sense of timing, that the moment had come for him again to take decisive action. He was then at Ravenna, where he was accustomed to spend the winter months between his Gallic campaigns because this town, of all those in his province, was the one where he could keep in closest touch with Rome. Although the winter was over, he had been delaying his departure for the theater of war, presumably because he felt it more necessary than ever at this time to keep a close watch on the political situation at the capital. Crassus had recently gone north to meet him and to warn him against Pompey and Cicero—against Pompey because of his feud with Clodius, and against Cicero because of his successful defense of Sestius. The news which now came from Rome of Cicero's victory on the question of the Campanian lands must have confirmed the warnings, but Caesar reacted to it in a way different from what Crassus probably desired. He decided to come to terms with Pompey. The latter had already left Rome on his way to Sardinia to buy grain in his capacity as food commissioner, and Caesar invited him to meet him at a convenient halfway point. Since Caesar could not leave his province, the place selected was the little town of Lucca, on the border between Etruria and Liguria,[77] and there a conference was staged that was to be another landmark in Roman constitutional history.

On this occasion, as on so many others where he could draw advantage from it, Caesar indulged both his showmanship and sense of drama. Although he undoubtedly meant to offer concessions to Pompey, he wished to be sure that they were plainly seen as concessions, albeit gracious ones, and for this purpose he decided to make a display of his importance and power which neither Pompey nor any other Roman politician could misunderstand. Accordingly, the Lucca conference was planned as a full-dress affair, without counterpart in the history of Rome. Invitations were sent out judiciously but widely. When the guests were assembled, two hundred senators were found in attendance, and so many praetors, ex-consuls and provincial governors were on hand that one hundred and twenty fasces of Roman magistrates were displayed. These, Caesar seemed to be saying silently to Pompey and Cicero, and to the entire government and people of Rome, are the evidences of my power and importance, and of my connections in the state. Before this great throng of officials and grandees Caesar appeared as leader and chief. Many of them had not seen him since he left the city, and these he now welcomed as the conqueror of Gaul, the winner of the hardest fought battles in recent history, the peer if not the superior of any living Roman general. In order to understand the position Caesar had made for himself and now occupied in the Roman world, and hence to appreciate the significance of the conference at Lucca, it is necessary briefly to review the two years of amazing victories which he had achieved beyond the Alps.

III

Caesar's conquest of Gaul has been aptly termed "one of the most important events in the history of the world," [78] and its significance is such that it could not possibly have been apprehended by Caesar himself or any of his contemporaries. Its importance lies in the fact that it ensured the Romanization of western and much of northern Europe; it guaranteed that the countries which are now France, Belgium, Holland, England and southern Germany—countries which for centuries have been the heart of Western civilization —would be brought under Roman law and administration, and subjected to the influences of Graeco-Roman culture. It thus provided the channel and conduit through which the civilization of classical antiquity has flowed into the modern civilization of the West.[79] In this sense, Caesar was the founder of modern Europe.[80] Subsequent events were to blot out almost entirely the most important features of Greek culture in the countries where it seemed to have taken firmest root—in Greece itself, in Asia Minor, in Syria and in Egypt—and had it not been for Caesar's conquest of Gaul, the influence of Greek philosophy, art, science and literature might well have been lost to the world. The provision of the means whereby the culture of antiquity was transmitted to the modern world was Caesar's greatest constructive achievement, indeed, almost his only one; and it is one of the ironies of history that for all his extraordinary foresight, his grandest accomplishment was unpremeditated and unintended.

From Caesar's own standpoint, the conquest of Gaul was only an incident in the fulfillment of his personal ambition, the exercise ground for improving the strength of his army and heightening his own glory.[81] In selecting Gaul for his proconsular assignment, Caesar must have known, for it was common knowledge in Rome at the time, of the stirring among northern tribes which promised an opportunity for military enterprises and successes of which he might take advantage to attain the political preeminence he desired.[82] It is hardly likely that when he first went to his province he intended more than to conduct the campaigns that would be necessary to deal with the immediate situation as it then existed, but almost immediately he appears to have broadened his plans. It was of the essence of Caesar's genius that he could take in a situation at a glance and immediately grasp its possibilities for his own purposes. The situation which he found in Gaul seems to have convinced him almost from the outset that the most effective and practical way of dealing with it was by the conquest and annexation of the whole country.

In conceiving such a design in such a forthright way, Caesar was breaking with Roman precedents and traditions as boldly as he had in politics. Throughout the entire course of Rome's history, it had never been a policy to begin a war, except to meet the threat of imminent attack,[83] and never to annex conquered territory or assume the burden of its administration save as a last resort. To make war deliberately for the purpose of annexation was something new and unheard of. In this sense, "Caesar was the first candid imperialist of Rome," and "the Gallic war is the clearest instance of deliberate expansion in the history of the Roman republic." [84]

When Caesar took over his province beyond the Alps, the tribes of free Gaul were in a state of highly unstable equilibrium, both internally and in their relations with one another.[85] Through contact with Roman traders they had attained a stage of civilization far higher than is commonly assumed, and distinctly above that of mere barbarians. "Walled towns . . . the strongholds of the various tribes, were conspicuous on numerous hills. The plains were dotted by scores of open hamlets. The houses, built of timber and wickerwork, were large and well-thatched. The fields in summer were yellow with corn. Roads ran from town to town. Rude bridges spanned the rivers; and barges laden with merchandise floated along them. . . . Every tribe had its coinage. . . . The Aeduans were familiar with the plating of copper and of tin. The miners of Aquitaine, of Auvergne and of the Berri were celebrated for their skill." [86]

In their growth to this stage of civilization, many of the traditional institutions of the Gauls had proved unequal to the strain and were in process of dissolution. Their political organization was still tribal and had become wracked with private feuds and bitter rivalries. The dissensions and divisions within the tribes, which grew out of the rivalries of their chiefs, had become sharpened by contacts with the Romans because some of the tribal chieftains were attracted toward Roman ways and Roman friendship, while others adhered with increased tenacity to their traditional usages and habits of independence. These trends and tendencies were fully apparent in the conditions that existed in the part of Gaul where Caesar commenced his operations—the country above the confluence of the Rhône and Saône which is now called Burgundy, and the adjacent region stretching eastward to the Rhine and known in modern times as Franche-Comté. Burgundy was the seat of one of the greater Gallic tribes, the Aedui, and their eastern neighbors were another great tribe, the Sequani, with whom they stood in relations of chronic enmity. The Aedui, who were among the most advanced nations of Gaul, had early entered into cordial relations with Rome, and had been received as friends and allies of the Roman people seventy years before.[87] Although the Aedui were still loyal to Rome, a powerful group among them chafed at the Roman connection and were ready to make common cause with the Sequani or any other tribe that was prepared to create trouble. The whole situation was thus fluid and unstable, and in the years just prior to Caesar's consulship two highly disturbing elements had been injected into it.

Sometime about the year 63, the Sequani went to war with the Aedui and employed the German leader Ariovistus to cross the Rhine with a large army of his tribesmen and assist them. The Aedui were badly beaten, but the Sequani found that their German

allies had become their masters. Ariovistus demanded and obtained
the cession of a part of what is now Alsace, where he settled his army
and set about founding a German kingdom which became a standing threat to the Aedui and Sequani alike.

Soon afterwards a second and even more ominous development occurred. The Helvetians, a large tribe inhabiting the western
part of modern Switzerland between Geneva and Basle, decided to
migrate westward in a body and seek a new home in Gaul, and to
that end they entered into negotiations with the Sequani and the
anti-Roman party among the Aedui. Making no secret of their intentions, they began to prepare for the emigration by procuring
supplies, wagons and draught cattle. The migration of the Helvetians, comparable on a small scale to that of the Cimbri and the
Teutons of half a century before, was certain to precipitate a major
war among the Gallic tribes, with repercussions that would sweep
southward into the Roman province of Narbonne and possibly into
Italy itself. Accordingly, when the news first reached Rome in the
early part of 60, the senate showed its opinion of the seriousness
of the danger by authorizing a levy of troops throughout Italy,[88] but
there the matter was allowed to drop, and nothing further had been
done.

This dual threat in Gaul provided an inviting prospect for a
man who desired military action. First, there was the immediate
task of checking and conquering the Helvetians, and, if that could
be accomplished, there would remain the further task of driving
Ariovistus back across the Rhine. Probably this was all that Caesar
envisaged when he made his preparations to take up his Gallic command. At the outset, his chief anxiety seems to have been lest either
or both opportunities should escape him. If, for example, the Helvetians should take fright and decide not to migrate, Caesar's chance
of inaugurating his governorship with a resounding military success
would be lost. He therefore seems carefully to have avoided doing
anything that might head them off, or prevent them from commencing their march, and this appears to have been one reason why he
felt free to remain at Rome, aiding and abetting the schemes of
Clodius against Cicero long after he would normally have left for
Gaul.[89] Meanwhile, Ariovistus had been lulled into security by of-

ficial recognition as a friend of the Roman people, and the probability that he would attack the Romans when they were engaged with the Helvetians was thereby lessened.

Caesar almost overdid his policy of delay. Toward the end of March in 58, word was brought to Rome that the Helvetians would start on their great migration in eight days. Caesar at once left for the north in great haste. Traveling ninety miles a day, he crossed into Provence, picked up the legion that was stationed there, and proceeded up the east bank of the Rhône to Geneva, where he arrived before the migration had commenced. The Helvetians promptly sent envoys to request permission to use the safer and easier road which ran along the east bank of the Rhône within the Roman province. Caesar had no intention of letting them do this, but he replied that he would think about it and give them an answer in ten days. He thus obtained an interval to barricade the road they wished to use, and when the time came to give his answer, it was a refusal. The Helvetians thus had no choice but to use the steeper and more difficult road west of the river, and along this almost impossible passage their vast column and caravan of wagon trains, consisting of over three hundred thousand human beings with their property and provisions, began to move.[00] Caesar rightly estimated that over such a route the Helvetians would require many weeks to reach the low country where a battle could be fought. This gave him time to make further preparations and again to display his amazing quickness and decisiveness of action.

Throwing himself into his traveling carriage, Caesar returned over the Alps and crossed Lombardy to Aquileia, at the head of the Adriatic, where the three legions attached to the province of Cisalpine Gaul were stationed. There, without legal authorization, and in apparent violation of his own legislation of the preceding year, he proceeded to recruit two additional legions, and, with a total army of twenty-five or thirty thousand men, he crossed the Cottian Alps and marched up the Rhône, to the point of its confluence with the Saône, where he arrived about the first of June, and was joined by the legion he had left at Geneva. He was exactly on time. The Helvetians had just crossed the Saône and were marching into the territory of the Aedui. Caesar led his army across the river and followed them until a promising opportunity for a battle presented itself near the end of the month at a point southwest of Bibracte, the Aeduan capital. Here he slaughtered the migrants by the thousands until only about one-third remained to be driven back to their own country. Caesar thus commenced his career in Gaul with the kind of spectacular victory he desired.

It was now the turn of Ariovistus, whom Caesar was naturally anxious to find an excuse for attacking so as to remove the dangerous intruder from the Gallic scene. First, Caesar resorted to the processes of negotiation and asked for a conference. When the German made the mistake of declining, Caesar was given the opportunity to announce to him the terms of Roman friendship: no more Germans must cross the Rhine; the hostages of the Aedui must be restored; he must cease to molest that people or their allies. Ariovistus sent back word that he was not interested in the friendship of the Romans, that he was a conqueror and entitled to treat his subjects as he pleased, that, if the Aedui did not pay their tribute, their alliance with the Romans would not save them, for no one had ever resisted Ariovistus and lived. This defiance suited Caesar's plans. He marched up toward Alsace, through the famous Belfort Gap, to the neighborhood of Strasbourg, where battle was joined. The Romans were completely victorious. Only Ariovistus and a few companions were lucky enough to reach safety across the Rhine. The battle occurred near the end of September and brought to a close a fighting season in which Caesar had won two victories in his first year in Gaul.

Caesar's choice of winter quarters near Vesontio, the chief town of the Sequani and the modern Besançon, sheds a good deal of light on his purposes as they had taken shape at this time. It seems clear that he had become convinced of the necessity, at least for the time being, of defending the Rhine frontier against further German incursions. There were rumors that another German tribe, the Suevi, had been on the point of crossing the river until deterred by the defeat of Ariovistus. To withdraw now from this area would be to invite and encourage new invasions and confess weakness and indecision in the eyes of the Gallic population. It may also have occurred to Caesar that the necessity of defending the Rhine frontier was a continuing one which would entail the annexation of Gaul. If his thinking had not gone so far as this in the autumn of the year 58, it was driven to that point by the events of the ensuing winter.

The presence of Caesar's army during the winter provoked a group of Gallic tribes known as the Belgae, in northeastern Gaul, to think he had designs against their independence, and in the course of the ensuing months there was developed a military confederacy designed to drive the Romans out of Gaul. Caesar's intelligence service, which was alert and capable, kept him in touch with these developments and, while attending to administrative duties south of the Alps, he took advantage of the opportunity to recruit two more unauthorized legions in Cisalpine Gaul. When the spring opened, he brought up these reenforcements to join the six legions he had left behind at Besançon. With this enlarged force, now numbering almost fifty thousand men, he crossed the watershed between the Saône and the Marne in the neighborhood of Langres, and made one of his rapid forced marches northward to meet the vast army which the Gallic confederates had assembled. One by one he was able to obtain the submission of these tribes, which he treated with firmness and clemency, punishing no one, until only the more remote tribes remained in arms. Chief among these were the Nervii, who inhabited the marsh country along the lower Sheldt. These had the reputation of being a fierce people, resolute in adhering to their primitive way of life, who would let no traders cross their borders, used no wine, tolerated no luxuries, and who announced that they would exchange no embassies and consider no terms of peace.[91] Caesar marched into their territory and engaged in the first great critical battle of his career, one of the fiercest and most desperate he ever fought. Only his extraordinary personal bravery and quickness of decision, exhibited in this battle for the first time, succeeded in saving them and winning the battle which ended with the practical annihilation of the Nervii.

After the defeat of the Nervii, Caesar sent one of his legates with a single legion to the west and south to demand and receive the submission of the tribes. None dared refuse, and by the end of summer he had brought at least nominally under his sway Normandy, Brittany and all of France as far south as the Loire. Poitou, Aquitaine and the central massif of Berri and Auvergne were the only parts of Gaul which remained for subsequent annexation, and it seemed only a question of time and of Caesar's discretion when these would have to submit. To all appearances the conquest of Gaul was complete, the result of two summers' work.

Caesar took care that his achievements should not be underestimated at Rome. His dispatches—which probably formed the basis of his immortal *Commentaries*—created the impression that Gaul in its entirety was now conquered and annexed, and Ferrero has not hesitated to characterize Caesar's conduct in creating this impression as "probably the most skilful recorded exhibition of political charlatanism." [92] In any event, the news, which arrived in the latter part of September before the bitterness of party strife had had time to renew itself, produced a great sensation, and Caesar's reputation and popularity mounted to unprecedented heights. Cicero himself, with the concurrence of Pompey, moved a resolution by which the senate decreed in Caesar's honor a thanksgiving of fifteen days, the longest that had ever been known. [93] In public estimation as a military hero, the conqueror of Gaul had at last attained a position equal if not superior to that of Pompey.

Whether or not Caesar overstated his achievements to produce a public impression at Rome, there can be no doubt that in his first two campaigns in Gaul he had already revealed the qualities of a great general, indeed, one of the greatest in all history. What has continued to awe subsequent generations, no less than his own, is that in middle life he was able not only to rise to supreme eminence in an entirely new kind of career but to assume what, superficially at least, seems almost like a new character. That a man forty-five years old, who had spent almost all his life in the world of fashion and pleasure and in backstairs political intrigues, should suddenly develop into a supreme strategist and military administrator is extraordinary enough, but Caesar did more. Suddenly and without apparent preparation he showed himself a great soldier in the highest and most difficult aspects of the soldier's character. His superb success in this respect was by no means only the result of his greatness as a strategist and an organizer. Far more it resulted from the fact that he was a great leader of troops and a great master of military psychology. He knew what to do to make himself respected and obeyed and to cause his soldiers to love and follow him. In middle age, he was able suddenly to assume a new way of life, new habits, new aptitudes, and new kinds of self-control to which he was entirely unaccustomed. Suetonius recounts that on the march he used to go at the head of his troops, sometimes on his horse, but more often on foot, with his helmet off and his head bare in all kinds of weather, and that he was able to bear fatigue beyond all belief.[94] He shared the hardships which his men had to endure and fought side by side with them in the battle line. If his army gave way, he often rallied his troops single-handed, planting himself in the way of those who fled, even catching them by the throat.[95] His greatness as a general lay in possessing willpower and determination which he was able to communicate to others because he possessed them himself and thus had an extraordinary hold on the confidence of his troops. "In the practical psychology which is the root of all great generalship he has probably never had an equal. It is because he could read the feelings of his adversaries and of his own men at the same time and with the same accuracy that he achieved things hardly credible." [96] He thus applied to the task of military leadership the same psychology which had made him so effective as a "machine" politician. He knew how to work on human beings through their lower instincts. His soldiers, like the soldiers of Sulla, were encouraged to understand that if they did their duty as effective fighting men, their general would shut his eyes to much that they might do on their own, so long as they did not go so far as to interfere with his own plans.[97]

Throughout the Gallic campaigns Caesar's camp was a busy center of political management and intrigue. He used the many means which he had at his disposal to bind to himself by ties of personal obligation those who might be useful to him at Rome. He gave favored positions at his headquarters to those prominently recommended to him, and he permitted them to share the booty and the proceeds of the sale of prisoners. He saw to it that his entourage was always surrounded by a strong and attractive odor of corruption: there was money to be made with no inconvenient questions asked. He appealed especially to young men, whom he preferred because few of them had any party connection and would owe their successes to him. In this way, he surrounded himself with a group of aggressive and ambitious young followers who looked on their future as bound up with his.[98]

Caesar also employed more direct and immediate ways of quietly bringing under his influence an increasing number of important men at Rome while he was hundreds of miles away in the wilds of Gaul. Through him much of the gold of Gaul, long hoarded in temple treasuries or in the coffers of old and princely families, found its way into Roman hands.[99] Gallic chiefs who sought Roman favor or protection had to pay handsomely for it, and the proceeds of the slave market were now turned in a steady stream on Rome.[100] Although much of this money fell into the hands of Caesar's soldiery, officers, subalterns and enterprising privates in the ranks, the lion's share was undoubtedly kept by Caesar, who poured it out lavishly but discreetly to buy the influential Romans who could serve him.

The fruits of this quiet and assiduous policy, pursued over a period of two years, he suddenly and boldly displayed at the conference of Lucca. Openly he brought together the prominent Romans, senators and magistrates with whom he had dealt separately and privately, and each was revealed to the others who, like himself, had Caesar's mark upon them. Caesar now drew back the veil and let each into the others' secrets. Thereafter, any pretense of independence would be futile, and at the same time each would be confirmed in his subservience by confidence in the number of others who were in the same cause. Two hundred members of the senate, almost a working majority of the entire body, were shown to be ready to play Caesar's game. Against the background of this polite exhibition of the strength of his position, Caesar was ready to sit down and confer with Pompey.

IV

The course which Caesar took with Pompey at Lucca has remained a puzzle to many historians and political analysts. He did not trade closely or sharply with him, although Pompey was now certainly, if not in dire need, at least in a weak and precarious political position. Caesar seems to have decided that his own immediate goal must be to complete the conquest of Gaul, and that nothing should be allowed to interfere with that objective at this stage. Mommsen and Warde Fowler are of the opinion that this decision was the result of Caesar's overwhelming sense of a great public duty and responsibility, and that, having set his hand to a task of such major importance to later ages, he felt he must carry it through at whatever cost or danger to himself.[101] Now although Caesar was unquestionably aware of the importance of annexing Gaul, it is impossible that he could have understood the implications of the conquest in terms of its subsequent significance which modern scholars are able to attach to it. Moreover, there is nothing to indicate that he ever performed any task, however important in a public sense, without a main eye to its effect on his own future, and there appears to be no ground for assuming that he did so now.

The real reason why Caesar felt it necessary to go forward with the Gallic War at this time was because he undoubtedly recognized that, despite the impressions he had created at Rome, the conquest was in fact only half completed. If he left off now, all that he had accomplished would be quickly undone and the record of his achievement wiped out. It seems clear, moreover, that he was not yet ready to return to Rome, for there was not at present any place at the capital into which he could fit conveniently or consistently with his desire for position. He had begun to weld his army into the instrument of personal power that it was later to become, but there was much still to be done in that respect. If he were recalled now, or at the expiration of his present term of command, in two years' time, he would probably not be able to resist, without civil war, an order to disband his troops, and he was not yet certain that he had an army with which he could win. Anxious not to leave Gaul, and unwilling yet to run the risk of a civil war in Italy, he must nevertheless have perceived that both were conceivable unless there were some change in the present state of affairs at Rome.

If matters went on at Rome as they had recently been going, there was the possibility that Pompey and the conservatives might at last come together on the common ground of opposition to himself and thus ruin his personal prestige. There was also the possibility that he might be recalled from Gaul. Cato was expected back soon from Cyprus, and his brother-in-law, Domitius Ahenobarbus, a young man of enormous wealth and great ambition, had already announced publicly that he intended to terminate Caesar's Gallic command.[102] Moreover, it was common knowledge that some of the conservatives had been drawing close to Clodius, and Caesar knew as well as anyone that Clodius was not trustworthy. Cicero he discounted except as a voice, but if a combination between Pompey and the conservatives were formed, with Cato as a leader and Cicero as a mouthpiece, and if the conservatives could control or neutralize Clodius, all the subtle influences which Caesar had been at such pains to link to himself by the gold of Gaul would dissolve, and he would find himself in troubles which he was not yet ready to meet. There was, of course, a chance that Pompey could not be brought to play an active part in such a combination, but even if he remained inactive and stood aloof in disgruntled neutrality, the threat to Caesar's plans would hardly be greatly diminished. The risks involved in again building up Pompey as an important figure on his side were not so great as the risks on the other side.

A more subtle factor may well have entered into Caesar's calculations, in view of his sensitiveness to the imponderables of politics. To date, his successes in politics had been achieved principally through the device of making the republican constitution unworkable, through constantly taking advantage of its defects so as to make constitutional government publicly ineffective and contemptible. If he were to proceed farther along the same road toward fulfilling his ambitions for power and prestige, the constitution must continue to be made to appear unworkable. Yet he was confronted by a situation which threatened, at least for the moment, to put new life and a greater measure of effectiveness into the republic. If his land law were repealed, if his Gallic command were revoked, if these were done lawfully under forms of republican constitutionality, if Cicero were to advocate them with his appealing eloquence, and if Cato or Cato's supporters were to take the lead in promoting them— then notice would be served on the Roman public and throughout the Roman world that the old republican constitution was still alive and was vigorous enough to assert its supremacy over the irregular and arbitrary kind of government to which Caesar owed his continuing success. This was an eventuality that he could not allow to occur if it could be prevented. Something must accordingly be done to proclaim anew, in a spectacular and unmistakable way, that constitutional government was defunct at Rome and that the kind of government which the triumvirs had introduced during his consulship was to be permanent. For such an effort he again needed Pompey's prestige, respectability and cooperation. Most of all, Caesar needed him because he could not afford to let it be thought that the triumvirate had fallen apart. Hence, Caesar seems to have concluded that it was essential to renew the partnership on terms that would satisfy Pompey and for the moment ensure his complete and enthusiastic cooperation.

Surprise has often been expressed at Caesar's generosity in the terms on which the triumvirate was renewed at Lucca. They were generous not only to Pompey but to Crassus, who up to now had played only an insignificant role in the partnership. Yet Crassus still controlled a strong bloc of senatorial votes and still had some sort of hold over Clodius, so that it was desirable to placate him. It was even more important to do so in order to exhibit to the public the unimpaired unity and solidarity of the triumvirate. Liberal terms for Crassus and Pompey were necessary not only for this purpose but also to ensure that the conduct of both of them in the months to come would contribute further to the breakdown of constitutional government. There cannot be much doubt that these were the considerations which dictated the terms presented to, and agreed on by, his partners.

Caesar's terms for himself were very modest. He asked only two things: a renewal of his Gallic command for another five years after the expiration of his present term and legal authorization for the extra legions which he had recruited without authority, as well as provision for their pay and maintenance at government expense. For his partners, whose cooperation and assent he badly wanted, he was willing to agree to far more important and spectacular rewards. Each of them was to have another term as consul, as a stepping-stone to further honors and opportunities, and they were to serve together for the year 55, just as they had fifteen years before. Thereafter, Crassus should have as his proconsular assignment the rich province of Syria, where plenty of money was to be made and where there was also a possibility that he might be able to renew his early reputation as a general by leading an expedition against Parthia, now proving an uneasy neighbor on Rome's eastern frontier. Pompey's province was to be Spain, for a period of five years, commensurate with Caesar's renewed term in Gaul, and he was to have the command of a suitable army. For the further convenience and accommodation of Pompey, he was to be relieved of the necessity of residing in his province but might remain at Rome if he chose and perform his provincial duties through deputies. To improve Pompey's position at home, and to relieve him of the chief cause of his embarrassments, Caesar and Crassus engaged not only to bridle Clodius but to bring him over to Pompey's support. Thus, as when the triumvirate was first formed, "all that Pompey had been in vain endeavouring by painful intrigues to extract from his natural allies, the constitutionalists, was granted to him in a word by his magnificent rival." [103] One other provision was agreed to in the compact: in exchange for the promises made to him, Pompey was to bring pressure on Cicero, to muzzle him and to keep him from making any further moves against Caesar.

Mommsen, with his characteristic lack of political acumen, represents Caesar as the great loser by these concessions to Pompey and finds it "difficult to say what motives induced Caesar to surrender without necessity his superior position" and enable his rival to exchange his former powerlessness for an important command.[104] Caesar, says Mommsen, "unhesitatingly gave up his superiority over his rivals and granted to Pompeius sufficient power to settle matters with the senate and its adherents." [105] This was a grave political blunder, Mommsen thinks, if Caesar was pursuing schemes of personal ambition. As a matter of fact, the reasons, as just pointed out, seem fairly obvious, whereas the risks that Caesar ran were negligible.

With his usual insight into character, Caesar had taken the measure of Pompey and gambled on what he thought he could safely expect him to do. Events proved that he was right. If any danger was to be anticipated from again putting Pompey at the head of an army, that danger was now directed against the senate and not against himself. More importantly, from his own standpoint, he ensured the further breakdown of constitutional government by promoting the kind of regime of violence and anarchy which he had first tried to bring about by his support of Catiline. Furthermore, matters were so arranged in Caesar's characteristic fashion that this breakdown, as it occurred, would be chargeable not against himself, but against Pompey, who would continue to bear the stigma of destroyer of the constitution. Thus Caesar could safely turn his attention back to Gaul and be confident that the government at Rome would continue to deteriorate and disorder continue to increase, without his becoming directly involved. Undoubtedly, he did not foresee in exactly what way he could ultimately take advantage of these conditions, but it was almost certain that he could do so in some way. He shrewdly guessed that Pompey's days as a rigorous and effective military commander were over and that he had become too fond of leisure and his own self-importance. If matters should someday come to an open issue of arms between Pompey and the senate, there was strong likelihood that Pompey would have to call Caesar to his aid, and in such a situation Caesar might find it advantageous to play the part of mediator. Meanwhile, the strengthened position in which Pompey was placed by Caesar's concessions would work not against Caesar, as Mommsen supposed, but against the senate; and Caesar clearly had confidence enough in his own dexterity and finesse to feel assured that he could control the situation in the end, if and when the worse came to the worst. In the interval, he was content to deal with an immediate problem and gamble on being able to extricate himself successfully from more distant difficulties when the occasion arose.

The sacrificial victim of the Lucca conference was Cicero. In a sense this sacrifice was a symbolic act, and so doubtless Caesar intended it to be. Cicero, more than any other Roman in public life at this time, represented the spirit of the republic. His championship of the constitution and the *mos majorum* was not, like that of Cato and his clique, dependent on membership in an exclusive caste which looked on the constitution and the republic as its private property and sought to perpetuate it for class purposes. Rather it was founded on a conscious, intellectual conviction and civic spirit which were open to be shared by Roman citizens of all degrees alike, a conviction and spirit which, if sufficiently widespread and persistent, would guarantee the vitality and permanence of republican institutions. Time after time Cicero had been able to ignite that spirit into a flame that momentarily threatened to inspire the ancient carcass of the republic with new life. Alone among the republican leaders Cicero had the gift of making the republic mean something to a wider circle of Romans than the conservative nobility and their dependents, and it was precisely this capacity which ran counter to Caesar's policy of making the republic unworkable and contemptible. To silence Cicero was in effect to deprive the republic of its voice; to humiliate him was to humiliate the republic in its most representative figure.

Pompey was in a position to humiliate Cicero, and, in return for the favors which Caesar lavished on him at Lucca, he stooped to do so. He sent Cicero a curt request, which had the note of a command, that he should not concern himself further about Caesar's Campanian land law and should not bring on his motion that had been set for discussion in the senate on the fifteenth of May. He then called in Cicero's brother Quintus, who was serving under him as one of his deputy grain commissioners, and told him with brutal frankness, "Unless you remonstrate earnestly with your brother, you will be held responsible for the guarantees you gave me." [106] He said that he had had to give pledges to Caesar for Cicero's good conduct and that, if Cicero could not defend Caesar's acts, at least he must not attack them.

These announcements came as a crushing blow to Cicero. The ground on which he was taking his stand had shifted under his feet. On the 15th of May, he absented himself from the senate and the discussion fell through. "So far Cicero had no choice but to submit, but he had still to decide how to shape his general policy in view of the altered circumstances." [107]

The renewal of the alliance between Pompey and Caesar compelled Cicero to recognize that he had lost what basis he had ever had for an independent political position. As between the senate

and Pompey, the voters whom Cicero could most effectively influence would for the most part almost certainly follow Pompey
rather than the senatorial conservatives. Yet if Cicero did not follow
Pompey, which now meant following Caesar, he had no choice but
to join the ranks of the conservatives. This was a bitter alternative.
Cicero's relations with the conservatives had been strained ever
since the critical weeks just before his exile when he felt that they
had not given him the support that he had a right to expect from
them. Ever since his return they had done everything in their
power to defeat his efforts to heal the breach between Pompey and
the senate, and by this attitude they had been the principal cause of
Pompey's reunion with Caesar. Cicero had therefore lost what confidence he had ever had in their political acumen and statesmanship.
He also felt very deeply the snobbish exclusiveness and petty class
spirit that led them to refuse to follow his leadership in the fundamental matters on which he was in entire agreement with them.[108]
This resentment against the conservatives had been rankling in his
mind ever since his return from exile, when he had written, that
"those very people . . . who clipped my wings do not wish to see
them growing again." [109] Most of all he resented and feared the
willingness which the conservatives had shown during the winter
just past to cooperate with Clodius. From the standpoint of his own
safety, therefore, as well as from his interest in the good order of
the state, Cicero could not help distrusting the conservatives when,
as he says, he saw them embracing, fondling, making much of his
enemy, the enemy of the country, of the laws, and of all honorable
men.[110]

Under these circumstances, the prospect which Cicero had to
face was this: if he broke with Pompey and defied him by defying
Caesar, his only possible support would have to come from the
conservatives. The conservatives, however, would not only not accept him as a leader and follow the policies which he recommended,
but they could not even be trusted to support him against new enemies. Instead, he strongly suspected that they would desert him when
a critical moment came and take a malicious pleasure in leaving
him to the vengeance of Clodius or Caesar. This prospect left him
a narrow choice of alternatives. Either he could go into exile at once,

which would do no good to anyone and would be only a gesture of despair, or he could stay on at Rome. If he stayed on, he could either cooperate with the conservatives in futile opposition to Pompey and Caesar, and run the risk of their sacrificing him to his enemies, or he could refrain from opposition to the triumvirs and at least secure himself from attack until the situation should once more change.

To take the latter course, as he did, was a galling and humiliating choice for Cicero. Like his decision to go into exile, it was a blow to his pride and self-esteem. It destroyed for a second time the picture of himself which he wished to go down in history as the fearless and successful vindicator of the constitution and the republic. Instead, as he feared, it afforded an opportunity which historians have employed ever since to represent him as a time-serving turncoat, a timid and vacillating schemer, a hollow mouther of big words which he was not courageous enough to make good by brave deeds. He foresaw that this would be the consequence, and once again he contributed to that very interpretation of his conduct by indulging in expressions of self-reproach in his correspondence, as he had done in the letters written during his exile.[111]

It has been customary for historians to speak of Cicero during the next few years as in the service of the triumvirs. This is not a strictly accurate description of the course which he mapped out for himself and in the main followed. What he did was to refrain from active opposition and take a position on the sidelines, making a point of maintaining friendly personal relations both with the triumvirs and their friends and with such conservatives as shared his interests and enjoyed his society. His attitude was one of acquiescence in a situation which he could do nothing to change. Occasionally he made a speech in the triumvirs' interest on some point of their policy which he could consistently support, as when he advocated the renewal of Caesar's Gallic command on the ground that it would be foolish to leave the Romanizing of Gaul half finished.[112] Occasionally he handled a law case for one of their retainers, as by defending the citizenship of Caesar's confidential agent, Balbus,[113] and he even stooped to defend his old enemy, Pompey's henchman Gabinius.[114] On the other hand, he did not hesitate to attack Caesar's father-in-law Piso in one of the fiercest and most savage of all his orations, and he continued his warfare with Clodius by defending a client who was accused of attempting to poison the demagogue's notorious sister Clodia.[115]

The fact is that during this time Cicero was to all intents and purposes out of politics and out of public life. For the next five years he played no part in any important political matter and exerted no influence on the course of events. To all appearances his career as a statesman closed. Although he remained active at the bar,[116] he had largely lost his taste for this kind of work that had sustained him in earlier days when he looked forward to an eminent position as a statesman.[117] Now, he wrote, the time had come to turn to writing.[118] This time he was really serious in his intention of turning to authorship; as Caesar at forty-five commenced to make himself a great general, so Cicero at fifty commenced to compose the works which were to earn him his reputation as a great author. In April of the year 56—only a few weeks after the conference of Lucca—he wrote to his friend Atticus that he was having his books unpacked and arranged at his seaside villa at Anzio.[119] A year later found him at Cumae "devouring the library of Faustus," which contained the Aristotelian manuscripts Sulla had brought home from Athens.[120] During this year he was composing his first major literary work, his treatise on oratory, which he published near the end of the year 55, and which became the standard textbook on the subject for the remaining centuries of classical culture. Then he turned to the other great subject to which he had devoted his life, statesmanship, and set to work on a treatise on political philosophy, the *Republic*, which is the subject of detailed discussion in a subsequent chapter.[121]

Thus Cicero passed for a time out of the current of Roman history in which he had played so conspicuous if ineffectual a role, but the sequence of his letters accompanies the course of events almost like the entries in a diary, or like the chorus of a Greek tragedy. Read with care and with due allowance for the personality and bias of the writer, they furnish a more intimate running commentary on the last age of the Roman republic than exists for any other period of ancient history.

4

Disintegration
and
Collapse

I

THE conference of Lucca marked a last turning point in the long history of the Roman republic: thenceforward, after a few months of uncertainty, the movement was straight and rapid toward disintegration and total collapse.

Until Caesar's consulship in 59 B.C. the operation of the republican constitution had been clumsy, corrupt, frequently frustrated by the conflicts and intrigues of selfish cliques and coteries, and constantly menaced by the danger of plots and conspiracies. In short, it had been in a state of highly unstable equilibrium, yet somehow it had managed to function and to provide a government under which, in the course of a few years, Rome's empire abroad had been extended and consolidated more successfully than ever before. Caesar had shown how easily the equilibrium could be upset and the normal procedures of the constitution thwarted and overborne by a bold and unabashed application of force to the deliberative processes of the senate and assemblies. Once his resolute hand was withdrawn, however, the republican system gave signs of renewed vitality, and the recall of Cicero provides an illustration of ways in which the old equilibrium, unstable as it was, tended to reestablish itself.

With what little specific information as there is about Caesar's mental processes and purposes, it seems clear from his acts that he was determined that this resuscitation should not occur again; hence the arrangements of Lucca. When those arrangements were put into effect, the constitutional procedures of the republic were not merely thwarted and choked, as they had been during his consulship; they were paralyzed, and the paralysis rapidly revealed itself in atrophy and putrefaction. For the next five years the history of the republic is the history of a body of living death, a corpse almost ready for interment.

The arrangements of Lucca were, of course, not publicly disclosed. All that was made known was that important decisions of some kind had been reached, and their very secrecy again infected the political atmosphere with a sense of uncertainty and strain. It was clear that in some way the importance and power of Caesar had been enhanced and his hold on the government strengthened, with the result that the senate was anxious to display a conciliatory temper and hastened to accommodate itself to his wishes. Accordingly, recruitment of the legions which he had raised without legal authority was duly authorized by senatorial decree and their current as well as their back pay charged to the treasury. At the same time Caesar was empowered to appoint the usual number of ten lieutenant-generals. "All this," writes Cicero, "which they hardly expected to obtain even from the popular assembly without an insurrection, they have obtained from the senate." [1]

Shortly afterwards, the senate gave another proof of its willingness to appease Caesar. Under the so-called Sempronian law, the question of allotting provinces to the consuls of the ensuing year was as usual brought up in advance of the summer elections at which those consuls were to be chosen. The conservative members took advantage of this opportunity to propose the removal of Caesar from

Transalpine Gaul, so that it might be allotted to one of the new consuls and Caesar's career of conquest brought to a close. Of course Caesar could not be ousted by senatorial action from Cisalpine Gaul, which he held until March of the year 54 by the Vatinian plebiscite; but he held Transalpine Gaul only by vote of the senate and for no special term, and it could therefore be taken from him at any time that the senate refused to review his appointment. This the conservatives now proposed to do. In the debate which followed, Cicero delivered his oration *De Provinciis Consularibus* in favor of retaining Caesar in Gaul. This speech, which amounted to a public announcement of his refusal henceforth to follow the conservative party line, he describes somewhat shamefacedly as a "recantation." [2] Since the practical arguments against removing Caesar from Gaul at this time were overwhelming, the conservatives' proposal was lost, and Macedonia and Syria were designated as the provinces of the new consuls.

It was now summer of the year 56, and not only were politics at Rome at a stalemate, but the motives which governed the actions of the different groups are impossible to decipher with plausibility. The one outstanding fact is that Pompey and Crassus were reluctant to come out into the open as candidates for the consulships in accordance with the arrangements of Lucca, and they carefully delayed showing their hands. Nevertheless, the rumor spread that they would run, but when publicly asked, they took refuge in equivocation. At this time the leading candidate for the consulate was Cato's brother-in-law, Domitius Ahenobarbus, whose exalted birth and enormous wealth made him a formidable contender. His chances were improved by the fact that Cato had by now returned from Cyprus and was exerting himself actively in Domitius' behalf. In addition, he was dallying with a strange alliance. The fact that he had accepted office under Clodius seemed to make him feel that he was under an obligation to justify the proceedings of the demagogue, and he now came to the defense of Clodius when the latter was under attack in the senate. So far as outsiders were concerned, the tie of noble birth was strong between them, and, although Clodius was restrained by the arrangements of Lucca from openly opposing

Pompey, Cato's blandishments might well prevent him from giving Pompey active assistance in the forthcoming election.

It was doubtless this situation which made Pompey and Crassus proceed circumspectly in furthering their consular ambitions. The body from which they would have to seek election would be the centuriate assembly, the first to be convened since the meeting which had recalled Cicero in the previous summer. If the membership of the forthcoming assembly at all resembled its predecessor, Pompey and Crassus might well expect serious trouble in winning its support, for the well-to-do country voters whose attendance had been drummed up in the interest of Cicero might decide to return again in the present year, and they were not likely to prove willing tools of the triumvirs. If bribery were resorted to, Domitius was rich enough to hold his own against even Crassus and Pompey. At all events, the two partners seem to have been reluctant for these or other reasons to face a test of strength at the polls at this time.

It may be presumed that the postponement of the elections from month to month throughout the summer and fall was their doing. What they were aiming at was to push the voting well into the winter, and beyond the turn of the year. For this decision several reasons may have presented themselves. One was doubtless that by that time the present conservative consuls would be out of office and would not be in a position to preside over the comitia and use the presiding officer's large prerogatives to the disadvantage of the two triumvirs.[3] The most likely reason, however, is disclosed in a sentence in Plutarch's account of the conference of Lucca, in which he says that the arrangements there agreed on included an understanding "that Caesar on his part should send a number of his soldiers to give their votes at the election."[4] Caesar could hardly send to Rome enough soldiers to influence the outcome by the mere number of their votes, but the arrangement is clear and intelligible if it means that Caesar's soldiers would be available to control the election by force. For this purpose, an outside supply of men-at-arms such as Caesar could furnish seems to have been necessary. Pompey could not rely on the gangs of Clodius, and without those gangs the preponderance of local force at Rome seems at this time to have been in the hands of Milo and other gang leaders who worked for the conservatives.[5] So far as the *comitia centuriata* were concerned, the balance of sentiment, public opinion, bribery and even force were thus all on the conservative side. Caesar must have sensed this situation when he hastened to patch up the new deal at Lucca. As usual, he placed his confidence in superior force to redress the balance, and he was in a position to furnish that kind of force if the meeting of the comitia were deferred until his troops were in winter quarters. The meeting was deferred, and when the election was held in January, the soldiers sent by Caesar were on the scene.

Contemporary sources make it clear that the election was in fact carried by force and violence. Domitius, who was present to see that his name was presented, was chased away from the Campus Martius by armed men, one of his servants was killed, and Cato and others among his retinue were wounded. Although Cato urged him to remain on the field and keep up the struggle as long as a spark of life was left in him, Domitius had no stomach for such heroism and was glad to be allowed to get back to his house alive. Thereafter, the names of Pompey and Crassus were the only ones placed in nomination, and they were duly elected. Through the management of Caesar, the army was thus employed again to control the civil government of Rome.

Pompey and Crassus entered on their consulship of the year 55 in the same spirit of "thorough" which Caesar had exhibited four years before. The capture of the election by force at the beginning of the year was a token of what was to follow and an indication of their intent to rule in defiance of everybody who stood in the way of their plans. Their first step was to muzzle Cato, on whom the leadership of the conservative opposition to the triumvirs had devolved. Undaunted by the defeat of Domitius, Cato now prepared to be a candidate for the praetorship, for which the polling had been postponed. Since there were no praetors in office, the successful candidates would commence their terms immediately after the election, and there would thus be no interval in which they would be subject to prosecution for electoral abuses. This situation created an opportunity for the employment of wholesale bribery, and the consuls were quick to seize upon it to ensure the success of their own nominees. Cato's friends tried to intervene by causing the senate to decree that after the election the new praetors should remain private citizens and therefore be subject to prosecution for an interval of sixty days. However, as Cicero reports, although the senate groaned aloud, the consuls refused to put the motion. "On that day, they unmistakably repudiated Cato. . . . They have everything in their own hands, and they want everyone to understand that that is the case." [6]

Cato was not, however, deterred from pursuing his candidacy, and when the election was held and the first century was called, it gave its vote in his favor. Usually, the first vote was indicative of the final outcome, but Pompey, who was presiding, immediately adjourned the meeting to a later date, and the consuls employed the interval to administer bribery in larger doses. When the assembly reconvened, they were also careful to have on hand the necessary array of force, and the outcome was the election of Caesar's henchman Vatinius. Cato remained on the field throughout the proceedings, and, after the result was announced, he made a speech to the crowd in which he is said to have "foretold all the miseries that afterward befell the state, exhorted them to beware of Pompey and Crassus, who were guilty of such things, and had laid such designs, that they might well fear to have Cato praetor." [7] When he had ended this speech, he was escorted home by a vast crowd.

From this point, the consuls moved forward to ensure themselves the provincial commands for which they had bargained at Lucca. Again, as during Caesar's consulship, the senate was ignored, and the matter was handled through the readily controllable tribal assembly. A tribune named Tribonius, a dependent of Caesar, was delegated to propose a law appointing Pompey to Spain and Crassus to Syria, with power to make war by sea and land as they should see fit. Cato appeared on the rostrum and was allowed to speak against the proposal for several hours, but although Tribonius then had him forcefully removed, he succeeded in breaking up the meeting. When it reconvened, there was the usual riot. Cato, who tried to speak again, was driven out of the Forum, "many were wounded, and some slain; and at length by open force they passed the law." [8]

The next item of the triumvirs' program was to carry out the

engagements entered into for the benefit of Caesar, and for this purpose a bill was sponsored by the consuls themselves that gave Caesar
both Gallic provinces for an additional terms of five years. It is
unfortunate for the understanding of later events that information
is lacking as to whether, under this Pompeian-Licinian law, Caesar's
new appointment was to terminate at the end of the year 50 or on
March 1, 49, for that question was to furnish one of the principal
pretexts for the outbreak of civil war five years later. However, it is
known that the law contained a provision to the effect that the
senate should not consider the question of Caesar's successor in Gaul
before March 1st of the year 50. Cato made no public opposition to
this proposal, but instead he made a personal appeal to Pompey, saying that he should consider that he was setting Caesar on his own
shoulders and that the latter would shortly grow too heavy for him.
Eventually, "not able to lay down the burden, nor yet to bear it any
longer, he would precipitate both it and himself with it upon the
commonwealth; and then he would remember Cato's advice, which
was no less advantageous to him, than just and honest in itself." [9]

If this story is true—and there seems to be no good reason
to doubt it—it foreshadowed a new alignment in Roman politics.
It means that at this point Cato became converted to the idea
of wooing Pompey away from Caesar and, if possible, bringing
him into an alliance with the conservatives. Certainly he was later
to pursue this course, which in substance was nothing but the old
policy of Cicero, who had vainly tried to convert Cato and the conservatives thereto six years before. Since then, the latter had done
everything in their power to defeat it because it was the policy of
Cicero. Now that Cicero was disposed of, his position was adopted
by the conservatives who had hitherto opposed it. That this should
have come about is a notable tribute to Cicero's political sagacity and
soundness of judgment, but their *volte-face* illustrates how impossible it was for him to become an effective political leader in the Rome
of his age.

No actual alliance was formed between Pompey and the conservatives at this time—there was merely the faint beginning of a
rapprochement on the conservative side, indicated by a number of
different bits of evidence. For example, from now on Caesar rather

than Pompey bore the brunt of the conservatives' denunciation. During the summer Cato attacked him in a speech of great bitterness for his behavior toward two German tribes, the Usipites and Tenctheri. As will appear,[10] Caesar had extricated himself from a difficult situation with those barbarians by conduct which was not entirely in accord with traditional Roman standards of good faith and fair play, and Cato took advantage of the incident to denounce Caesar and declare that Roman honor demanded that he should be surrendered to the Germans whom he had unrighteously deceived. Caesar took this attack so much to heart when he heard of it that he wrote a public letter to the senate, bringing countercharges against Cato, and Cato was thus afforded further opportunity to review the course of Caesar's career and to warn the senate that it was not Gauls or Britons that they had to fear but Caesar himself.[11]

There is only one indication, but a seemingly significant one, that as early as this Pompey may have lent a not unfriendly ear to the approaches of Cato. In the consular elections of that same summer, Cato's man, Domitius Ahenobarbus, was again a candidate, but Pompey apparently made no effort to defeat him. The explanation may be that without the aid of Caesar's troops Pompey saw no hope of controlling the election, but at least he did not, as in the preceding year, seek to postpone it until winter, as he could have done. Furthermore, it is significant that the colleague chosen with Domitius was Appius Clodius, the respectable older brother of the demagogue, whose daughter had just been married to Pompey's son. Appius may thus be regarded as a kind of personal candidate of Pompey, and his choice, together with Domitius, the candidate of the conservatives, suggests that some sort of arrangement had been worked out between the latter and Pompey. At the election Cato was chosen praetor without opposition from Pompey, and subsequently several tribunes hostile to the triumvirs were named. Pompey did not in any way bestir himself to force matters in favor of his partners after the measures agreed on at Lucca had been carried through at the beginning of the year.

During much of his year as consul in 55, Pompey seems to have been engaged in a vast campaign to rebuild his popularity. This effort took two forms—first, the exhibition of games and spectacles on a more colossal scale than ever before, and, second, the completion and opening of the first permanent stone and marble theater which, until the end of the Empire, remained the largest and most important theater at Rome.[12] Size and grandiosity, even beyond the bad taste of the typical Roman, were always characteristic of Pompey's displays,[13] but this time the slaughter of hundreds of lions, as well as eighteen elephants, in the course of one spectacle disgusted even the heartless Roman proletariat. According to Pliny, the crowd was so moved by the sufferings of the animals that they broke out into loud curses against Pompey.[14] Thus Pompey, "clumsy and tactless as ever in dealing with his fellow-citizens, seems to have gained little popularity by all his outlay." [15]

During the second half of his consulship, Pompey became involved in a matter which enhanced neither his popularity nor his reputation. It will be remembered that when, in the early months of the year 56, King Ptolemy, "the flute-player," was asking the Romans to restore him to his lost throne of Egypt, it was strongly suspected that Pompey desired the commission,[16] but in the end the matter had been left by the senate in the hands of the governor of Cilicia, who was instructed not to use force in Ptolemy's behalf. Those instructions were equivalent to a senatorial decision in favor of inaction, and they were so interpreted by Ptolemy, who had taken sanctuary from his creditors in the temple of Diana at Ephesus. Ptolemy then appears to have made a direct appeal to Pompey, doubtless with a reminder of the promises Caesar had made during his own consulship.[17] Pompey was now in a position to bring about action by the use of informal and unofficial pressure. His henchman Gabinius was governor of Syria and in command of a substantial army, and Pompey apparently wrote to him in the spring of the year 55, ordering him to march into Egypt and restore the "flute-player" to his throne. Shortly afterwards, Ptolemy himself appeared at the headquarters of Gabinius and added the inducement of a large bribe, which persuaded Gabinius to turn aside from his other duties and invade Egypt. Two battles were fought against the troops of the established Egyptian government, now headed by Ptolemy's eldest daughter, Berenice. All Egypt soon surrendered, and Ptolemy, after his restoration, proceeded to put Berenice and the richest Egyptians to death in order to obtain their property.

"The scandal of this business," says Heitland, "was something quite out of the common, even in that corrupt age." [18] The bribery was bad enough, but what was worse was the direct and open defiance of the senate's authority in a matter upon which it had acted, and with the use of troops of the Roman state. Obviously no government could continue to function under such conditions, and it was not surprising that the blame for the whole affair devolved on Pompey. It was strongly suspected, and not without reason, that the lion's share of the bribe money had come into his hands and that Gabinius, who was known to be Pompey's henchman, was only acting as agent for his chief. Pompey's part in this business can certainly not be defended, but it seems likely that money may not have been his sole object. With Crassus about to set out for the East, Pompey may well have thought that it would be dangerous to leave so tempting a bait as Egypt in his greedy partner's path, for Crassus had had his eye on the kingdom of the Ptolemies for a decade [19] and might take this opportunity to possess himself of the richest country in the world. Any Roman politician of this era was well aware that whoever was master of Egypt could perhaps become master of the Roman world, and Pompey certainly did not intend that Crassus should be able to avail himself of that opportunity.

Throughout the year of his consulship with Pompey, Crassus seems to have taken little part in public affairs. Instead, he devoted himself to making preparations for his great expedition to the East and did not even wait to leave for his province until the expiration of his term of office. He seems to have set out with the fixed intention of making war against the Parthians, with whom at the time Rome had no quarrel, and thereby provided another flagrant example of the new policy of aggression which Caesar had initiated in Gaul. The expedition did not have even the excuse which Caesar's Gallic policy could allege for itself in the supposed need of preventing German incursions from across the Rhine. It was aggression pure and simple, war for conquest, and personal aggrandizement. It ended two years later, in 53, in the death of Crassus in one of the most humiliating and disgraceful defeats ever suffered by Roman arms.[20]

It has been customary from almost the time of contemporary observers to see in the death of Crassus a principal cause of the ultimate breach between Pompey and Caesar,[21] but it is not easy to accept this traditional view. Throughout the history of the triumvirate, Crassus appears nowhere in the part of a mediator or balancing influence; in fact, his role was remarkably passive and insignificant. Insofar as he filled a role at all, it was by lending certain additional strength to Caesar through his ability to furnish money and through his control of a number of senators who might otherwise have leaned to the conservative side. Yet Caesar, with the gold of Gaul at his disposal, no longer required Crassus for these purposes, so that his disappearance from the political scene can be regarded neither as weakening Caesar nor as strengthening Pompey in any important respect.

II

The commencement of the year 54 found Pompey in a position which, from a constitutional standpoint, was anomalous and certainly unprecedented. He was still commissioner of the grain supply, with power over all ports, warehouses and markets throughout the Roman world for the two years which remained of his five-year term in that office. He was now also governor of the two Spanish provinces for five years and in command of four legions. At the same time, he was legally authorized to remain in Rome and exercise his functions abroad by lieutenants and deputies. Such a combination of powers hardly accorded with preexisting constitutional standards. In particular, his position as an absentee provincial governor was without precedent. Yet it seems incorrect to suggest that at this time Pompey was already "emperor" of Rome. Although he occupied a position and exercised powers which were inconsistent with the old constitution, and which plainly showed that that constitution was breaking down, he did not yet combine proconsular functions abroad with the holding of any of the regular domestic magistracies at Rome, which was to be the essence of the imperial office which Augustus subsequently established.

Meanwhile, despite the accumulation of large nominal powers, Pompey's character and temperament were such that he was in no sense the master of affairs at Rome. His "mysterious and shifty ways were a constant source of weakness; to act with him was always embarrassing, and to be led by him was to feel the want of a leader." [22] He had no settled policy or drive toward any certain objective, not even the enhancement of his own power, and his habit of aimless drifting soon caused matters to get out of hand. The unconstitutional accumulation of powers which he held, so far from enhancing his actual power or introducing vigor into the government, actually produced confusion and contributed to the general breakdown of orderly governmental processes.

The year 54 was mainly taken up by a series of wholesale political prosecutions, instituted by conservative influences against minions of the triumvirs, and by counterprosecutions directed against conservatives in retaliation. The incipient rapprochement between Pompey and the conservatives had not reached the point where Cato and his followers were willing to desist from attacks on the underlings of Pompey, no less than of Caesar, and their chief targets were Caesar's man Vatinius and Pompey's man Gabinius. The careers of men like Vatinius and Gabinius were a characteristic feature of the rise of dictatorial government at Rome. Both owed their promotion to the fact that as tribunes they had been willing to use their offices to further the ambitions of their leaders. Having proved their loyalty, they continued to be employed in carrying on the dirty business which was incidental to the methods used by both Caesar and Pompey in advancing their power. These satellites were doubtless no more dishonest or corrupt as individuals than the greedy members of the nobility who looked to a political career as a source of wealth and fortune, but they were part of a general system of corruption which was regarded with alarm by honest men and with envy by others who were not permitted to share in its spoils. Vatinius was acquitted,[23] but Gabinius had a more difficult time. First prosecuted under Sulla's law of *majestas,* on the ground that he had restored Ptolemy to his throne without senatorial authorization, he was acquitted on this charge by a very narrow margin, but he immediately had to face a new trial for extortion in his province. Pompey made every effort to save him. While the trial was going on, he called a mass meeting and read a letter from Caesar in favor of the accused. He even sent a petition to the jury. Yet, in spite of these unseemly exertions on behalf of Gabinius, the latter was convicted and fined the equivalent of $10,000,000, which he avoided paying by going into exile.[24]

Throughout the year 54 there were signs of a drawing apart of Caesar and Pompey. It is customary to date the beginning of their breach from the death of Caesar's daughter Julia, which apparently occurred in September. As a matter of fact, it seems clear that they were at variance as early as July over the consular election, when Caesar put forward a candidate of his own. Plainly Caesar was again seeking a direct part in Roman politics independent of Pompey, as before the conference of Lucca, and Pompey resented it. Nevertheless, Caesar was not yet ready to break with his old ally, and after Julia's death he offered Pompey a new marriage alliance, this time with Octavia, sister of the future emperor Augustus and herself destined to be the ill-fated wife of the triumvir Mark Antony.[25] Pompey declined the offer and thereby indicated his intention of acting independently of Caesar. For the moment no cause of conflict arose to bring them into collision, but henceforth each pursued his own way.

Pompey entered the year 53 with the obvious intention of controlling the elections and placing in office for the following year consuls of his own choice. He put forward as candidates one Publius Plautius Hypsaeus, an old officer of his in the Mithridatic Wars, and his new father-in-law Quintus Caecilius Metellus Scipio, whose daughter he had just taken as another girl-wife to succeed Julia. It was apparent from the outset that the contest would be hard fought, for there was a third resolute and determined candidate in the field. This was Milo, who for five years had been the chief swordsman and effective mob leader of the conservatives. Since the days of his persecution by Clodius, Pompey had owed much to Milo for helping to hold Clodius at bay. Now, however, Pompey had not only become reconciled to Clodius but had entered into a political alliance with the faction of the nobility to which Clodius belonged. In fact, Clodius was now presenting himself with Pompey's support as a candidate for praetor at the same time that Milo was canvassing for the consulship, and their clashes and collisions in the streets revived the conditions of five years before. Once again, when summer came, the elections were postponed. Pompey seems to have favored this delay, either because he was afraid his candidates could not win, or because he was toying with the idea of a dictatorship for himself to take the place of an interregnum. At all events, months passed and the year ran out without an election, and in the early days of the new year one of those incidents occurred which in an unstable and revolutionary political situation are likely to have far-reaching consequences.

Late one afternoon in January of the year 52, at the little cross-roads village of Bovillae on the Appian Way, Milo and Clodius, each accompanied by a troop of armed guards, happened to meet. A fight ensued, and in the course of it Clodius was wounded and carried into a roadside tavern. Here he was followed by some of Milo's guards, who dispatched him, it was subsequently charged, by Milo's orders. The news spread quickly to Rome, and, when the corpse reached the city, conditions were ripe for a riot. Clodius's associates in the Roman underworld, and in the ward clubs and guilds which he had been so active in organizing, led their followers into the Forum, where the body was exhibited. Through the mob which milled around the bier ran surges of grief and rage, and inflammatory speeches against Milo whipped them into a frenzy of excitement. The climax came when the crowd carried the body into the senate house and set about burning it on a great pyre of benches, tables, and other combustibles that could be heaped together. The conflagration set fire to the building and burned it down, with serious damage to adjacent structures. Then the mob ran off to the house of Milo, where they demonstrated in favor of Pompey's consular candidates and cheered for Pompey, demanding that he be made dictator.[26]

The riot at Clodius's funeral played into Pompey's hands, whether he had anything to do with instigating it or not. Many senators were frightened into thinking that a large-scale uprising was imminent and that an army should be gotten together to repress it. Pompey as proconsul had full military imperium, and the senate now passed a decree authorizing him to recruit troops in Italy. Meanwhile, no action was taken to settle the crisis by holding the elections. Milo offered to withdraw as a candidate if Pompey would request it, but Pompey did not wish either to obligate himself to Milo in any way or to deprive himself of the opportunities which the continuance of the crisis afforded him. He therefore did nothing, the deadlock persisted, and the republic remained without consuls. In the absence of constitutional chief magistrates, Pompey at the head of his army was in effect head of the state.

Under such circumstances it was natural that the movement to make Pompey dictator should revive. As Plutarch afterwards wrote in an effort to reproduce the thinking of this time, the lack of good government of Rome had reached a point where the city was without any government at all. "Some were so bold as to declare openly, that the government was incurable but by a monarchy, and that they ought to take that remedy from the hands of the gentlest physician, meaning Pompey, who, though in words he pretended to decline it, yet in reality made his utmost efforts to be declared dictator." [27] The tension was enhanced by another proposal which seems to have been put forward at this crisis, namely to have Caesar and Pompey jointly elected consuls.[28] It appeared that the latent rivalry between the two might thus come to a head.

In the face of this dangerous situation Cato came forward with a compromise proposal that departed radically from the policy he had hitherto always followed. He seems to have convinced himself that the existing disorder would go from bad to worse unless Pompey's wish for some more distinguished position were gratified, and that if this were not arranged, an opportunity might be afforded Caesar to advance his ambitions. As between Pompey and Caesar, Cato had long ago reached the conclusion that, much as he disapproved of Pompey, Caesar was more to be feared, and that the time had come to begin to think of what to do about Caesar when the term of his Gallic command expired. From the standpoint of the constitutionalists generally, nothing was more alarming than the idea of a second consulship for Caesar, either before or after the expiration of his Gallic command. Several years earlier, Cato had recognized that if Caesar were to be headed off the conservatives had no choice but to build up Pompey against him. Up to this time, however, Pompey's selfish and unconstitutional maneuvers had been so repugnant to Cato that he had refused to cooperate on Pompey's terms, and Pompey would tolerate no other kind of cooperation. Now, however, the time had come to reconsider the situation. It was clear that Pompey was a different kind of man from Caesar and that power in Pompey's hands was a different thing from power in Caesar's. Experience had shown that Caesar wanted the use of power, Pompey only its trappings and appearance. Caesar, if vested with power, would stop at nothing; hitherto, whenever Pompey had been vested with political power, he had not abused it. Although it had taken Cato a long while to perceive this distinction, which Cicero had seen from the outset, he was at last willing to recognize it and act accordingly.

The compromise which Cato and his conservative followers proposed was something short of making Pompey a dictator, but the proposal was as unprecedented as it was unconstitutional. Bibulus proposed in the senate, and Cato seconded, a resolution that at a meeting of the *comitia centuriata* the only candidate presented should be Pompey, and that if elected he should be sole consul, but with power after a lapse of two months to provide himself with a colleague by appointment. The resolution was carried, the meeting of the *comitia* was held, and Pompey was elected.[29] Cato consoled himself that "it was necessary to make use of a lesser illegality as a remedy against the greatest of all," [30] and that it was better to set up a "more legal sort of monarchy" to terminate the disorder in the state than to have recourse to a dictatorship.[31] Nothing better shows the force of a trend in thinking, the power of an idea that something has become inevitable, than the way in which even Cato was thus led to the belief that something approaching monarchy was indispensable.

The position which Pompey had thus finally attained in the Roman state does at last suggest that comparison with the subsequent status of the emperors which historians have been so anxious to find evidenced at earlier stages of his career. Now he was at one and the same time a proconsul in the provinces, commander-in-chief in Italy, and holder of a regular magistracy at Rome. No Roman had hitherto combined so many constitutionally inconsistent offices or held so much power under the supposed forms of law in the absence of a revolutionary dictatorship; yet Pompey, as usual, made no far-reaching or revolutionary use of his powers, although he exercised them in ways that were highly arbitrary and irritatingly directed toward personal ends. He did not attempt to make his position permanent, and, after appointing his father-in-law Metellus Scipio as his colleague for the balance of his term, he proceeded to hold the consular elections for the following year at their usual date. Cato was a candidate but was defeated, it is said, because he declined either to make the usual appeals to the voters or to resort to the customary flattery, much less to bribery.[32] The two successful candidates were sound conservatives, Servius Sulpicius Rufus, the great jurisconsult, and Marcus Marcellus, an outspoken opponent of Caesar.

A large part of the year 52 was again taken up with political prosecutions. Pompey's first concern as consul was to gratify the partisans of Clodius by prosecuting Milo. Immediately on entering office he proposed a bill that substantially altered the procedure in cases involving public violence by limiting the length of trials, forbidding the testimony of character witnesses for the accused, and in some way reserving to himself a part in the selection of the jurors.[33] Apparently another bill was specifically directed to the case of Milo. When the bills came before the assembly, they were resisted by some of the tribunes, but when Pompey announced that if necesary he would have them carried by force, all opposition melted away.[34] The interval before Milo's trial was filled with a succession of mass meetings at which Milo was assailed in embittered speeches by the retainers of Pompey and the partisans of Clodius. When the trial came on at the beginning of April, Pompey filled the Forum and its approaches with soldiers and watched the proceedings himself from the front of the Treasury, surrounded by an armed guard. Around the court the mob was packed in threatening masses and was harangued during the progress of the trial by orators who demanded that the defendant should not be allowed to escape. When Cicero, representing Milo, had to speak for his client under these conditions, the great orator lost his composure and delivered a disconnected and ineffective speech.[35] The result was a foregone conclusion. Milo was convicted and went into exile at Marseilles.

When the situation was reversed and the object of prosecution was Pompey's own father-in-law, Metellus Scipio, who was charged with bribery, Pompey showed equal disregard of law, this time in behalf of the accused. He summoned the jury panel to his house and expressed his desire for an acquittal as a personal favor to himself, with the result that the prosecutor abandoned the case. In another instance, he was not so successful. Cicero brought a prosecution for public violence against a tribune, Lucius Munatius Plancus, who had acted as the principal mob leader of the Clodian faction throughout the proceedings from the riot at Clodius's bier down to the trial of Milo. Again Pompey interfered by sending the jury a eulogy of Plancus and a personal request for his acquittal, but the jurors showed their independence and found Plancus guilty. In spite of this conviction and the convictions of other leading Clodians, there is ample basis for the discouraged comment of Cicero in a letter to one of the victims then in exile:

The state of our legislation, law courts and the times . . . is such that that man would seem to have taken the best course who has left this republic with the lightest possible penalty.[36]

It is of interest to speculate on the strategy and policy that dictated Pompey's line of action at this time. Although his course was seldom clear or decisive, it is possible to see a kind of strategic purpose in what he was doing. Apparently he was attempting to maneuver himself between Caesar and the senate into an independent middle position in which he would be free to throw his weight to one side or the other as his interests demanded. The events of the past few years had shown that in the final analysis the conservatives feared Caesar more than they feared Pompey. With this fear to rely on, Pompey doubtless reasoned that he could go far in opposing them without losing their support, and that there was therefore no need to hamper his freedom of action by tying himself to them in a close alliance. He could thus afford to continue to cooperate with Caesar, whenever it seemed advantageous, but on more independent terms than before. However, he had learned from Caesar that to maintain such an independent position it was necessary to have the support of the mob of Rome. This was undoubtedly why Pompey thought Clodius and his organization so important to him; he could not use Milo because Milo was independent and obstinate and, besides, was irretrievably tied to the conservatives. The alliance with Clodius also carried with it the support of a substantial faction in the senate through which the opposition of that body could in some degree be neutralized. Now that Clodius was dead, it was essential to this strategy that Pompey continue in alliance with the organization which the great demagogue had built up, and this required that he should retain the loyalty of that organization by destroying the influence of Milo and his supporters. If Pompey could successfully carry out this policy, he had reasonable assurance that he might be able to maintain his position against possible attack from Caesar on the one hand or from the senate on the other. If this was his reasoning, it failed to take account of two weaknesses in his position. The first of these was that in a contest with Caesar he might not be able to rely on the loyalty of the Clodian mob leaders, who were more likely to follow Caesar than himself. His second weakness was that he was no match for Caesar in the game of finesse and intrigue. Hence, in the end, his maneuvers of this year, while disgusting many of his would-be supporters by presenting him in the unusual and unfavorable aspect of a tyrant, ultimately failed of their intended results.

Pompey's ineptitude at pursuing a devious and double-faced policy is illustrated by his course with respect to Caesar during this year. Clearly when the conservatives capitulated to Pompey and made him sole consul, he was not yet ready for anything like a definite break with Caesar. If, therefore, the conservatives' purpose in going over to Pompey was to check Caesar, it seemed at first that they had achieved nothing for their pains. As already mentioned, the point which was in everyone's mind, and especially in the minds of the conservatives and of Caesar, was the question of a second consulship for the latter. Caesar not only desired a second consulship, but he desired it to commence before, or at least simultaneously with, the termination of his Gallic command. This was because, as pointed out, he was almost abnormally fearful of prosecution for his illegal acts during his consulship and during his governorship of Gaul. "He knew that his enemies lay in wait for him, and hoped to ruin him by the votes of a jury, the moment he became a private citizen. He was resolved to give them no chance of doing so: there must be no such interval as that on which they reckoned." [37] Accordingly, when the term of his governorship expired, he must be able to step into a second consulship at once. This required that he be elected while still proconsul of Gaul. Since, technically, no proconsul could enter Rome while still vested with military imperium unless exempted by a special law such as had been passed in favor of Pompey, Caesar must either obtain such a law for himself or have the benefit of a lesser exemption which would enable him to be a candidate *in absentia*. Caesar preferred the latter alternative, and, in order to ensure his position well in advance, he requested both Pompey and Cicero to help him obtain the necessary legislation in the spring of 52. Apparently at that time Pompey was not willing to offend Caesar by objecting, and a law sponsored and supported by the tribunes with Pompey's sanction granted the authority that Caesar desired.[38]

There was, however, a further weakness in Caesar's position. In order that he might step at once from his Gallic governorship into the consulate, it was necessary that his term as governor should be prolonged as far as possible and not expire until his consular term began. As already stated,[39] it is unfortunate that the precise expiration date set for Caesar's proconsulship under the Pompeian-Licinian law is not known, but it seems almost certain that it was either near the end of the year 50, or at the latest on March 1st, 49.[40] Caesar had set his mind on the consulate for the year 48, and he would therefore be vulnerable between the expiration of his governorship and December 31st, 49, unless allowed to retain his provincial command during that interval. No question about the extension seems originally to have entered his mind, since it was the long-established practice that a proconsul who found himself in office during part of a year might round out the year if he so desired. It was therefore apparently Caesar's plan to continue to govern Gaul throughout the year 49, have himself elected consul during the summer, and return to Rome just in time to commence his term on January 1st, 48. This plan was put in serious jeopardy, however, by certain legislation which Pompey sponsored and carried through to enactment in the latter part of the year 52.

Sincere advocates of reform had been concerned for some time by the obvious fact that the civil magistracies at Rome were the object of corrupt ambition, chiefly because of the lucrative provincial governorships by which they were followed. This aftermath, it was thought, was what caused the fierce contests for the consulships and the widespread resort to bribery that accompanied them. Accordingly, a recommendation had been adopted by the senate in the preceding year that, in the future, consuls and praetors should not succeed to provincial governorships immediately on going out of office but must wait for an interval of five years.[41] The argument in favor of the proposal was that if greedy politicians found that they would have to wait for so long an interval before being able to satisfy their appetites, they would no longer be willing to risk such large sums on a speculation that was henceforth to be long deferred and uncertain. Pompey now took up this proposal and embodied it in a bill which was enacted into law. In order to give effect to the scheme, certain time-honored practices had to be abandoned. Thus, if a consul were not to receive a province until five years after the expiration of his term, it was no longer appropriate to designate consular provinces annually in advance of the consular elections, as required by the Sempronian law, and that law was therefore repealed.

The effective administration of the new plan required that the assignments of provincial governorships should be largely a matter of senatorial discretion. The law seems also to have contained a provision that expressly authorized the senate to terminate a provincial governor's appointment and bring him home at any time. The latter provision was obviously disadvantageous to Caesar, who no longer had the assurance he had before that he could remain in his province until he was ready to begin his new consular term at Rome, for that assurance depended on his being able to retain his provincial governorship throughout the entire year 49. Now, under Pompey's law, the senate could order him home at any time after the expiration of his command and thus expose him to prosecution by his enemies.

Whether Pompey's "law of the five-year interval" was enacted with Caesar's situation primarily in mind is doubtful, but it seems significant that a reform which had never previously enlisted Pompey's interest should suddenly do so now when it presented an opportunity to embarrass Caesar. Moreover, there is little doubt that, as the year advanced, Pompey became progressively less unwilling to play the conservatives' game of undermining Caesar. Feeling that he occupied a new position of strength through his alliance with the conservatives on the one side and with the Clodian mobs on the other, he seems to have been not averse that Caesar should see that he could make trouble for him, and ought therefore to be deferred to. In his vanity he appears to have felt that the unprecedented position in the state which he now held required him to show his superiority to Caesar and make the latter yield obeisance to him. He wanted to make Caesar feel uneasy and in need of help. Hence the provision of his new law which destroyed Caesar's assurance on the matter of the termination of his proconsulate; and hence a further provision in that law which threatened Caesar on an even more vital point.

As already explained, early in the year 52 a tribunician law had been enacted permitting Caesar to be a candidate for the consulship *in absentia*. Now, when the text of the new law of the five-year interval was published, it was found to contain a clause reinstating the old rule against standing for the consulship without being present at Rome in person. When this provision was discovered, the complaints of Caesar's friends were loud and indignant. Pompey so far gave way as to show favor to Caesar by tampering with the text of the law, and he is said to have inserted in the official copy in his own hand a proviso reserving the rights of anyone to whom a special exemption had been or should be voted by name. With this Caesar had to be satisfied, but his legal position, as a result of Pompey's maneuvers, was left in confusion and uncertainty. Doubtless Pompey thought that he could thereby keep Caesar more completely in dependence on himself, but in fact his course served to warn Caesar that he could not be trusted and so to place Caesar on his guard. Pompey had thus aroused Caesar's suspicions without gaining any real advantage for himself.

It is possible that Pompey might not have been willing to go as far as he did in showing his hand against Caesar if the latter had not stood at just this time at the most difficult and perilous point of his entire military career. During the summer of the year 52 he was confronted with a vast rebellion of united Gaul against Roman rule, and so great were the odds he had to face that for several months it looked as if he would be engulfed by the uprising. The story of this rebellion and of the events leading up to it is a necessary prelude to an understanding of Caesar's position during the next phase of the political struggle at Rome.

III

Although Caesar's spectacular success in reducing Gaul in two summer campaigns had already been achieved and had brought him unprecedented honors and acclaim before the conference of Lucca, it was in the years following that conference, while he was consolidating and confirming his conquests, that he displayed some of his most extraordinary abilities as a general and a soldier: his rapidity of decision and action, his ingenuity and fertility of invention, his ability to produce moral and psychological effects by spectacular feats, his boldness and resolution in overcoming unexpected difficulties.

Certain of the Gallic tribes which had participated in the wholesale capitulations of the year 57, particularly the tribes of the far west, were neither very earnest nor sincere in their submission and soon began to repent of it. This was especially true of the Veneti, the tribes inhabiting the peninsula of Britanny, who were seafaring folk with large fleets of clumsy sailing vessels used for carrying on a regular trade with the island of Britain. It is suggested by Strabo [42] that they were afraid the Romans would interfere with this trade, but in any event they were preparing for an uprising during the early part of 56, while Caesar was absent in Lombardy and attending the conference of Lucca. Immediately after that conference he hurried back to Gaul and established his headquarters near Nantes. To hold the other tribes in check and prevent them from overwhelming him in the event of defeat by the Veneti, he distributed forces through the interior and sent one of his ablest lieutenants, young Publius Licinius Crassus, who afterwards perished with his father at Carrhae, to hold Aquitaine. Caesar then undertook to subdue the Veneti through a series of naval engagements successfully conducted by another of his young generals, Decimus Brutus. The other tribes along the Channel coast were then restored to obedience, while Crassus in a brilliant campaign completed the conquest of Aquitaine.[43]

While Caesar was in his Cisalpine province in the winter of 56–55, news reached him that a vast new influx of Germans had crossed the lower Rhine in what is now Holland and had settled in territory west of the river. These were two hordes known as Usipites and Tenctheri, who were fleeing before the advance of more powerful tribes in the interior of Germany. Caesar could not with safety to his prestige among the Gallic tribes permit these invaders to settle in Gaul. "At all costs they must be driven out. An obscure but effective campaign followed. . . . Caesar found himself in great danger. . . . From his own narrative we may gather that he stooped to gain an advantage by treacherous dealing. He seized the German leaders who had come to deal with him and fell upon their main body unawares. They were either cut down or driven into the river. So he saved his army." [44] This was the affair which led Cato to make the bitter speech in the senate, referred to above, in which he demanded that Caesar should be surrendered to the Germans for his violation of Rome's traditions of honor and good faith.[45]

After the defeat of the Usipites and Tenctheri, and before the end of the summer, Caesar accomplished two dramatic feats which not only greatly increased his prestige in Gaul but made him the most talked-of man in the Roman world. He decided to produce a moral effect on the Germans by leading a Roman army across the Rhine. Believing that to transport his men in boats was not sufficiently spectacular, he sought to make a display of Roman power by bridging the river. For this purpose he set his army to work building the trestlework bridge which he describes with such technical accuracy in the passage of the fourth book of his *Commentaries* [46] and which has been a nightmare for schoolboys ever since. The work was completed in ten days, and for the first time a Roman army stood on the soil of Germany.[47] The expedition was merely in the nature of a demonstration, and the Romans soon returned across the river, after breaking the bridge down behind them.

A still more dramatic expedition occupied the remainder of the season. Caesar ordered his fleet to meet him near Calais and proceeded to ferry a small force across the straits to the island of Britain. Here again Roman soldiers were treading on soil where Romans had never ventured before. Because of the lateness of the season and the relative smallness of his force, this expedition likewise could only serve the purpose of a demonstration, and after a few minor skirmishes with the natives Caesar brought his force back to Gaul.[48] However, the boldness of the attempt, and the quality of imagination it displayed, fired the enthusiasm of the Roman public and greatly increased Caesar's popularity.

In the next summer (54 B.C.) he played upon the same theme of popularity and attracted renewed attention at Rome by a second expedition to Britain, this time on a much larger scale. For this purpose, an armada of six hundred ships, built on a new model and completely equipped, was constructed during the winter. With this fleet he ferried across to Britain an army of five legions, which penetrated the island some distance to the north of the Thames. There was no real conquest, but the tribes made nominal submission, and for form's sake a yearly tribute was imposed and a Roman protectorate declared. The real conquest of Britain and its incorporation into the Roman Empire did not occur for another century.

When Caesar returned from his second British expedition in the fall of 54, he established his headquarters at Amiens and did not immediately leave for Cisalpine Gaul as had been his custom. Moreover, he distributed his legions throughout central and northern Gaul at stations not more than a hundred miles apart. These precautions indicate that he was aware of signs of uneasiness and threatened revolts. Discontent had already flared up among the Treveri in the northeast but had been temporarily checked by support given to the pro-Roman party within the tribe. Nevertheless, discontent was widespread and general. "Since the coming of Caesar the position of the Gaulish chiefs was not what it had been. A strong hand was over them, and they could no longer plot and squabble among themselves freely and go to ruin in their own way." [49] Furthermore, they saw the profits of war and intrigue being drained off by the Romans instead of remaining in their own coffers. Caesar and his entourage were taking the lion's share and not admitting the old masters of the country to participate in the booty to the extent that they thought themselves entitled. The discontent was so obvious that Caesar had taken many of the chiefs with him to Britain as hostages.

Caesar did not go south of the Alps at all during the winter of 54-53, and the event proved that he was wise in not doing so. A dangerous uprising soon occurred among the Eburones, who were the northern neighbors of the Treveri, living along the upper Meuse. This portion of the frontier was under the command of Cicero's brother Quintus, whom Caesar had appointed as one of his lieutenants to please the orator and maintain friendly relations with him. Cicero's camp near Namur was surprised by an attack in force but was held with a desperate resistance and bravery which holds a high place in the annals of heroism. At last a message got through to Caesar, who arrived with a relieving force just in time to save the garrison, of whom not one man in ten was unwounded.[50] In consequence, a great general rebellion of the tribes was averted.

Caesar spent the entire campaigning season of the year 53 in checking and repressing incipient outbreaks in northern and northeastern Gaul. He took time, however, during the summer to make a display of confidence and strength by leading a second expedition into Germany, and for this purpose he again bridged the Rhine. From this demonstration he returned to deal with disaffection among the tribes along the upper Seine, and, after distributing his army in winter quarters near Trier, Langres and Sens,[51] he finally set out for Cisalpine Gaul.

The year 52 was the most critical of Caesar's career. From a military standpoint, it witnessed a crisis that was nothing less than a test of survival, while politically it brought him to the lowest point of the balance in his rivalry with Pompey. It was in January of this year that the latter had been made sole consul, holding a greater combination of powers than had ever before been concentrated in the hands of a single Roman, short of a revolutionary dictatorship.

As already pointed out, Pompey had been careful not to come to any real breach with Caesar; but the vast enhancement of Pompey's power and position, following so quickly on the death of Julia, boded ill for the continuance of their harmonious relationship. Pompey's position was now so independent and powerful that Caesar had no choice but to conciliate Pompey in every way. Meanwhile, trouble of a most serious nature was brewing for Caesar in Gaul; and, when the storm broke, and he seemed likely to succumb to it, Pompey's attitude, as might have been expected, underwent a change.

The uprisings in the winter of 54–53 and in the summer of 53 were confined to the northern and northeastern parts of Gaul. In the early spring of 52, however, there broke out a far vaster and more deeply prepared revolt of the tribes of central Gaul—those of the Loire country, Berri and Auvergne. The revolt was led by an extraordinarily able and energetic young chief of the Arverni named Vercingetorix, and under his leadership it rapidly grew to proportions which not only taxed all Caesar's abilities and resources to the utmost but, under the pressure of necessity, drew from him a supreme exhibition of military skill. In the short summer season of this one year Caesar exceeded all his previous exploits as a general. The campaign opened with a series of brilliant successes, beginning with a remarkable stratagem whereby he defeated the efforts of Vercingetorix to prevent him from joining his legions in the north, and ending with the burning of Orléans and the capture of Bourges, where he massacred the entire population. At this point, the fortunes of the war took a decisive turn.

Vercingetorix blockaded himself in the hill town of Gergovia (near Clermont-Ferrand), the capital of Auvergne, and Caesar was unable either to cut it off or to take it by storm. Vercingetorix knew better than to come out and give battle, and while Caesar was thus immobilized the revolt was spreading in his rear, notably among the hitherto loyal Aedui, who threatened to cut Caesar off from that part of his army which was holding the lines of the Loire and the Seine. For almost the only time in his life he confessed failure. He drew off his troops and left Vercingetorix in possession. Not only was his withdrawal a great blow to his prestige, but it increased immensely the confidence of the Gauls and seemed to change all the probabilities of the outcome of the war.

Caesar's one concern seems to have been to extricate himself and make good his retreat. Exchanging his usual policy of boldness for one of extreme caution, he prepared his retreat with great care. Among the steps that he took was to recruit an auxiliary force of German horsemen from beyond the Rhine, thereby inaugurating a policy which five centuries later was to number among the causes of the downfall of the Roman Empire. With these and other preparations completed, Caesar apparently moved off toward the territory of the Sequani.[52] Vercingetorix seems to have felt that he had no choice but to pursue, lest the enthusiasm of the Gallic insurgents should cool without the stimulant of action and victory. However, the battle that ensued was disastrous to his cause. The engagement was short but decisive, and the onslaught of the German horsemen, supported by the solid strength of the legions, succeeded in scattering the Gallic army.

Vercingetorix therefore decided to repeat the strategy which had proved so successful at Gergovia and reassembled his troops in the hill town of Alesia. Excavations, commenced and largely conducted under the auspices of the Emperor Napoleon III, have established beyond doubt that Alesia was located on the top of Mont Auxois, within a few miles of the great mediaeval monastery of Flavigny, and about twenty-five miles northwest of Dijon.[53] Caesar's strategic eye perceived that Alesia was not Gergovia and that the place could be effectively blockaded. He therefore proceeded to surround the walls of the town with a great earthwork in order to starve out the horde of Gauls entrapped on the summit. Faced with this prospect, Vercingetorix sent out calls for help to all the allied tribes, and Caesar soon learned that a vast outpouring of Gallic tribesmen was on the way to convert his position from besieger to besieged. He accordingly began to construct another great earthwork ring, with trenches, ramparts, redoubts and towers around the outside of his own position so that his army would be enclosed in two concentric rings of fortifications surrounding the hill. The tribesmen were slow in arriving, and there was ample time to construct these extraordinary works. When at last the Gauls arrived, they numbered almost two hundred and fifty thousand, more than ten times the number of troops enclosed within Caesar's lines, so that his situation was perilous and threatened to become desperate. Fortunately, the tribesmen were a mere mob rather than an army, undisciplined and impatient and without either the facilities or the organization to conduct an effective siege. Their one thought was to fight, and fight immediately, and for three days his lines on both sides, within and without, were assailed by wild and furious assaults, the last of which was nearly successful. Then, gradually, the Gallic host began to disintegrate, and in a few days more had dispersed to their homes, leaving Vercingetorix and his men entrapped on the hill. He had no recourse but to surrender. The revolt of Gaul was over, and the remaining task was merely to stamp out its embers and pacify the country.

Caesar's victory at Alesia was regarded in his own time as stupendous. Even in the next generation it was said that "near Alesia such feats were accomplished as it was scarcely possible for a mortal to attempt, or for almost any except a god to perform." [54] This spectacular success not only restored Caesar's damaged prestige but raised it to a height that it had never reached before. Only a few months earlier, after his failure at Gergovia, it had seemed for a time as if his career might be ruined. Now the situation was entirely altered, and Caesar was in a stronger position than ever. The question in Caesar's mind and in the minds of all the ambitious politicians at Rome was whether Pompey would again reverse himself or would move farther toward a definite break with his rival.

IV

When Pompey's extraordinary consulship ended at the close of the year 52, he again subsided into a position of relative inactivity, taking care only to procure an extension of his proconsular command in Spain for an additional five years. The question of Caesar he left to the senatorial conservatives, who were becoming increasingly agitated over the matter under the leadership of Marcus Claudius Marcellus, one of the two consuls for the year 51. On this group the enhancement of Caesar's prestige since his victory at Alesia had not had the same effect as on the public generally. Far from causing them to conciliate him, it stiffened their resolution to prevent him from employing his prestige to acquire greater power in the future.

The issue between Caesar and the conservatives seems to have been opened up by Caesar himself in his anxiety to protect his position. He had hardly disposed of the Gallic rebellion before he made an appeal to the senate early in the spring of 51 to grant him express permission to retain his province until the close of the year 49, thereby neutralizing the adverse effect of the Pompeian legislation of the year 52.[55] At the same time, he seems also to have asserted that he would stand upon the tribunician legislation of the same year, which authorized his candidacy in absentia, and would insist that the effect of that authorization was not impaired by Pompey's subsequent law.[56] This communication squarely presented the issues that were to be the subject of unceasing argument and negotiation for the next two years. What Caesar wanted above all was to be consul again, and, in addition, to become consul without having to leave his province and run the risk of prosecution at Rome. What the conservatives wanted was, first and foremost, that Caesar should not again be consul. To this end they were anxious to get him out of his province as soon as possible, and they saw in Pompey's law of 52 too favorable an opportunity to bring about that result to surrender it at Caesar's mere asking.

In April of 51, Marcellus called a meeting of the senate expressly to discuss the subject of Caesar's position. A good deal of his speech seems to have been devoted to a general attack on Caesar's alleged illegal conduct in his province, especially in the matter of bestowing grants of Roman citizenship on provincials and colonists, with a view to imposing a censure. However, the proposal was vetoed by a tribune, and so came to nothing. Marcellus then proceeded to emphasize the importance of making as early a provision as possible for a successor to Caesar as proconsul. No immediate action was recommended, and the matter was allowed to stand over for further debate, which occurred late in July.[57]

Until this time Pompey seems successfully to have avoided taking a position vis-à-vis Caesar. As usual, his attitude was perplexed and obscure. It is reasonable to suppose that he expected some approach from Caesar, some appeal for help, but, contrary to that expectation, none came. Caesar made no effort to come to terms with him, doubtless because he was impatient with Pompey's shiftiness and thought himself now strong enough to do without him. When no request came to mediate Caesar's controversy with the conservatives, Pompey was piqued and his sensitiveness wounded. Taking stock of the situation at last, he apparently realized, doubtless with a shock, how far Caesar had outdistanced him, and all of Pompey's resentment was awakened. From now on he consistently aligned himself with Caesar's opponents.

In September, there was another debate in the senate relating to Caesar. Marcellus proposed that a definite date should be fixed for a meeting of the senate to consider and settle the question of Caesar's successor, and he recommended March 1st of the following year. Probably that date was selected because, as will be remembered, the Pompeian-Licinian Law of 55 B.C., under which Caesar held his province, contained a clause naming March 1st, 50, as the earliest date on which his successor could be discussed. However, it now appeared that that date would still be too early for Caesar's convenience. Under the subsequent legislation of Pompey, Caesar would be succeeded by whomever the senate might appoint, and the date of his supersession would therefore be the actual date on which his term expired. To this Caesar interposed a strong objection, apparently asserting that he was entitled to the benefit of the law as it stood at the date of his original appointment, and not as it had been subsequently altered. Accordingly, his supporters in the senate opposed taking up consideration of his successor before March 1st.

It was during this debate in September of 51 that Pompey was at last brought to indicate, if not actually to declare, his position. He said that under the law he could not rightfully give his opinion concerning Caesar's provinces before the first of March, but that after that date he would have no hesitation. He was then asked what his position would be if the senate's decision should be vetoed by a tribune. He replied that it would make no difference whether Caesar directly refused to obey the senate's decree or procured a tribune to prevent a decree from being passed; in either case his contumacy would be the same. Then, suppose, Pompey was asked, that Caesar should wish both to be consul and at the same time keep his army? This supposition Pompey refused to entertain, saying that it might as well be supposed that "my son would wish to apply a cudgel to my back." [58] Some thought that by these words Pompey was expressing private knowledge of Caesar's pacific intentions, but others concluded more correctly that he was intimating to Caesar that he would oppose him.[59] Gradually Pompey's attitude became more plainly defined, and shortly afterwards it was reported that he opposed permitting Caesar to become consul-designate before he had given up his army and his province.[60] At the same time it was said that "Caesar . . . is persuaded that he cannot be safe if he quits his army." [61]

Meanwhile, the consular elections for the year 50 had been held, and Caesar's candidate was defeated. On one of the two victors at the polls, however, he could feel that he had claims of a sort. This was Gaius Claudius Marcellus, then the husband of Caesar's great-niece Octavia, whom he had offered in marriage to Pompey not long before and who was afterwards to be the unhappy mate of Mark Antony. Gaius Marcellus, however, proved to be much more under the influence of his cousin Marcus, his predecessor as consul, than of Caesar, and in fact turned out to be one of the stiffest anti-Caesarians of his day. The other consul, Lucius Aemilius Paullus, was also elected as a conservative, but Caesar thought it worthwhile to test whether he was made of equally stern stuff and discovered that he was not. An enormous sum of money, part of the gold of Gaul, accordingly changed hands to enable the new consul to build a monument to himself, the Basilica Aemiliana, and for other purposes besides.

Caesar seems at this time to have engaged upon a new and wholesale campaign to purchase goodwill. He paid off the debts of many senators and other men of high places and "gratified the people with buildings, with funeral games, and other displays in honor of his daughter Julia; [and] gained the favour of . . . the more important [Italian] municipalities by lavish expenditures of his Gallic gold." [62] The funeral games of Julia were especially magnificent, and, by honoring the dead wife of Pompey, they carried a covert suggestion of reproach for the defection and ingratitude of Caesar's former son-in-law. In the end, the wisest of Caesar's investments in goodwill, from his standpoint, was his acquisition of the support of a young aristocrat Gaius Scribonius Curio, who had just been chosen one of the new tribunes. A dozen years before, Curio had figured as a leader of the set of fashionable young rakes who had gathered around Catiline. In the interval, he had returned to the conservatives and had for a time been one of Cicero's circle of young admirers. However, his reckless and profligate life had burdened him with heavy debts, and he now attached himself to Caesar at the price of having these paid off. Seemingly, it was part of the bargain that he should give an appearance of continuing to act with the conservatives, but that he should be ready to come over to Caesar at the critical moment. As a young man of great resourcefulness, boldness and high oratorical abilities, Curio played a leading part in the maneuvers which ultimately brought on the civil war in such a way as to seem to give Caesar just cause for conflict.

Caesar's constant emphasis on appearances, and his habitual attention to producing on the public the impression that he desired, is at no point in his career better illustrated than in the year 50. His sense of the importance of public psychology made him more than ever anxious to seem to have right on his side. That a man of his astuteness should have put so much emphasis on this point seems to indicate that public opinion counted for more at this time than might otherwise be supposed. With government operating as habitually under the influence of force and bribery as it did at Rome during the 50's, it is hard to understand what room there was for public opinion, as it is understood today, or what part it could have played. Certainly it did not directly determine the outcome of elections or the content of legislative enactments. Probably it played a passive rather than an active part in the overall balance of political forces as something to be assuaged and mollified into friendly acquiescent assent, rather than as a power and instrument of guidance and determination. In this sense, if public opinion were favorable to a leading politician, he would be left free to manipulate the government in his own way without the opposition and resistance that might otherwise have to be faced. The general public, and more particularly people of social and financial standing, would be led to look on his doings with acquiescence, even though he undertook to rule without direct regard for their wishes in particular matters. This is the kind of public opinion which is always needed by a politician of Caesar's stamp and which supplies the essential background and atmosphere of Caesarism.

Among the results of Caesar's efforts to mold public sentiment was what proved to be a masterpiece of historical writing—his account of his campaigns in Gaul, which he sent to Rome sometime during the year 51 to be published under the title of *Commentaries on the Gallic War*. The object of the treatise, as suggested earlier, was to justify his conduct and glorify his accomplishments.[63] His manner of presentation for this purpose sheds important light on his psychological insight, for it is far removed from comparable efforts of politicians of our own day. Caesar avoids the slightest appearance of self-laudation; he writes in a dry, hard style, lacking in adjectives, and tells a factual story without seeming to embellish it. The result is an appearance of utter honesty and simplicity; and, told in such a style, his remarkable feats seem more remarkable still. Reading this plain, straightforward story, large numbers of Romans must have come to the conclusion that Caesar had done nothing in Gaul that he was not compelled by circumstances to do, that he had behaved honorably and in the best interests of the Roman people, and that the charges brought against him for improper conduct and for waging aggressive war to gratify his ambitions were baseless calumnies. At the same time, the matter-of-fact tale of his daring deeds, decisive stratagems and hair-breadth captures of victory from the jaws of defeat was bound to attract and hold the spellbound interest of the young and adventurous, and to win their enthusiastic admiration for the hero of the tale. Caesar was a past master at depicting and changing the public image that he wished his contemporaries to see, and the *Commentaries* succeeded entirely in wiping out the earlier image of Caesar as a nonchalant and luxurious man of fashion and in replacing it with a portrait of a tireless, efficient and victorious representative of the best traditions of Rome. No one could say that the factual basis on which this impression was founded was in any respect wanting in truthfulness. Through publication of his *Commentaries* at just this time, Caesar completed the picture of himself as Rome's outstanding man of power and promise, and thereby helped not only to assure his position as hero of the hour but at the same time to quell and deaden the spirit of opposition.

Caesar's investment in the consul Paullus soon began to yield him a satisfactory return. In accordance with the senate's resolution of the previous September, the debate on the termination of Caesar's proconsulship was resumed on March 1st, 50. No conclusion, however, was reached, for Paullus kept adjourning and postponing the discussion before action could be taken. In the course of these delays a new proposal emerged, in appearance conciliatory to Caesar, that he should retire not on March 1st, 49, or on any earlier date, but on the first of July of that year, and that he should come to Rome at once to stand for the consulship. Such a proposal, of course, could not be satisfactory to Caesar, since it did not meet his primary difficulty, for it would still leave an interval of six months between the date when he would cease to be proconsul and the commencement of his consulship if he were elected. His supporter Curio accordingly vetoed the proposal, and matters remained at a standstill. Other proposals were apparently suggested and discussed, but no action on them was taken. Meanwhile, the months were passing by. In the summer, the consular elections were held and resulted in the choice of two men who were strong opponents of Caesar— Gaius Claudius Marcellus (a cousin of the consul in 50) and Lucius Cornelius Lentulus Crus.

The picture presented by the events of the year 50 is one of ceaseless jockeying for position, each side seeking to justify itself from a constitutional point of view and to put the other in the wrong. In this contest and on this field of rivalry, Caesar had a distinct advantage. His demands had every appearance of moderation and involved no serious violation of precedent. His desire to be a candidate *in absentia* had been sanctioned by the tribunician law of the year 52, passed expressly for that purpose. Even Pompey's law of the five-year interval did not affirmatively require the senate to terminate his proconsulship at any particular date, for it left to the senate full discretionary power to prolong his command in the same way that in the past the commands of other proconsuls had been prolonged. Such moderation on Caesar's part stood in marked contrast with the strikingly unconstitutional position of Pompey, built up for him by the same group which was now resisting Caesar. Pompey had been both a proconsul and consul at the same time, whereas all that Caesar now asked was to step from one office into the other. Pompey had been twice elected consul (55 and 52) within a period of four years, whereas Caesar was observing the regularly established ten years' interval. Pompey as proconsul had maintained and commanded an army in Italy, whereas Caesar was not asking for any such power. The conservatives, by vesting Pompey with thoroughly unconstitutional and unrepublican powers, had in effect disabled themselves from making convincing or even plausible arguments against the concessions which Caesar was now seeking. To many Romans of that time, it seemed perverse and illogical for a party which had been willing to overlook constitutional scruples on such a wholesale scale in favor of Pompey to assume an attitude of high-minded insistence on strict constitutional regularity insofar as Caesar was concerned. Such an attitude could be made to seem very like personal persecution of Rome's greatest hero on the part of the conservatives who were not in a position openly to allege the real ground of their opposition to Caesar.

The ground of opposition was, of course, the fear of Caesar's holding consular office at all, for it was believed that if he were allowed to hold the consulship for a second time he would use it to complete the destruction of the processes of traditional government which he had begun ten years before. The experience of his first consulship, viewed in retrospect and supplemented by the subsequent immense increase in his prestige and power as a result of his Gallic victories, confirmed the conservatives in their fear. During his first consulship Caesar had shown that he knew how to rule without the assistance of the senate and that he could force the popular assemblies to act at his bidding. It was reasoned that if he were again elected consul, Rome would be given up to the one-man rule of one who had shown his contempt for legal procedures and who had relied habitually on force and violence. Pompey, talking with

Cicero, expressed the belief that Caesar would subvert the state even if elected consul without his army.[64]

While the conservatives were engaged in proposals, counter-proposals and obstructionist tactics, unable to admit to their real purpose, Caesar, in characteristic fashion, was active in endeavoring to arouse a backfire by stirring up the old type of popular agitation. Through Curio, who had now come out openly as Caesar's friend, a liberalization of the grain dole was proposed, and a measure affecting the Campanian lands was introduced.[65] Both these moves naturally infuriated the conservatives, and Pompey in particular was alarmed by the second because of its possible effect on his veterans. The lines were becoming so obviously drawn that men were already beginning to talk of civil war.[66] It is conceivable that if Pompey and Caesar could have been brought into communication, some solution might still have been found and some adjustment made. On the other hand, Caesar clearly felt himself so strong that he no longer needed Pompey and was no longer willing to make concessions to him, whereas Pompey in his jealous pride would make no approach to Caesar. Early in August one of Cicero's correspondents in Rome wrote that "the detestable alliance" between Pompey and Caesar was at last about to break out into open war,[67] and in October Cicero himself, writing to Atticus from Greece, said, "I think I foresee . . . such a violent struggle as there has never been before." [68]

Matters came to a head on December 1st with a great debate in the senate. On that day, Gaius Marcellus, the consul, opened fire in a violent speech in which he called Caesar no better than a brigand and demanded that he be declared a public enemy unless he surrendered his province and army by a fixed date. Curio then entered the debate and, assuming a position of moderation, argued that the only fair and reasonable course was for both Caesar and Pompey to give up their commands simultaneously. The suggestion was brushed aside, and the consul put a motion that a successor should immediately be sent to supersede Caesar. The motion was carried by a great majority, but was vetoed by Curio. Then a motion was put that Pompey should also be relieved of his command, and this was voted down by a large majority. Up to this point the conservatives had had their way and had apparently attained their objective, but Curio now threw a bombshell into the proceedings. He demanded that a motion be put embodying his earlier suggestion that Caesar and Pompey should both be relieved simultaneously. To the consternation of the consul and the conservative managers, the motion was carried by the enormous majority of three hundred and seventy against twenty-two.[69]

The success of Curio's maneuver threw the whole situation into doubt. The vote revealed that although a large majority of the senators wished to terminate Caesar's command and were unwilling to put an end to Pompey's so long as Caesar's continued, nevertheless, nearly the entire senate was heartily anxious to be rid of both the great rivals. In other words, there was little evidence of any loyalty or devotion to Pompey, and the vote therefore dangerously weakened his prestige. At the same time, Curio's motion confronted Pompey with a difficult choice and fixed on him a large share of the responsibility for the future course of events, whatever direction they might take. If he resigned at once, he would be open to the charge of deserting his senatorial supporters and leaving them defenseless and at the mercy of Caesar; whereas if he did not resign, this would be regarded as a proof of his insincerity and as a justification for Caesar's retaining his command. Thus, whatever eventuated, Pompey could be held responsible and Caesar absolved from blame. In this way Curio's clever trick made the action of the senate seem directed not against Caesar but against Pompey. So despondent was the conservative leadership by this turn of events that Marcellus is said to have declared "this vote means slavery to Caesar." [70]

A few days later, returning from his province of Cilicia, Cicero arrived in the neighborhood of Rome, and henceforth the guidance of his letters is again available. Immediately he began to pick up news and express his opinion to correspondents, and from this source comes much information about what was happening. On December 10th he visited Pompey and had a talk of two hours with him which he reported as follows:

As to the political situation, he spoke as if there were no doubt as to war. He held out no hope of maintaining peace. He said that although he had felt before that Caesar was alienated from him, now he was quite sure of it. Caesar's intimate friend Hirtius had been in the neighborhood, but had not called on him . . . and had started to join Caesar late in the night. This seemed to him clear evidence of a split between them.[71]

To Pompey, apparently, a split between himself and Caesar was ample evidence of a state of war; if Caesar meant to press forward his own ambitions, the only course conceivable was to resist him by force. This was naturally not the logic of the conservatives, but their reasoning led them to the same result. Their object was to bring Caesar's provincial command to an end at once by whatever means were available, including resort to war if that should be needed. That it was needed the more extreme among them seemed by now to have convinced themselves, and that conviction henceforth guided their action.

Acting upon that conviction, the consul Marcellus convened the senate on December 9th and proposed a resolution declaring Caesar a public enemy, on the basis of an unfounded rumor that he was marching against Rome at the head of his army. At the same time Marcellus also proposed to authorize Pompey to take command of all the troops in Italy for the defense of the republic. These motions led to a violent altercation with Curio, who vetoed them after delivering an eloquent speech in favor of Caesar. Then Marcellus told the senate that he meant to provide for the public safety on his own responsibility and in his own way. This he did by leaving Rome the next day, accompanied by the consuls-elect, to meet Pompey on the thirteenth at Naples. There he undertook formally to commission him to assume command of the two legions in Italy, now in camp at Luceria, and to raise further forces and march against Caesar. Pompey was well aware that Marcellus had no constitutional right to offer him such a commission, and he knew or should have known that to accept it meant war. Nevertheless, he accepted and went to Luceria the next day. In consequence, as Heitland says, "the breach of the constitution was a fact accomplished beyond recall." [72]

In retrospect, the proceedings of the anti-Caesarians, commencing with the first of December, seem incredibly stupid. At each step they played directly into Caesar's hands and put themselves in a more indefensible and unconstitutional position. They consciously and deliberately initiated the appeal to arms and introduced civil war into the state without adequately assessing their strength or their ability to win. Thus, in the end, they ruined their own cause while they split the state apart and made way for Caesar. It must be recognized, however, that they acted under strong provocation. That provocation was the persistent and conclusive exercise of the veto power against the senate's action by a single tribune, in this instance Curio. There was no doubt that the senate was lawfully entitled to supersede a provincial governor immediately on the expiration of his term of office; yet that power could not now be exercised against Caesar because he happened to have been shrewd enough to obtain control of one member of a board of ten magistrates. Furthermore, the occasion and the subject matter of the veto were novel and startling: there seems to have been no previous instance in which a tribune had undertaken to interfere with senatorial power over provincial administration. Yet, novel as was the application of the veto in such a situation, there was no way of testing by legal procedures whether it constitutionally extended that far. In the absence of such a test, Caesar could coolly retain his province against any decree the senate might pass, so long as he could control one tribune, and already he had taken care to have another of his henchmen, young Mark Antony, elected tribune for the following year. The prospect was therefore that, through the device of the tribunician veto, Caesar would be able to ignore the senate and keep his province until he attained the consulship he desired.

In the absence of any judicial procedure to resolve such a constitutional deadlock, resort to force was inevitable, unless one side or the other gave way, and it was obvious that Caesar at least did not intend to yield. The senatorial party, therefore, had no choice but to surrender to Caesar without more ado, or else prepare to fight. Accordingly, although we may believe that they were not circumspect in choosing the ground that they did for the contest, or in adopting the particular measures of military preparation which they decided upon, it seems impossible not to conclude that war was now the only way by which Caesar could be removed from his province and kept out of a second consulship. If such a war was to be initiated, it could, of course, be initiated only by the conservatives.

Thus, what seems their stupidity may properly be regarded as the necessary counsel of desperation; they saw that in the end they would have to fight, and if this were so, then the sooner the better.

The immediate practical question was, of course, what were the chances of success in such a contest, and this was the question which perplexed Cicero in particular. He saw only weakness, disunity and irresolution on the side of the constitutionalists, only strength on the side of Caesar:

The political crisis makes me more fearful every day, for the constitutionalists are not, as people think, united. How many Roman knights, how many senators, have I seen prepared to inveigh most bitterly against everything and especially against this journey of Pompey [to levy troops]! [73]

In pointing out the disunity and weakness of the republicans, Cicero expresses himself as in no way approving Caesar's course, but only as recognizing his superior strength:

We should have resisted him when he was weak. . . . Now we are confronted by eleven legions, as much cavalry as he may wish, the people of the Po Valley, the city rabble, so many tribunes of the people, a corrupt youthful generation, a leader of enormous influence and audacity. With such a man we must either fight a pitched battle, or admit his candidacy in accordance with the law. "Fight," say you, "rather than be a slave." To what end? To be proscribed if defeated; to be a slave, in the end, even if victorious. [74]

The last sentence is significant. It shows that from a constitutional standpoint Cicero had no illusions about Pompey and feared him as well as Caesar. In another letter, written at about the same time, he says: "Peace is what we need. Victory will bring many evils, and one will certainly be a tyrant." [75] For years Cicero had watched Pompey ignoring and disregarding the constitution and helping others to do likewise, and he had no expectation that such a man, if seated in power as a result of civil war, would rule within the limits of law. Cicero therefore did not deceive himself into thinking that a victory for Pompey would be a victory for the constitution, and this was one reason why he was so anxious for peace. If, however, peace should prove impossible, he saw that so far as he himself was concerned, in the light of the past, his connections and his convictions, he would in the end have no choice but to be on Pompey's side. It was a choice of evils, but Pompey was the lesser evil, and Cicero felt that he had to stand on the ground which the conservative leaders had chosen.

Pompey, however, was by now already so far committed that Cicero despaired of persuading him to avoid war. After a long conversation with him on December 25, Cicero reported that Pompey appeared "not only not to seek peace but even to fear it." [76] Reviewing the alternatives open to the conservatives, Cicero concluded that one was to cease resisting Caesar's second consulship, but to insist that he resign his province and disband his army; the other was to give in to Caesar's wishes and to permit a prolongation of his proconsulship to any date he desired. Of the two alternatives Cicero preferred the former but thought it no longer practical because Caesar would certainly not accept it. If the conservatives, then, would not consent to the second alternative, war was certain, for no other course was open to them.

Meanwhile, Curio had gone north to meet Caesar at Ravenna and to inform him of developments. Caesar at once ordered the single legion that he had with him to leave its winter quarters, and he sent orders for two other legions to cross the Alps from Gaul. He then prepared for the senate a formal letter which Curio, by traveling post-haste, was able to bring back to Rome by the first of the year. On that day, as soon as the new consuls had been sworn in, Curio handed them the letter and asked them to place it before the senate. This they declined to do.[77] In the end they allowed the tribune Mark Antony to read it out,[78] but they refused to permit any motion respecting it to be put to the house.[79]

In this letter Caesar reminded the senate that he had already made an offer to surrender Transalpine Gaul, provided he might retain Cisalpine Gaul and Illyricum with two legions until the end of the year. Now he offered to give up the Cisalpine province also, if he might still keep Illyricum and one legion. In short, all that he insisted on was retaining his proconsular status until his consulship began. That was a minimum demand from which he would not recede for fear of exposing himself to prosecution. He pleaded self-defense, recited his services to the state and refused to be handed over to the mercy of his enemies. He was even ready, he said "to resign all his provinces and his army, provided Pompey would do the same. But he added that the refusal of these terms would compel him to take measures for asserting his own rights and the freedom of the Roman people." [80] Although Caesar afterwards referred to his demands as "of the mildest kind," [81] Cicero denounced Caesar as insolent and spoke of the letter as "menacing and bitter." [82]

After Caesar's letter had been read, a debate "on the whole state of the republic" began and took up four days. On the first day, the lead was taken by the ex-consul Metellus Scipio, who was understood to be speaking for his son-in-law Pompey. [83] After stating that it was Pompey's intention not to abandon the republic, Scipio moved that Caesar should surrender his command by a certain day or else be declared a public enemy. After a long and confused discussion in which many senators clearly showed their reluctance to bring matters to a crisis, Scipio's motion was carried, but was immediately vetoed by Mark Antony and by another tribune friendly to Caesar. The veto was challenged, apparently on the ground that, since the question was one which properly lay within the senate's exclusive control of provincial administration and foreign affairs, it was not constitutionally subject to tribunician obstruction. [84] A motion was then made that if the two tribunes persisted in their veto, they should be treated as attempting a revolution and punished accordingly. [85] No action was taken on this motion, and the senate adjourned.

In the evening, Pompey invited the senators to an informal meeting at which he sought to win over waverers and rouse feeling against Caesar. [86] An effort was also made to secure attendance in the senate of as many of Caesar's enemies as possible on the following day. When the senate reconvened and the debate was resumed, there was still a wide difference of opinion. A proposal was made to open negotiations with Caesar, another to send commissioners to him to notify him of the senate's pleasure. Mark Antony seems to have revived the proposal put forward in Caesar's letter, that both Caesar and Pompey should resign at once. Metellus Scipio opposed these proposals with the support of Cato. [87] It was probably at this point that, as reported by Plutarch, "Cato cried out, what he had foretold was come to pass; now it was manifest that Caesar was using his forces to compel their judgment, and was turning against the state those armies he had got from it by imposture and trickery." [88] Once more there was an adjournment without definite action.

On the fourth of January, one of the days the senate did not sit, Cicero arrived outside the walls and tried his hand at working out a compromise.[89] Apparently he made some progress with Pompey, who was inclined to accept a proposal that Caesar should retain one legion and be allowed to keep the Cisalpine provinces. To this, however, the new consul, Lentulus Crus, who was one of the most violent of the anti-Caesarians, would not assent.[90] "Although I desired," writes Cicero, "to find a remedy, and, I think could have done so, I was prevented by the passions of certain men, for on both sides there are those who are determined to fight." [91]

When the senate reconvened on the fifth, it met outside the walls, so that Pompey and Cicero, both still vested with proconsular imperium, could attend and participate in the discussion. Cicero brought up his compromise proposal and spoke for it, but in vain. "Lentulus and the men who saw that it meant their ruin would not hear of it. Cato would not make the public interests the subject of a bargain," [92] and insisted that it was better for them to die than for the state to listen to offers from a private citizen.[93] Pompey apparently did not speak. Again there was adjournment without action. The next day seems to have passed without a session and was probably spent by Cato and Pompey in whipping up votes.

The critical and decisive session came on the seventh. It commenced with a discussion of the motion, which had stood over from January first, to punish the recalcitrant tribunes for their allegedly unlawful veto of the original proposal of Metellus Scipio. For the senate to decree such punishment would have been unprecedented. Tribunes had been prosecuted before for illegal conduct in office, but the prosecutions had taken the form of a trial for *lèse majesté,* or unlawful violence, before the regular courts and after the expiration of the defendants' official immunity.[94] The conservative leaders accordingly seem to have reconsidered their position and decided on a different plan. Apparently they concluded that the only legally defensible way to eliminate the obstruction of the tribunes controlled by Caesar was by resorting to a *senatus consultum ultimum,* or "last decree." Not only was this not subject to tribunician veto, but it would remove from the operation of the veto any steps that the senate might thereafter take, or orders it might issue, to give effect to the decree. The consuls accordingly informed Antony and his colleague that if they did not withdraw their veto, the "last decree" would be voted, and, if they did not intend to obey it, they should now leave the city peaceably. Mark Antony took this occasion to deliver an impassioned speech, in which he protested against the violation of the sacrosanct tribunate. The senate nevertheless proceeded to vote the "last decree," and Antony and his colleague, although no violence was offered them, dramatized their supposed danger by fleeing to Caesar's headquarters at Ravenna disguised as slaves.

It is interesting to observe the grounds on which Caesar afterwards voiced his objection to these proceedings. He did not contend that the senate had no right to pass the "last decree" in a proper case, and he did not attempt to argue that after the passage of that decree the tribunes would have the right to veto measures intended to give it effect. Instead, he limited himself to the argument that the present case was not a proper one for the "last decree." He took his stand entirely on precedent, arguing that that extreme and final decree of the senate was never resorted to except when the city was in danger of being set on fire, or when the public safety was despaired of.[95] Whenever such a decree had been passed, he wrote, it was only "when pernicious laws were proposed, when the tribunes attempted violent measures, when the people seceded, when the temples and high places of the city were seized; . . . none of those things was attempted now, or even thought of; no law was proposed, no intrigue with the people was going on, and there was no secession." [96]

This was a far narrower ground than Caesar had seemed to take at either the time of the prosecution of Rabirius [97] or of the execution of the Catilinarian conspirators.[98] It was, however, all that was needed for an assertion that an unlawful outrage had been committed against the tribunes, and that such an outrage was an attack on the dignity and liberties of the Roman people. This was the ground on which Caesar decided to justify his future course, so as to be enabled to identify his cause with that of the Roman people and claim that he was fighting in defense of "liberty." He assembled his little army and made to them one of those characteristic speeches, in the nature of a public proclamation or pronunciamento, which he was a master hand at framing. Outlining his own position, he developed his constitutional argument, contrasted the illegal accumulation of Pompey's powers with his own modest demands, and hinted that his veterans could safely look to no one but himself to provide them with the rewards which they had a right to expect. At this point, says Caesar, the soldiers all cried out that they "were prepared to defend their general and the tribunes of the people from injuries." [99]

Caesar saw the importance of surprising his enemies by seizing the initiative. Without waiting for additional troops, he set out with his single legion to conquer Italy. He sent his little force forward into Italian territory to capture Rimini, the town nearest the border. When he followed and crossed the river Rubicon, which was the boundary of his province, he committed an overt act of war against the state. It is then, we are told, that he uttered the famous words, "The die is cast." [100]

5

Civil War
and
Dictatorship

I

CAESAR's audacity in seizing the initiative and setting out to conquer Italy with only one legion presaged the policy and strategy which he was to follow throughout the civil war that ensued. In that conflict he displayed a rapidity of action, a boldness—even rashness—of strategy, and a willingness to trust to luck that outstripped all his previous performances. He revealed himself as a thunderbolt of war, able to overcome his enemies by speed and surprise and to extricate himself from critical difficulties with an ingenuity and persistence that is little short of amazing.

On the eleventh of January, Caesar took Rimini without resistance. At approximately the same time, Mark Antony crossed the Appenines and seized Arrezzo in Etruria, with the result that Caesar acquired control of both the great roads leading from the north to Rome. He then commenced moving down the east coast, taking town after town without a blow. Such was the temper of the inhabitants that the senatorial garrisons were withdrawn by their commanders, and even some of Pompey's troops went over to Caesar.[1]

These developments, following as quickly as they did after Caesar crossed the Rubicon, suggest that his decision to begin the conquest of Italy with a single legion was not nearly so rash as it may now seem. So competent was his intelligence service that he must have been reasonably well informed of the state of mind among the leaders in the Italian municipalities and countryside who were anything but favorable to his opponents. Pompey, to his astonishment and chagrin, had also begun to find this out. Ever since the time of the great Italian insurrection forty years before, his family had been supposedly all-powerful in the district of Picenum, where their estates lay; now the towns in that area were all going over to Caesar. For five years—ever since his second consulship—Pompey had been courting the municipal communities throughout Italy, and now he was not only finding great difficulty in recruiting troops in those communities but was discovering that their sentiment was more favorable to his rival than to himself. Apparently, he had sought to attach to himself in each community the more staid and wealthy inhabitants, substantial elderly men who, under normal conditions, were the leaders in community affairs. Yet these men now proved irresolute, averse to taking risks, and of no use in a crisis.

Caesar had pursued a different policy. The legions with which he conquered Gaul were made up almost entirely of recruits from the Italian countryside. His soldiers had friends and connections in every Italian community. They had sent home tales of their success, of the riches they were accumulating, and doubtless a good deal of those riches found their way back to Italy. Young men were infected with a spirit of emulation and ambition, and that spirit kindled the hopes of aggressive young leaders anxious to serve under Caesar and to bring themselves to his notice so as to reap the rewards of becoming lieutenants of the man who, above all others, stood for success. For some time Caesar had been lavish in his efforts to win over these enterprising younger men, and now that policy was bearing fruit as they rallied to his party nearly everywhere.

Against a movement of this kind Pompey's cautious, substantial friends, in spite of their wealth and position, were powerless. In the general sentiment of the people they found little or no support. Most Italians who were not tempted by the prospect of making money in Caesar's service had no more interest in Pompey than in Caesar. Above all else they wanted peace, and if there was to be war, they did not much care which side won. They had no interest in the Roman constitution, from which they had been excluded until so recent a date that they had not yet come to regard it as their own; and they had no love for the senate or the Roman aristocracy, whom they rightly blamed for their long exclusion. They therefore preferred not to become involved in a conflict which was not theirs. Thus the active Caesarian party, while doubtless everywhere in a minority, was able to carry all before it, and the result became apparent in the rapidly mounting size of Caesar's army. Recruits flocked to his standard, whole detachments of senatorial troops deserted to him, two of his legions of veterans joined him from beyond the Alps, and within six weeks after crossing the Rubicon he was in command of an army of six legions, a far larger force than the Pompeians had yet been able to muster.

In the weeks following the senate's "last decree," something like consternation came over the conservative party at Rome because of Pompey's inability to recruit an adequate army. In December, Pompey had made his famous boast that he had but to stamp his foot and an army would spring from the ground. Late in the month he had assured Cicero that he "felt confident of his own and the state's resources." [2] The day after the "last decree" was voted, a general levy of troops throughout Italy was ordered, and the municipal towns were called on to furnish arms and contribute money. Pompey had left Rome at once to put these orders into effect, but he was disheartened at his lack of success. The levy dragged; men would not enlist, and those who did so were men reluctant to serve and averse to fighting. [3]

Meanwhile, Caesar's rapid advance injected a decisive element into the psychology of the situation: on his side, all was confidence, hope and assurance; on the other was gloom, confusion and discouragement, typified by a decision on the sixteenth of January that the government and the senate should abandon Rome. Cicero, on whom this decision fell as an unexpected blow, and who doubtless reflected the general sentiment of the upper class, denounced it as "rash and insane," [4] but it was carried out, and Rome was left without a government. Pompey became more active, but no results were visible. "As to what Pompey is doing," writes Cicero, "I do not think he knows himself, certainly none of us do. . . . Nobody knows whether he means to make a stand anywhere, or to cross the sea. If he stays in Italy, I am afraid he cannot have a dependable army." [5]

Pompey now decided to try for a compromise with Caesar, and for this purpose he sent an agent, one of Caesar's relatives, to confer with him and inquire as to what terms he would consent to. Caesar's answer, which was delivered on January 23rd, was amazingly moderate.[6] "Let Pompey go to his own province [Spain]; let both sides disband their armies; let all persons in Italy lay down their arms; let all fear be removed from the city; let free elections . . . be held." [7] Cicero wrote of these proposed terms somewhat more explicitly: "Proposals have arrived from Caesar that Pompey should go to Spain; that the levies already completed, and our garrisons, should be disbanded; that he will hand over Transalpine Gaul and Cisalpine Gaul [to the new governors already appointed by the senate] . . . ; that he will come to Rome to canvass for the consulship and no longer demand that his candidacy be admitted in his absence; that he will be in the city as a candidate for the full legal period [of twenty-four days]." [8]

Apparently Caesar was now willing to yield on what had hitherto always been the sticking point in the negotiations, doubtless because he felt that he no longer had anything to fear from a prosecution. Immediately, the consuls called together all the members of the senate who could be assembled at Capua to consider his terms, which were accepted with enthusiasm. However, they insisted that Caesar first withdraw his garrisons from the towns he had occupied "so that the senate might meet in Rome to debate the terms without apprehension." [9]

The matter of the withdrawal of Caesar's garrisons became a new subject of controversy, particularly from the standpoint of timing. Apparently Caesar refused to perform his part of the pact until after Pompey left for Spain. He took the position that it was not enough for Pompey to promise to go without specifying a date, for Pompey would still be in a position to make new levies after Caesar's troops had been disbanded.[10] The conservatives, on the other hand, insisted on the withdrawal of Caesar's troops from Italy as a preliminary condition of the arrangement, since otherwise they would have no security that Caesar would keep his promise.[11] On this point negotiations broke down, and for the last time. The truth of the matter was that neither side trusted the other enough to make an agreement, and the Pompeians were unwilling to admit that the effective bargaining power was all on Caesar's side. Thus the last prospect of peace disappeared, and Pompey had no choice but to go forward with the unpromising task of trying to counteract Caesar's resistless advance.

Caesar's southward progress brought him to the hill country, where the old Italian capital, Corfinium, had been occupied by the Pompeians with a strong force of recruits equivalent to two legions. The town was a strategically located outpost which Caesar could not afford to leave in his rear, whether he proceeded in a southeasterly direction down the coast or turned toward the west and Rome. Accordingly, he besieged it on the fourteenth of February. Pompey sent orders to withdraw, but the garrison's commander, the ex-consul Domitius Ahenobarbus, was conceited and stubborn, and he refused. The result justified Pompey's worst fears: Corfinium surrendered, and, what was still worse, the army which had held it for the Pompeians went over *en masse* to Caesar, and Pompey lost the best troops he had.

After the fall of Corfinium, Pompey decided on a step which for some time he had been considering as a possibility—to abandon Italy, and, after assembling and training an efficient army, make a stand in the East. Doubtless for this reason he had been concentrating his troops near Luceria, and now he hurried them as fast as possible to Brindisi for embarkation. At this time he seems to have had only five legions against Caesar's eight.[12] As soon as the plan became evident, Caesar hurried down the coast to intercept him, but when he reached Brindisi, the greater part of Pompey's army had already sailed. Pompey had taken care to protect the port and gain possession of all the available shipping, so that Caesar could neither prevent the embarkation of the remaining troops nor follow them. He therefore had no course open but to turn back and complete the subjugation of Italy.

Modern scholars have seen in Pompey's abandonment of Italy a grand and farsighted strategic plan. One recent historian has stated that "his plan was no mere makeshift . . . but subtle and grandiose—to evacuate Italy, leaving Caesar entrapped between the legions of Spain and the hosts of all the East, and then to return, like Sulla, to victory and to power." [13] If Pompey's strategy was thus to entrap Caesar between hostile pincers, one in Spain and one in the East, it was singularly inept for so experienced and cautious a general, because the ends of the pincers were much too far apart. Pompey must have known that he would lose all touch with, and control over, his Spanish army, and such proved to be the case. Moreover, separated from his command, that army could not be depended on. Caesar pointed out the fatal flaw in the pincer strategy in a witticism to the effect that he was first going to Spain to fight an army without a general and then going to the East to fight a general without an army.[14]

It is not likely that Pompey was so obtuse from a military standpoint as not to understand the situation as well as Caesar. It must be concluded, therefore, that Pompey left Italy because he felt he could not hold it and because he could not afford to suffer a crushing defeat at the outset of the war. His only chance to remain in the contest was by withdrawing to build up his strength. Moreover, in considering withdrawal, there was no place for him to go, with ultimate hope of success, except the East. Not only did he still have influence and important connections in the eastern provinces which he had so recently added to the Empire, but those provinces were from a material standpoint by far the richest part of Rome's dominions. Above all there was Egypt, which now again, as so often during these critical years, exerted its influence on the strategy of Roman politics. The vast wealth of that country was such that the minds of the leading Roman politicians constantly recurred to it as furnishing a prospective fulcrum from which to control the balance of power in the Roman state. Thus not only did it seem necessary to Pompey to get between Caesar and Egypt, but control of the wealth of Egypt offered Pompey his best prospect of equipping himself with the resources that he would need to sustain a long war. It is not without significance that when he was again forced to withdraw before Caesar after his defeat at Pharsalus, it was to Egypt that he turned.

Pompey's withdrawal from Italy with the nucleus of an army made it plain what the character of the coming civil war was to be. It was to be a war between armies of professional soldiers for the victory of one of two opposing generals. Political issues had become subordinated to their personal rivalry which overshadowed political differences. Thus, the conflict that was now in prospect was "in the hands of trained soldiers, men who had taken an oath of allegiance to their commander and were fighting to bring about his victory and the bonus he had promised them. Although the Civil War was technically a war between Caesar and the senate, actually it was fought by the personal armies of Pompey and Caesar." [15] It was thus an essentially different kind of civil war from that between Charles the First and Parliament, or the American Civil War between the southern and northern states. It is true that Pompey was regarded as having greater respect for the senate and the established processes of the constitution than had Caesar, but it was common knowledge that throughout his career Pompey had never hesitated to override the senate and the constitution whenever it had seemed to his advantage to do so. The difference between the two rivals was thus only one of degree, which could not be expected to make much impression on average minds, or to arouse any very keen interest. A difference of this kind was not powerful enough to dispel the apathy which had been the striking feature of the general Roman attitude toward politics ever since the time of Sulla. Even if Pompey could be regarded as now fighting for the traditional distribution of powers in the state, which many must have doubted, there was no longer any real or living interest in preserving that distribution on the part of the great body of citizens, Romans and Italians alike.

In this state of affairs, the determining considerations which drew supporters to Caesar on one side, or Pompey on the other, were bound to be mainly personal ones, and those personal considerations operated with different force and effect on some groups than on others. There seems little doubt that the cause of Caesar made a strong appeal everywhere to those who were anxious to rise in the world and who saw their best chance for attaining this ambition in attaching themselves to a leader who had the reputation of opening up profitable opportunities for his followers. The fact that Caesar was opposed by the senate also attracted to him all who had been unsuccessful in achieving their hopes of wealth and fortune and who attributed their failure in that direction to the family favoritism and class exclusiveness of the aristocracy. Many of Caesar's followers were broken adventurers of the kind who had followed Catiline. "What a following," exclaims Cicero, "What corpses! . . . What a lost cause, what a gang of desperadoes!" [16] Yet besides these unsavory characters, there were other ambitious men of more respectable standing, particularly among the middle class, who saw in Caesar's victory the prospect of careers open to talent and were honestly anxious to do away with the exclusive proprietorship of the lucrative and important state offices which the aristocrats had so long enjoyed.

Since the choice between Caesar and Pompey turned so largely on personal factors, it is not surprising that Caesar found many supporters even among the senatorial group in an age when the Roman aristocracy had grown accustomed to administering public offices for private ends. Individual senators made their decisions to a great extent not on public or constitutional grounds, but on the basis of friendship, family connection, and prospects of personal gain. Thus Caesar's father-in-law, Piso, naturally refused to oppose him. So even did Gaius Marcellus, the consul of the previous year, who had given Pompey his commission to defend the state against Caesar.[17] Asinius Pollio, afterwards famous as a historian, man of letters and the early patron of Vergil, who was now winning fame as a rising orator, chose Caesar's side because, as he explained later to Cicero, "he treated me as one of his oldest friends, though he had not known me until he reached his highest position. . . ." [18] The same course was likewise followed by the great jurist Sulpicius Rufus, who had been consul in the year 51. [19] Caesar was also joined by the younger Hortensius, son of the orator, and by Cicero's son-in-law Dolabella.

It was easy for many of these aristocrats to side with Caesar, or at least not to oppose him, because, as pointed out, the constitutional and political issues at this time were far from being clear-cut and well-defined. With those issues in doubt, many considerations other than purely personal ones influenced in one degree or another the choice of particular individuals. Several of these considerations are presented in Cicero's letters, written in an anguish which was so excruciating that even at this distance of time the pain he felt is still vivid. First, there was the loss of confidence in Pompey's ability and leadership occasioned by his abandonment of Italy, which looked unpleasantly like cowardice and flight. He "flies before he knows from whom he is flying, or whither; he has betrayed our interests, abandoned his country and deserted Italy." [20] "He declined any terms of peace but he had made no preparation for war; . . . he went off to Greece without a word, leaving us uninformed of a move on his part so important and unprecedented." [21] Even if there was an undisclosed strategy in Pompey's retreat, the prospect was still more terrifying, since the strategy appeared to be that of Sulla —to fall back on the East and return with the hosts of the Orient to overwhelm his country. "He did not abandon the city because he was unable to protect it, nor Italy because he was driven out of it; his idea from the first has been to stir up every land and sea, to arouse foreign princes, to bring savage tribes under arms into Italy and to collect huge armies." [22] "A kind of Sullan regime has long been his objective and is desired by many of his followers. . . . I know what I am saying. He never made less of a secret of anything." [23] Even aside from proscriptions, a war for Italy was bound to be cruel and devastating beyond belief. "I say that you will see poor Italy trodden under foot next summer, or in the hands of the slaves of both leaders gathered from all quarters. It is not so much a proscription that is to be feared . . . as general destruction." [24] Pompey's plan was apparently "to choke off the city and Italy by starving them, and then devastate and burn the country and not keep their hands off the money of the wealthy." [25] Meanwhile, the constitution was already lost beyond recovery, whichever side might win.[26] "I see that we can never have our constitution back while these two men are both alive, or with either one remaining." [27]

With thoughts like these running through the mind of even such a man as Cicero, it was not remarkable that many members of the Italian upper classes were unwilling to exert themselves actively or to incur serious risks in the Pompeian cause. Caesar set himself to win their support, or at least their acquiescence, by appealing to the consideration which was uppermost in their minds. If their coolness toward Pompey was largely the result of fear of his vengeance and destructiveness, Caesar was prepared to do all in his power to show that his own course would be marked by conciliation and mildness. This was the origin of that famous policy of "clemency" or "mercy," which from now on he did so much to emphasize, and which he succeeded in making a part of the public image of himself that has come down in history as one of its most characteristic features. In a letter written at this time to his agents Balbus and Oppius, and meant for public consumption, he discourses on this policy and says that he had resolved to act with the utmost leniency. "Let us exert ourselves to recover by such means, if it be possible, the good-will of all men, and so secure a lasting victory; our predecessors did not escape the hatred which their cruelty aroused; none of them could permanently hold his ground, excepting only Sulla, and him I will never imitate. Let us conquer on a new plan, and fortify ourselves with mercy and kindness." [28] The success with which he created this impression of his policy is evident throughout Cicero's letters of this period. Caesar, he writes, "is regarded as the preserver of his enemies, the other as the traitor to his friends." [29] If Caesar "refrains from putting anyone to death, and from despoiling anyone of anything, he will be most adored by those who formerly feared him most." [30]

Undoubtedly Caesar's course in this respect was the result of deliberate and careful calculation, rather than of a merely humanitarian disposition. He had shown in Gaul that he could be both hard and cruel when the occasion demanded, but the circumstances now seemed to require a different course. In the present instance, his policy had three objectives. From a general standpoint, he did not wish to rule over an Italy that was a shambles, as it had been after Sulla's ruthless seizure of power. He wanted, so far as possible, to have the normal processes of economic and social life go on, if for no better reason than to ensure that the maintenance of his own position might be less costly and more secure. He seems also to have had two more immediate purposes. Every man of prominence he was able to win to his side meant one less center of disaffection and of possibly dangerous opposition. Furthermore, he wanted to give his regime an aura of respectability if not of luster. Like Napoleon, who resembled or imitated him in so many respects, he desired to gather around him a circle of the nobility and prominent figures of the old regime, which would be impossible if he were to butcher or pillage them or their kinsmen and friends. Of course he did not intend to share his power with them, or to let them have any real influence on his policies. In his personal associations, he was no democrat. Although he had to spend a great deal of his time with rough soldiers and with the disreputable instruments of his political intrigues, he was all the more desirous of indulging his own tastes in the pleasures of a polite and elegant society to which he had grown accustomed in his early years. His famous policy of "clemency" was undoubtedly motivated in differing degrees by all these considerations. As one of his intimates told Cicero, "Caesar was not by taste or nature averse to bloodshed, but he thought that clemency would make him popular." [31]

In pursuit of this policy, Caesar attached great importance to winning over Cicero. With Italy now at his disposal, after the departure of Pompey and the consuls, his immediate task was to go to Rome and organize some kind of *de facto* government. If in this he could appear to have the assistance, or at least the acquiescence, of so eminent a republican as Cicero, the seeming legality and propriety of his proceedings would be greatly enhanced. Accordingly, on his way to Rome from Brindisi he wrote to Cicero that he would be very much obliged if Cicero would meet him in the capital, "that I may as always avail myself in all matters of your advice and influence." [32] Not content with this, he stopped to visit Cicero at his villa at Formiae and had a conversation with him which is vividly reported in one of Cicero's letters. [33]

To those who conclude from Cicero's lifelong habit of viewing both sides of a question that he was necessarily wanting in courage or decision, the story of this famous interview furnishes an answer. Doubtless he was sometimes slow in coming to a conclusion when opposing considerations, which he saw more clearly than others, were nearly in balance; but that he did not lack courage in a crisis calling for decisiveness is shown by the calm and frank way in which he now confronted Caesar in the moment of the latter's triumph. Caesar repeated his request that Cicero should come to Rome and take his place in a session of the senators which Caesar proposed to call. Cicero declined. "I found myself mistaken," he writes, "in thinking that he would be easily satisfied. I never saw any one less so. He kept repeating that my decision amounted to condemning him, that the rest would be more reluctant to attend if I did not come. I told him that their position was not the same as mine. . . . 'Well then,' he said, 'at least come and discuss peace.' 'At my own discretion?' I asked. 'You do not think that I would dictate to you, do you?' he asked. 'Then,' I replied, 'I shall propose that the senate does not approve that you should go to Spain or that an army should cross the sea to Greece; and I shall also express my sympathy for Pompey.' 'But of course,' he answered, 'I don't wish such things said.' 'That is what I supposed,' I replied, 'but I must decline being present, because I must either speak in this sense if I am there, and say many other things which I could not leave unsaid, if I were present, or else I must decline to be there at all.' The result was that, by way of ending the discussion, I was to think the matter over. I could not refuse, and so we parted. After this I feel certain that he has no love for me, but at least I have a liking for myself, which has not been the case for a long time. . . . His closing remark, which I had almost forgotten to mention, was ominous— that if he was not allowed to avail himself of my counsel, he would take advice where he could get it, and would go to any length." [34]

Accordingly, Caesar went on to Rome, and Cicero was left with his doubts and uncertainties. He was resolved more firmly than ever not to join Caesar or become a party to his proceedings, but he still doubted whether any good would come of his leaving Italy and joining the Pompeians in Greece. "Matters are impossible," he wrote. "Everything has to be left to chance. We are struggling along without hope. If anything better turns up, it will be a surprise." [35] "One leader is inflamed with madness and crime which is not cooling but becomes worse every day. . . . The other . . . is preparing war by land and sea. The war . . . will be fatal to his fellow citizens unless he proves victorious, fraught with disaster even if he is victorious. . . . If the republic still existed, I should know what to do by way of severity and kindness." [36]

In the end, Caesar himself drove Cicero to a decision by assuming a tone of menace. On his way to Spain, he wrote a letter to the orator suggesting that if Cicero left Italy he would regard it as an unfriendly act. "You will have done a serious injury to our friendship and not consulted your best interests if you make it clear that you are not following fortune (for everything has been most favorable to us and most unfavorable to them) . . . and that you have condemned some act of mine, whereby no greater harm could be done to me by you." [37] Caesar's man, Mark Antony, whom he had left in charge in Italy, also wrote to warn Cicero not to compromise himself and to urge him not to flee from one who, "although he will not love you, which is impossible, will always wish you to be safe and in the highest position." [38] At this, Cicero decided to depart. Either one must approve the measures now being taken, he wrote to Servius Sulpicius Rufus, "or be a party to them in spite of disapproving them. The one alternative is in my eyes discreditable, the other is dangerous as well. . . . I must go." [39] Accordingly he secretly caused a vessel to be prepared, and on the third of June sailed to join Pompey.

On arriving at the headquarters of the constitutionalists, Cicero had an interview with Cato, which, if Plutarch's account is to be believed,[40] must have been somewhat of a shock to him. Cato reproached him for coming. Cato said that he himself could not desert the party he had chosen from the beginning and with which he had acted consistently throughout his entire career. Cicero, however, would have been more useful to his country if he had stayed in

Italy in a neutral position and adjusted himself to the ultimate result, and if he had not assumed an attitude of hostility to Caesar on grounds of principle, but only insofar as compelled to do so by necessity. Coming from Cato, such a comment must have shaken Cicero severely, for he thought he had chosen the side of honor, consistency and principle, and now Cato, the great exponent of those virtues, told him he had been wrong. Perhaps Cato was merely in a perverse mood and indulging in Stoic paradoxes at Cicero's expense; perhaps Cato wished him to feel that a new man like Cicero had no proper place among the hereditary proprietors of the constitution; perhaps, for once, he hearkened to the appeal of worldly wisdom, and really believed, as Cicero himself at times did, that a moment might come when a neutral mediator of sufficient authority could work out a compromise between the opposing leaders. In any event, Cicero had now chosen his side, and from that choice there was no retreating, but he found little to comfort or encourage him among the aristocratic clique that surrounded Pompey. Neither they nor their general took him into their confidence; he hung about the outer fringes of their circle, useless and unhappy, and contributing nothing to the cause he had espoused. He hardly made matters better by indulging in caustic comments about the things that disheartened him, as by saying, when criticized for coming late, that he was not late at all, for nothing was yet ready.[41]

It has seemed appropriate to follow in detail the story of Cicero's doubts and hesitations because it not only furnishes an opportunity to study the vagueness and uncertainty of the issue between Caesar and Pompey, as seen through the medium of a first-class contemporary mind, but also because, in a broader sense, it illustrates the difficulty of making political choices which often exists at a moment of crisis that may afterwards prove to be a turning point in history. A political choice is often—perhaps more often than not—nothing but a choice between two evils, and of what seems the lesser of the two. Historians often overlook this. With the benefit of hindsight, they are able to see the outcome of the course which prevailed, and so tend to pass judgment in black-and-white terms on the conduct of contemporaries according as they approve or disapprove of the result. For the student of politics it is important to see the issues not in this way—not in the light of the outcome—but as they actually presented themselves at the time to men who did not have the gift of prophecy. In politics, as in human relations generally, the outcome of any course of action is largely veiled in uncertainty; and, while that uncertainty persists, the basis for a clear-cut decision is usually absent, so that competing considerations and probabilities weight the scales on either side in determining a preference. Sometimes the grounds of preference in favor of one side or the other are reasonably clear; but often this is not true at the very moments of supreme crisis in the history of a nation or civilization. It is with crises of this kind that students of politics as an art need to familiarize themselves; and for such a study there is no better laboratory material than the letters of Cicero, written during the first half of the year 49, in which he balances and counterbalances the arguments in favor of Caesar and Pompey.

In the letter in which Cicero announced his decision finally to join Pompey, he wrote that if he did not do so, he must either "approve the measures now being taken" or be a party to them in spite of disapproving them.[42] By "the measures now being taken" he was undoubtedly referring to Caesar's actions at Rome following their conversation at Formiae. When Caesar reached the city, he caused Antony, in his capacity of tribune, to summon a meeting of the senators who had remained behind and ask them to undertake the administration of the state in conjunction with himself. That much deference he paid to form, in accordance with his professions that he was fighting in defense of the constitution. However, that he did not greatly care for the senate's assistance, or mean to be hampered by it, he showed by going on to tell them that if they were afraid to accept his proposal he would not trouble them further and would take the administration into his own hands, and that he proceeded to do. He then set about making the arrangements which he regarded as necessary during his absence on his campaign against Pompey's armies in Spain. Without any basis of legal authority, he named a governor for Rome and appointed Antony military commander of Italy. The most urgent problem was to safeguard the food supply, which was endangered by the fact that the

Pompeians had control of the two nearest grain-growing provinces, Sicily and Sardinia.[43] He therefore lost no time in despatching troops to take over those islands. His attitude toward the senate was again displayed in the appointment of the commanders of these expeditions. Curio, who was named to lead one of them, told Cicero that he wanted to get authority from a decree of the senate, "but Caesar now dislikes the senate more than ever. 'All authority,' he says, 'will come from me.' "[44] Asinius Pollio, another of Caesar's appointees, when asked to show his authority, replied, "The master of Italy has sent me on this business."[45]

Before leaving Rome, Caesar felt it necessary to take a step which kindled a momentary spark of opposition. He needed money, a large amount of money, for the prosecution of the war. Locked up in the treasury was a reserve fund, amounting to roughly seventeen million dollars, the equivalent of almost an entire year's revenue of the state, which was regarded with special sanctity, not to be touched except to save Rome from invasion. Caesar wanted to take possession of this fund in a legal way, and a motion to put it at his disposal was accordingly made in the senate, but it was vetoed by a tribune named Metellus. Caesar at once showed his lack of respect for the sanctity of the tribunician office which he was professedly fighting to maintain. He not only disregarded the veto and proceeded with an armed force to the treasury, but, when Metellus placed himself before the door to prevent the money from being taken, Caesar ordered him to be killed if he persisted in his opposition. Metellus then yielded, and Caesar took the money.

In order to appease the Roman populace during his stay in the city, it seems that Caesar had promised a cash distribution to every citizen.[46] However, his seizure of the sacred fund in the treasury had roused such a storm of popular ill-feeling, probably on superstitious grounds, that he felt it would be futile to make a bid for popularity at this time, and he accordingly canceled the distribution. He also canceled a speech which he had intended to make to the people and took pains to ensure that his displeasure with the populace, no less than with the senate, should be made plain in no uncertain terms. He had reached the point where his temper was becoming short and where he felt that he could afford to show it. The Roman people were in his power, and he had no objection to their knowing it. In this spirit he set out for Spain.

II

Hurrying north to join the legions which he had left in Gaul, Caesar encountered a troublesome interruption on his way to Spain from the attitude of Rome's ancient ally, Marseilles. This old Greek city professed to be neutral but closed its gates against him and named the Pompeian general, Domitius Ahenobarbus, commander of its troops. Caesar invested the city by land and sea and began what was to be one of the greatest siege operations of antiquity; but he had no time to direct the siege himself, and left Decimus Brutus and another officer in charge, so that he could hasten across the Pyrenees with six legions.

Pompey's two deputies in northern and western Spain, with five legions and a large body of native auxiliaries, combined their forces and awaited Caesar's coming a short distance south of the mountains on a tributary of the Ebro. The two armies faced each other by the end of June. Caesar was in a hurry and ready to take chances, whereas the Pompeian generals wished to play a safe game and stand on the defensive. The result was that, although at several points during the campaign Caesar's army was in great danger, from which it was extricated only by his boldness and skill, he finally maneuvered his opponents into an impossible situation where they were without food or water and entirely at his mercy. Then, instead of closing in and butchering them, as his own men wished him to do, Caesar granted a truce on condition that he might address the trapped Pompeian army. He told them that all he wanted was to make sure they would not fight against him again and therefore required only that they should be disbanded. All were to go free, but no one was to return to Italy as a soldier of Pompey. In this way, Pompey's best legions ceased to exist, and once again Caesar's "clemency" won him gratitude and allegiance in thousands of Italian homes.

Caesar then moved on into southern Spain, the most Romanized part of the peninsula, which was held for Pompey by the antiquary Varro with two legions. This was the province where on two previous occasions Caesar had served terms of office, once as quaestor and afterwards as governor. He had friends everywhere among Romans and Spaniards alike, especially in the principal cities of Cordova and Cadiz. Both of these now declared themselves on his side, and the leading men of the local communities were thereupon summoned to meet him at Cordova. In this way, Varro, whose position was already weakened by the harshness with which he had levied exactions for defense, found his authority thoroughly undermined. His efforts proved vain, and his troops and garrisons began deserting to Caesar in a steady stream. Varro had no choice but to surrender. He handed over his remaining troops and the public funds in his possession. Caesar restored to the provincials the money which Varro had exacted from them. He also promised citizenship and other rewards to the communities and individuals who had taken the lead in his cause. Thus the conquest of Spain was completed in two months, and Caesar returned to supervise the subjugation of Marseilles.[47]

After receiving the surrender of that city, Caesar returned to Rome, where he arrived about the first of October. Here he found that his lieutenant Lepidus, whom he had left in charge as prefect of the city, had proclaimed him dictator. In this capacity, he now proceeded to promulgate, apparently on his sole authority, a number of measures of no lasting or fundamental importance, but designed to improve and strengthen his political alliances and meet temporary emergencies. For example, he pardoned and recalled all persons who had been condemned for political offenses during Pompey's second consulship, except Milo, who alone was expressly exempted from the pardon. This action was intended not only to enhance Caesar's reputation for "clemency," in contrast with Pompey's supposed severity, but to bring back into public life a number of former "democratic" politicians who might be useful to him in the future in controlling the city populace. He kept his promise to the Cisalpine Gauls and certain Spanish communities, notably Cadiz, by conferring Roman citizenship on them. Finally, he provided a temporary expedient for the financial depression into which Rome had fallen in consequence of the war.

These economic measures were rendered necessary by the severe drop in prices, particularly of real estate, which occurred because of the uncertainties of the outcome of the war. Debtors could not meet their obligations or creditors realize on their securities. As might have been expected, the situation encouraged a revival of the old Catilinarian cry for cancellation of debts. Caesar seems to have been glad to have an opportunity to show his lack of sympathy with such a program and to win the favor of the moneyed men whose support he desired. Accordingly, he issued an edict under which embarrassed debtors were required to turn their property over to liquidators for the benefit of their creditors. However, the property was to be applied against the debt at an assessed valuation based not on the current depressed market price but reflecting the more normal price-level which had prevailed before the war. Moreover, debtors were to have the advantage of deducting interest payments already made from the principal amount remaining due on the debt. By these means, some measure of relief was extended to debtors without impairing the rights of their creditors as harshly as they had been led to fear. Caesar coupled this program of debt relief with another measure designed to bolster prices: he limited the amount of specie, or liquid funds, which a man might lawfully possess, and he thus compelled men to invest the balance, thereby creating a market for investment property which might be expected to enhance its price. It is not known how effectively these measures accomplished their intended economic results, but they seem at least to have had the political consequence of attaching Roman business interests to Caesar's cause. It is strongly to be suspected that for Caesar, as for many another politician before and afterwards, economics were primarily an instrument of political strategy.

In the midst of these arrangements, Caesar held the elections and had himself chosen consul for the year 48. Thus the ambition which he had so long pursued with such fateful consequences was at last attained without postponement of his original schedule. He could now proceed against Pompey in the legal status of chief magistrate of republican Rome. This appearance of legality seems to have been the more highly prized by Caesar, in order to divert attention from his willingness to override law whenever it stood in the path of his will. A full complement of occupants of the various public offices were elected at the same time, governors were appointed for the provinces under Caesar's control, and a respectable aristocrat, the younger Publius Servilius Isauricus, was named as his colleague. After these dispositions were completed, Caesar left the city, not to return for almost two years.

Once again Caesar decided to throw his enemies into confusion by doing the unexpected. Winter was approaching, and at Pompey's headquarters in Greece it was apparently not supposed that he would venture to cross the straits until the following spring. For this reason, although the Pompeians had control of the sea, their admiral, Bibulus, Caesar's old colleague in the consulship, had done nothing to bar his passage. Even so, Caesar was not able to collect enough shipping to transport all the twelve legions with which he had marched to Brindisi. He therefore had to leave six of them behind under Mark Antony, who from now on generally acted as his second in command, to find their way across at the first opportunity. With the other legions Caesar landed on the Greek coast near Apollonia without meeting opposition.

With reasonable foresight and diligence, it ought to have been possible for the Pompeians to prevent Caesar from landing in force on the Greek shore; but the Pompeians had been careless and were not ready, and Caesar took them by surprise. Pompey hurried his army west from Macedonia, where he had gone into winter quarters, and arrived just in time to occupy the port of Durazzo and keep it from falling into Caesar's hands. Yet it was not only sluggishness and ineptitude that encumbered Pompey; as on so many other occasions, luck and chance contributed to Caesar's success. When Antony made a dash to bring over four of the legions which had been left at Brindisi, his transports slipped away under the eyes of a blockading Pompeian squadron, and with the aid of a favoring wind eluded pursuit and made a safe landing.

With nine legions Pompey was now encamped along the beach outside Durazzo, but he did not trust the temper and quality of his troops sufficiently to challenge Caesar to battle. His army was still a raw and makeshift affair, not yet welded into an efficient fighting machine. Five of these legions he had brought with him from Italy, and only two of them had seen service; one was a veteran legion which he had summoned from Cilicia; and three had just been recruited in Asia, Macedonia and the islands. Thus two-thirds of his force consisted of raw levies. Two more veteran legions from Syria were marching to join him under his father-in-law Matellus Scipio and were in the course of crossing from Asia into Thrace. Although Pompey had a large body of six or seven thousand excellent horsemen, it was impractical to use cavalry in the rugged coastal terrain where the two armies faced each other. He therefore sat still and did nothing. Having control of the port, his army could be supplied by sea, whereas Caesar's troops soon found themselves on short rations because of the barrenness of the country to which they were confined.

Under these circumstances, Caesar resorted to another of those bold expedients of which the history of his campaigns is so full. He constructed a line of circumvallation around Pompey's army, confining it to a narrow strip of coast and thus preventing interference with his foraging parties. This was an extraordinary attempt to blockade a well-provisioned army by a starving one. Pompey made Caesar's plan increasingly difficult by lengthening his own lines, so that Caesar was gradually forced to extend his circuit over a distance of fourteen miles until it was very thinly defended. Pompey watched for an opportunity, and one morning at dawn delivered a sudden assault, broke through Caesar's line, and started to roll it back. Although Caesar threw additional troops into the breach, they, too, were rolled back, with the victorious Pompeians pursuing the flying veterans of Caesar pell-mell into their camp. Pompey, however, did not follow up this success by a general attack, and Caesar is said to have remarked afterwards that if Pompey had known his business, he could then and there have ended the war.[48]

After this reverse, Caesar resolved to change his whole plan of operations.[49] He broke camp, drew off his force from before Durazzo, and started to march away into the interior. For this he had a double motive. Some time before, he had sent two legions into Macedonia to head off the section of the Pompeian army that was advancing from Syria under Metellus Scipio. By moving to the support of those two legions which were retreating before Scipio, Caesar could not only save them from possible defeat but prevent the junction of Scipio with Pompey. At the same time, he could lure Pompey from the safety of his base on the coast and in all probability force him to expose his unseasoned troops to the unequal hazard of a pitched battle.

Caesar's move presented Pompey with a difficult decision. He had two courses open. On the one hand, he could do what Caesar expected and pursue him into inland Greece; on the other hand, master as he was of the seacoast and the sea, he could ferry his army back to Italy and recover Rome. At a council of war some of his advisers are said to have urged him to take the latter course, recover Gaul and Spain, and seal off Caesar in the East.[50] However, the opposing arguments were overwhelming. Not only would it take long, hard fighting to recover Gaul and Spain, but, in the meanwhile, Caesar would gain possession of the vast resources of the East, which Pompey could not afford to let him do. In the end, he would return much stronger than he was now, and Pompey would have lost his hold on the only part of the Empire on which he could rely to support his forces. The hard fact had to be faced that Pompey and his associates could never be safe until Caesar's legions were destroyed, and this could not be accomplished by always running away from them. Moreover, Scipio and his army could not be abandoned without dishonor. It was true that Pompey's levies were raw and unseasoned compared with Caesar's veteran troops; but, at the moment, they were in high courage and confidence because of their victory at Durazzo, whereas Caesar's men were gloomy and disheartened by that defeat.

In this last calculation, Pompey committed a serious error. With his superb understanding of practical psychology, Caesar knew how to win advantage from the disheartened temper of his men and turn it into an instrument of victory. Indeed, no better instance could be cited of Caesar's manipulation of psychology as an ingredient of leadership than his conduct toward his troops at this juncture. He permitted "no signs of dejection, nor of a sense of difficulty to appear in his conduct. He had so artfully soothed the vanity of his soldiers by extenuating their defeat, and imputing it to any cause rather than to a want of courage or zeal on their part, that the men were less dismayed than irritated by their disaster; and feeling grateful to their general for the kindness of his behaviour towards them, they were impatient for an opportunity of retrieving their disgrace, and of proving to him that his confidence in them had not been bestowed unworthily." [51] Caesar himself tells us that the chagrin and disappointment of his soldiers burned down into a bitter rage, which showed itself in more than ordinary devotion to duty and a grim determination to wipe out their disgrace. He knew that there was no more potent incentive to victory than the memory of a defeat to be avenged. On the other hand, the taste of success which had come to Pompey's fledgeling soldiers inspired them with a rash and dangerous confidence. "Pompey's young troops now fancied themselves invincible, and . . . were fatally elated." [52] This mood seems to have misled the general himself, and Pompey appears to have concluded that, since Caesar would ultimately have to be faced, it might be well to humor the enthusiasm of his men by going after him in pursuit while the mood of victory was still upon them.

Leading his army inland in a southeasterly direction by a hard and difficult track up the steep valley of the Aous to a pass in the Pindus range, near Janina, Caesar crossed over into the high uplands of northwestern Thessaly. Pompey correctly saw the folly of being drawn into country where the enemy could turn and make a stand at countless vantage points in the mountains, and he accordingly took a different route which had an important strategic advantage. He followed the Egnatian Way, the broad and easy highroad which the Romans had built from Durazzo to Thessalonica, with the intention of there turning southward along the coast, and thus keeping between Caesar and the sea. In this way he ensured that his own troops would be adequately provisioned by water, and he could confine Caesar to upland terrain where the forage would soon be exhausted. However, as he marched his army eastward along the Egnatian Way, he met another of those strokes of ill-fortune which had so large a share in defeating him. Domitius Calvinus,

who headed the two legions of Caesar's army which had been sent
into Macedonia, and with which he had been unable to communicate, was retiring westward along the same road before Metellus
Scipio. Because of inadequate scouting, Pompey was not aware of
this, and the news of Caesar's retreat into Thessaly reached Calvinus
just a few hours before Pompey would have met and overwhelmed
him with superior numbers. Calvinus was thus enabled to turn aside
and join his chief safely on the eastern slopes of the Pindus. Pompey
continued on and, after effecting a junction with Scipio, disposed his
enlarged forces in the important lowland city of Larissa.

Meanwhile, Caesar had come down from the mountains for
the purpose of finding better country to provision his troops. The
first town before which he arrived refused to open its gates, and
again Caesar showed his mastery of military psychology by seizing
this opportunity to revive the spirits of his men in a way that he
knew would, and did, appeal to them. He ordered the town to be
taken by storm and sacrificed the unfortunate inhabitants to a wild
orgy of drunken lust and blood-letting. The incident also served as
a warning to other towns, and he was soon master of all northwestern Thessaly. Pompey was thus presented with the problem of
what to do next. It seems to have been his hope that if Caesar could
be confined in the interior, his supplies would run out, but that outcome, of course, would provide no final solution. Deprived of supplies, Caesar would almost certainly try to break out toward the
east or south, and Pompey would either have to pursue the Fabian
strategy of dogging his footsteps and trying to lay waste the country on which he relied for subsistence, or else squarely meet him in
battle. The former course offered no assurance of success, and it had
the disadvantage of requiring a degree of stamina and patient persistence that could hardly be expected from such troops as he had.

It was a tradition in antiquity, repeated by almost all historians,
that Pompey was forced to fight by the insistence of his aristocratic
advisers—the senators, knights and others who accompanied him—
when he had not the strength of will to resist. It is said that he himself decided, "on the most prudent calculation to protract the war
and wear out the enemy by hunger from day to day. Pompey was
surrounded by a great number of senators, of equal rank with him-

self, . . . [who] by reason of their inexperience in war, others because they were too much elated by the victory at Dyrrachium [Durazzo], others because they outnumbered the enemy, and others because they were tired of the war and preferred a quick decision rather than a sound one—all urged him to fight. . . . Yet harassed by the whole army, which was unduly puffed up by the victories at Dyrrachium, and by men of rank who accused him of being fond of power and of delaying purposely in order to prolong his authority over so many men of his own rank—and for this reason called him derisively king of kings and Agamemnon because that general also ruled over kings while war lasted—he allowed himself to be moved from his purpose and gave in to them, . . . and he prepared for battle against his will, to his own hurt and that of the men who had persuaded him to it." [53]

This is the traditional story. Doubtless it is true that throughout the campaign Pompey had trouble with the opinionated and self-important aristocrats around him who chafed at his authority and went out of their way to make him feel that they were his equals. Doubtless it is also true that many of these nobles were by now tired of the war and anxious to bring it to a quick conclusion so that they could return to the comforts and luxuries of the capital. Yet, on reviewing the history of the campaign as a whole, and in the light of the circumstances in which Pompey found himself, and of the alternatives with which he was presented, it seems unreasonable to believe that he offered battle wholly against his own military judgment and because of the impatience of the nobles in his camp. There was wisdom in fighting before his men lost the feeling of confidence which they had gained at Durazzo. "Nothing in Pompey's career hitherto as a general suggests that he would have permitted his calculations to be influenced by the clamour of mere impatience. He must, therefore, be credited with the belief that . . . he could not expect in the near future a more favourable opportunity." [54] This conclusion is justified by the nature of his army. As already stated, his legions were inexperienced and undependable. A large proportion of his troops was composed of foreign auxiliaries brought together from Eastern tribes and dependencies, and they were certain to grow restive and melt away if the war was protracted. The issue could not, therefore, be long deferred, and, if it was to be promptly decided, the present situation seemed to present one highly advantageous circumstance. Pompey's position was superior to that of Caesar chiefly because of the number and excellence of his cavalry; and, now that Caesar had come down into the plains, there was no terrain on which Pompey's cavalry could be used to greater advantage. As the event proved, he relied on them to win the battle; and this circumstance, taken in conjunction with the others, may well have been the determining factor of his decision. At all events, as Caesar moved toward the east and south, Pompey led his troops out of Larissa and advanced southwestward, and thus the two armies came face to face.

On a slope above a nameless river was fought the great "battle in Thessaly," as Caesar calls it, giving it no other name, but which after ages have spoken of as "Pharsalus" or "Pharsalia." The site of the battlefield remains unknown, but it is believed to have been not far from Cynoscephalae, the "hill of dogs' heads," below which the Romans had defeated Philip of Macedon in their first victory on Greek soil a century and a half earlier. When the battle lines were drawn up opposite each other, Pompey's was somewhat higher up the slope and with its back to the hill. He massed his cavalry on his left wing, intending it to charge around Caesar's right flank and take the latter's infantry in the rear. The cavalry charge was made as planned, but Caesar knew of it in advance and devised a simple but novel expedient to frustrate it. He detached six of his best cohorts—perhaps as many as three thousand men—and drew them up slightly behind the corner of his right wing, at right angles to his main line and facing in the direction from which Pompey's cavalry would come. Accordingly, when the latter charged around Caesar's flank, they found themselves unexpectedly confronted by a wall of spears. Caesar had instructed these troops not to hurl their weapons, but to stand fast and thrust at the faces of the charging horsemen.

The result was all that Caesar intended. Pompey's horsemen, surprised and unexpectedly halted, were thrown into confusion and then broke in flight back to their own lines with Caesar's men in pursuit. Meanwhile, Pompey's infantry, on which he had hesitated to rely, had stood firm against the charge of Caesar's main battle line, but were now displaced and broken on their left by the flight of their returning horsemen. At this juncture, Caesar threw against Pompey's right and center the reserves which he had held back to protect his rear. This decided the battle, which turned into a rout. Caesar took Pompey's camp but did not permit his men to halt for rest or plunder; instead, he pressed on after the fugitives, most of whom he succeeded in entrapping before nightfall among the hills. He received their surrender mercifully on the following morning and extended amnesty to all who laid down their arms. He had instructed his men even during the fighting to spare all the Roman soldiers who gave themselves up, and after the battle no blood was shed. Pompey's eastern auxiliaries did not enjoy the same fate, and large numbers of them were put to the sword.

The battle of Pharsalus destroyed Pompey's army and deprived him of the means of continuing the war, at least on land. He took refuge in Larissa with the survivors of his headquarters staff, but the senatorial group which had followed him to Greece rapidly disintegrated. Several senators had fallen on the field. Cicero and Cato had not accompanied Pompey to Thessaly, and the former now returned to Italy, while the latter sailed for Africa, which was still in the hands of the Pompeians. The rest made their way to the places where they thought they would be safe. Some went on to the East, and others joined the Pompeian fleet based on Durazzo, which still controlled the Adriatic and the waters surrounding Sicily. It has been suggested that Pompey's soundest course after the battle would have been to join his fleet and, using Africa as his base, make the most of the supremacy at sea which still remained to him.[55] He did not do so, however, but with a few companions made his way to the Thessalian coast and embarked in a merchant ship for Egypt, a refuge which he seems to have had in mind from the beginning.

Pompey's flight to Egypt had momentous and unforeseen consequences. It had the immediate effect of involving Caesar in a new and essentially different war, which introduced into Roman history a novel and extrinsic factor that persisted for almost two decades and came near to determining the ultimate direction of Roman political development. Hitherto, as already explained, Egypt

had been a lure for more than one powerful Roman politician because of its enormous revenue-producing capacity, but up to now all
had stopped short of bringing Egyptian influences actively into the
politics of Rome. At last, however, that step was imminent as an
indirect consequence of Pompey's decision to take refuge in Egypt.

The sequence of events took its start from the fact that at this
time the internal affairs of Egypt were once more involved in deep
confusion. Pompey's protégé, Ptolemy Auletes, the "flute-player,"
was dead. He had left four surviving children, two sons and two
daughters, of whom the daughters were the eldest. In his will he
had named his elder daughter, Cleopatra, a girl of less than twenty,
and his elder son, Ptolemy Dionysus, a boy in his early teens, as joint
heirs to the throne, reigning together under one of those brother-
sister marriages which were traditional in the Ptolemaic dynasty.
The power which was legally and nominally in the hands of these
child-princes was actually, after the fashion of the East, wielded
by the chief palace eunuch, one Pothinus, acting in conjunction
with the commander of the royal mercenary army. Apparently
Pothinus had no difficulty in controlling the boy-king, but Cleopatra
was a girl of independent mind, clever and masterful, and she
wished personally to exercise the powers of her station. Accordingly
the palace ring drove her into Syria, where she collected an army
to effect her restoration. This force was now facing the royal troops
before Pelusium, a fortress near the eastern mouth of the Nile, at
the moment when Pompey was approaching the coast of Egypt.[56]

The girl-queen Cleopatra made her first appearance with a
display of independence and resolute self-will and was destined for
a generation to be one of the principal figures on the stage of Roman
history. In the years that were to follow she was to wield an influence and have a part in shaping the course of Roman political
development far more important than that of most senators and
generals, and inferior only to two or three others among the great
figures of an age when politics were dominated by personalities.
The character and temperament, the ambitions and stratagems of
this remarkable woman are so unlike any which had figured in
Roman history before that it is easy to forget that she was only one
in a long line of other Cleopatras, queens and princesses who pre-

ceded her in the royal house of Egypt, and who differed from her only in the extent by which she surpassed them in their familiar traits, and in the breadth and scope of her field of action. As Professor Mahaffy has put it:

She was one of a race in which almost every reigning princess for the last 200 years had been swayed by like storms of passion, or had been guilty of like daring violations of common humanity. What . . . Cleopatra, from the first to the last, had hesitated to murder a brother or a husband, to assume the throne, to raise and command armies, to discard or adopt a partner of her throne from caprice in policy, or policy in caprice? But hitherto this desperate gambling with life had been carried on in Egypt and Syria; the play had been with Hellenistic pawns— Egyptian or Syrian princes; the last Cleopatra came to play with Roman pieces, easier apparently to move than the others, but implying higher stakes, greater glory in the victory, greater disaster in the defeat. Therefore is it that this last Cleopatra, probably no more than an average specimen of the beauty, talent, daring, and cruelty of her ancestors, has taken an unique place among them in the imagination of the world, and holds her own even now and for ever as a familiar name throughout the world.[57]

That this Cleopatra was able to attain her unique position in the world's portrait gallery of drama and romance was primarily the result of Pompey's decision to take refuge in Egypt. It was that decision which gave her her opportunity, although Pompey himself was not aware of it, and Cleopatra certainly did not enter into his calculations. At the outset, she was merely an unimportant collateral factor in a situation she was soon to dominate. Pompey's decision to go to Egypt was undoubtedly founded on the fact that many of the veterans of Gabinius were now soldiers in the royal Egyptian army. These men had originally served under Pompey in his eastern campaigns and might be expected to feel some loyalty and affection for their old commander. He might therefore expect not merely to find a welcome among them but through them to attain a position of importance and power at the court of a dynasty which owed so much to his intervention and support. If he could in this way get a foothold of influence in the government of a country having the vast financial resources of Egypt, where those resources were at the absolute disposal of the government, he might hope again to become a factor in the power politics of the Mediterranean world. As he made his way eastward, he assembled a small force of about two thousand armed men at Cyprus, and with this little army and a considerable sum of money he set sail for the camp of the young king at Pelusium, where he expected to find a cordial welcome.[58]

Pompey's calculations in making for Egypt were clearly divined in two quarters where they aroused no sympathetic response. Caesar understood them at once when he crossed over to Asia with part of his army and learned that Pompey had gone on to the East. So important did he think the matter, and so needful of haste, that with only three thousand men and ten ships of war he started at once in pursuit. Apparently he thought it imperative that Pompey should not be allowed to establish a footing in Egypt, and Caesar's judgment in this respect suggests that Pompey's decision may have been sounder than it might otherwise seem.

Caesar was not the only one to be alarmed: others, too, saw their position threatened if Pompey's plans should work out as he intended. These were the members of the palace ring who ruled Egypt in the name of the boy king. They saw their power menaced if so important a personage as Pompey, who had such claims on the loyalty of the Egyptian army, were received in their midst. Accordingly, they decided that "a dead man does not bite," [59] and when Pompey's ship dropped anchor in the harbor before the royal camp at Pelusium he was set upon and stabbed to death. In this almost casual way, a great career came to an end, and the man who for a generation had overshadowed the public life of Rome, who had been so largely responsible for vast changes that he neither intended nor understood, faded from the scene for reasons in no way connected with Rome or the issues of Roman politics. With Pompey's death an era came to a close. The future was now open to Caesar.

III

When Caesar followed Pompey to Egypt, it is clear from his subsequent actions that he had in view very much the same object as his rival—to bring under his control the government and re-sources of the country which was the treasure house of the world. He wanted money and wanted it immediately, for apparently the funds he had seized the year before from the treasury at Rome were now giving out; and, with a favorable or compliant government in Egypt, he saw a way of gaining possession of further riches. He was prepared to make his demands in the form of a claim of legal right. When Ptolemy the "flute-player" had needed money in his dealing with Rome, and particularly to pay his great bribe to Gabinius, he had borrowed it from a company of Roman financiers headed by one Gaius Rabirius Postumus, who had tried to obtain repayment by having Ptolemy make him his collector of taxes. Rabirius seems to have recovered only a small amount in this way, whereupon he and his associates assigned the debt to Caesar. Caesar thus appeared in Egypt with a claim for many millions against the Egyptian government as assignee of the late king's credi-tors.[60]

It is proof of Caesar's reckless boldness at this stage of his career that he descended on Egypt with a mere handful of soldiers. Pompey, at least, had grounds for anticipating that he would be re-ceived as a leader by his former troops now in the Egyptian army, but Caesar had no such expectation. If Pompey's hopes had been realized and he had won the support of the Egyptian army forces, as there was at least a chance that he might do, it is interesting to speculate what fate might have befallen Caesar when matched against those forces under the command of a Roman general. Once again, however, fortune befriended him, and his luck held good. When he arrived at Alexandria, Pompey was dead, and his slayers were miserably anxious to make friends with his successful rival and win gratitude for their act.

Caesar had no intention of allowing the Egyptians to use him, or of complying with their expectation of gratitude. Instead, he treated their cowardly murder of a prominent Roman as ground for assuming an attitude of stern severity, and he announced that as consul of the Roman republic he had come to exercise his jurisdic-tion to hear and decide the dispute over the succession to the Egyptian throne.[61] His bold assurance momentarily cowed opposition, and he was able with his troops to take possession of the royal palace, a strong citadel fronting on the inner harbor of Alexandria. From there he issued a summons to the young king and his sister Cleopatra, ordering them to disband their armies, lay their case before him and abide by his decision. Meanwhile, he obtained possession of the person of the king and kept him in protective custody. At the same time, he presented to Pothinus, as administrative head of the government, his demand for payment of the late king's debt.

This was hardly what Pothinus and the other ruling courtiers expected. When they recovered from their surprise, they began to intrigue against their unwelcome guest. With the royal army as well as the turbulent city mob of Alexandria at their disposal, they had reason to suppose that it would not be difficult to overpower Caesar's small force and do away with him almost as easily as they had done away with Pompey. They were, of course, prepared to act in the name of the young Ptolemy and professedly for the purpose of liberating their monarch from captivity in the hands of a foreign invader. The cause of the young king thus became the cause of the enemies of Caesar. Before they were ready to act, however, an important development occurred. It became apparent both to Caesar and to Cleopatra that they could be of use to each other. If Ptolemy's claims were to be made a rallying point of opposition to Caesar, the latter could make capital out of supporting the claim of Ptolemy's rival. Cleopatra, on the other hand, whose Syrian army seems to have been beaten off or melted away, could save her position only through Caesar's support. She desperately needed help and was willing to pay for it in her own way.

Whether Caesar sent for Cleopatra, as Plutarch supposes, or whether she sensed that he would be willing to aid her and so went to him of her own accord, she made her way to Alexandria in a boat and disembarked by night at the landing-stage of the palace where Caesar was lodged. The familiar story is that to avoid detection she was smuggled inside by her slaves, wrapped in a roll of oriental carpets, and had herself carried to his apartment, where Caesar saw for the first time the seductiveness of her charms. The connection then and there formed between them would be beneath notice had it been only a casual amour, but it was destined to have an extraordinary importance in the history of Rome and of the West which dwarfs the romantic aspect of the liaison. Cleopatra was a young woman of great personal beauty and magnetism, combining elegance and wit with a capacity for raw animalism. She was already skilled in the arts of seduction, and Caesar throughout his life had always been ready to be tempted by beautiful women. It is hardly surprising that she was able to appeal as excitingly and intensely as she did to the jaded sensibilities of a man in his middle fifties.

Caesar, however, had always been too cool and calculating by temperament to allow himself to be diverted from his main objectives by indulgence in casual pleasures. Wherever possible he combined business with pleasure, and in his affair with Cleopatra his keen intelligence saw the opportunity of securing control of the government and resources of Egypt. It seems soon to have occurred to him that the cheapest and most effective way of securing Egypt was by a personal and more or less permanent union with the sovereign of the country. If such a union could be cemented and maintained on an amatory basis, many difficulties might be avoided; and the boldness and novelty of the conception from a Roman viewpoint were precisely such as to appeal to Caesar's imagination. Doubtless the plan did not take shape in his mind at the beginning of their liaison, when Cleopatra must have seemed a mere pawn in the petty game of Egyptian intrigue; but when he became aware, as he soon did, of her remarkable intelligence and strength of will, he came to see her as a valuable partner for the attainment of his objectives. Yet their relationship did not stop at this point. She soon began to exercise a real influence over his thoughts and ambitions. She had more to teach him than the art of love, and in the end she probably had more influence upon him than any single individual. Through him she helped to introduce into the stream of Western political thought the concept of the divinity of secular rulers.

The first days and weeks of Caesar's affair with Cleopatra in the palace of Alexandria were passed in the midst of great perils.[62] Indeed, during those days Caesar was in more desperate personal danger than at any other time in his life. The Egyptian army, with the aid of the infuriated city mob, were now blockading the palace on the land side, so that it was imperative for Caesar to preserve his communications at sea by maintaining control of the inner harbor. He seized the famous lighthouse island of Pharos, but after desperate water fighting it was lost again to the Egyptians. Help finally arrived from Syria under one Mithridates of Pergamum, whom Caesar had commissioned to raise whatever troops he could as quickly as possible. Caesar ferried his own small contingent across the harbor to join this motley array, but before leaving he was astute enough to release the young Ptolemy, who at once joined the Egyptian army and thus placed himself in open opposition to Caesar. A battle was fought near the Nile; the king was slain, and Caesar was overwhelmingly victorious. Pothinus and his associates were wiped out, and Caesar was now master of Egypt. He thereupon recognized Cleopatra as queen and regularized her position under the Ptolemaic system by marrying her to her surviving younger brother, a mere child. At the same time, he safeguarded his own hold on the country by substituting for the former royal army a Roman garrison consisting of the troops which he had brought to Egypt, reenforced by a legion from Syria and commanded by a Roman professional soldier appointed by himself.[63]

It was now March of the year 47. Caesar had been in Egypt almost half a year. Eight months had passed since his victory at Pharsalus, and nearly fifteen months since he had last been in Rome. There and in the provinces the situation had been rapidly deteriorating. Nominally, Rome had been under the government of Servilius, his colleague in the consulate, but after Pharsalus, Caesar had sent home the greater part of his army under Mark Antony, and Antony seems to have resumed the position of military commander of Italy, relegating Servilius to a subordinate status. Agitation for radical economic measures had again broken out at the capital. A program for the cancellation of debts was proposed, the city was disturbed by rioting, and the troops, who had not yet been paid off, were becoming mutinous. No arrangements had been made for holding the elections, and as the end of the year approached the prospect was imminent that the state would again be left without lawfully constituted magistrates. In this situation it was natural that a proposal was made, probably at the instance of Antony, that Caesar should be named dictator again, with the right to fill all the magistracies and provincial governorships and, in addition, to exercise tribunician powers. The program was carried out, and Antony was designated as the dictator's deputy, or "master of the horse." In the absence of his principal, however, Antony hesitated to act with firmness, and the disorders increased. Meanwhile, the conservatives were gathering in force and building up a formidable power in the province of Africa. "There the fragments of the army scattered at Pharsalus, the troops that had garrisoned Dyrrhachium, Corcyra and the Peloponnesus, the remains of the Illyrian fleet, gradually congregated; there the second commander-in-chief Metellus Scipio, the two sons of Pompeius, Gnaeus and Sextus, the political leader of the republicans Marcus Cato, the able officers Labienus, Afranius, Petreius, Octavius and others met. . . . As neither Caesar himself nor any of his lieutenants undertook the smallest movement against Africa, the coalition had full time to acquire political and military reorganization." [64] Finally, there was danger that the entire East might be lost to Rome, or could be retained only at the cost of a great war. "Pharnaces, the son and successor of Mithradates, had been left in possession of his father's Bosporan kingdom when the Pontic territories in Asia Minor were either made into Roman provinces or handed over to client-kings. The outbreak of the civil war had emboldened him to attempt the reconquest of his father's lost empire. . . . Instead of joining Pompey, he invaded Pontus and the adjacent countries. . . . There was for the moment nothing to stop him. He overran great part of Cappadocia . . . and occupied the Lesser Armenia." [65] Calvinus, whom Caesar had left in charge in Asia Minor, at last managed to collect sufficient troops to march against him but was completely defeated in a battle fought near Nicopolis, in western Armenia, where most of his army was scattered or destroyed. Pharnaces then went into winter quarters in Pontus with every prospect of overrunning and taking posssession of Asia Minor in the following spring.

In the face of all these gathering storms, Caesar made no haste to leave Egypt after the close of the Alexandrian war. Instead he lingered on for several months, allowing his men to rest and enjoy themselves, and indulging himself in a belated honeymoon with Cleopatra. The spell of the country seems to have affected him profoundly, emotionally and intellectually. With the coming of spring he allowed her to take him on an extended excursion up the Nile to visit the monuments of Egypt's former glory. They traveled with all the stupendous magnificence which the sovereigns of Egypt's royal house affected, and their flotilla is said to have numbered no less than four hundred sail—yachts, barges, supply boats and other craft.[66] Only after the termination of this royal progress did he at last consent to tear himself away from the classic land of enchantment and from the romantic enchantress whom he had set up to rule over it. Some months after his departure, Cleopatra gave birth to a male child whose paternity she ascribed to him, and to whom she gave the name of Caesarion; but Caesar never publicly acknowledged or displayed any particular interest in the child, and the ascription of paternity was indignantly repudiated by his partisans on the ground of the well-known character of the mother.

Caesar was severely criticized in his own time, and has been criticized ever since, for his delay in Egypt and for his apparent surrender to the sybaritic lethargy of the country. There is no doubt that he played a risky game and took long chances in postponing the necessary steps to meet the dangers with which he was beset; but it was a characteristic of Caesar's, and one that grew on him as he became older, to take long chances, and his conduct in this instance suggests a strategy which was not out of keeping with his temperament and should surprise no one familiar with his career. A number of considerations suggest themselves as reasons for his delay. The first of these was his fixed resolution to bring as much money as possible out of Egypt, and the accomplishment of this design undoubtedly required much coaxing and wheedling of Cleopatra. In the existing state of their personal relations, he could hardly resort to the hasty method of crude force, and he therefore had to await a favorable opportunity. At this point the need for money appears to have been Caesar's foremost consideration, and it remained so throughout his stay in the East. In the second place, so far as the disorderly conditions prevailing at Rome were concerned, Caesar's delay in meeting them was consonant with a strategy that was also characteristic of him. He always counted on deriving advantage from a state of disorder in the capital, and, in the present instance, if he intervened before the disorder became serious enough, he might create expectations in one group or another which he could not satisfy, and thus incur needless enmities. If, on the other hand, he stayed his hand until the disorder became severe enough to be regarded as intolerable by a preponderance of the population, he could count on overwhelming support in suppressing it in whatever manner he pleased, and so could not only avoid dangerous criticism of his actions but expect to have a favorable opportunity to enhance his power still further. His apparent lack of concern about the revival and reorganization of the republican forces in Africa seems to have stemmed from a different cause. Caesar's uninterrupted and almost incredible series of successes over a period of more than ten years had unquestionably made a deep impression on his mental processes and attitude. He had always had a superstitious belief in his "star," or "fortune," and there is little doubt but that he had by now come to look on himself as invincible. From a coldly practical standpoint, he must have recognized his superiority in strategy, organizing ability and willpower over the republican leaders who were once more gathering against him. Now, however, there was an additional element in his mental outlook. Always possessed of a supreme faith in himself, he now identified that faith with something higher—fate, fortune or divinity—and regarded himself as proved by his unprecedented success to be the embodiment and incarnation of an unseen power. His cool, clear and calculating intellect lost none of its acuteness in passing under the spell of this self-centered mysticism, but the union of calculating intelligence with mystical self-exaltation made him what he was to be for the remainder of his life.

Caesar's stay in Egypt and his subjection to its influence helped to feed this mystical identification of himself with the supernatural and brought it, perhaps for the first time, to self-conscious realization. It may well have been for this reason, among others, that he desired to linger in an atmosphere which was so congenial to the new conception of himself that was taking shape within him. As he sailed up the Nile with Cleopatra and beheld the stupendous temples of the eighteenth and nineteenth dynasties at Thebes and

Karnak, "he must have looked upon the reliefs depicting the divine birth of the queen Hatsheput at Deir el Bahri, and have visited the shrine of Seti I, which lay beside the sanctuaries of the great gods, Isis, Osiris and Ammon at Abydos. With these monuments of the Pharaohs of old he must have beheld the reliefs that showed the Ptolemies as the heir of all their power and divinity—the great pylons of Ptolemy Euergetes at Karnak, for instance, or the gateways but lately erected by Ptolemy the Flute Player at Edfu and Philae. And Caesar saw not merely the hollow shell which makes an unforgettable impression on the modern visitor to Egypt. He probably witnessed the ceremonies with which the Egyptian people were erecting statues in all their temples to their new queen, worshipping as a revealed divinity among them the last of the house of the Ptolemies, the divine Cleopatra. At every stage of the journey he must have stood by and beheld his companion adored in actual divinity and he doubtless noted how her orders were accepted not merely as the words of a ruler but as the commands of a god." [67]

It cannot have been without significance for Caesar that he was the master as well as the lover of Cleopatra, this goddess-queen and earthly embodiment of divinity, and that she owed to him and to him alone her royal station. If he was thus master of a living god dess, and, in a sense, the creator of a goddess, what was he to think of himself? There cannot be much doubt that Cleopatra contributed at least in some degree to Caesar's conception of himself as having transcended ordinary human limitations and that this conception, apart from obvious practical advantages, grew to be one of the reasons for which he valued the connection. His mind went back to the traditions of his own ancient family and to the legend that represented the Julian race as descended from Venus, a legend in which he had long before publicly professed his belief, in delivering the funeral oration of his aunt Julia.[68] In Cleopatra he saw a reincarnation of the goddess of love and passion, an identification which he afterward suggested when he placed the queen's statue in the temple of Venus at Rome.[69]

For all these reasons, and in all these various ways, Caesar seems to have been converted or almost converted, to a belief in his own divinity, the conviction that he was, or was becoming, a god—"the unconquered god," as he afterwards openly avowed. In the conventional fashion of the East, he had already been hailed as divine by several Greek cities in honor of his victory at Pharsalus,[70] and now he was coming to regard the honor seriously. The illusion seems to have taken possession of him in Egypt, and it was in keeping with the atmosphere of the place; whether it could survive in another atmosphere his clear intelligence must have questioned. It was, however, an exhilarating and comforting illusion, and he wished to enjoy it.

To reduce so complex a mind and temperament as Caesar's to a simple and consistent pattern of beliefs and impulses is hardly possible. Yet some historians, such as Professor Adcock, have attempted to do so in rejecting the idea that he could ever have consented to take advantage for his own purposes of a willingness on the part of others to deify him. Such a possibility, it is said, must be "rejected as little suited to what we know of Caesar's own acts and of his attitude of mind."[71] "Amid the honours paid to him he presumably remained coolly detached."[72] Under that view it must be supposed that Caesar could never have sought on his own initiative, or by any effort of his own, to bolster his authority by making a claim to divinity for political reasons, since such a claim would be so inconsistent with the cool and skeptical mentality that he elsewhere displayed as to be out of character. If this view is accepted, it would even more definitely exclude the possibility that Caesar could for a moment have deluded himself with a belief that he was divine.

This view, however, is too rationalistic and simple. To maintain that Caesar did not, from now on, seek on more than one occasion to find support for his authority in a claim of divinity would be to disregard or misinterpret well-attested historical evidence. Moreover, that a man like Caesar should have been willing to make such a claim, as he indubitably did in the final stages of his life, although explicable as policy, can hardly be attributed to policy alone. The fact that Caesar would initiate such a claim, even for the sake of policy, indicates in itself that his mentality was no longer entirely normal and that it must already have been suffused with such egotism as to be unable clearly to distinguish between pretensions and reality. However cool and impersonal Caesar's intellect may always have been, and have still remained, in its aspect of calculating intelligence, the vastness to which his ambition, fed by success, had now attained, denotes abnormality, and abnormality of precisely the kind to which a claim of divinity would be congenial. That Caesar was too shrewd to make a public display of this claim at all times and places, and especially before he was quite sure that he could make it effective, is doubtless true. He would have to test out by degrees the extent to which he could advance it at Rome, and this again furnishes a reason for his having lingered where he could for the moment indulge it without fear of opposition or ridicule.

Caesar seems to have left Alexandria about the first of July in the year 47. He had two immediate objectives before him. His indispensable business was to dispose of Pharnaces, but he apparently had such implicit confidence in his success in that undertaking that he combined it with the complicated and time-consuming task of readjusting the organization of the provinces and client-states of the entire Roman East. The latter task was more to his taste and, in a sense, more important from his standpoint, since he intended to make it a profitable source of additional funds. This objective he was able to accomplish, partly by imposing fines on those princes or cities which had given aid to Pompey, partly by levying requisitions on temple treasuries and partly by exacting a price for the titles or privileges which he granted or confirmed to cities and individuals.[73] He held court first at Antioch and then at Tarsus, and the obsequious Eastern states and potentates were glad to accept whatever terms he meted out to them and pay whatever price he asked. At Tarsus he collected a small army and marched inland over the mountains to deal with Pharnaces. As usual, his luck held good. Had Pharnaces acted promptly and commenced the campaign before Caesar was upon him, he might have overrun the interior of Asia Minor and threatened the favorable outcome of the war; as it was, he allowed Caesar to seize the initiative and stood on the defensive on the Pontic frontier. There, at Zela, near the spot where Mithridates had defeated Triarius twenty years before, a stiff, hard battle was fought in August and resulted in a complete victory for Caesar and the flight of Pharnaces to the Crimea. Nowhere are

Caesar's pride of success and assurance of invincibility more clearly displayed than in the famous dispatch of three words in which he reported his victory to Rome, *"veni, vidi, vici"*—"I came, I saw, I conquered."

Thereafter, Caesar moved westward through Asia Minor, adjusting boundaries, confirming privileges, levying fines and collecting money as before. From Bithynia he sailed for Italy and landed at Taranto on the 24th of September.[74] In Italy he found, as he doubtless expected, a scene of utter confusion and governmental paralysis within Rome and without. Some of his partisans, consisting of young experimentalists led by Cicero's aristocratic son-in-law Dolabella, had put forward a program in the tradition of Catiline looking to the further reduction or total cancellation of debts. One feature of that program which proved extremely popular was to relieve tenants from the payment of rent to their landlords. Another faction of Caesar's partisans, consisting no doubt of his supporters among the business classes, strongly resisted these proposals, and rioting and street fighting ensued. While this agitation went on, mutiny broke out among the legions quartered in Campania. Antony, who was the only person vested with any semblance of authority, put Rome in charge of a governor of his own choosing and went to the scene of the trouble, but he found himself unable to accomplish anything, and he returned to the city. There matters went from bad to worse. At first Antony hesitated to offend either faction by taking sides. He sought to gain time by temporizing but discovered that Dolabella was winning so much support as to threaten his own supremacy. The chief source of Dolabella's strength was his "no-rent" campaign, and he prepared to carry his measure by force in the fashion made familiar by Caesar and Clodius. Antony thereupon decided to meet force with force, and when the day for voting arrived he filled the Forum with soldiers. A ptiched battle resulted, in which eight hundred persons are said to have lost their lives.[75] The fighting ended on the eve of Caesar's return.

As usual, Caesar did the unexpected. It might have been supposed that the mutiny of a formidable army would have engaged his immediate attention, but his shrewd sense persuaded him that the most effective strategy for dealing with it was to show that he was not afraid of it by ignoring it. He therefore turned to the internal situation in Rome without taking any step to deal with the mutineers. The measures which he took in response to the economic agitation were once more of a purely tentative and makeshift character, but looked in a decidedly different direction from those which he had adopted when he had been in Rome two years before. Then, he had been careful to allay the fears of the moneyed interests; now, surprisingly, he supported, at least in part, the radical program of Dolabella. Caesar never did anything without a view to its effect on his power and position, and he must have concluded that he no longer had anything to fear from the business classes and had no further need of them in view of the enormous amounts of money and gold that he had brought back from the East. At the same time, he doubtless felt that he could not afford to alienate the urban populace, for, under the influence of agitators like Dolabella, they could give him serious trouble while he was dealing with the mutinous legions and during the war that he would soon have to wage against the republicans in Africa. He must have believed that he had to satisfy at least to some extent the expectations that Dolabella's agitation had raised. He therefore enacted a measure remitting house rents for a year at the expense of landlords, but applied it only to lower-class properties renting for the equivalent of approximately $100 a year or less, thus limiting the benefit to the low-income groups.[76] At the same time, he revised and liberalized the provisions of the law of debt relief which he had put into effect two years before. He also remitted all interest which had become due since the commencement of his war with Pompey, and he provided for a new and presumably higher valuation of property sold for debt.[77] He sought to create further support for the declining value of Italian real estate by requiring that all persons having capital to invest must invest a percentage of it—perhaps as high as two-thirds—in Italian land.[78] Of the economic effects of these measures we know nothing, but politically they seem to have succeeded in subduing agitation for the time being.

Caesar then turned to the mutineers. He sent Sallust, the historian, as an emissary to promise them each an extra cash bonus of the equivalent of $200 in addition to what he had already promised them after Pharsalus, but they drove him away, saying they were tired of promises and wanted cash. They then proceeded to march on Rome. It was significant of the existing state of affairs, as Heitland points out, "that we hear of no prominent leader, nor of any anti-Caesarian partisan trying to turn their fury to account. Though mutinous, they were still Caesar's army; they dealt with him only, he only could deal with them. There was no real alternative to Caesar, and he faced the situation with his usual nerve." [79] Appearing suddenly before them, he mounted a tribunal and asked what they wanted. Taken aback, no one mentioned a bonus, but when some called out that they wanted their discharge, Caesar at once replied "I discharge you," adding that he would pay them in full when he returned from Africa to celebrate his triumph with a new army. In this speech he used the forms of civil address, calling them "fellow citizens" and not "soldiers," so as to bring home to them that their military days were over. "It was they who were now in a dilemma. To destroy Caesar was to destroy their hopes of reward. To accept discharge, and leave him to go to Africa without them, would answer their purpose no better. Either he would perish, and their hopes with him, or he would return with a new victorious army, an army whose claims to glory and reward would override their own. This was not what they wanted. They had no effective means of extorting ready money from a master who was proof against intimidation, and they were in no hurry to exchange the sword and *pilum* for the spade and plough. They begged to be forgiven, and with affected reluctance he consented to accept their service as volunteers. In short he was master of them on his own terms." [80] Thus Caesar's shrewd psychological insight and extraordinary presence of mind rescued him again with entire success from a position of critical danger. In many ways, it was a greater victory than Pharsalus.[81]

With the mutiny disposed of, Caesar turned to making the most of his political position at Rome. He wished to replenish still further his cash resources and apparently thought the time had come when his policy of "clemency" could be somewhat relaxed in favor of his increasing financial requirements. Although he planned no proscriptions or bloodshed, he proceeded to confiscate the property of Pompeians who had been killed or were absent abroad. Further funds he obtained through the general exaction of forced "loans" from wealthy individuals and Italian communities. He seems, in other words, to have pursued the same policy in Italy as in the East, collecting as much money as possible from whatever sources and by whatever methods he could, and in these ways he continued to amass a vast fund entirely under his own control and for which he was not liable to account—a fund that could be used at his discretion for military, political and personal purposes indiscriminately.

Before leaving Rome, Caesar had to arrange for the government of the city during his absence. For this purpose he had his dictatorship renewed and also had himself elected consul for the following year, with Marcus Lepidus as his colleague. He seems at this time to have cooled toward Mark Antony and apparently intended that Lepidus should from now on be his personal representative in Italy. After making these arrangements, he left Rome in December for Sicily, where he mustered an expeditionary force of six legions for the conquest of the republicans in Africa.

In the period of almost eighteen months which had passed since Pharsalus, the republicans in Africa had collected under Metellus Scipio a formidable army of ten legions, besides a large force of cavalry and enough additional troops to garrison the principal towns on the northern and eastern coasts. They also had the support and alliance of King Juba of Numidia, who placed at their disposal the services of his strong native army. This alliance with a "barbarian" was highly repugnant to many Roman inhabitants of the African towns, who were further alienated by the heavy contributions that Scipio exacted. As a result, they were permeated with strongly pro-Caesar sentiment which was held in check only by the military preponderance of the republicans. So complete was the control exercised by the latter that when Caesar brought over the first part of his army from Sicily, he found all the ports closed against him and no landing place available execpt at the extreme southeastern corner of the province. The republican army marched at once to meet him, but he succeeded in fortifying a plateau above the beach and was able to resist attack as well as to maintain his communications by sea. As proved to be the case throughout this war, the republicans were unable to employ their naval strength effectively, and Caesar was thus able to receive supplies and reenforcements by sea.

Scipio sought to bring on a battle before his superiority in numbers was lost through the arrival of more of Caesar's legions, but the latter successfully eluded these efforts and in the meanwhile resorted to diplomacy in order to draw off the native allies of the republicans. By creating a diversion on the western frontier of Juba's kingdom, Caesar forced the latter to withdraw a large part of his troops from the support of Scipio, and meanwhile reenforcements soon brought Caesar's strength up to twelve legions. Preponderance in numbers thus passed to Caesar, who was now ready to bring on a battle. He massed his troops before the town of Thapsus and laid siege to it. Scipio brought up his army to hem in the besiegers but was compelled to divide his forces on the two sides of a lagoon in the rear of the city. This gave Caesar his opportunity. He threw his entire strength against one wing of Scipio's army and overwhelmed it; the other wing fled. Caesar was unable to check the fury of his veterans who fell upon, and butchered wholesale, enormous numbers of the foot soldiers. Most of Scipio's subordinate officers were spared but sent into exile. The republican leaders, including the two sons of Pompey, fled toward Spain, where a revolt against Caesar's deputies had already broken out, but many perished on the way. Juba killed himself, and Caesar annexed the kingdom of Numidia as a province after taking care to exact large fines from the individuals and communities that had supported the defeated side.

The dramatic climax of the war for Africa was not Caesar's victory at Thapsus but the death of Cato. Cato was not present at the battle, for he had been left in command of Utica, the republican headquarters. In that city there was a substantial colony of Roman businessmen and financiers who were by no means firm in their loyalty to the republican cause, and when the news arrived of the disaster at Thapsus, Cato permitted them to choose what course they would take. The story of their debates, hesitations and divided counsels, as told by Plutarch, affords a typical example of the behavior of prosperous human beings, with no interest in politics and with property at stake in a moment of crisis.[81] The episode helps to explain very clearly how Caesar won the civil war largely by his reputation for success and by the impression he created that it was futile to resist him. In the end, the Roman residents of Utica told Cato that they wished to submit to Caesar, and he did not oppose them. However, by tact and diplomacy he persuaded them to postpone their surrender until all the republican leaders, to the last man, had successfully made their way through the town to the ships that were to carry them abroad, or had equipped themselves for flight overland. In the meanwhile, he was able to protect the timid city dwellers from the fury of the returning fugitives from the republican army.

On the evening when the last republicans were leaving Utica, Cato invited some of the more prominent Roman residents to supper, at which he brought the conversation around to the Stoic theme that a good man is always free, since he always has it in his power to refrain from doing, or participating in, acts which do not conform to the standard of right and wrong. It seems clear that he did not admit defeat but contended that he now had the victory over Caesar from the standpoint of justice and honesty; that it was Caesar who should be looked on as vanquished, for he had now shown himself guilty of those very designs against his country which he had so long practiced and so consistently lied about. A good man, Cato said, would not be beholden to a tyrant for his preservation, since by so doing he would admit the tyrant's right over the lives of men whom he had no title to govern. After the party broke up, Cato withdrew to his room where he read Plato's dialogue, the *Phaedo,* on the immortality of the soul; later on in the night, when he had had word that the last refugee was safe on shipboard, he called for his sword and calmly killed himself.[82] Cato's suicide was, and was meant to be, a symbolic act. It was the end of the republic.

IV

Caesar's African victory not only enormously strengthened his prestige but seemed to have eliminated all organized opposition to his power, and when he returned to Rome the question began to be asked what steps he would take to reorganize the government and what changes, if any, he would introduce permanently into the constitution. He made no haste, however, to take up measures of long-range constructive reform. From the course which he followed, it seems likely that he thought some additional and more spectacular demonstration of his unprecedented success and supremacy was needed to cause the public mind to acquiesce still further in his position. For this purpose, he planned and carried out a triumph more stupendous than any which had been celebrated before, eclipsing by far the mammoth spectacle which Pompey had presented on his return from the East fifteen years earlier. The great pageant consumed four days, consisting in fact of four separate triumphs presented on alternate days.[83] With intentional delicacy of feeling and respect for what may be called "national" sensibilities, all direct allusion to the civil war was omitted, and no reference was made to the conflicts in Spain or at Pharsalus. Instead, the four triumphs were presented as celebrating victories over foreign nations, Gaul, Egypt, Pontus and Numidia, respectively, a separate day devoted to each. The processions included famous prisoners in chains: the great Gallic chief Vercingetorix, who had spent six years in a Roman dungeon; Arsinoë, the rebellious sister of Cleopatra; and the little prince Juba, son of the Numidian king. There was a vast display of banners and of pictures depicting scenes from the wars, such as the burning Pharos, or lighthouse, at Alexandria, the deaths of Pothinus, Juba, Metellus Scipio, and, remarkably enough, Cato. Each day, behind the great procession of marching and singing men, rode Caesar in gorgeous robes in his triumphal car drawn by white horses and preceded by forty-eight lictors.

In some respects the most remarkable feature of the pageant was the frank and open display of the immense mass of money and other tangible treasure which Caesar had accumulated from every land he had conquered—bullion, coined money, plate, jewels, gold and silver statues and ornaments. It was Pompey who had initiated the practice of exhibiting such collections as part of the spoils of war; now Caesar far outdid him. Whereas the gold, silver and jewels that heaped the wagons in Pompey's triumph had been valued at the rough equivalent of about twenty million dollars, the treasure that was exhibited in Caesar's triumph is said to have reached the then stupendous sum of seventy-five million.[84] To display such wealth to public gaze as the spoils of war was tantamount to a public announcement that Rome under her present leadership was frankly waging war as a money-making business and was treating her subject lands as tributaries to be milked for the advantage of those who controlled the military machine. The old senatorial conception of a hundred years before, that Rome's function was to rule as a just judge or arbiter between nations, had been supplanted by the "democratic" conception advanced by Gaius Gracchus, that Rome should extract the wealth of foreigners for the benefit of such of her people as were in a position to enforce their will.

That this had become for the moment a dominant philosophy is further borne out by the uses to which Caesar proceeded to put the wealth he had exhibited in his triumph immediately after the great spectacle was over. The largest part of it he distributed as an immense donation to his troops—more than a thousand dollars apiece to every private in the ranks, and equal to twenty-five years' pay at a time when twenty-five dollars in today's money was the annual wage of a Roman legionary.[85] What was left of the money after this enormous disbursement Caesar laid out in dazzling spectacles and entertainments for the civilian populace of Rome on a scale never dreamed of before. Games, gladiatorial shows, wild-beast fights went on for a month. A sham naval battle was exhibited on an artificial lake dug for the purpose in the Campus Martius, which set the fashion for the expensive type of entertainment that long retained its vogue under the Empire. The spectators at the games were shaded from the sun by awnings of silk brought from China, a fabric which for the first time now made its appearance in the West. On one day during the festivities, an immense feast with costly wines was spread for all who would partake, and 22,000 couches were required to seat the diners, three to a couch. On another day, the equivalent of twenty dollars apiece was distributed to all citizens entitled to receive the grain dole. During the celebration, the amount of that dole was enlarged and supplemented by free distributions of wine and oil. Rome in these days was mad with a frenzy of excitement and enjoyment, and the madness reached its pitch when two men were offered up for human sacrifice in a ceremony on the Campus Martius under the presidency of the pontiffs and the High Priest of Mars.[86] To this extent Caesar unleashed and played on the irrational mass instincts of the crowd to break down the resistance that reason and institutionalized self-restraint might offer to the dominance of his will. It is not without interest that there is no mention of this orgy of hysteria anywhere in the writings of Cicero, perhaps because, as a civilized Roman steeped in the traditions of Rome's past, he was unwilling to take notice of what was happening around him.

When the frenzy was over and had performed the function that Caesar intended, he turned, with his usual practical hardheadedness, to further consolidating his position. Enormous as were the expenditures he had made, and they must have consumed all the wealth he had publicly displayed in his triumph, he had certainly held back further amounts to provide for the ordinary expenses of government, for the maintenance of his army, and to build up the great private fortune which he was to leave at his death eighteen months later. Even so, however, it behooved him to practice economy, and he proceeded to do so in a way that was characteristically bold and contemptuous of public opinion. After stupifying the Roman populace with unparalleled largesse for the month of his triumph, he now curtailed at a single stroke, and in the most drastic way, their cherished privilege of the grain dole by ordering a complete revision of the list of those entitled to participate in its distribution and reducing the number from 320,000 to 150,000.[87] When it is recalled that the list had been inflated by Clodius, at a time when he was Caesar's agent, and that the dole had only recently been liberalized by Curio, another political henchman of Caesar's,[88] much light is shed on the sincerity of the dictator's belief in the "democratic" program on which he had so largely relied to advance himself to power.

In his repudiation of his "democratic" past, Caesar did not stop with curtailment of the grain dole. He went on to undo the other principal measure of Clodius's tribunate by again outlawing the ward clubs and guilds of which he and Clodius had made such effective use in controlling the Roman assemblies. He abolished those organizations as ruthlessly as the conservatives had attempted to do eighteen years before, except for a few geniuine trade guilds of ancient origin and certain clubs of Jews, for whom he always displayed a decided preference.

Caesar's apparent inconsistency in withdrawing time-honored privileges from the urban proletariat after courting their favor by the most lavish bounties and entertainments ever showered upon them illustrates his shrewd understanding of mob psychology and his strategy in manipulating it. He was obviously anxious to be rid of the continuing burden of the grain dole and of the ever-present threat from the ward organizations which might become serious at any moment. He therefore chose to strike at these popular institutions suddenly and unexpectedly just when he had made himself the object of an overwhelming passion of hysterical enthusiasm. He counted on the fact that such a mood would not suddenly reverse itself and that, before his popularity had cooled, the memory of his unpopular measures would already have been forgotten.

Caesar next proceeded to renew his dictatorship in such a way as to make it in effect permanent. This he did by making it an annual office, but providing at the same time that he should hold it continuously for ten yearly terms without the need for a renewal of his tenure. He then made himself consul for the ensuing year, 45 B.C., without a colleague. He had already been vested permanently with the tribunician power,[89] which gave him a veto on the acts of all other officials, as well as on the proceedings of the senate. It was further decreed that he should have a seat in the senate between the two consuls of the year if there should be other consuls than himself, and that he should always deliver his opinion first. He was given the right to appoint not only all provincial governors, but also the prefects who took over the functions traditionally performed by the praetors, aediles and questors.[90] He was made sole censor for three years, which carried with it the usual powers of the censorship to bestow citizenship, expel and create senators, and to let and supervise all public contracts. He was still, as he had long been,[91] chief pontiff, and, as such, he now resumed, after his many absences, the personal leadership of the Roman religion, with power to invoke or remit sacramental authority for governmental action.

With such an accumulation of powers there was no phase of Roman government which was not directly and immediately under Caesar's personal control. The Roman state had ceased to be a republic in the sense of a thing belonging to the people: it had become the property of an individual.

With Caesar's supremacy thus established and confirmed, thoughtful Romans still awaited an answer to the question of how he would use it, but again an answer was delayed by a new threat to Caesar's power. That threat proceeded from a formidable concentration of disaffected elements in Spain. Ever since the Spanish peninsula had afforded a refuge to the remnants of the Marian party in the days of Sulla, its possibilities as a foothold for malcontents awaiting an opportunity to strike a blow for their restoration had been well understood. Many of the leading Pompeians defeated at Thapsus had found their way to Spain and had been so favorably received that they were now in control of much of the peninsula.

The trouble in Spain had its origin in Caesar's habit of neglecting everything which he could not personally attend to, and of leaving power in the hands of political henchmen who often proved to be irresponsible if not disreputable. This proved to be the case with Cassius Longinus, a former tribune, whom he had left in command in Spain after conquering the peninsula in the first year of the civil war. During the ensuing two years, Longinus had made everything he could out of his position. "He had contracted great debt there, and he determined to release himself by imposing heavy demands on the province. Requisitions of money were made on the rich, and Cassius not only allowed, but ordered this money to be set down as paid to his account. Slight grounds of offence were invented; and no manner of gain either great or small was neglected, whether the profit came direct to the governor's residence or reached his hands through the courts of justice. No man who had anything to lose escaped from being either brought into court or charged with some offence; and thus the fear of personal injury was added to loss of property." [92] Soon the provincials were on the verge of revolt, and to meet this threat Longinus raised additional troops but did not pay them, with the result that mutiny broke out and developed into a full-fledged rebellion. Although Caesar replaced Longinus when he returned from Egypt in the autumn of 47, so bitter was the feeling that had developed against Caesar that a strong Pompeian party had sprung up which attracted the fugitives from Thapsus. Under the command of Gnaeus, son of Pompey, a formidable army of thirteen legions had taken possession of practically all of southern Spain.

In November of the year 46, Caesar left Rome in haste to deal with the insurgents. Traveling at his usual speed, he reached Spain in twenty-seven days. He made an unsuccessful attack on Gnaeus's headquarters at Cordova, and then began a hide-and-seek campaign in an effort to maneuver him into battle. Finally, Caesar decided to give battle on terrain where his enemies had the advantage. Gnaeus drew up his army along the summit of a slope near a town called Munda, not far east of Seville, and Caesar's men charged the slope. The conflict was one of the closest in Caesar's military career and lasted for hours. At last, a misunderstood tactical move by part of the Pompeian army threw the rest into confusion, and they broke in flight. Caesar's troops poured after them and killed or rode them down in a scene of unrestrained butchery. All the Pompeian leaders were slain or perished in their efforts to escape, with the exception of Sextus Pompey, brother of Gnaeus, who survived to make trouble a decade later.

V

Munda was Caesar's last campaign, and important though it was as marking the final end of the civil war, it was but the convulsive death agony of a political party whose defeat had come at Thapsus. That battle was the end of the republic, and Cato's death symbolized its extinction. His suicide announced to the world, as he intended it should, that the political forms and institutions which the old Roman spirit had worn as its outward integument for five centuries had at last perished from the earth. The remarkable fact is that Cato's act was recognized immediately for what it was, and the shock of the recognition among thoughtful men of the upper class at Rome caused a resurgence of a sense of the value of what had been lost at the moment when they realized that it could not be recovered. A mood developed, like that at a funeral, a mood which dwelt on the virtues and loss of the departed, and at the same time suggested the excellence of the things Cato had loved and stood for. Cicero, who was now living at Rome by the sufferance of Caesar, again showed his courage by taking the lead in raising his voice to give expression to this mood, and with his gift of language endowed it with the permanence and stability of words. He published a eulogy of Cato which won immediate and widespread popularity. Unfortunately the eulogy has not survived, but its essence is suggested in a letter written by Cicero while he was composing it:

> . . . I cannot succeed in writing what your guests can read not only gladly but with complacency. Even if I make no mention of his [Cato's] speeches in the senate, and of every wish and purpose which he entertained in politics, and use merely general terms to eulogize his firmness and consistency, this in itself would be an unpleasant tale for them. But that man cannot be truly praised unless these topics are fully developed: his having foreseen that the present state of things would come to pass; his having exerted himself to the utmost to prevent them, and his having laid down his life to avoid seeing what has now happened.[93]

With his usual sense of Cicero's influence on intelligent public opinion, Caesar thought it so important to counteract the eulogy that he took time in the midst of his Spanish campaign to write an answering tract in the form of an attack on Cato, in which he descended to making scurrilous charges of drunkenness, avarice and even incest.[94] Caesar's fears proved well-founded, and his book, with its bitter tone, did nothing to check the growth of a "Cato legend," which went on gathering strength until a hundred years later it reached its climax in the noble panegyric of Lucan:

> These were the manners, this was the unswerving rule of life of inflexible Cato: to hold to just measure and be true to his purpose: . . . to follow nature and lay down his life for his country; not to believe that he was born for himself, but rather for the world. . . . He was a worshipper of justice, an observer of strict honor, a friend and lover of the common weal.[95]

And again:

Behold the true father of his country, the man most worthy, Rome, of your altars; the man by whose name it will never shame you to swear; and if the day ever comes when your neck is freed from the yoke of servitude, it is he whom you will make your god.[96]

Nothing in Latin literature reaches a higher pitch of ethical sublimity than the reply which Lucan puts in Cato's mouth when urged to consult the oracle of Jupiter Ammon in the desert:

. . . What, Labienus, would you have me ask? Whether I ought to die in arms rather than behold a tyranny? . . . Whether violence can harm a good man? . . . Whether fortune when virtue opposes her is enhanced by success? . . . These things I know already and Ammon's voice will not make me surer of it. We all depend on heaven, and though the oracles are silent, we cannot act otherwise than in accord with the will of God. God needs no endorser and no witness; once and for all at our birth he gave us knowledge of what we are allowed to know, . . . nor has he hidden truth in the desert. Where earth and sea and air and sky and virtue are, there is God. Why should we seek heaven elsewhere? [97]

This picture of Cato became inextricably identified with the republic for which he had died and which Caesar extinguished. His memory became the heritage of the republic:

. . . [As] a statesman he was a failure. But as a moral force his character and his career left an impression on after generations deeper than that made by those of any other Roman. . . . Once the Empire was established, the worship of Cato became a fashion and a passion with all the bolder and loftier spirits who chafed under the restraints of the new order of things and sighed for an idealized past. The abominations of the Republic were forgotten, and Cato appeared as the champion whose heroism had dignified its fall, the martyr in a lost but worthy cause.[98]

The impression of the value and significance of the republic which Cato's death produced was set in bold relief by its contrast with what Caesar seemed every day to be more clearly intending as the destiny of Rome. If Cato was the symbol of the past, Romans now had before their eyes the visible symbol of the future that seemed to await them, and that symbol was Cleopatra. With dramatic effect, and just after Cato passed off the scene, Cleopatra entered upon the stage. Caesar sent for her before he was called away to Spain and installed her in a villa set among gardens across the Tiber, while his lawful wife Calpurnia adjusted herself to the situation with deferential acquiescence. Cleopatra in Rome was the embodiment of the new order which Caesar's success portended.

There is evidence that Cleopatra's presence in Rome under Caesar's protection caused uneasiness among many Romans who were otherwise willing enough to submit to Caesar's supremacy.[99] She was a symbol of the direction in which that supremacy was tending, and many Romans who had lost their loyalty to the constitution and the republic still cherished in their submerged consciousness a repugnance to what they felt she represented. She was openly and blatantly of the East, an Oriental in the fullest sense, and her presence at Caesar's side was more than a suggestion that Caesar meant to orientalize the government and social institutions of Rome. Ever since the great wars of the Persians against the Greeks four centuries and a half earlier, the civilized thought and traditions of the West, of Greece and of Italy, had been charged with a sense of the deep-seated differences and antagonisms between Western and Oriental civilization, especially in the sphere of government and politics. "Since the days of Herodotus Greek and Roman historians had developed a cumulative skill . . . in portraying the despotic rule of their oriental neighbors—a despotism which to them represented the very incarnation of [insolence], as opposed to the measure, the ordered liberty of a polity as they knew it." [100]

Accordingly, many Romans who felt no particular emotion over the accumulation of power in Caesar's hands became alert to a sense of danger when they saw that power associated with oriental royalty and threatening itself to assume an oriental form. Men otherwise selfish and cynical felt subconsciously that "it was apostasy and cowardice to slide back from the political faith which Greece had delivered once for all to the world, that it was of the essence of the higher civilisation of the West to protest against arbitrary power, to believe in government by discussion and consent, and in the rule of reason and of law." [101] This was the faith that Cato's death brought back vividly for a moment to men's minds, and now its significance was underscored by Cleopatra's presence in Rome. No doubt the feeling was only nascent and as yet not entirely self-conscious, for there was still no certainty as to how Caesar intended to develop his power or in what ways he would use it. Yet, from the moment of his return from Munda, the way was being prepared for a conflict, vaguely sensed but deeply felt, between ideals and points of view rather than between political programs. It was a conflict that assumed progressively clearer shape until it was at last brought to the decision of arms fifteen years later at the battle of Actium. Although Caesar was to live but a few months longer before he was stabbed by the daggers of assassins, those remaining months helped to shape and to define, as the civil war had never done, a political choice of fundamental magnitude between two rival theories of government.

Notes

CHAPTER 1

1. Horace, *Odes*, II, 1, 1.
2. *Supra*, pp. 17–19.
3. *Cambridge Ancient History*, IX, 396.
4. Mommsen, IV, 24.
5. Ferrero, I, 153.
6. Heitland, III, 452.
7. E.g., Cicero. See Plutarch, "Caesar," *Lives*, IV, 259.
8. Mommsen, IV, 539.
9. A. Trollope, *The Life of Cicero* (New York, 1881), I, 266–267.
10. See Suetonius, *Julius*, ch. 54.
11. Ferrero, I, 216.
12. Plutarch, "Caesar," *Lives*, IV, 260–261.
13. *Cambridge Ancient History*, IX, 480.
14. T. Frank, *A History of Rome* (New York, 1923), 263.
15. Quintilian, *Institutio Oratoria*, VIII, 3, 3.

16. C. T. Cruttwell, *A History of Roman Literature* (New York, 1878), 165.

17. Plutarch, "Demosthenes and Cicero," *Lives*, V, 90.

18. Ferrero, I, 230.

19. Cicero, *Oratio Pro Sex. Roscio Amerino*, ch. 52.

20. Ben Jonson, *Catiline*, Act II, Scene 1.

21. *Childe Harold*, Canto IV, xliv.

22. Cruttwell, *supra* note 16 at 181.

23. Cicero, *Oratio II De Lege Agraria*, ch. 13.

24. *Id., Oratio Pro C. Rabirio*.

25. Long, III, 268.

26. Cicero, *In L. Catilinam Orationes*.

27. Sallust, *De Catilinae Coniuratione*, ch. 51.

28. *Id.* at ch. 52. See Cicero's tribute to the decisive effect of Cato's argument in *Oratio Pro P. Sestio*, ch. 28.

29. Sallust, *supra* note 27 at ch. 55.

30. See J. L. Strachan-Davidson, *Cicero and the Fall of the Roman Republic* (New York, 1894), 151; Mommsen, IV, 221.

31. W. Forsythe, *Life of Marcus Tullius Cicero* (London, 1864), I, 124.

32. T. Mommsen, *Römisches Staatsrecht* (Leipzig, 1888), III, 1246.

33. Cicero, *Att.* I, 14.

34. *Ibid.*

35. Appian, *Bell. Civ.* II, ii, 14.

36. Cicero, *Att.* I, 13.

37. *Id.* at I, 16.

38. *Id.* at I, 18.

39. *Id.* at I, 16.

40. Long, III, 382.

41. See his earlier reference to this conception in *Oratio Pro C. Rabirio*, ch. 1.

42. Cicero, *Att.*, II, 1.

43. Plutarch, "Caesar," *Lives*, IV, 267.

44. B. R. Abeken, *An Account of the Life and Letters of Cicero* (C. Merivale transl., London, 1854), 76.

45. Suetonius, *Julius*, chs. 18, 19.

46. Cicero, *Att.*, II, 3. Balbus was a Spaniard from Cadiz on whom Pompey had conferred Roman citizenship. Ferrero, I, 285.

47. Dio Cassius, *Roman History*, xxxviii, 56–58.

48. Suetonius, *Julius*, ch. 19.

49. *Ibid.*

50. Cicero, *Att.*, II, 3.

51. *Ibid.*

52. *Id.* at II, 1.

CHAPTER 2

1. Heitland, III, 127 n. 2.
2. Cicero, *Att.*, II, 6.
3. *Id.* at II, 7.
4. *Id.* at II, 5.
5. *Id.* at II, 9.
6. See Cicero, *Oratio de Domo Sua.*
7. See generally, A. H. J. Greenidge, *Roman Public Life* (London, 1901), 162 *et seq.*
8. Long, III, 422.
9. Dio Cassius, *Roman History,* xxxviii, 4.
10. *Id.* at xxxviii, 5.
11. Heitland, III, 128–129.
12. Dio Cassius, *supra,* note 9 at ch. xxxviii, 6.
13. Appian, *Bell. Civ.,* II, ii, 11.
14. Heitland, III, 135.
15. Dio Cassius, *supra,* note 9 at ch. xxxviii, 8.
16. Suetonius, *Julius,* ch. 54.
17. Heitland, III, 130.
18. Plutarch, "Pompey," *Lives,* IV, 110–111.
19. Heitland, III, 131.
20. Dio Cassius, *supra,* note 9 at ch. xxxviii, 7.
21. Heitland, III, 131.
22. T. Frank, *A History of Rome* (New York, 1923), 279.
23. Cicero, *Att.,* II, 17.
24. Cicero, *Q.F.,* I, 2.
25. Cicero, *Att.,* II, 21.
26. *Ibid.*
27. *Id.* at II, 14.
28. *Id.* at II, 18.
29. *Id.* at II, 20.
30. *Id.* at II, 19.
31. *Id.* at II, 19, 20.
32. *Id.* at II, 20.
33. *Id.* at II, 21.
34. *Id.* at II, 22.
35. Cicero, *Q.F.,* I, 2.
36. See B. R. Abeken, *An Account of the Life and Letters of Cicero* (C. Merivale, transl., London, 1854), 94.
37. Cicero, *Att.,* II, 19.
38. *Ibid.*

39. *Id.* at II, 16.
40. *Id.* at II, 5.
41. See Heitland, III, 101.
42. Cicero, *Oratio Pro L. Valerio Flacco*, ch. 2.
43. *Id.* at ch. 38.
44. Cicero, *Q.F.*, I, 2.
45. *Supra*, p. 89.
46. Cicero, *Att.*, II, 24.
47. J. L. Strachan-Davidson, *Cicero and the Fall of the Roman Republic* (New York, 1894), 221.
48. W. Warde Fowler, *Julius Caesar* (New York, 1892), 125.
49. It is of interest that a eulogistic life of Caesar was written by Carlyle's disciple, James Froude.
50. Mommsen, III, 472–473.

CHAPTER 3

1. *Supra*, p. 84.
2. Cicero, *Oratio In L. Calpurnium Pisonem*, ch. 35.
3. Long, III, 457.
4. Dio Cassius, *Roman History*, xxxix, 24.
5. Long, III, 446.
6. Suetonius, *Julius*, ch. 41.
7. Cicero, *Oratio Pro P. Sestio*, ch. 25.
8. See *id.* at ch. 19.
9. L. R. Taylor, *Party Politics in the Age of Caesar* (Berkeley, 1949), 138.
10. Heitland, III, 150.
11. Long, III, 450.
12. Cicero, *Att.*, III, 15.
13. Cicero, *Oratio Pro T. Annio Milone*, ch. 14.
14. Cicero, *Oratio In L. Calpurnium Pisonem*, ch. 6.
15. *Id.* at ch. 8.
16. *Id.* at ch. 31.
17. Long, III, 455–456.
18. E. G. Sihler, *Cicero of Arpinum* (New York, 1933), 207.
19. Cicero, *Fam.*, XIV, 4.
20. Cicero, *Oratio Pro P. Sestio*, chs. 19–20.
21. *Id.* at chs. 17–20.
22. Heitland, III, 151.
23. *Ibid.*
24. Cicero, *Oratio Pro P. Sestio*, ch. 26.
25. *Id.*, *Oratio de Haruspicum Responsis*, ch. 13.
26. Long, IV, 73; Cicero, *Oratio De Domo Sua*, chs. 47–48.
27. Cicero, *Att.*, III, 18.

28. *Id.* at III, 23.
29. Cicero, *Oratio Pro P. Sestio,* ch. 33.
30. *Id.* at ch. 35. See also Long, IV, 85–86.
31. See Taylor, *supra,* note 9 at 59.
32. Long, IV, 90.
33. Heitland, III, 175.
34. Cicero, *Oratio De Domo Sua,* ch. 10.
35. Cicero, *Att.,* IV, 1.
36. Cicero, *Oratio De Domo Sua,* chs. 3–7.
37. Cicero, *Att.,* IV, 2.
38. Cicero, *Oratio Pro A. Caecina,* ch. 33.
39. Cicero, *Oratio De Domo Sua,* chs. 13–14.
40. *Id.* at ch. 17.
41. *Id.* at chs. 20–21.
42. *Id.* at chs. 24–29.
43. *Id.* at ch. 30.
44. Cicero, *Att.,* IV, 3.
45. *Supra,* p. 82.
46. Cicero, *Att.,* IV, 9.
47. Cicero, *Fam.,* I, 2.
48. *Id.* at I, 1–2.
49. Cicero, *Q.F.,* II, 3.
50. In *Oratio De Haruspicum Responsis.*
51. *Id.* at ch. 25.
52. *Id.* at chs. 22, 24.
53. *Id.* at ch. 25.
54. *Id.* at ch. 28.
55. *Supra,* p. 100.
56. *Oratio Pro P. Sestio,* ch. 42.
57. *Id.* at ch. 45.
58. *Id.* at ch. 56.
59. *Id.* at ch. 46.
60. *Id.* at ch. 46.
61. *Id.* at ch. 47.
62. *Id.* at ch. 48.
63. *Id.* at ch. 49.
64. *Id.* at ch. 49.
65. *Id.* at ch. 50.
66. *Id.* at ch. 23.
67. *Supra,* p. 80.
68. Cicero, *Oratio Pro Sex. Roscio Amerino,* ch. 45.
69. *Supra,* p. 54.
70. *Supra,* p. 114.
71. *Supra,* p. 78.

72. Cicero, *Q.F.*, II, 1.
73. *Id.* at II, 5.
74. Cicero, *Fam.*, I, 9.
75. *Ibid.*
76. *Ibid.*
77. Suetonius, *Julius*, ch. 24.
78. E. A. Freeman, *General Sketch of European History* (London, 1905), 79.
79. See generally, C. H. Haskins, *The Renaissance of the Twelfth Century* (Cambridge, Mass., 1927), especially 104–105, 193 *et seq.*
80. Ferrero, II, 37.
81. Plutarch, "Caesar," *Lives*, IV, 286.
82. *Supra*, ch. II, p. 80.
83. Almost the only exception is the unhappy instance of the declaration of war on Mithridates by Aquillius in 88 B.C.
84. T. Frank, *Roman Imperialism* (New York, 1914), 329.
85. The account of the Gallic War that follows is based upon Caesar's *Commentaries* and the valuable text of T. Rice Holmes, *Caesar's Conquest of Gaul* (London, 1899).
86. *Id.* at 11.
87. Heitland, II, 332.
88. Frank, *supra* note 84, at 335; Cicero, *Att.* I, 19.
89. *Supra*, p. 103.
90. Heitland, III, 162–163.
91. Caesar, *Bell. Gall.*, II, 15.
92. Ferrero, II, 37.
93. Cicero, *Oratio De Provinciis Consularibus*, ch. 9.
94. Suetonius, *Julius*, ch. 57.
95. *Id.* at ch. 62.
96. Heitland, III, 159.
97. See Suetonius, *Julius*, chs. 65, 67.
98. G. Boissier, *Cicero and His Friends* (A. D. Jones, transl., London, 1897), 242–244.
99. Heitland, IV, 222–223.
100. Long, IV, 271.
101. E.g., Mommsen, IV, 373.
102. J. L. Strachan-Davidson, *Cicero and the Fall of the Roman Republic* (New York, 1894), 263.
103. *Id.* at 264.
104. Mommsen, IV, 372.
105. *Id.* at IV, 373.
106. Cicero, *Fam.*, I, 9.
107. Strachan-Davidson, *supra*, 102 at 266.
108. Cicero, *Att.*, IV, 5.

109. *Id.* at IV, 2.
110. Cicero, *Fam.*, I, 9.
111. *Supra,* p. 101.
112. Cicero, *Oratio De Provinciis Consularibus.*
113. *Id., Oratio Pro L. Cornelio Balbo.*
114. This speech is not preserved.
115. Cicero, *Oratio Pro M. Caelio.*
116. Cicero, *Q.F.*, II, 4.
117. Cicero, *Fam.*, VII, 1.
118. Cicero, *Q.F.*, III, 9.
119. Cicero, *Att.*, IV, 4-a.
120. *Id.* at IV, 10.
121. *Infra,* ch. VI.

CHAPTER 4

1. Cicero, *Fam.*, I, 7.
2. Cicero, *Att.*, IV, 5.
3. Heitland, III, 189.
4. Plutarch, "Pompey," *Lives,* IV, 114.
5. Heitland, III, 226.
6. Cicero, *Q.F.*, II, 9.
7. Plutarch, "Cato," *Lives,* IV, 412.
8. *Id.* at 413.
9. *Id.* at 414.
10. *Infra,* p. 165.
11. Plutarch, "Cato," *Lives,* IV, 422.
12. S. B. Platner, *The Topography and Monuments of Ancient Rome* (Boston, 1911), 366.
13. Plutarch, "Pompey," *Lives,* IV, 67.
14. Heitland, III, 228.
15. *Ibid.*
16. *Supra,* p. 112.
17. *Supra.* p. 82.
18. Heitland, III, 228.
19. *Supra,* p. 40.
20. For an account of the Roman defeat at Carrhae, see *Cambridge Ancient History,* IX, 609–611.
21. Lucan, *Pharsalia,* I, 100–106.
22. Heitland, III, 228–229.
23. *Id.* at III, 234.
24. *Id.* at III, 236–237.
25. Suetonius, *Julius,* ch. 27.
26. Heitland, III, 242.

27. Plutarch, "Caesar," *Lives,* IV, 287.

28. Heitland, III, 243.

29. *Ibid.*

30. Plutarch, "Cato," *Lives,* IV, 418.

31. *Id.,* "Caesar," *Lives,* IV, 287.

32. Heitland, III, 248–249.

33. Long, IV, 357–358.

34. *Id.* at IV, 359.

35. The speech subsequently published, the famous and much admired *Oratio Pro T. Annio Milone,* is a rhetorical exercise composed after the trial.

36. Cicero, *Fam.,* V, 18.

37. Heitland, III, 244.

38. Cicero, *Att.,* VIII, 3.

39. *Supra,* p. 77.

40. See Heitland, III, 274–275.

41. *Id.* at III, 241.

42. Strabo, *Geographica,* IV, 4, 1.

43. For the history of these campaigns, see T. Rice Holmes, *Caesar's Conquest of Gaul* (London, 1899), 62–68.

44. W. E. Heitland, *A Short History of the Roman Republic* (Cambridge, 1911), 421.

45. *Supra,* p. 82.

46. Caesar, *Bell. Gall.,* IV, 17.

47. The older view has been that the bridge was in the neighborhood of Bonn, but Rice Holmes believes it was near Coblenz. Rice Holmes, *supra,* note 43 at 75.

48. Caesar, *Bell. Gall.,* IV, 20 *et seq.*

49. Heitland, III, 199–200.

50. Rice Holmes, *supra,* n. 43 at 90.

51. Caesar, *Bell. Gall.,* VI, 44.

52. Heitland, III, 217.

53. See E. M. Hatch, *Burgundy Past and Present* (London, 1927), 74–80.

54. Velleius Paterculus, II, 47.

55. F. B. Marsh, *The Founding of the Roman Empire* (Austin, Tex., 1922), 135.

56. Heitland, III, 250.

57. *Id.* at III, 250–251.

58. Cicero, *Fam.,* VIII, 8.

59. *Ibid.*

60. *Id.* at VIII, 9.

61. *Id.* at VIII, 14.

62. R. Y. Tyrell and L. C. Purser, eds., *The Correspondence of M. Tullius Cicero* (Dublin, 1890), III, lxvi.

63. *Supra,* p. 130.
64. Cicero, *Att.,* VII, 8.
65. Cicero, *Fam.,* VIII, 6.
66. Cicero, *Att.,* VII, 9.
67. Cicero, *Fam.,* VIII, 14.
68. Cicero, *Att.,* VII, 1.
69. Appian, II, iv, 30.
70. Heitland, III, 267.
71. Cicero, *Att.,* VII, 4.
72. Heitland, III, 269.
73. Cicero, *Att.,* VII, 5.
74. *Id.* at VII, 7.
75. *Id.* at VII, 5.
76. *Id.* at VII, 8.
77. Caesar, *Bell. Civ.,* I, 1.
78. Plutarch, "Caesar," *Lives,* IV, 289.
79. Caesar, *Bell. Civ.,* I, 1.
80. Heitland, III, 270.
81. Caesar, *Bell. Civ.,* I, 5.
82. Cicero, *Fam.,* XVI, 11.
83. Caesar, *Bell. Civ.,* I, 2.
84. *Ibid.*
85. See note in C. E. Moberly, ed., *The Commentaries of C. Julius Caesar: The Civil War* (Oxford, 1897), 138, n. 21.
86. Caesar, *Bell. Civ.,* I, 3.
87. *Id.* at I, 4.
88. Plutarch, "Cato," *Lives,* IV, 422.
89. Cicero, *Fam.,* XVI, 11.
90. Plutarch, "Caesar," *Lives,* IV, 289.
91. Cicero, *Fam.,* XVI, 11.
92. Heitland, III, 273.
93. Velleius Paterculus, II, 49.
94. *Supra,* p. 159.
95. Caesar, *Bell. Civ.,* I, 5.
96. *Id.* at I, 7.
97. *Supra,* pp. 55 *et seq.*
98. *Supra,* pp. 57 *et seq.*
99. Caesar, *Bell. Civ.,* I, 7.
100. Plutarch, "Caesar," *Lives,* 291.

CHAPTER 5

1. See Heitland, III, 279–280.
2. Cicero, *Att.,* VII, 8.

252 THE COURSE OF DESTRUCTION

3. *Id.* at VII, 21 (Feb. 8), 23 (Feb. 10).

4. *Id.* at VII, 10.

5. *Id.* at VII, 12.

6. *Id.* at VII, 14.

7. Caesar, *Bell. Civ.,* I, 9.

8. Cicero, *Fam.,* XVI, 12.

9. *Ibid.*

10. Caesar, *Bell. Civ.,* I, 11.

11. *Id.* at I, 10.

12. H. M. D. Parker, *The Roman Legions* (Oxford, 1928), 61.

13. R. Syme, *The Roman Revolution* (Oxford, 1960), 49.

14. Suetonius, *Julius,* ch. 34.

15. L. R. Taylor, *Party Politics in the Age of Caesar* (Berkeley, 1949), 162.

16. Cicero, *Att.,* IX, 18.

17. Taylor, *supra* note 15 at 163–164.

18. Cicero, *Fam.,* X, 31.

19. H. J. Roby, *An Introduction to the Study of Justinian's Digest* (Cambridge, 1884), cxi–cxii.

20. Cicero, *Att.,* VIII, 7.

21. *Id.* at VIII, 8.

22. *Id.* at VIII, 11.

23. *Id.* at VIII, 11; IX, 7.

24. *Id.* at VIII, 11.

25. *Id.* at IX, 7.

26. *Id.* at IX, 5.

27. *Id.* at IX, 7.

28. J. L. Strachan-Davidson, *Cicero and the Fall of the Roman Republic* (New York, 1894), 336.

29. Cicero, *Att.,* VIII, 9.

30. *Id.* at VIII, 13.

31. *Id.* at X, 4.

32. *Id.* at IX, 16.

33. *Id.* at IX, 18.

34. *Ibid.*

35. *Id.* at X, 2.

36. *Id.* at X, 4.

37. *Id.* at X, 8-b.

38. *Id.* at X, 8-a.

39. Cicero, *Fam.,* IV, 2.

40. Plutarch, "Cato," *Lives,* V, 75.

41. E. G. Sihler, *Cicero of Arpinum* (New York, 1933), 321.

42. Cicero, *Fam.,* IV, 2.

43. Appian, *Bell. Civ.,* II, vi, 40.

44. Cicero, *Att.,* X, 4.

45. Appian, *Bell. Civ.*, II, vi, 40.
46. Dio Cassius, XLI, 16.
47. Caesar, *Bell. Civ.*, II, 8–12.
48. Heitland, III, 304.
49. Caesar, *Bell. Civ.*, III, 73.
50. Appian, *Bell. Civ.*, II, vi, 5.
51. T. Arnold, *History of the Later Roman Commonwealth* (London, 1845), I, 516–517.
52. Heitland, III, 304.
53. Appian, *Bell. Civ.*, II, x, 66–67.
54. *Cambridge Ancient History*, IX, 664.
55. B. G. Niebuhr, *The History of Rome* (L. Schmitz, transl., London, 1844), II, 72.
56. Heitland, III, 309–310.
57. J. D. Mahaffy, *The Empire of the Ptolemies* (London, 1895), 445–446.
58. Long, V, 225.
59. *Id.* at V, 227.
60. Mahaffy, *supra,* note 57 at 438.
61. Caesar, *Bell. Civ.*, III, 107.
62. Heitland, III, 313–314.
63. Mommsen, IV, 516.
64. *Id.* at IV, 521.
65. Heitland, III, 315–316.
66. Appian, *Bell. Civ.*, II, xiii, 90.
67. L. R. Taylor, *The Divinity of the Roman Emperor* (Middletown, Conn., 1931), 61–62.
68. *Supra,* p. 36.
69. Appian, *Bell. Civ.*, II, xv, 102.
70. *Cambridge Ancient History*, IX, 722.
71. *Ibid.*
72. *Id.* at IX, 721.
73. Dio Cassius, XLII, 49.
74. Long, V, 300; Heitland, III, 317.
75. Long, V, 303.
76. Heitland, III, 324.
77. Long, V, 308.
78. Heitland, III, 324.
79. *Id.* at III, 326.
80. *Ibid.*
81. Plutarch, "Cato," *Lives,* IV, 431 *et seq.*
82. Heitland, III, 332.
83. *Id.* at III, 336.
84. *Ibid.*
85. Parker, *supra,* note 12 at 215.

86. Long, V, 372, note 7.
87. *Id.* at V, 374.
88. *Supra,* p. 178.
89. *Supra,* p. 222.
90. Heitland, III, 350.
91. *Supra,* p. 54.
92. Long, V, 234.
93. Cicero, *Att.,* XII, 4.
94. Long, V, 411; Taylor, *supra,* note 15 at 171.
95. Lucan, *Pharsalia,* II, 380–390.
96. *Id.* at IX, 601–604.
97. *Id.* at IX, 566–586.
98. Heitland, III, 332; Taylor, *supra,* note 15 at 178–182.
99. *Cambridge Ancient History,* IX, 713.
100. A. D. Winspear, *Augustus and the Reconstruction of Roman Government and Society* (Madison, Wis., 1935), 12–13.
101. Strachan-Davidson, *supra,* note 28 at 354.

Part THREE

RIVAL PHILOSOPHIES
OF GOVERNMENT

6

Cicero
the
Institutionalist

I

In the first year of the civil war between Caesar and
Pompey there died at Rome an obscure and ancient senator, Marcus Perperna, who had lived to the great age of
ninety-eight years.[1] He had been born only two years after the
death of Cato the Censor, and Cato had been born in 234 B.C. The
span of these two human lives, almost touching end-to-end, thus
reached back from the final collapse of the republic to the era of the
First Punic War—to the heroic days of Regulus, when Rome acquired her first province and was still only a country town heading
a confederacy of other country towns and tribes of rural Italy. The
vast changes which had occurred in the meanwhile in the political
arrangements of the whole Mediterranean world, in the social and
economic condition of Rome and above all in the workings of the
Roman constitution take on a dramatic intensity from the fact that

257

they had all taken place within the comparatively short stretch of two human lives.

Few peoples of the world have had so strong a consciousness of history as did the Romans. Although Cicero complained that "our national literature is deficient in history," [2] he was obviously thinking of artistic historical masterpieces comparable to the great works of Herodotus and Thucydides, and his complaint was directed to what he regarded as deficiencies in style and literary composition. In fact, Roman life was lived in a veritable museum of history. The temples, the public buildings, the Forum were replete with bronze tablets on which the texts of ancient laws and treaties were set forth and displayed. The *tabularium*, or record office, was filled almost to capacity with scrolls recording the day-to-day transactions of public business. The methodical and regular habits which were so marked a feature of the Romans' character—their addiction to records, accounts and their emphasis on precedents and established practice—caused them to accumulate with care and consult with assiduity these muniments of the past. Some of the materials were very old. The archives of the Pontifical College went back to the commencement of the republic, and perhaps farther, recording not only prodigies, eclipses and earthquakes, but the names and offices of the magistrates of each year, laws and treaties, the foundation of colonies, the dedication of temples and the deaths of great men. A disastrous gap in these records had been made by the destruction of Rome by the Gauls in 390 B.C., but what had been preserved had been pieced together, filled out with other materials, and re-edited as the foundation for more recent series of the same kind.[3] Besides the pontifical records were those kept by the various civil magistrates—consuls, praetors and censors—and also stored in the record office. In addition, each great aristocratic house had a family register of its honors and achievements, kept and treasured with particular care.[4]

From the time of the Second Punic War, when Rome first became self-conscious of her position as a world power, a succession of chroniclers and annalists had drawn upon these raw materials of history and had attempted to tell the story of the rise and successes of the great republic. None of these writers, however, was a literary craftsman of a high order, and none was a philosophical historian. All confined themselves to a bare recital of events and did not undertake to analyze the operation of cause and effect in the history of the republic. Only once had this been attempted, by the Greek Polybius, on the eve of the fatal breach in the constitution which was made by the Gracchi. Nearly all other chroniclers were typical Roman aristocrats, too cautious and legalistic to venture far beyond the facts in an effort to discover their meaning. The time was again ripe, as it had been in the age of Polybius, for such an attempt: the great changes which had taken place in the two lifetimes between the birth of Cato and the death of Perperna challenged interpretation. What had happened to the Roman republic in the intervening years and why?

The Romans, unlike the Greeks, had no natural bent for philosophical speculation. Their characteristic concern with the practical and the immediately useful kept them from reflecting on the broad principles implicit in their own political arrangements and still more from embarking on an even broader examination of the principles of politics in general. Yet reflection and examination were now suggested by something more than mere mental curiosity. Such introspection was vital if the Romans were to take stock of themselves and consider how to shape their course most intelligently for the future. Significant efforts in the field of political thought have always been reactions, favorable or unfavorable, to a political situation which registers marked and visible changes in the state, and the changes which had taken place in the Roman state during the two centuries since the birth of Cato were by now sufficiently glaring to draw forth comment of major importance. The man who was to perform this task was Cicero. With his broad and sympathetic scholarship nurtured in Greek learning, he was free from the inhibitions which made most Romans timorous about discussing general principles. The chief issue that concerned him was central to his own entire career in politics—the issue between absolutism and republicanism. In discoursing upon this theme, which became of increasing contemporary significance with the rise of Caesar, Cicero formulated a statement of principles which supplied the guide and outline of most of the basic political thought of the

Western world for the next nineteen centuries, and his formulation is of living interest in our own time because men are again confronted today by the same central issue in a greater degree of dramatic worldwide intensity than at any other single epoch during the interval.

It is appropriate, therefore, to conclude the narrative of the downfall of the Roman republic with a review of the two opposing views of government and political power which, latent in every age, come into open and striking conflict in all great periods of change. One of these views is represented in the political writings of Cicero and is set forth with perhaps greater simplicity and clarity than by any other publicist in the history of Western thought. The other view is represented by the policies of Caesar, who wrote no books about politics, but whose acts speak more plainly and expressly than most men's words. These two men stand on opposing sides of the conflict between two views of government which in large measure have repeatedly come into open prominence in most of the great crises in Western political development. This chapter is accordingly devoted to a summary of Cicero's political views; the next is concerned with those of Caesar.

Cicero's philosophic views about the basic principles of government are contained chiefly in three works written during the last dozen years of his life—the *Republic,* the *Laws* and the treatise on practical morality which he entitled *De Officiis.*

The *Republic* was the second major work to which Cicero turned his hand during the years after the Conference of Lucca when he left politics for literature.[5] Although begun in the spring of 54, it was apparently not completed for publication until three years later. Unfortunately, the text has come down to us in a very mangled and fragmentary state. For centuries it was wholly lost and known only through a few scattered quotations by later writers until the famous discovery of the Vatican palimpsest by Cardinal Mai in 1820, which restored the first and second books and the first part of the third book almost in their entirety. The barest fragments are left of the remainder, except for the famous Dream of Scipio at the end of the sixth book.

Of Cicero's other major work on politics, the *Laws,* only three books survive, and it is not known whether more were ever written. Although part of the work appears to have been composed in the year 52,[6] Cicero evidently laid it aside, for there is some evidence that he was engaged on it in the year 46;[7] but it also seems clear that he never published it in his lifetime and that it was probably issued after his death by Tiro, his secretary and literary executor.[8] The *De Officiis* came last and was written in the year 44.[9] It should be noted that there is a close and important connection between these three works in that the *Laws* amplify matters dealt with in the third book of the *Republic* and that the *De Officiis* is an amplification of many matters discussed in the *Laws*. Consequently, the three can, and indeed must, be considered together.

The titles which Cicero gave to his *Republic* and *Laws* inevitably suggest that he followed Plato as his model, but the inference is unjustified. Nothing, in fact, could be more different in spirit and approach than Cicero's treatment of politics from Plato's great expositions of Utopianism. Plato's political works are abstract constructions, existing neither in space nor time, and arbitrarily designed to illustrate political problems in a vacuum, like a work on mathematics. Cicero's books, on the contrary, are historical commentaries limited to the vicissitudes of actual states and more specifically to the facts of Roman history. Plato may have supplied an inspiration for them, but certainly neither the model nor pattern.

There has been much misunderstanding of the relation of Cicero's political writings to those of Greek thinkers. Although in some of his works on general philosophy he contented himself with following closely the text of a Greek original, he did not do so in either the *Republic* or the *Laws*. In them Cicero speaks directly on his own authority, supplementing and correcting what he had derived from Greek thought by Roman maxims and by his own practical experience. He is clearly thinking of himself when he puts these words into the mouth of Scipio in the *Republic:*

. . . I ask you to listen to me as to one who is neither entirely ignorant of Greek authorities, nor, on the other hand, prefers their views, particularly on this subject, to our own, but rather as to a Roman who, though provided by a father's care with a liberal education and eager for knowledge from boyhood, yet has been trained by experience and the maxims learned at home much more than by books.[10]

Hence, as Professor Conway puts it:

As we leave the pages of Plato's Republic, beautiful and perennially stimulating as they are, still more as we turn from the cold reasoning of Aristotle, despite the value of his shrewd comments on Greek history, to Cicero's political writings, we feel that we have passed from the atmosphere of the study to the free air of actual life, passed from rainbows or cobwebs to reality.[11]

In other words, Cicero added to the technical insights of the academic philosophers the vivid observations of a man of practical experience, and he clothed them in language which carried meaning to men of the world like himself. It is not without significance that so long as classical scholars continued to be men of the world, Cicero's reputation remained in the ascendant; after classical scholarship became an academic discipline, its votaries have not always known what to make of him.

In the *De Officiis,* written with almost unbelievable haste in three months of the last year of his life, Cicero followed closely, in the first two of the three books, the plan and exposition of a treatise by the Stoic philosopher Panaetius, but Cicero's work is full of examples from Roman history, enriched by his own comments and observations. The last and most important of the three books is almost wholly Cicero's own, and, partly for this reason, the *De Officiis* is Cicero's best and most perfect work. Although it is not equal in beauty and polish of prose style to the superb perfection of some parts of the *Republic,* the contents and arrangement are so admirable that it is still more than readable today. Moreover, it is the work of Cicero which held its popularity longest and most influenced the European mind of later ages. In the fourth century it helped shape some of the most important Christian teachings on morality and government,[12] and in the Renaissance it was translated into several vernacular tongues and issued in numerous editions.

Aside from Cicero's three major political works, expressions of his thought about politics are naturally scattered through his speeches and letters, and in this connection special reference must be made to his oration in defense of Sestius,[13] which in its published form is an extended political tract comparable to some of the published speeches of Edmund Burke. That oration is in effect an essay which served as a medium for the initial development of certain ideas that later found a place in the *Republic*.

Inevitably, when the expression of a man's political views is contained in a series of writings extending over a period of years there are bound to be certain inconsistencies, or at least differences in emphasis. In Cicero's case the striking thing is that the differences and inconsistencies are so few, and there is a remarkable stability in the major outlines of his thought from beginning to end. Unlike Plato and some other thinkers, he did not shift from one position to another after reflection on the shortcomings of his earlier theories. At most, he became franker, as time went on, and more emphatic about such matters as the aims and consequences of the career of a man like Caesar, especially after Caesar was dead and it was less dangerous to speak out.

II

Practical Roman that he was, Cicero began his first work on politics, the *Republic*, with a statement of the purpose and utility of government and of the state. This introduction he casts in the form of an appeal to citizens to take a part in politics, which has a very modern, indeed a late nineteenth century, ring. Marcus Cato, the Censor, he begins, might have lived his life at Tusculum in the leisurely enjoyment of a delightful place, but, madman that he was, he preferred, "though no necessity constrained him, to be tossed by the billows and storms of our public life . . . than to live a life of complete happiness in the calm and ease of such retirement." [14] Here Cicero undoubtedly had in mind his close but shrewd friend Atticus, who deliberately chose to keep out of politics and managed to established good relations with whatever group or individual was in control of the government. Deeply as Cicero loved Atticus, he saw in this calculated refusal to perform the duties of a citizen, and in the less deliberate apathy of the more intelligent part of the Roman civic body, one of the chief causes of the downfall of constitutional government.

The appeal to intelligent citizens to participate in politics does not have the conventional quality of similar appeals made in America in the nineteenth century. From the days of Cicero's youth, the age of Marius and Sulla, politics had been a desperately dangerous business which might lead at any time to violent and sudden death. Accordingly, those who are reluctant to enter politics, he says, refer to the dangers to which public life is exposed and which present to brave men the dishonorable fear of death; even if death can be avoided, they nevertheless point to the misfortunes of the most illustrious men and the wrongs they have suffered at the hands of their fellow citizens.[15] Hence these objectors allege that for the most part worthless men turn to public affairs, men with whom it is too sordid to be associated, whereas to contend with them is both deplorable and beset with danger, especially when the mob is aroused. "Therefore, they maintain, a wise man should not attempt to take the reins, as he cannot restrain the insane and untamed fury of the common herd; nor is it proper for a freeman, by contending with vile and wicked opponents, to submit to the scourgings of abuse or expose himself to wrongs which are intolerable to the wise." [16] Such people, when they say that no wise man will take part in politics, admit only one exception, namely, when some emergency compels him to do so.[17] To this Cicero answers that the opportunity of serving the state in a time of great danger does not come suddenly to those who wish it, unless they are already there and available for it.[18]

In the couse of explaining why, in the face of the admitted inconveniences and dangers of public life, sensible men should take part therein, Cicero develops his view of the purpose and usefulness of government. Government, he says, is a service, and public office is a moral duty, not a mere honor or source of profit.[19] It is a duty to participate in it because men desire, or should desire, to bring about a better life for others and to undergo the greatest toil and trouble for the sake of aiding mankind when possible.[20] "[W]e feel a mighty urge to increase the resources of mankind, since we desire to make human life safer and richer by our thought and effort, and are goaded on to the fulfilment of this desire by Nature herself. . . ." [21]

Cicero then proceeds to emphasize that government is of the highest utility to mankind and hence deserving of the best efforts of all good men. Obviously, however, to be useful it must be good government, one that seeks the greatest happiness of the governed.[22] He is thus led to consider the question of the good and the bad in governments and the kind of institutional arrangements which best promote the proper objects of government. He begins this discussion,[23] by striking down to a more fundamental issue—the essential nature of the social aggregate or political community within which government functions. He deals with this problem in a way which, although doubtless not particularly original for a Roman, represents the appearance of a novel element in Western political thought. The bond of civil society, he says, is law; [24] a state exists only when the individuals who compose it are held together by a consensual compact in legal rights.[25] "[A] commonwealth is the property of a people. But a people is not any collection of human beings brought together in any sort of way, but an assemblage of people in large numbers associated in an agreement with respect to justice and a partnership for the common good." [26] Again, he asks, what is a state but an association in law? [27]

This clear, explicit and constantly reiterated emphasis on law in its broadest sense as the essential basis of the state and civil society is the most fundamental and original of Cicero's contributions to political thought. It is a characteristic Roman contribution which he probably drew unconsciously from his own traditions without being clearly aware that there was any novelty in it. Yet it is a distinct landmark and starting point in the development of Western political philosophy: it initiates the concept of the law-state, which was to dominate the entire thought of the West until the end of the eighteenth century, and which was to be the parent of modern constitutional government in the form in which it won the assent of the nineteenth. Among Greek thinkers, notably Plato and Aristotle, the constitution is conceived largely as an ethical relationship between the citizens of the state rather than as a legal organization of institutions.[28] On the other hand, Cicero's "whole theory is far more dependent on law . . . a theory of rights in a sense with which the Greeks were unacquainted; and this legalistic character, apparently of Roman and not Greek origin, confirmed by the later Roman jurists, was handed on by them to remain one of the distinguishing marks of western political thought almost to our own day. . . ." [29]

How firmly rooted and familiar Cicero's basic conception is, even today, at least in our American thinking, is shown by the following passage from the pen of an able American lawyer, Judge John Parker, which might almost have been written by Cicero himself:

Society, whether a free society or not, is not a mere aggregation of individuals. It is an organism. The law is the life principle of that organism. It is not something imposed from without but something that arises from within. There is something in the nature . . . of human beings and of the society that they compose that determines how society should act and how the members of society should act towards each other. This is law in its true sense. It must be interpreted in terms of rules and these rules must be enforced by the power of the State; but it must never be forgotten that the source of law is not the power that enforces the rules but the life that gives rise to the power, and that the source of the rules is not the power but reason applied to the life from which the power arises.[30]

On one point Cicero would almost certainly have differed from Judge Parker, for to him a society ruled in accordance with law was a "free society." Nothing is more characteristic of Cicero's thinking than his view of the relation between law and the concept of freedom or liberty, which he was the first to emphasize in political thought. "[N]othing," he writes, "is sweeter than liberty, even to wild beasts." [31] Yet law is the mother of liberty and its indispensable condition:

You must allow that nothing is more unworthy in a state which is governed by laws than to depart from the laws. For that is the bond of that human dignity which we enjoy in a republic, the foundation of liberty, the source and origin of equity. The mind and soul and judgment and purpose of a state have their seat in the laws. As is a body without a mind, so a state without laws cannot make use of its constituent parts, its nerves, blood and members. The magistrates are but servants of the laws, the judges are their interpreters: in short and finally we are all slaves of the laws in order that we may be free.[32]

Accordingly, for Cicero the essential feature of a state is that it shall be governed in accordance with law; if not so governed, it is not a state at all, but a tyranny.[33] The state is thus a mere instrument or agency of law, and the good and bad aspects of governmental arrangements are to be tested by the state's effectiveness to serve as such an instrument. The capacity to promote justice according to law is the standard and touchstone of government, whatever its form. Law demands government, and even if law and justice are superior and anterior to government and provide the rules in accordance with which government should act, they nevertheless require the existence and operation of government in order to give effect to them. "Nothing, moreover, is so completely in accordance with the principles of justice and the demands of Nature (and when I use these expressions, I wish it understood that I mean Law) as is government, without which existence is impossible for a household, a city, a nation, the human race . . . and the universe itself." [34]

Yet, if government is thus essential to give effect to law, it must itself be organized in accordance with law and be a system of legal arrangements. A government, Cicero writes, "consists of its magistrates and those who direct its affairs." [35] The differences between various forms of government consist therefore in the different legal arrangements for the distribution and exercise of power.[36]

With these preliminary postulates established, Cicero proceeds to assess the merits of different systems of governmental arrangements, that is, different types or forms of government. Of these he recognizes the three basic varieties which had been commonly recoganized since the days of Herodotus—monarchy, aristocracy, democracy. Either "a just and wise king, or a select number of leading citizens, or even the people itself . . . can . . . form a government that is not unstable, provided that no elements of injustice or greed are mingled with it." [37] No one of these three types of government is necessarily or inherently bad, and if it holds fast to that bond of law and justice which originally bound men together in the association of the state, although it may not be perfect or even the best, it is nevertheless tolerable.[38] An important practical consideration, however, is that the form of government must always be congenial to the particular circumstances which have brought any given state into being.[39]

The great difficulty about these primary or simple forms of government, says Cicero, is their instability and the likelihood that they will become perverted. At this point, he swings into the established tradition of Greek political thought and lends his voice to views already developed with basic consistency by Plato, Aristotle and Polybius. In this part, his debt to Polybius in particular is great. Plato [40] and Aristotle [41] had identified three perverted or corrupt kinds of government corresponding to each of the three simple types —tyranny corresponding to monarchy, oligarchy to aristocracy and ochlocracy or mob-rule to democracy. Polybius had developed the view that there is an inherent tendency in each simple form to degenerate into its perverted correlative. Beginning with monarchy, kings succumb to the temptation of using their power to set themselves above their subjects and gratify their greed. Kingship is then turned into tyranny, which in due course is overthrown by high-minded and courageous men of noblest birth because they are the most intolerant of the tyrannical acts of their rulers.[42] The aristocracy which has thus supplanted a tyranny in turn degenerates in the next generation because the sons of many of these aristocrats, bred in the shadow of their fathers' authority and preeminent position,

gave themselves up with passion to avarice and unscrupulous love of money . . . and so they turned an *aristocracy* into an *oligarchy*. But it was not long before they roused in the minds of the people the same feelings as before; and their fall therefore was very like the disaster which befel the tyrants. . . . Having then got rid of these rulers by assassination or exile, they do not venture to set up a king again, being still in terror of the injustice to which this led before; nor dare they intrust the common interests again to more than one, considering the recent example of their misconduct: and therefore, as the only sound hope left them is that which depends upon themselves, they are driven to take refuge in that; and so changed the constitution from an oligarchy to a *democracy,* and took upon themselves the superintendence and charge of the state. . . . But as soon as a new generation has arisen, and the democracy has descended to their children's children, long association weakens their value for equality and freedom, and some seek to become more powerful than the ordinary citizens; and the most liable to this temptation are the rich. . . . [W]hen, in their senseless mania for reputation, they have made the populace ready and greedy to receive bribes, the virtue of democracy is destroyed, and it is transformed into a government of violence and the strong hand. For the mob, habituated to feed at the expense of others, and to have its hopes of a livelihood in the property of its neighbours, as soon as it has got a leader sufficiently ambitious and daring, . . . produces a reign of mere violence. Then come tumultuous assemblies, massacres, banishments, redivisions of land; until, after losing all trace of civilization, it has once more found a master and a despot.

This is the regular cycle of constitutional revolutions, and the natural order in which constitutions change, are transformed, and return again to their original stage.[43]

This clear and straightforward exposition of Polybius, however oversimplified we may consider it, bore enough resemblance to the known facts of Roman history, and particularly that part of Roman history which had ensued since his own death, to carry conviction to Cicero, and he accordingly employs it, at least in its main outlines, as the basis for his discussion of government. Ahead of every one of the three simple forms of government, he says, lies a steep and slippery way leading to something that is evil.[44] The first and most certain of these changes is the one that occurs in a kingship: "when the king begins to be unjust, that form of government is immediately at an end, and the king has become a tyrant. This is the worst sort of government. . . ." [45] Tyrants snatch the ruling power in the state, as though it were a ball, then princes or the people seize it from tyrants, oligarchical factions or tyrants from these, and the same form of government never long maintains itself.[46]

From this last sentence it appears that Cicero was not quite so dogmatic as Polybius about the precise and inevitable sequence of the different governmental changes. He thinks that tyranny, for example, may be followed by popular government and popular government by oligarchy, whereas Polybius seems to lay down the formula that tyranny is always followed by aristocracy and popular government by mob-rule. However, Cicero expresses essential agreement with the Greek historian on the point that the simple or primary varieties of government, because of their instability, are subject to a never-ending succession of cyclical changes.[47] The leading principle of political wisdom toward which this discourse is aimed, he says, is to see the paths and variations of governments so that when it is known in what direction a particular one is tending it will be possible to take measures to hold it back or meet the change in advance.[48]

Another main difference between Cicero and Polybius, which likewise goes to a fundamental point and beyond a difference of emphasis, is that Cicero's basic objection to the simple forms of government is directed not merely, as with Polybius, to their instability and short duration but to the underlying reason which causes the instability. That cause he finds in the tendency of governments to degenerate without reference to form. For Cicero the essence of tyranny is lawlessness; the two are synonymous. Where there is tyranny, there cannot be a state in any proper sense, since the essential characteristic of a state is law. "Therefore, wherever a tyrant rules, we ought not to say that we have a bad form of commonwealth . . . but . . . that we really have no commonwealth at all." [49] It is this lawlessness which causes revolutions and leads to changes in the state, for men are so constituted that they resent injustice and will rise in rebellion against it. Only a government which pursues justice is stable, for justice is the quality and virtue which is concerned with holding together and conserving organized society. Accordingly, a government that wishes to maintain itself in power and avoid the danger of overturn should so rule as to be loved rather than feared. Of all motives, writes Cicero, none is better adapted to win influence and hold it than to be esteemed; nothing is more foreign to that object than to be feared; no amount of power can successfully withstand the hatred of the many.[50]

Accordingly, for Cicero, the chief weakness of the simple governmental forms and the cause of their instability is the innate tendency of all of them to degenerate into tyranny and lawlessness. The monarchical form of government is most subject to change, he thought, because the vices of a single man easily sweep it headlong to destruction.[51] Precarious is the lot of a people, he says, when it depends on the caprice or character of one man,[52] for as soon as a king has adopted a form of rule which is less just than formerly, he forthwith becomes a tyrant.[53] Cicero puts the same thought in another way in one of his letters: "From the man who has all power in his hands I see nothing to fear, except that everything is uncertain when once there has been a departure from law . . . it is impossible to guarantee what sort of future there may be when it depends on the will, not to say the whim, of a single individual." [54] Hence, he says, when we speak of a king, the idea of an unjust king presents itself to our minds.[55]

The inevitable connection in Cicero's mind between tyranny and revolution is revealed by the assent he gives to a doctrine which both before and after him has played a considerable part in political thought—the doctrine of tyrannicide. From his view that the tyrant has placed himself outside the law it follows simply and logically that men have no ties of fellowship with a tyrant, but rather a bitter feud. It is not, he says, "opposed to Nature to rob, if one can, a man whom it is morally right to kill;—nay, all that pestilent and abominable race should be exterminated from human society." [56] The younger Africanus, he argues, did no greater service to the state by conquering Numantia than was done at the same time by Publius Scipio Nasica when he slew Tiberius Gracchus.[57] The Gracchi, he continues, were not approved by good men while they lived, and when dead they were included in the number of those who have been rightly slain.[58] These statements, it should be noted, are drawn from the De Officiis, written after the assassination of Caesar.

Aristocracy, like monarchy, has a natural tendency to deteriorate. This arises from "the false notions of men, who, through their ignorance of virtue . . . think that the best men are those who are rich, prosperous, or born of famous families. For when, on account of this mistaken notion of the common people, the State begins to be ruled by the riches, instead of the virtue, of a few men, these rulers tenaciously retain the title, though they do not possess the character, of the 'best.' " [59]

Finally, popular government, too, is subject to perversion. The extent of good or bad qualities therein may depend in part on its origin. Thus, if the people themselves have killed or driven out a tyrant, they govern with restraint as long as they are prudent and wise; taking pride in their accomplishment, they are willing to preserve the constitution they have established. If, on the other hand, the people have risen in rebellion against a just king, or if they have tasted the blood of the aristocracy, they subject the whole state to their caprices and passions.[60] No state, he writes, less deserves the name of commonwealth than one in which everything is in the hands of the masses.[61] No fire is so hard to check as the vengeance of the unbridled mob.[62] At this point, Cicero paraphrases a section of Plato's *Republic* to the effect that the final result of boundless license is that, if the least restraint of government is applied, men cannot endure it and thereafter begin to neglect the laws as well, and thus they are finally without any kind of rule.[63] He then continues by saying that from such extreme license, which is viewed as liberty, tyrants spring up as from a root. Just as excess of power in the hands of aristocrats leads to the overthrow of aristocracy, so when the people have too much liberty, liberty itself brings them to slavery. Thus, any extreme condition, whether in climate, in agriculture, or in health, is usually followed by the opposite extreme. From extreme liberty is born a tyrant and with him cruel slavery, for out of this untamed populace someone is generally chosen a leader against those leading citizens who have already been overwhelmed and driven from their position—some bold, vicious man who wantonly persecutes those who have earned the gratitude of the state, and who curries favor with the people by giving them the property of others as well as his own. To such a man, because he is a private citizen and because he is beset with fear, great powers are given and continually renewed; as was the case with Pisistratus at Athens, he is surrounded by armed guards. Finally, he emerges as a tyrant over the very people who have elevated him to power.[64]

Having developed in this way the particular perverse tendencies characteristic of each of the three simple types of government, Cicero continues to follow Polybius in adopting the view that, in order to have reasonable assurance of stability and just government, a state must have a constitution in which all three simple forms are combined, that is, it must have a government of the so-called "mixed" type.[65] He then goes on to say that "unless there is in the State an even balance of rights, duties, and functions, so that the magistrates have enough power, the counsels of the eminent citizens enough influence, and the people enough liberty, this kind of government cannot be safe from revolution." [66] Thus "there should be a supreme and royal element in the State, some power also ought to be granted to the leading citizens, and certain matters should be left to the judgment and desires of the masses. Such a constitution in the first place, offers in a high degree a sort of equality, which is a thing free men can hardly do without for any considerable length of time, and, secondly, it has stability. For the primary forms already mentioned degenerate easily into the corresponding perverted forms . . . but whereas these forms are frequently changed into new ones, this does not usually happen in the case of the mixed and evenly balanced constitution, except through great faults in the governing class. For there is no reason for a change when every citizen is firmly established in his own station, and there underlies it no perverted form into which it can plunge and sink." [67]

Thus, fundamentally, Cicero's preference for mixed government is that it removes the chief cause of revolution by its superior ability to protect each citizen in his rights—in other words, by its superior ability to maintain a regime of law. Since such a government offers the best guarantee of the rule of law, it also offers the best guarantee of stability, for departure from law and justice provokes first discontent and then revolution. With mixed government thus identified as the best practicable type, Cicero finds, as Polybius did, the best illustration of mixed government in the historic institutions of Rome. He accordingly concludes the first book of the *Republic* with the remark that "no other form of government is comparable, either in its general character, in its distribution of powers, or in the training it gives, with that which our ancestors received from their own forefathers. . . ." [68]

III

Cicero's discussion of mixed government takes the form of a commentary on Roman constitutional history as he and his contemporaries understood it. This commentary is to be found in the second book of the *Republic,* the third book of the *Laws,* and various passages scattered through the *De Officiis.* The second book of the *Republic* deals with early constitutional development down to the completion of the republican constitution—the degeneration of kingship into tyranny under the Tarquins, the original aristocratic republic, the attainment of power by the plebeians, and the establishment of the tribunate. The third book of the *Laws* discusses problems of the later republic, the suffrage, the ballot, the power of the tribunes, and the like. Some of these latter topics are also touched on in the *De Officiis* in connection with particular historical incidents.

At the beginning of the second book of the *Republic* Cicero shows his awareness of the development of the Roman constitution as an organic growth rather than an artificial construction, and he emphasizes that feature as the principal ground of its health and vigor. "Cato used to say," he writes, "that our constitution was superior to those of other States on account of the fact that . . . our own commonwealth . . . was founded, not in one generation, but in a long period of several centuries and many ages of men. For, said he, . . . the combined powers of all the men living at one time [could not] possibly make all necessary provisions for the future without the aid of actual experience and the test of time." [69]

This conception of a sound constitution as the product of organic growth had been foreshadowed by both Aristotle and Polybius, but Cicero added substance to it by suggesting that its essential feature consisted in developing old principles in the light of new experience and permitting time to fuse old and new together into a living whole which would be capable of further development. It is interesting to observe that Cato's words, as Cicero reproduces them, bear a strong resemblance to similar remarks by Lord Coke with reference to the growth of the English common law:

[O]ur daies upon the earth are but as a shadow, in respect of the old and ancient dayes and times past, wherein the Laws have been by the wisdom of the most excellent men, in many successions of ages, by long and continual experience (the trial of right and truth) fined and refined, which no one man (being of so short a time) albeit he had in his head the wisdom of all the men in the world, in any one age could never have effected or attained unto.[70]

With this sense of growth, Cicero recognized various stages in the development of the Roman republic, and it was this recognition which almost certainly caused him to revert to his original plan of choosing the age of the younger Africanus as the vantage point from which to review the republican constitution. There were two obvious reasons for this choice. The first was that in that era, which coincided with the advent of the Gracchi, the fatal fissures in the constitution which afterwards destroyed it had already begun to make themselves felt; the second was that in the Scipionic circle Romans first commenced to employ the tools of Greek thought in an effort to understand and appraise their institutions. The age of Scipio (which was also the age of Polybius) thus constituted a watershed and great divide; it was the natural vantage point for an effort to understand what had gone before in the light of what was to come afterwards. Cicero nowhere makes this thought explicit, but it can be read everywhere between the lines of his book. Thus, at the very beginning, he causes one of his speakers to ask, "why, in one State, we have almost reached the point where there are two senates and two separate peoples? For . . . the death of Tiberius Gracchus . . . divided one people into two factions." [71] While, "as to our having a united senate and people, it is possible, and unless it is brought about, we shall have serious trouble; we know and observe that the situation is far from being as it should be, and that, if this can be brought about, our lives will be better and happier." [72]

Cicero seems to have felt that in the Scipionic era the happy achievement of concord was still not beyond the bounds of possibility; for any later time he doubtless hesitated to commit himself. To understand the republic, it was therefore necessary to revert to the last epoch in which the government was still functioning normally. For Cicero there was perhaps another reason, a personal and sentimental one, for reverting to this particular epoch of the past. In his youth, as a country lad in Rome, he had had the good fortune to be received into the company and sit at the feet of distinguished men who had been part of the Scipionic circle, and he thus undoubtedly felt that he was in a sense a channel of the direct tradition stemming from that older and more wholesome time. In this connection it is interesting that he pretends that the dialogue which he reproduces in the *Republic* had been reported to him by

Publius Rutilius Rufus when as a young man he had visited that distinguished exile at Smyrna.[73]

Cicero's account of the Roman constitution in the *Republic* accordingly leads up to, and terminates at, the Scipionic era, when in his judgment it had reached its maturity and was at the end of its strong and healthy condition.[74] He begins his review with a discussion of the deterioration of the primitive monarchy of Romulus into the tyranny of the Tarquins and makes the important observation that "the tyrant overthrows the whole monarchical constitution, not by seizing any new powers, but by his misuse of the powers he already possesses."[75] The overthrow of the Tarquins is represented not as the work of the aristocracy but of the whole Roman people, under the leadership of Lucius Brutus, a man preeminent for wisdom and bravery, who "freed his fellow-citizens from the unjust yoke of cruel servitude."[76] The foundation of the republic thus owed its beginnings to the leadership of a single man. "And though Brutus was only a private citizen, he sustained the whole burden of the government, and was the first in our State to demonstrate that no one is a mere private citizen when the liberty of his fellows needs protection."[77] Such a leader stands out in vivid contrast to the tyrant—"the good, wise, and skilful guardian and protector, as one may say, of the practical interests and of the self-respect of the citizens of the State; for these are titles which will be granted to one who is truly the guide and pilot of a nation. See to it that you are able to recognize such a man, for he is one who can maintain the safety of the State both by counsel and by action."[78]

Speaking of the Roman constitution immediately after the expulsion of the Tarquins and the foundation of the republic, Cicero says that in that period "the government was so administered by the senate that, though the people were free, few political acts were performed by them, practically everything being done by the authority of the senate. . . . Another principle that was most important to the retention of the power by the aristocracy was also strictly maintained, namely, that no act of a popular assembly should be valid unless ratified by the Fathers. . . ."[79] Yet the whole government was kept, with the people's consent, in the strong hands of the aristocracy. . . ." [80] However, "the people, freed from the domination of kings, claimed a somewhat greater measure of rights. Such a claim may have been unreasonable, but the essential nature of the commonwealth often defeats reason. For you must keep in mind a fact which I mentioned at the beginning: unless there is in the State an even balance of rights, duties, and functions, so that the magistrates have enough power, the counsels of the eminent citizens enough influence, and the people enough liberty, this kind of government cannot be safe from revolution . . . just as at Rome the plebeian tribunes were chosen to counterbalance the power of the consuls." [81] "[T]he people were given an occasion, through the creation of two plebeian tribunes . . . for curtailing the power and influence of the senate. This power, however, remained great and respected, because the wisest and bravest still guarded the State by arms and counsel, and their influence continued to be supreme because, while they surpassed the masses in preferment, they had a smaller share of the pleasures of life, and in property were not, as a rule, better off than their fellows." [82]

From the history of the republic Cicero draws the conclusion that even for a sound constitution to function in an orderly and effective way there must above all else be concord and agreement among the different orders or classes composing the state. "[A] State [is] made harmonious by agreement among dissimilar elements, brought about by a fair and reasonable blending together of the upper, middle, and lower classes, just as if they were musical tones. What the musicians call harmony in song is concord in a State, the strongest and best bond of permanent union in any commonwealth; and such concord can never be brought about without the aid of justice." [83]

Cicero says that in many instances in the course of Roman history the desire of the multitude and the whim of the people have been at variance with the true interests of the state.[84] To guard against this danger he praises the distribution of voting strength by the early king Servius Tullius, who parceled it out among the different centuries, and says that "the principle . . . ought always to be adhered to in the commonwealth, that the greatest number should not have the greatest power." [85] Under the system of Servius, "while no one was deprived of the suffrage, the majority of votes was in the hands of those to whom the highest welfare of the State was the most important." [86] Elsewhere he says that "in civil strife, when virtue is of greater importance than numbers, . . . the citizens ought to be weighed rather than counted." [87] Absolute equality of political rights for all is injustice, for "when all the power is in the people's hands, even though they exercise it with justice and moderation, yet the resulting equality itself is inequitable, since it allows no distinctions in rank." [88] "For that equality of legal rights of which free peoples are so fond . . . is really most inequitable. For when equal honour is given to the highest and the lowest—for men of both types must exist in every nation—then this very 'fairness' is most unfair. . . ." [89]

Yet with this recognition of the injustices and dangers inherent in popular rule, Cicero recommends no diminution of the democratic element in the Roman constitution. His attitude is most plainly stated in a discussion of the tribunate in the third book of the *Laws*, where he and his brother Quintus are the speakers. Cicero says that the tribunes were set up to check and balance the consuls because "if one magistrate is to rule over all the others, it will seem that it was merely the name of king that was abolished, the institution remaining." [90] Thus it was not without good reason that the tribunes were created in opposition to the consuls and to balance them. Admittedly "it was the institution of this office that brought about the decline in the influence of the aristocracy and the growth of the power of the multitude." [91] Hereupon a debate ensues between Cicero and Quintus in which Quintus attacks the tribunate and Cicero defends it.

The power of the tribunes, Quintus is made to say, "seems to me a mischievous thing, born in civil strife and tending to civil strife. . . . Of what crimes has it not been guilty! Its first acts . . . were to deprive the senators of all their privileges, to make the lowest equal to the highest everywhere, and to produce utter confusion and disorder. But even after destroying the authority of the aristocracy, it never rested. For . . . what rights did the tribunate of Tiberius Gracchus leave to the best citizens? . . . Furthermore, was it not the overthrow of Gaius Gracchus and the casting of daggers into the forum . . . that brought about, through the tribunate, a complete revolution in the State? Why should I go on to mention Saturninus, Sulpicius, and all the other tribunes from whom the republic could not protect herself without resorting to the sword? . . . Wherefore I heartily approve of Sulla's laws on this subject, which took from the plebeian tribunes the power of doing mischief, and left them only the right to give relief; and as for our friend Pompey . . . as regards his attitude toward the power of the tribunes I have nothing to say, for I do not wish to criticize him and I cannot praise him." [92]

Cicero replies that "in an attack on any institution it is unfair to omit all mention of its advantages, and enumerate only its disadvantages. . . . I acknowledge that there is an element of evil in the very power of the tribunate; but we could not have the good aimed at when the office was established without the evil you refer to. 'The tribunes of the plebs have too much power,' you say. Who can deny it? But the power of the people themselves is much more cruel, much more violent; and yet this power is sometimes milder in practice because there is a leader to control it than if there were none. . . . 'But,' you object, 'the tribunes sometimes excite the people.' Yes, and they often calm them too. . . . But consider the wisdom of our ancestors in this matter. When the Senate had granted this power to the plebeians, conflict ceased, rebellion was at an end, and a measure of compromise was discovered which . . . was the only salvation of the State. 'But we have had the two Gracchi,' you say. Yes, and you could mention many more besides . . . whose activities are harmful . . . but in the meantime . . . the common people make no desperate struggles for their rights. Thus it is clear that either the monarchy ought never to have been abolished, or else that real liberty . . . had to be given to the common people; but this liberty has been granted in such a manner that the people were induced by many excellent provisions to yield to the authority of the nobles." [93] In dealing with the restoration of the tribunician power, Pompey "had to determine, not merely what was ideally best, but also what was practically necessary. For he realized that this office was indispensable in our republic. . . . It was the duty of a wise citizen, in dealing with an institution not evil in itself and so dear to the people . . . not to leave its defence to a popular leader, which would have had evil consequences." [94]

These remarks of Cicero about the tribunate supply a key to his attitude toward the democratic element in government. Although it must be balanced with other elements to provide for proper moderation and leadership, it cannot and should not be either suppressed or too strongly checked. This conclusion rests on both moral and practical grounds. A free people is entitled to liberty in fact as well as in name, and this means that they must have a large participation in political rights and adequate protection for those rights.[95] On practical grounds the case for democracy is even stronger. In the last analysis it is in the power of the people, and nowhere else, to overturn any government; and, accordingly, if government is to be stable, the people must be satisfied to the extent they must in the last analysis be supreme. "It is not easy to resist the people in their might if you give them no legal rights or only a few." [96] Thus, as one commentator has expressed it, in Cicero's ideal state:

Absolute power is given to the People, but as many opportunities as possible are provided for the play of senatorial influence upon this all-powerful democracy. . . . If he thinks of the common people as entirely lacking in political wisdom, why has he given them the supreme power in the state? Simply because he recognizes the great fact that, in any form of state, they actually possess the supreme power. This fact he had doubtless learned from practical experience. . . . This point of view . . . gives a complete explanation of Cicero's Constitution as we have it. Only the aristocracy can govern the state wisely, but it cannot govern the state at all, except with the full approval of the People. . . . Cicero, of course, . . . thinks of the People's combination of political power with entire lack of political wisdom as an evil, but he differs basically from the extreme conservatives in his realization that the maintenance of this power is absolutely necessary.[97]

In one important respect, dissent must be expressed from this otherwise sound interpretation of Cicero's thought: he did not believe that the people must inevitably be totally lacking in political wisdom, for without a certain kind of political wisdom on their part not even an adequately balanced or mixed constitution could function or endure. For such a constitution to be effective the people must at least be willing to work harmoniously with the other parts of the government and must be imbued with a spirit of concord and compromise, or what he had previously called a sense of, and will toward, justice.[98] "[A]s to our having a united senate and people, it is possible, and unless it is brought about, we shall have serious trouble." [99] "This, then, ought to be the chief end of all men, to make the interest of each individual and of the whole body politic identical." [100] In other words, if the citizens are to play their part rightly in the state—a part of which they cannot practically or morally be deprived—they must have the proper objectives and give their support to the policies of leaders who are furthering those objectives; otherwise the state will fall. The citizen must consider not his own interest alone but his interest in relation to the other interests which are comprehended in the community of which he is a part. Although doubtless this ideal state of affairs can never be completely attained, unless it is attained to a certain minimum degree, not even a mixed constitution will work.

The idea of concord between the different elements of the state—"concord between the orders" as he called it—had been the basic and favorite policy to which Cicero had devoted his efforts throughout his political career and which he had repeatedly emphasized in his speeches. It was most fully elaborated in his speech in defense of Sestius from which quotations have been given in an earlier chapter [101] and which was a plea for a party of good citizens of all ranks and classes in opposition to those who would split the state in support of their selfish interests. As to who are the best citizens, he said:

They are the chief men in our public councils and those who follow their leadership; they are the men of highest position to whom the senate-house stands open; they are the citizens of the Italian municipalities and the Romans of the country-side; they are the businessmen; there are even freedmen who belong to the party of good citizens. The number of men of this kind is distributed far and wide, but, to avoid misunderstanding, the entire group can be briefly defined and described. All men belong to the party of good citizens who are neither bent on wrong-doing nor unjust or revolutionary by nature, nor involved in private difficulties. . . . Those who are guided by the views of these good citizens, who consult their interests and opinions in the government of the republic, belong to the party of good citizens. . . . What then is the object kept in view and pursued by these governors of the republic and which they should keep before their eyes and by which they should direct their course? It is that good which is the best and most desirable for all sane and good and happy citizens—public tranquillity and private self-respect.[102]

Cicero's observation and experience led him to the view that the chief obstacle to the concord and cooperation which was the objective of the "party of good citizens" came from the agitation of those who desired change for selfish reasons of their own. "For in so great a number of citizens there is always a large body of those who . . . are anxious for changes and revolutions in the state, or who on account of some innate lack of mental balance feed on the discords and sedition of the citizens, or who on account of the embarrassment of their private fortunes and estates would rather perish in one general conflagration than in one of their own. And when these men have found instigators, leaders and promoters for their vicious purposes, great upheavals are stirred up in the state." [103]

The party of change has unfortunately an inherent advantage over the party of stability and concord; the former is fighting to gain something, the latter only to defend what they have, and attack is always more vigorous than defense. The constitution is always attacked with greater force than that by which it is defended.

Bold and reckless men are touched off by a nod, and of their own accord they are incited to overturn the established order of things. On the other hand, good men are somehow slower to act, they overlook the first beginnings of evil until they are aroused by necessity to face the last extremity, so that sometimes through their hesitations and delays, while they wish to preserve their tranquility even without self-respect, they lose both. Moreover, those who wish to be defenders of the constitution, if they are men of little resolution, give up the task; if they are somewhat timid, they are not to be found; only those remain and risk all for the republic . . . whom no violence, no threats and no unpopularity have caused to waver.[104]

In these passages, Cicero diagnoses one of the chief reasons for the strength of the anti-senatorial movement of his day. That strength arose from the fact that energetic and aggressive "new men," who were anxious to improve their personal fortunes and felt that their opportunities were too restricted under the existing governmental arrangements, were willing to go to all lengths to overturn those arrangements, whereas those who had an established position at stake were unwilling to risk it by opposing too openly new forces which might in the end prove successful. Such an unequal balance of parties Cicero regarded as necessarily fatal to the constitution without an overall devotion on the part of the civic body to the welfare of the state, as opposed to complete devotion to either party. This thought he expresses in a passage in the *De Officiis* as follows:

Now, those who care for the interests of a part of the citizens and neglect another part, introduce into the civil service a dangerous element—dissension and party strife. The result is that some are found to be loyal supporters of the democratic, others of the aristocratic party, and a few of the nation as a whole. As a result of this party spirit . . . not only dissensions but also disastrous civil wars broke out. All this the citizen who is patriotic, brave, and worthy of a leading place in the state will shun with abhorrence; he will dedicate himself unreservedly to his country, without aiming at influence or power for himself; and he will devote himself to the state in its entirety in such a way as to further the interests of all.[105]

It is apparent from these expressions that Cicero believed a sound civic spirit, a sense of justice, and self-restraint in promoting private interests were essential on the part of the civic body to enable the democratic element to play its indispensable part in a mixed constitution like that of the Roman republic. Without them there could not be the requisite degree and kind of cooperation between the people and their leaders, the sort which a mixed type of government was meant to provide. For although, as in all governments, the people must in the final analysis be the supreme source of power, Cicero did not regard it as desirable or in accord with Rome's traditional constitutional forms that they should exercise the full measure of their power directly; indeed, it was the essence of the mixed type of government that they should not. The most desirable arrangement was that which he describes in a passage, already quoted, in which he says, referring to the government of the early republic, that although the people were free, "few political acts were performed by them, practically everything being done by the authority of the senate. . . . Yet the whole government was kept, with the people's consent, in the strong hands of the aristocracy. . . ." [106]

Cicero conceived that the function of the senate was twofold. In the first place, it was to conduct the day-to-day details of governmental administration, instead of leaving them to be supervised directly by the popular assembly, as in a typical ancient democratic city-state; secondly, and more importantly, the senate was to be vested with leadership in the determination of broad matters of public policy. Our ancestors, says Cicero in his speech on behalf of Sestius, "placed the senate in the position of guardian, presiding body and defender of the state; they wished the magistrates to act under the authority of this body and be as it were the ministers of its wise counsels." [107] Again, in the *Laws,* he says, "if the Senate is recognized as the leader of public policy, and all the other orders defend its decrees, and are willing to allow the highest order to conduct the government by its wisdom, then this compromise, by which supreme power is granted to the people and actual authority to the Senate, will make possible the maintenance of that balanced and harmonious constitution which I have described. . . ." [108]

Thus in Cicero's conception of the Roman constitution, "the Senate is the mainspring of the machine," [109] the instrument and agency for carrying on the business of government in matters large and small. He was even prepared to recognize its authority to legislate, and among his few suggestions for constitutional change was that its decrees should have the force of law, [110] and that it should also have direct administrative supervision over the minor magistrates. [111] Cicero obviously believed that for a balanced constitution to be workable there must be some central organ in a position to make government function, and in his conception the proper organ for that task was the senate, which should embody the concentrated competence and political wisdom of the state. [112] More realistic and practical than Polybius, Cicero sees that a state must have a center of gravity. "Polybius balances his three powers, Magistrates, Senate and People as accurately as a skilful juggler; Cicero finds in the Senate the true center of gravity in the Roman constitution." [113]

Cicero's conception of the senate was not that of a self-perpetuating aristocracy or oligarchy, ruling by virtue of birth, descent, social position or wealth. The basis for the powers with which he would vest it lay in competence, political wisdom and personal leadership derived from recognition of merit. For this reason, its membership should consist of the ex-magistrates of the republic, who had been chosen to their offices by popular vote from the entire citizen-body. This, says Cicero, is certainly a measure embodying democratic principles, since "it ensures that no one shall enter that exalted order except by popular election, the censors being deprived of the right of free choice." [114] This is in accord, he thinks, with the historical principles of the Roman constitution, for it was there decreed that the members of the senate should be chosen by the entire people and that entry into that supreme order of all citizens should be the consequence of industry and worth.[115] Cicero assumes that in a reasonable, sound political community election will be for merit and not for less worthy reasons. Thus the senate of his ideal Roman state "is to be no narrow Roman oligarchy, but representative of all that is best in the whole of Italy, merit, and not birth, being the passport to it." [116]

This was no ignoble ideal. It was a return to that better Rome which Cicero, like Polybius, believed had existed during the Punic wars, and which was beginning to break up just before the advent of the Gracchi. It has been said that we "may partly call the sum of his political theory a system of enlightened aristocracy"; [117] it would seem more fair to call it a system of conservative democracy. He recognized what has become a commonplace in modern democratic thinking that the formulation of policy and the details of administration cannot be performed by the entire civic body in mass meetings, as had been attempted in the democratic city-states of the ancient world; but he also believed that the governing body which formulates policy and superintends administration must consist of elected representatives of the people. The obvious difference is that Cicero would have these representatives chosen for life and not change with the fluctuating views and wishes of the electorate; what he sought was a stable governing body of experience and political wisdom and not a mere registering instrument of the popular will. In this sense he believed not in direct democracy but in a republic with a democratic basis.

Just as Cicero recognized that a balanced or mixed government, no matter how admirable its institutional arrangements, could not function successfully without a sound civic spirit and sense of justice among the people,[118] so likewise he recognized that the senate, to perform the part in government which he assigned to it, must consist of leaders who on the whole had a proper sense of responsibility, a will to do justice, and a willingness to subordinate their personal interests to the interests of the community. He frankly admitted that he no longer found these qualities present in adequate measure in the senate of his own time. In fact, he attributed the sickness of the republic mainly to the shortcomings and vices of the senatorial leaders. This thought was constantly in his mind. Not only did those leaders, in their rivalry for wealth and power and in their personal jealousies and hatreds, make the senate ineffective as an organ of leadership in the state, but many of them were personally the most active agents in promoting and stirring up dissension and sedition among the populace and thus destroying the civic spirit without which no kind of orderly government could go on. Accordingly, in the *Laws* Cicero adds a final provision with respect to the functions of the senate: "That order shall be free from dishonor, and shall be a model for the rest of the citizens." One of the other speakers then breaks in to say that the task of punishing misdeeds of the members of that order would take the time of all the judges. To this Cicero replies: "We need not enter into that. . . . For we are not talking about the present Senate or the men of our own day, but about those of the future; that is, in case any of them ever are willing to obey these laws of mine. For as our law requires that senators shall be free from all dishonour, no one who is guilty of anything dishonourable will so much as enter that order. Of course this is difficult of accomplishment except through education and training." [119]

One thought expressed by Cicero in this passage reflects a most important phase of his political philosophy, namely, that the members of the senate, the aristocracy, should "be a model for the rest of the citizens." He believed that inevitably the masses will imitate the classes. He was conscious of a fact which was largely lost sight of during the era of nineteenth century optimism—the fact that it is generally a relatively small part of any given society or community which sets the tone, creates the mental and moral atmosphere, and prescribes the standards of the entire group. Those who thus set the standards are the leaders, by whatever name we call them. Cicero called them "nobles" or *principes,* men of rank, and thought of them as the aristocracy and as furnishing the bulk of the membership of the senate. Therefore, he says, "a transformation takes place in a nation's character when the habits and mode of living of its aristocracy are changed. For that reason men of the upper class [*principes*] who do wrong are especially dangerous to the State, because they not only indulge in vicious practices themselves, but also infect the whole commonwealth with their vices; and not only because they are corrupt, but also because they corrupt others, and do more harm by their bad examples than by their sins." [120]

In this connection Cicero tells of a reply of the great Lucullus to a criticism of the luxury of his country seat at Tusculum. Lucullus said that he had two neighbors, a Roman knight living immediately above him and a rich freedman immediately below; and, since their seats displayed the height of luxury, he thought he ought to have at least the same privilege as men of less distinguished position. This reply was thought very neat and witty; but, asks Cicero, "Lucullus, do you not see that even their desire for luxury is your own fault? If you had not indulged in it, it would not have been permissible for them to do so. . . . Who would not put an end to their inordinate desires, if those very men whose duty it was to put an end to them were not guilty of the same passions? For it is not so mischievous that men of high position do evil—though that is bad enough in itself—as it is that these men have so many imitators. For, if you will turn your thoughts back to our early history, you will see that the character of our most prominent men has been reproduced in the whole State. . . ." [121] Just as the whole state "is habitually corrupted by the evil desires and the vices of its prominent men, so is it improved and reformed by self-restraint on their part." [122] Every state is "such as its ruler's character and will make it." [123]

Nothing is more fundamental in Cicero's philosophy of government than his conviction that no matter how good the political institutions of a state may be in themselves, they will not work, or result in just and stable government, unless those who must be relied on to work them, both the citizen body and its leaders, are in the main human individuals of reasonably sound and disciplined character. Institutions will not produce results of themselves; they need the right kind of human beings to make them function. Hence in the fifth book of the *Republic,* where he admits that the Roman constitution has broken down, he places the blame on a breakdown of Roman character. "[I]t is through our own faults, not by any accident, that we retain only the form of the commonwealth, but have long since lost its substance." [124] "But though the republic, when it came to us, was like a beautiful painting, whose colours, however, were already fading with age, our own time not only has neglected to freshen it by renewing the original colours, but has not even taken the trouble to preserve its . . . general outlines. For what is now left of the 'ancient customs' on which [the poet] said 'the commonwealth of Rome' was 'founded firm'? They have been, as we see, so completely buried in oblivion that they are not only no longer practised, but are already unknown." [125]

This phase of Cicero's thought may seem to identify it with what has been called the "good man" theory of government, which so largely permeated the political philosophy of the Middle Ages and carries a perennial appeal in every age to well-meaning people who are impatient of detailed analysis. This theory contents itself with the view that so long as the wielders of political power are personally "good," institutional arrangements and governmental forms are immaterial. It is apparent from everything said thus far that this was not Cicero's view at all. He attached great importance, as we have seen, to the form and institutional arrangements of government, but he did not believe that good institutions are self-operative or will produce good government automatically. He recognized that political institutions are but one element in a complex social pattern, which is made up of countless individual patterns, and that government always functions in relation to all the other elements in society and ultimately to the human individuals who compose the community for which it acts.

The great problem with which Cicero was thus concerned— a problem to which he certainly contributed no novel solution but which he was one of the few political thinkers to emphasize—is expressed in his observation that relatively good institutions deteriorate and cease to function effectively as changes occur in the human character of the civic body and of the leaders who attain political power. The essence of this problem is how to relate impersonal institutional arrangements to the personal factor of human character on the part of both the rulers and the ruled. The only answer which Cicero had to offer was education and the maintenance of such social institutions of an educational and disciplinary kind as might be expected to build sound individual character.[126] To these subjects he devoted the last three books of the *Republic,* one-half of the entire treatise, which in itself illustrates his opinion of their supreme importance to the problem of government. Unfortunately the text of these books is almost entirely lost.

Cicero's approach to the problem of the relation of human character and behavior to the working of government differs basically from that of twentieth century students of sociology and social institutions. Inevitably, they regard that approach as old-fashioned and even primitive, although it was the approach of most would-be reformers down to the end of the nineteenth century. Cicero did not undertake to explain, as modern students would like to do, the urges, ambitions, inhibitions or lack of inhibitions of individuals, groups and classes by their enonomic and social conditions, the circumstances of the times and the opportunities and temptations which those circumstances present. He did not undertake to account for human character and behavior by environment or existing social and economic arrangements, but pointed instead to moral defects and aberrations. Thus he does not explain the failure of the Roman constitution in institutional terms but in moral terms—in terms of wrong individual motivation.

This approach is natural and inevitable for a thinker whose

whole theory, like that of Cicero, was preeminently a moral one. Since, from the moral point of view, man is a free agent with a capacity for distinguishing right from wrong, what he does, whether good or bad, depends on whether he is guided by good or bad motives. In making his choice, a man of character has the capacity, and as a moral agent is under a duty, to rise above external circumstances and be resistant to them. A man of character is expected to set himself outside his environment, and it is precisely in the ability to do this that character or moral goodness consists. The man who cannot or will not do it is not a man of character. This doctrine may seem old-fashioned today, but it is one which was usually taken for granted down to the end of the nineteenth century. In Cicero's day it was a doctrine on which both the great rival philosophical schools, Stoic and Epicurean, opposed in practically all else, were for once agreed. In the view of both those schools "the normal man . . . is . . . he who knows how to free himself from the external world. . . ." [127]

Cicero's moral theory, and his conception of the relation of morality, as he understood it, to government, are outgrowths of his theory of human nature and its capacities. This theory is developed in his consideration of the nature and possibility of justice, to which he turns in the third book of the *Republic* and elaborates more fully in the first book of the *Laws*.

IV

After Cicero has reached the conclusion at the end of the second book of the *Republic* that institutions depend for their successful working on human character, he is remitted to a more thorough examination of the major postulate of his treatise, namely, that government must be founded on, and bring about, justice. Clearly, however, if in the last analysis government reflects human character with its passions and weaknesses, and its constant tendency to lapse into injustice, the question arises whether as a practical matter government can ever be carried on without injustice; or, in other words, whether justice is really possible. Cicero faces this question candidly at the end of the second book of the *Republic* where he says: "we have no basis whatever for further progress, unless we can not merely disprove the contention that a government cannot be carried on without injustice, but are also able to prove positively that it cannot be carried on without the strictest justice." [128] Accordingly in the third book he takes up the question whether it is futile to hope that a state can be ruled by justice and law. Differently put, the question is whether justice is not a mere sham and pretense—whether men do not inevitably prefer and practice injustice.

Unfortunately what is left of this book of the *Republic* is only a fragment, devoted to reproducing the stock arguments of Greek philosophers in favor of injustice, which Cicero intends afterwards to refute. These fall broadly into two classes—what may be called the prudential or utilitarian argument on the one hand, and the skeptical argument on the other. Cicero states both of them plausibly and forcefully.

The prudential or utilitarian argument against justice proceeds from the proposition that prudence or practical wisdom and justice are in fundamental disagreement.[129] "Wisdom urges us to increase our resources, to multiply our wealth, to extend our boundaries . . . to rule over as many subjects as possible, to enjoy pleasures, to become rich, to be rulers and masters; justice, on the other hand, instructs us to spare all men, to consider the interests of the whole human race, to give everyone his due, and not to touch sacred or public property, or that which belongs to others. What, then, is the result if you obey wisdom? Wealth, power, riches, public office, military commands, and royal authority, whether we are speaking of individuals or of nations . . . [D]id our own people . . . whose empire now embraces the whole world, [grow] from the smallest [to the greatest] through justice or through wisdom?" [130] No people "would be so foolish as not to prefer to be unjust masters rather than just slaves." [131]

If justice is thus so disadvantageous to those who practice it, how did such an idea ever come to win widespread acceptance? Because, answered the school of Epicurus, it was a compromise of convenience and necessity, a convention and artifice, contrived by men living in a group to save some slight measure of advantage for themselves and avoid greater disadvantages. "But when there is

mutual fear, man fearing man and class fearing class, then, because
no one is confident in his own strength, a sort of bargain is made
between the common people and the powerful; this results in that
mixed form of government which Scipio has been recommending;
and thus, not nature or desire, but weakness, is the mother of justice.
For we must choose one of three things—to do injustice and not to
suffer it, or both to do it and to suffer it, or else neither to do it nor
to suffer it. The happiest choice is to do it with impunity, if you
can; the second best is neither to do it nor to suffer it; and the
worst fate of all is to engage in the everlasting struggle of doing
and suffering injustice." [132]

If justice originates in this way—if it is merely the product of
the weakness and compromise out of which government is supposed
to spring—then justice is itself only a product of government, and
it is therefore whatever government for the moment chooses to
say it is. Thus, justice is only a "civil" or governmental thing, not
something which originates in, or exists by nature.[133]

With justice thus reduced by the utilitarian theory of the Epi-
cureans to convention and artifice, a mere creation of government,
the way is prepared for the skeptical theory which denies that there
is anything which can properly be called justice at all. According
to this view, advocated by a younger school of the so-called Middle
Academy,[134] the concept of justice upon examination and analysis
fades away altogether and melts into nothingness. It cannot be
regarded as something which has any inherent or characteristic quality of its own—in other words, it does not "exist by nature," it is
not something which can be felt or recognized or defined, it is
nothing in itself. If justice and the distinction between right and
wrong existed by nature, "then, like heat and cold, or bitter and
sweet, justice and injustice would be the same thing to all men." [135]
"But if I wished to describe the conceptions of justice, and the
principles, customs, and habits which have existed, I could show
you, not merely differences in all the different nations, but that
there have been a thousand changes in a single city, even in our
own, in regard to these things. For example, our friend Manilius
here, being an interpreter of the law, would give you different advice about the rights of women in regard to legacies and inheritances

from that which he used to give in his youth, before the passage of the Voconian Law." [136] If god or nature had provided laws, "then all men would obey the same laws, and the same men would not have different laws at different times. But, I ask, if it is the duty of a just and good man to obey the laws, what laws is he to obey? All the different laws that exist?" [137] It is a characteristic of virtue that it does not admit of inconsistencies, just as nature does not admit of variations.[138] Therefore, since laws are subject to infinite variations from place to place and time to time, it follows that "laws are imposed upon us by fear of punishment, not by our sense of justice. Therefore there is no such thing as natural justice, and from this it follows that neither are men just by nature. Or will they tell us that, though laws vary, good men naturally follow what is truly just, not what is thought to be so? For, they say, it is the duty of a good and just man to give everyone that which is his due." [139]

It is unfortunate that the latter part of the third book of the *Republic,* which undoubtedy contained Cicero's answers to the prudential and skeptical denials of natural justice, is almost wholly lost. However, this loss is largely supplied by the first book of the *Laws,* in which the same topics are treated with great elaboration, and also by the third book of the *De Officiis,* which discusses in practical detail the conflicting claims of justice and prudential expedience. It is in these places that we find the clearest and most explicit statement of Cicero's own theory of justice.

Cicero's approach to the problem is not to answer the prudential and skeptical arguments directly but to go behind and beyond them —to transcend them by appealing to what he regarded as more fundamental issues and more relevant data of observation and experience regarding the facts of human nature. The nature of justice, he writes, must be sought in the nature of man.[140] His theory of justice is therefore based on a theory of human nature which underlies his whole political philosophy—a conception of human dignity and a conviction that human beings are entitled to respect as such. Men, he says, are born for justice,[141] and "there is no human being of any race who, if he finds a guide, cannot attain to virtue." [142] Men possess reason and therefore, if not virtue, at least the capacity for it; and because of this they have an innate ability to recognize the difference between right and wrong, or in other words justice. Man has been given a distinctive status by the supreme god who created him, "for he is the only one among so many different kinds and varieties of living beings who has a share in reason and thought, while all the rest are deprived of it." Therefore, since reason "exists both in man and God, the first common possession of man and God is reason." [143] "For when the nature of man is examined . . . while the other elements of which man consists were derived from what is mortal, and are therefore fragile and perishable, the soul was generated in us by God. Hence we are justified in saying that there is a blood relationship between ourselves and the celestial beings. . . . Therefore among all the varieties of living beings, there is no creature except man which has any knowledge of God." [144] "Moreover, virtue exists in man and God alike, but in no other creature besides; virtue, however, is nothing else than Nature perfected and developed to its highest point; therefore there is a likeness between man and God." [145] It is from these characteristics of human nature, and especially man's capacity for virtue and the respect to which this entitles him, that Cicero draws the conclusion that there is such a thing as natural justice and that men are "born" for it. Cicero nowhere expressly says that in their mutual dealings men should never treat one another as mere things or instruments, or as persons not entitled to respect, but this is everywhere implied in his thought, and it is the basis for his belief that all men have certain claims and interests which other men should recognize, irrespective of existing political arrangements or commands. This recognition is imposed by a law of our nature as human beings, and the rights so recognized supply the core and substance of natural justice.

The steps in the argument by which Cicero derives not only natural justice but law and the origin of civil society from the dignity of human nature and its participation in the god-given attribute of reason will have to be discussed subsequently, but at this point it is important to note the fundamental change registered by this approach to the problems of law and government from the approach represented by classical Greek thought in the writings of Plato and Aristotle. For Plato and Aristotle, justice consisted essentially in each individual's fulfilling his part properly in a well-ordered state; in this sense, man derived his title to respect and consideration solely as a unit in a civic body. For Cicero, on the other hand, the right of a state to be regarded as well-ordered, or even to be considered as a state in a proper sense at all, depended on its respect for the rights of human beings and its ability and will to protect and serve them. By this shift in emphasis Cicero marks a sharp dividing line, a major watershed, in the history of political thought. For the first time the emphasis shifts from the state or political community to the human beings who compose it, and the reason for this shift is no less important than the shift itself. That Cicero marks such a sharp line of change in political theory between what precedes and what follows is attributable to the fact that he bases his political thought on the innate dignity of human nature—on the worth of the human individual as a person —and that he bases this worth and dignity in turn on man's kinship with the divine and his participation in some of the attributes of a supreme being. This is what caused the doctors of the Church to find Cicero's writings so congenial when they turned to political speculation, and through the channel of their influence his fundamental ideas and attitudes toward political problems became part of the heritage of Western Christendom and have remained interwoven in its fabric and texture long after political thought ceased to be guided by mainly theological influences. The abiding stamp imprinted by Cicero on Western habits of thought and expression is illustrated by a passage in an article by John Foster Dulles, which almost certainly would not have been written as it was had Cicero not thought and written as he did. In this article, Mr. Dulles makes the point that the principal reason for giving freedom to the individual is that men are the children of God, created in his image. Hence, the human personality is sacred and must not be trampled upon by government. That idea is given expression in the American Constitution in the Bill of Rights. He then goes on to say that if a society ceases to be founded on religion, it is both logical and practical to suppress human freedom so that men, like domesticated animals, may be more secure.[146]

Scholars never tire of pointing out that Cicero's theory of human nature and especially his emphasis on its divine elements are derived from Greek thought of the period subsequent to Aristotle and particularly from doctrines of the Stoic school, whose writings have unfortunately nearly all perished.[147] There cannot be any doubt that Cicero was familiar with the doctrines of the Stoics and that many of the ideas initiated by their teaching were congenial to his way of thought; but here, as elsewhere in his political works, there is no evidence that he slavishly copied earlier texts, while on the other hand it is clear that in some important particulars he departed radically from orthodox Stoic tenets. It is true that the Stoics believed in a divine "world-reason" expressing itself in "natural" law in which men had by nature a capacity for participating, so that true morality, when realized, "coincides with genuine, complete humanity and with the reasonableness which is valid in like measure for all." [148] In the Stoic view, however, this participation was an ideal achieved by only a very few human individuals—the narrowly limited number who could measure up to the standard of the Stoic "sage" or "wise man," to which Cicero's contemporary, the younger Cato, so earnestly aspired. "According to the view of the Stoics, therefore, the few sages stood as perfect men over against the great mass of fools and sinners, and in many declamations they lamented the baseness of men with the Pharisaic pessimism. . . ." [149] This is a far cry from Cicero's conception that men in general have a capacity for virtue in such sense as to entitle all of them to respect. Again, in the Stoic view, political institutions and actual governmental arrangements were of little or no concern to the "wise man," who was primarily interested in the spiritual and ethical community of "wise men" everywhere. Thus, "both the particular forms of the state and the individual historical states were held to be ultimately indifferent to him." [150] Indeed, insofar as the Stoics had a preference among different kinds of government it was for absolute monarchy, which they thought would afford scope and opportunity for the talents of the "wise man" if he should happen to be king. This disregard of the differences between governmental forms and this depreciation of historical institutions are entirely different from the views of Cicero. Although much that he wrote about man's participation in the divine reason, the intrinsic worth of moral personality, and the subordination of men and governments to natural law was undoubtedly suggested by Stoic thought, it seems clear that he used these suggestions as starting points for his own thinking and did not merely follow a pattern of ideas borrowed from an outside source. While his basic and most important conception of the dignity of human nature had been receiving increasing recognition for a century at the hands of the Stoics, it had never been given such a central and controlling position in political and legal thought as it received from Cicero. It is inevitable that Cicero borrowed much from the schools, and particularly from the Stoics, but his choice of emphasis is so novel as to amount almost to originality. Above all, he breathed warmth and power into their dry technicalities and thereby assured that his words would survive as a living force and influence for men who could never have been moved by mere academic philosophy.

Cicero's derivation of natural justice from a conception of the dignity of human nature was part of a more comprehensive theory which sought to deduce human society, the state, government and law from one and the same source. In his view, all were interrelated manifestations and emanations of the same original cause. From this point of view, human nature could be considered as displaying two basic characteristics—man's possession of reason on the one hand and his natural sociability on the other. In Cicero's view the latter was a consequence of the former. The participation of all men in the reasoning faculty draws them together into fellowship and communication.[151] Because they reason they communicate. This innate social tendency, combined with man's capacity for reason, is the source of the virtues. All men "are bound together by a certain natural feeling of kindliness and good-will." [152] Generosity, love of home and country, loyalty, the wish to be of service to others and to show gratitude for favors received—all these originate in our natural inclination to love our fellowmen.[153] "What nation does not love courtesy, kindliness, gratitude and remembrance of favours bestowed? What people does not hate and despise the haughty, the wicked, the cruel and the ungrateful?" Man's social nature, expressing itself in these virtues, is the parent of both justice and of the state.

The basis of the state is "not so much the weakness of the

individual as a certain social spirit which nature has implanted in man." [154] "And it is not true, as certain people maintain, that the bonds of union in human society were instituted in order to provide for the needs of daily life; for, they say, without the aid of others we could not secure for ourselves or supply to others the things that Nature requires; but if all that is essential to our wants and comfort were supplied by some magic wand, as in the stories, then every man of first-rate ability could drop all other responsibility and devote himself exclusively to learning and study. Not at all. For he would seek to escape from his loneliness and to find someone to share his studies; he would wish to teach, as well as to learn; to hear, as well as to speak." [155] It was the inclination of man to associate with man, he says elsewhere, that caused cities to be founded and peopled, as a result of which laws and customs were established, followed by the definition of private rights and a definite discipline of living. [156]

Just as man's reasoning powers and his natural sociability are the parent of the state or civil society, so also they are the source of justice and of the other social virtues. Men "are so constituted by Nature as to share the sense of Justice with one another" and to communicate it among themselves. [157] The mind and reason of the intelligent man provide the rule and standard of justice and injustice. [158] All good men recognize and love fairness and justice for its own sake. [159]

That justice should express itself in law was, in Cicero's view, a necessary consequence of man's possession of reason. [160] Man's perception of cause and effect produces an understanding of and respect for law, order and propriety. [161] The most learned men are right in defining law as the highest form of reason, inherent in nature, "which commands what ought to be done and forbids the opposite. This reason, when firmly fixed and fully developed in the human mind, is Law. And so they believe that Law is intelligence, whose natural function it is to command right conduct and forbid wrongdoing. . . . Now if this is correct, as I think it to be in general, then the origin of Justice is to be found in Law, for Law is a natural force; it is the mind and reason of the intelligent man, the standard by which Justice and Injustice are measured." [162]

This theory that law and justice form a pattern implicit in

nature and capable of apprehension by human reason encounters, of
course, the skeptical argument outlined above that, if this were
the case, then all peoples at all times would have the same laws and
that the obvious variations in legal institutions between different
states and within the same state at different times would be impossible.[163] Cicero produces a number of answers to this argument,
and he brings them forward at different points in the development
of his own views. The first answer which he advances is that the
human perception of justice is often interfered with and impaired
by countervailing influences. Thus, he says that right is founded not
on men's opinions, which may fluctuate, but upon Nature.[164]
"Wherefore since both good and evil are judged by Nature and are
natural principles, surely honourable and base actions must also
be distinguished in a similar way and referred to the standard of
Nature. But we are confused by the variety of men's beliefs and
by their disagreements, and because this same variation is not found
in the senses, we think that Nature has made these accurate, and
say that those things about which different people have different
opinions and the same people not always identical opinions are un-
real. However, this is far from being the case. For our senses are
not perverted by parent, nurse, teacher, poet, or the stage, nor led
astray by popular feeling; but against our minds all sorts of plots
are constantly being laid, either by those whom I have just mentioned, who, taking possession of them while still tender and un-
formed, colour and bend them as they wish, or else by that enemy
which lurks deep within us, entwined in our every sense—that
counterfeit of good, which is, however, the mother of all evils—
pleasure. Corrupted by her allurements, we fail to discern clearly
what things are by Nature good. . . ."[165]

If justice and law in the true sense are implicit in nature, they
are obviously anterior to and independent of the enactments or
judicially prescribed rules and customs of any particular state or
states. The popular definition of law is that which in the form of a
written enactment decrees or forbids whatever it pleases. "But in
determining what Justice is, let us begin with that supreme Law
which had its origin ages before any written law existed or any State
had been established."[166] Therefore, law is not to be learned from

the praetor's edict, as most people think, nor from the Twelve Tables.[167] "Even if there was no written law against rape at Rome in the reign of Lucius Tarquinius, we cannot say on that account that Sextus Tarquinius did not break that eternal Law by violating Lucretia. . . . For reason did exist, derived from the Nature of the universe, urging men to right conduct and diverting them from wrong-doing, and this reason did not first become Law when it was written down, but when it first came into existence; and it came into existence simultaneously with the divine mind." [168] The most foolish notion "is the belief that everything is just which is found in the customs or laws of nations. Would that be true, even if these laws had been enacted by tyrants? If the well-known Thirty had desired to enact a set of laws at Athens, or if the Athenians without exception were delighted by the tyrants' laws, that would not entitle such laws to be regarded as just, would it?" [169] "[I]f the principles of Justice were founded on the decrees of peoples, the edicts of princes, or the decisions of judges, then Justice would sanction robbery and adultery and forgery of wills, in case these acts were approved by the votes or decrees of the populace. But if so great a power belongs to the decisions and decrees of fools that the laws of Nature can be changed by their votes, then why do they not ordain that what is bad and baneful shall be considered good and salutary? Or, if a law can make Justice out of Injustice, can it not also make good out of bad? . . . [O]nly a madman would conclude that these judgments are matters of opinion, and not fixed by Nature." [170]

Another indication to Cicero's mind that law does not consist of the enactments of governments but of the dictates of man's nature is his conviction that law cannot be made effective through political sanctions alone but chiefly through men's own sense of guilt. Men pay the penalty for their crimes, he says, "not so much through decisions of the courts (for once there were no courts anywhere, and to-day there are none in many lands; and where they do exist, they often act unjustly after all); but guilty men are tormented . . . with the anguish of remorse and the torture of a guilty conscience. . . . [I]n fact there has never been a villain so brazen as not to deny that he had committed a crime, or else invent some story of just anger to excuse its commission, and seek justification for his crime in some natural principle of right. Now if even the wicked dare to appeal to such principles, how jealously should they be guarded by the good! But if it is a penalty, the fear of punishment, and not the wickedness itself, that is to keep men from a life of wrongdoing and crime, then no one can be called unjust. . . . For to what lengths will that man go in the dark who fears nothing but a witness and a judge?" [171] Thus, it is a "function of Law to win some measure of approval, and not always compel by threats of force." [172] Men are not "deterred from crime so much by the fear of the penalties ordained by law as by the sense of shame which Nature has given to man in the form of a certain fear of justified censure." [173]

From these various aspects of the operation of natural law, as Cicero conceived it, there emerges a reasonably clear notion of the idea that he had in mind. He was obviously thinking of certain broad fundamental principles that make a compelling appeal to man's unconscious sense of fairness, the disregard of which results in a feeling of outrage. Cicero believed so strongly in the basic unity and uniformity of human nature that he thought all men would recognize these principles and respond to them in the same way. Thus, to him natural law is not a detailed code of specific rules or precepts but a broad body of axioms, a set of human values, with which the specific rules enacted for different times and places should be consistent. Within the limits of such consistency, peoples are free to select what shall be their particular local or "civil" laws ("positive" laws, as they are now called), and Cicero even went so far as to derive the etymology of the Latin word for law, *lex,* from the idea of selection or choice between possible alternatives involved in the verb *legere.* Our forefathers, he says, "chose to understand one thing by the universal law and another by the civil law. The civil law is not necessarily also the universal law; but the universal law ought to be also the civil law." [174] Elsewhere he writes that "those rules which, in varying forms and for the need of the moment, have been formulated for the guidance of nations, bear the title of laws rather by favour than because they are really such. It is agreed . . . that laws were invented for the safety of citizens, the preservation of States, and the tranquillity and happiness of human life, and that those who first put statutes of this kind in force convinced their people that it was their intention to write down and put into effect such rules as, once accepted and adopted, would make possible for them an honourable and happy life; and when such rules were drawn up and put in force, it is clear that men called them 'laws.' " [175] Hence that variation in the detailed provisions of actual legal rules which skeptical analysis sought to use as an argument against the existence of natural justice.

Since law in the true sense—natural law or the highest law or law as right-reason, as Cicero variously calls it—is thus essentially a standard or yardstick by which to test the justice or properly legal character of specific detailed rules and enactments, one of the most useful functions of that standard is negative, namely, to cancel and invalidate the enactments and edicts of political agencies which are contrary to, or inconsistent with, it. "[T]he function of a magistrate is to govern, and to give commands which are just and . . . in conformity with the law. For as the laws govern the magistrate, so the magistrate governs the people. . . ." [176] Again, "those who formulated wicked and unjust statutes for nations, thereby breaking their promises and agreements, put into effect anything but 'laws.' . . . What of the many deadly, the many pestilential statutes which nations put in force? These no more deserve to be called laws than the rules a band of robbers might pass in their assembly. For if ignorant and unskilful men have prescribed deadly poisons instead of healing drugs, these cannot possibly be called physicians' prescriptions; neither in a nation can a statute of any sort be called a law, even though the nation . . . has accepted it." "Then," asks one of the speakers in the dialogue, "you do not think the Titian or Apuleian Laws [177] were really laws at all?" "No; nor the Livian Laws either." [178] "And you are right, especially as the Senate repealed them in one sentence and in a single moment." [179]

The thought which Cicero here expresses, and which he was the first publicist clearly to formulate, is that an enactment of the political lawmaking body which is contrary to fundamental principles of natural justice is not law in the proper sense and is not entitled to the obedience which law should receive. At an earlier time, the Athenians had recognized the beginning of the idea that the ordinary day-to-day enactments of a governing body should conform to a pattern of more permanent and fundamental laws of the state, but the latter were not conceived as necessarily founded in natural or universal justice, and the lack of conformity was not regarded as automatically invalidating the former. In these two respects Cicero's idea is novel and marks another point at which his thinking may be compared to a watershed between what went before and what came afterward. From his time onward, the idea of an invalid enactment is never completely absent from legal and political thought; it hovers over the surface of speculation through the centuries and gathers impetus in the Middle Ages from the force of Christian tradition, which was never willing to recognize the absolute sovereignty of the state. The difficulty, of course, was how to ensure and enforce the supremacy of natural or fundamental law over the commands of political rulers, and for this problem Cicero and his successors had no practical answer. He seems simply to have assumed that an enactment or decree which was void for inconsistency with natural or higher law should be disregarded, as he had argued in his speech *De Domo,*[180] in any proceeding—judicial, legislative or otherwise—in which it came in question and where reliance was sought to be placed on it. An individual, likewise, might also disregard it with impunity. This obviously left the validity of state-enacted law in a condition of permanent uncertainty, for no orderly institutional way was provided to decide the question of validity or invalidity with clearness or finality. It was left for the American political thinkers who framed our state and federal constitutions in the last quarter of the eighteenth century to find a way by attempting to formulate the basic principles of natural justice in written constitutions which the ordinary courts of judicature had jurisdiction to enforce against the acts of the political departments of government. The later American doctrine of judicial review of legislation and executive action thus rests ultimately on the basis of Cicero's thought, and after nineteen centuries that doctrine at last supplied the key by which his conception was made workable in practice.

Much of the difficulty involved in discussions of natural law and natural justice throughout the history of political speculation has sprung from failure to fill out the abstract terms with concrete content. Cicero attempted to meet this difficulty by identifying some of the specific requirements of natural justice, as he conceived it, both in the *Laws* and more fully in the *De Officiis,* which is devoted to considering the practical aspects of justice as applied to human conduct. It is interesting to note how closely Cicero's formulations of some of the specific requirements of natural justice correspond to principles which have been embodied in American constitutional law.

In the first place, according to Cicero, enactments in order to be just and therefore valid, must be of general application and not directed against particular individuals.[181] This ancient mandate of the Twelve Tables is a corollary of the very nature of law, whose essential character and function is to be applicable generally.[182] "For what people have always sought is equality of rights before the law. For rights that were not open to all alike would be no rights. . . . [L]aws were invented, to speak to all men at all times in one and the same voice." [183]

As to the content of just laws, justice is that virtue which renders every man his due.[184] "The first office of justice is to keep one man from doing harm to another, unless provoked by wrong." [185] Unlawful injury may be to the property as well as to the person. Nature's laws do not permit any one to appropriate to himself anything that he has taken from others.[186] The firmest bond of human society, he says, is "the conviction that it is more repugnant to Nature for man to rob a fellow-man for his own gain than to endure all possible loss." [187] Another basic requirement of natural justice is good faith, abstention from fraud and the performance of contracts. Justice commands "the faithful discharge of obligations assumed." [188] "The foundation of justice . . . is good faith—that is, truth and fidelity to promises and agreements." [189] Injustice, he says, "is fatal to social life and fellowship between man and man. For, if we are so disposed that each, to gain some personal profit, will defraud or injure his neighbour, then those bonds of human society, which are most in accord with Nature's laws, must of necessity be broken." [190]

It was of the essence of Cicero's theory that just as each man must observe the principles of natural justice in his dealings with other men, so the state must observe the same principles in its dealings with individuals. It is in those cases where it fails to do so that its decrees and edicts, whether or not cast in the form of legal enactments, are invalid and not entitled to be regarded as laws. Since two of the fundamental principles of natural justice, according to Cicero, are respect for private property and respect for the obligations of contracts, laws which override the rights of individuals in these respects are unjust and invalid. Accordingly Cicero condemns specifically not only directly confiscatory legislation but also the agrarian laws and laws for the relief of debtors which were so constantly agitated in his own time.

The primary duty, he says, of one who administers public office in a true commonwealth or republic is to "make it his first care that everyone shall have what belongs to him and that private citizens suffer no invasion of their property rights by act of the state. . . . For the chief purpose in the establishment of constitutional state and municipal governments was that individual property rights might be secured. For, although it was by Nature's guidance that men were drawn together into communities, it was in the hope of safeguarding their possessions that they sought the protection of cities." [191] Everyone "shall be protected in the possession of his own property by the fair administration of the law and the courts, that the poorer classes shall not be oppressed because of their helplessness, and that envy shall not stand in the way of the rich, to prevent them from keeping or recovering possession of what justly belongs to them." [192] Those who wish to safeguard the commonwealth "will refrain from that form of liberality which robs one man to enrich another." [193]

It is from this point of view that Cicero discusses agrarian and debt legislation, treating them together. Those who "pose as friends of the people," he says, "and who for that reason either attempt to have agrarian laws passed, in order that the occupants may be driven out of their homes, or propose that money loaned should be remitted to the borrowers, are undermining the foundations of the commonwealth: first of all, they are destroying harmony, which cannot exist when money is taken away from one party and bestowed upon another; and second, they do away with equity, which is utterly subverted, if the rights of property are not respected. For, as I said above, it is the peculiar function of the state and the city to guarantee to every man the free and undisturbed control of his own particular property." [194] "And how is it fair that a man who never had any property should take possession of lands that had been occupied for many years or even generations, and that he who had them before should lose possession of them? Now, it was on account of just this sort of wrong-doing that the Spartans banished their ephor Lysander, and put their king Agis to death. . . . What shall we say of our own Gracchi, the sons of that famous Tiberius Gracchus and grandsons of Africanus? Was it not strife over the agrarian issue that caused their downfall and death?" [195] "And this is the highest statesmanship and the soundest wisdom on the part of a good citizen, not to divide the interests of the citizens but to unite all on the basis of impartial justice. 'Let them live in their neighbour's house rent-free.' Why so? In order that, when I have bought, built, kept up, and spent my money upon a place, you may without my consent enjoy what belongs to me? What else is that but to rob one man of what belongs to him and to give to another what does not belong to him? And what is the meaning of an abolition of debts, except that you buy a farm with my money; that you have the farm, and I have not my money?" [196] Provision should therefore be made, he argues, to prevent in advance the existence of such indebtedness as may be harmful to the commonwealth, and this can be done in many ways without causing people of means to lose their property, or enriching debtors with the property of their neighbors. No stronger bond, he continues, holds the commonwealth together than its credit, but it can have no credit unless the payment of debts is insisted upon and made compulsory.[197]

Cicero could not have foreseen the effective instrumentality for transferring the property of one group to another that in later times would be afforded by taxation; nevertheless, he looked on taxation with dislike and suspicion. Taxes should be held down to a minimum except in an emergency. Government, he writes, "should also put forth every effort to prevent the levying of a property tax. . . . Such a tax was often levied in the times of our forefathers on account of the depleted state of their treasury and their incessant wars. But if any state . . . ever has to face a crisis requiring the imposition of such a burden, every effort must be made to let all the people realize that they must bow to the inevitable, if they wish to be saved." [198]

These expressions of Cicero provide a rough sketch of a rudimentary system of constitutional limitations resembling at many points those which have become familiar in American constitutional law, but in one important respect Cicero's sketch presents a conspicuous void or deficiency in contrast with the modern American system. It contains no guarantees of those so-called personal or civil rights, such as freedom of speech and religion, on which so much emphasis has been laid in our recent constitutional decisions. On the contrary, Cicero expressly repudiates both the latter rights: he takes for granted a state-established religion and favors a strict control of at least certain forms of public expression. "No one shall have gods to himself," he provides in his model code, "either new gods or alien gods, unless recognized by the State," [199] for "the worship of *private gods* . . . brings confusion into religion." [200] This position was natural and inevitable from the viewpoint of a man like Cicero, who frankly relied on religious sanctions to supplement state action and promote social discipline. This viewpoint remained the normal and prevalent one down to the final secularization of thought in the seventeenth and eighteenth centuries, when finally the opposite opinion found classic expression in Locke's *Essay on Toleration*. With regard to freedom of speech, Cicero's expressions are limited to only one form of public expression, the stage, but what he says on this subject shows clearly that he was no friend of an indiscriminate liberty of disseminating ideas among the masses. "Whom has [comedy] not attacked, or rather persecuted?" he asks. Yet it has always been "able to make its disgraceful exhibitions acceptable to the spectators. . . . On the other hand, our Twelve Tables, though they provided the death penalty for only a few crimes, did provide it for any person who sang or composed a song which contained a slander or insult to anyone else. This was an excellent rule; for our mode of life ought to be liable to judgment by the magistrates and the courts of law, but not by clever poets; nor ought we to be subject to disgrace unless we have an opportunity to answer and defend ourselves in a court of law." [201] It must be remembered that, when this passage was written, no private right of action for slander or libel had yet been developed.

One final and most important aspect of Cicero's conception of the relation between natural justice and governmental action remains to be mentioned. This was his view, repeatedly emphasized throughout his writings, that a state is under an obligation to observe the principles of justice toward foreigners and other nations as well as toward its own citizens. This conclusion followed logically and inevitably from his conception that justice had its source and sanction in human nature, for "all men have received reason; therefore all men have received Justice." [202] Moreover, "the whole human race is bound together in unity." [203] "And, if this be true, we are all subject to one and the same law of Nature. . . . Others again who say that regard should be had for the rights of fellow-citizens, but not of foreigners, would destroy the universal brotherhood of mankind; and, when this is annihilated, kindness, generosity, goodness, and justice must utterly perish." [204] Therefore, those commit injustice "who would debar foreigners from enjoying the advantages of their city and would exclude them from its borders. . . . It may not be right, of course, for one who is not a citizen to exercise the rights and privileges of citizenship. . . . Still, to debar foreigners from enjoying the advantages of the city is altogether contrary to the laws of humanity." [205] No view could differ more widely than does this from the basic presuppositions of the city-state as embodied in the works of Plato and Aristotle, and it foreshadows the liberal cosmopolitanism of the eighteenth century.

Cicero recognizes that if one state is obligated by the law of nature to deal justly with other states, a problem is presented by the fact that states so often go to war with one another. Is war unjust and contrary to the law of nature? Cicero's answer to this question is the earliest formulation of a theory which became the accepted doctrine of the publicists of the Middle Ages and is today a part of the international law of the Catholic Church. This is the theory that, since there is no judicial organ having jurisdiction to enforce the law against independent states, each is competent to protect its legal rights by using force against an aggressor. War for this purpose is a just war; other wars are not. "Those wars are unjust which are undertaken without provocation. . . . No war is considered just unless it has been proclaimed and declared, or unless reparation has first been demanded." [206] "Then, too, in the case of a state in its external relations, the rights of war must be strictly observed. For since there are two ways of settling a dispute: first, by discussion; second, by physical force; and since the former is characteristic of man, the latter of the brute, we must resort to force only in case we may not avail ourselves of discussion. The only excuse, therefore, for going to war is that we may live in peace unharmed." [207] "War . . . should be undertaken in such a way as to make it evident that it has no other object than to secure peace." [208] Even when a war becomes a contest for political supremacy, "it must still not fail to start from the same motives which . . . [are] the only righteous grounds for going to war." [209]

In this discussion Cicero stands out as the originator of a rudimentary international law, just as in his discussion of certain of the other matters reviewed above he appears as the forerunner of several doctrines of modern constitutional law. Although his treatment is fragmentary and goes no further than to deal with a few broad problems, it is significant of his originality that subsequent speculation, which fixed the mold for modern thought in these fields, proceeded on the premises which he laid down and has not only followed in general the approach which he indicated but has largely remained within the framework of his basic principles. This is one reason why it is so difficult to recognize Cicero's originality: his thought has become so much a part of our traditional heritage that it is apt to seem trite and obvious.

From his discussion of the rights of foreigners and of the mutual obligations of states, Cicero proceeds to consider the relations of Rome to her empire and to the allied and subject communities which composed it. Although the empire grew up in the main as the result of war, Romans long remained true to the principle, Cicero thinks, that not only "must we show consideration for those whom we have conquered by force of arms but we must also ensure protection to those who lay down their arms and throw themselves upon the mercy of our generals." [210] "Let me add . . . the empire of the Roman People maintained itself by acts of service, not of

oppression, wars were waged in the interest of our allies or to safeguard our supremacy; the end of our wars was marked by acts of
clemency or by only a necessary degree of severity; the senate was a
haven of refuge for kings, tribes, and nations; and the highest ambition of our magistrates and generals was to defend our provinces
and allies with justice and honour. And so our government could be
called more accurately a protectorate of the world than a dominion." [211]

From this high ideal and standard of imperial rule Cicero felt
that there had been a sad falling-off, which began with the Gracchi
and the onset of the deterioration of Rome's domestic constitution.
"Tiberius Gracchus," he says, "violated the treaty rights of our allies
and the Latins," and accordingly in the *Republic* Cicero puts in the
mouth of Scipio this warning: "If this habit of lawlessness begins
to spread and changes our rule from one of justice to one of force,
so that those who up to the present have obeyed us willingly are
held faithful by fear alone, then, though our own generation has
perhaps been vigilant enough to be safe, yet I am anxious for our
descendants, and for the permanent stability of our commonwealth,
which might live on for ever if the principles and customs of our
ancestors were maintained." [212]

The deterioration of Rome's imperial rule, Cicero thought, had
been particularly rapid after the time of Sulla. "This policy and
practice we had begun gradually to modify even before Sulla's
time. . . . For the time had gone by when any oppression of the
allies could appear wrong." [213] The source of much of this oppression
was, in Cicero's opinion, Rome's position as a tax-gatherer. "I do not
approve," he says, "of the same nation being the ruler of the world
and also its tax-gatherer." [214] With the consent of the senate, he
remarks, Sulla had exempted from taxation certain states upon re-
ceipt of a lump sum of money from them. "Philippus proposed that
they should again be reduced to the condition of tributary states,
without repayment on our part of the money that they had paid for
their exemption. And the senate accepted his proposal. Shame upon
our government! . . . 'But,' someone will say, 'the revenues were
increased, and therefore it was expedient.' How long will people
venture to say that a thing that is not morally right can be expedient?
Furthermore, can hatred and shame be expedient for any govern-

ment? For government ought to be founded upon fair fame and the loyalty of allies." [215]

With this contrast between expediency and moral right stated, Cicero returns to the utilitarian or prudential argument against justice which he had propounded at the beginning of the third book of the *Republic*. The whole last book of the *De Officiis* is devoted to refuting it by arguments based largely on practical situations and examples. It is unnecessary to reproduce these arguments, since they are drawn for the most part from private relations between individuals rather than from the field of political relations or the public acts of government. In substance, Cicero's position is that on mature reflection and analysis nothing will prove to be truly expedient that is not morally right, that is, in accordance with natural justice, because, from a long-range point of view, that which is apparently expedient but at the same time unjust carries with it the seeds of an ultimate retribution which more than counterbalances the immediate advantage. This ultimate retribution does not necessarily take the form of loss of wealth or power or station, or of physical suffering; but inevitably it consists in something worse—destruction of character, disintegration of personality and mental torture. Then he concludes: "Thus it is the error of men who are not strictly upright to seize upon something that seems to be expedient and straightway to dissociate that from the question of moral right. To this error the assassin's dagger, the poisoned cup, the forged wills owe their origin; this gives rise to theft, embezzlement of public funds, exploitation and plundering of provincials and citizens; this engenders also the lust for excessive wealth, for despotic power, and finally for making oneself king even in the midst of a free people; and anything more atrocious or repulsive than such a passion cannot be conceived. For with a false perspective they see the material rewards but not the punishment—I do not mean the penalty of the law, which they often escape, but the heaviest penalty of all, their own demoralization." [216]

V

Cicero's discussion of justice is designed to show that, since justice has its roots in human nature, it is not beyond the possibility of being to some degree realized in the actual conduct of government. Accordingly to make justice the goal and standard of governmental action is not to erect an impossible Utopian ideal. At the same time, experience had convinced Cicero that there was a constant tendency to fall away from that standard, even on the part of a state like Rome, which had the benefit of reasonably well devised governmental institutions. This tendency he attributed to the frailties and weaknesses of human character, as explained above.[217] Cicero believed that just as there is inherent in human nature a capacity for justice and virtue, so men are alike in their frailties and follies. "The similarity of the human race is clearly marked in its evil tendencies," he says, "as well as in its goodness. For pleasure also attracts all men; and even though it is an enticement to vice, yet it has some likeness to what is naturally good. . . . It is through a similar misconception that we shun death . . . and cling to life . . . and . . . look upon pain as one of the greatest of evils." [218] "In the same way, on account of the similarity between moral worth and renown, those who are publicly honoured are considered happy, while those who do not attain fame are thought miserable. Troubles, joys, desires, and fears haunt the minds of all men without distinction, and even if different men have different beliefs, that does not prove, for example, that it is not the same quality of superstition that besets those races which worship dogs and cats as gods, as that which torments other races." [219]

With these defects inherent in human nature, man's better tendencies and capacities are in constant danger of being submerged, unless they are strengthened into character by training and discipline. In this way, Cicero is brought back again to the question which emerged from his historical commentary on Roman government—the relation between institutions and the human character of both the governors and the governed. The formation of proper character in the civic body is accordingly the theme of the last three books of the *Republic*. Unfortunately, nearly the whole text of these books has perished, and only a few fragments are left from which to conjecture the course of the discussion.

Cicero believed that government and law are but two of the institutions of social life and that their functioning is related to and dependent on other social institutions. Thus, the qualities of good citizenship are largely formed by nongovernmental means—by customs, practices, ideals and educational influences which lie outside the properly political sphere. The association of citizens, he says, "in a happy and honorable life . . . is the original purpose of men's coming together, and it should be accomplished for them in their commonwealth partly by established customs and partly by laws." [220] He then quotes the historic verse of Ennius to the effect that Rome's commonwealth stands founded firm on ancient customs and on manly men.[221] These established customs include the education of youth, the treatment of women, the encouragement and inculcation of a proper sense of honor and shame, restraint of the abuses of the theater, and the like.[222] Not enough survives to enable us to know anything significant about Cicero's views on these subjects, but one very definite conclusion which can be pieced together from the fragments is that in all these matters he relied heavily on leadership and on the human instinct for imitation. He believed it was an invincible human tendency for the people to take their cue from a leader, and accordingly, at various places throughout the *Republic,* and particularly in the fragments of the fifth book, he seems to call for an outstanding figure in the state who can combine wise advice and guidance in public affairs with leadership by precept and example in the field of morals and right living. This outstanding leader of whom he expected so much he sometimes calls *moderator,* sometimes *rector,* of the state; and it is to such a leader that he seems to have referred when, in describing the content of the *Republic,* he says that the work dealt not only with the best form of state but also with the ideal citizen (*optimo cive*) of the state.[223]

The brief and fragmentary passages in which Cicero mentions a *moderator* or *rector* of the republic have aroused considerable controversy in recent years among scholars and historians. It has been suggested that in the lost parts of the *Republic* from which these passages survive Cicero must have intended to advocate a strongly monarchical element in the Roman constitution, and that he was in fact proposing to create a place in the Roman state for such a *princeps,* or chief of state, as Augustus made himself in the next generation. This view was propounded over forty years ago by the great historian Eduard Meyer in a book in which he argued that Cicero's conception of the *rector,* or *moderator,* was put forth in the immediate interest of Pompey to justify and legalize the quasi-dictatorial or monarchical position which the latter occupied at Rome in the year 52.[224] The same suggestion was somewhat differently developed and defended in an article published about the same time by Reitzenstein, who interprets the *Republic* as a *Tendenzschrift,* or tract for the times, in which Cicero, through his concept of the *rector* or *moderator,* is making a subtle and more or less veiled plea for monarchy of the kind later established by Augustus.[225] Reitzenstein bases his argument on the fact that while Cicero postulates a monarchical element as one of the three components of a "mixed" or balanced system of government, he nowhere emphasizes or even discusses the monarchical position of the consuls, and accordingly leaves the inference that this element must be supplied somewhere else in the state. It is also his contention that Cicero's concept of the *moderator* or *rector* suggests the Stoic doctrine of the "wise man," whose qualifications entitle him to guide the state by individual personal leadership and, in fact, demand that the state shall submit to such leadership, since it represents the rule of reason in contrast with the rule of passions represented by the conflict of contending parties.[226]

Reitzenstein's article received an elaborate answer from the distinguished classicist Richard Heinze.[227] Heinze argued that although Cicero speaks of the *moderator* or *rector* in the singular, he does so only in the sense in which he speaks of "the orator" as illustrating proficiency in oratory, or as one would speak of "the statesman" as illustrating statesmanship, not as implying that there can be only one orator or one statesman at a given time, or that the statesman, to qualify as such, must be vested with monarchical power. "So in his speech in defence of Rabirius,[228] Cicero gives a whole list of *custodes* (guardians) and *gubernatores* (governors) of the republic who bore arms against the demagogue Saturninus. These and similar expressions show plainly how self-understood it was in Cicero's thinking that the Roman state was guarded, guided and led by a large number of men, not by a single man." [229]

That the true import of Cicero's conception probably lies somewhere between the opposing views of Heinze and Reitzenstein is suggested by a careful reading of the relevant fragments of the *Republic* in connection with other parts of Cicero's writings where he speaks in similar terms of "moderators" or "rectors" or "governors" of the state. Heinze is clearly right in thinking that Cicero did not conceive his "leading" or "ruling" statesman in monarchical terms. Plainly he did not regard it as necessary that such a man should hold any official or recognized post in the government, and apparently he did not think it impossible that more than one such man might be acting on the political scene at a given time. The *moderator* or *rector* was simply a statesman who, by combining political with moral leadership, would be able to guide his fellow-citizens not only to sound political decisions but to what in Cicero's view was more important, a better way of life. "For just as the aim of the pilot is a successful voyage, of the physician, health, . . . so this director of the commonwealth has as his aim for his fellow-citizens a happy life, fortified by wealth, . . . great in glory and honoured for virtue." [230] In this *rector,* he says, one should expect prudence, which is derived from the verb to foresee. "Wherefore this citizen must see to it that he is always armed against those influences which disturb the stability of the State." [231] He should have almost no other duty than to examine and improve himself continually, to urge that others imitate him, and to hold himself up to his fellow-citizens by the excellence of his mind and conduct.[232] Men are not deterred from wrongdoing so much by fear of the punishment prescribed by laws as by the sense of shame. This feeling the *rector* strengthens by his guidance of public opinion and makes it effective by education.[233]

As Heinze says, it was Cicero's conviction, expressed again and again throughout the *Republic,* that alterations in the constitution were neither necessary nor useful. To restore the republic required simply the reestablishment of the old constitution in its rightful setting, not only literally but in its spirit. The restoration could not be accomplished through measures of compulsion, but only through the moral regeneration of the governing class, the leading citizens or *principes.* Thus, in discussing the cause of the civil dissensions that threatened the ruin of the state, it is to the vices of the *principes* that Cicero points in warning.[234] Those vices he believed were responsible for the state's having become a mere plaything between tyranny and mob rule. Not only had the *rectores* of the republic abdicated their position, but the whole body of citizens, and for this he said the *principes* were answerable because the people follow the example provided. The concept of a *rector* of the commonwealth, Heinze goes on to say, was one which Cicero was the first to bring to clear consciousness and expression. By it he intended what the Greeks originally meant by the word *politikos* or statesman, but also something more. He sought, in addition, to express what philosophers ever since Socrates had attempted to put into the concept with increasing definiteness. The goal by which the *rector* must regulate all his acts and omissions required, he believed, spiritual training, "the theoretical insights on which the practice of life depends, and above all a firm will and determination to practice virtue and become a model and example for all his fellow-citizens." [235]

Although the functions and responsibilities of the *rector* and *moderator* are such that they may well attach to more than one individual at a given time, and indeed are expected by Cicero to attach in some degree to all who hold high position in the state, it nevertheless seems clear—and this is the essential point of truth in Reitzenstein's view which seems not sufficiently recognized by Heinze—that Cicero did feel it necessary that at great crises in the life of the state some outstanding citizen should be available and should come forward, a man who possessed the qualifications of the *rector* and *moderator* in a preeminent degree and would be able to apply them to the work of reform, either in or out of public office. This conviction seems most clearly illustrated by his conception of the part played by Brutus in the foundation of the republic, which Cicero represented as essentially the work of a single man,[236] and attributable to one man's leadership. In referring to this, he makes Scipio say, "See to it that you are able to recognize such a man, for he is one who can maintain the safety of the State both by counsel and by action." [237]

It has not generally been observed in discussions of Cicero's conception of the *moderator* and *rector* that his references to Brutus and to the foundation of the republic supply an almost complete key to his meaning. That discussion shows that he was not thinking of the position of such a leader in terms of a public office forming part of the constitutional machinery, for essentially his position is extraofficial. Thus, says Cicero, "though Brutus was only a private citizen, he sustained the whole burden of the government, and was the first in our State to demonstrate that no one is a mere private citizen when the liberty of his fellows needs protection." [238] Such a leader is the antithesis of the tyrant and is the ruler who is good and wise and skillful in everything that contributes to the advantage and prestige of the commonwealth. [239]

In other words, it was apparently Cicero's view that there should always be in the state a group of public-spirited, farsighted and unselfish citizens who had risen to eminence by participating in public affairs, and that at moments of crisis or in times of tension at least one of these should come forward and assume the leading part in whatever needed to be done, without expecting any reward in emoluments or honors. Cicero's selection of Scipio as the chief speaker in the dialogue, and, indeed, the whole picture of Scipio which is built up throughout the *Republic,* shows that he was embodying in the person of that man his conception of the true *moderator* and *rector,* whose life and character supply leadership of the right kind to his fellow-citizens. This picture is developed to a noble climax in the beautiful concluding section of the *Republic,* "Scipio's Dream," which exhibits Cicero's prose style in its ultimate perfection which doubtless accounts for its having survived as a separate episode throughout the Middle Ages long after the rest of the work was lost. The theme of this concluding episode is the reward that comes to true moderators and rectors beyond the grave— the only reward they should look for. The hope of such a reward will never lead them astray into a violation of justice but will, on the contrary, supply the strongest motive to make them regard all earthly honors with disdain. Even the desire for fame, so deeply treasured in every true Roman heart, will, if it stands alone, lead the virtuous astray; and if even fame must thus be recognized in the end for a worthless thing and set aside as of no account, how much less can any other supposed good carry weight? Therefore Scipio, in his dream, as he looks down from heaven on the earth, must before all else learn to despise fame, and this theme, more than the hope of immortality, is the central and basic idea of "Scipio's Dream."

While Cicero was thinking of Scipio, he was also undoubtedly thinking of himself. As Heinze puts it: "The last beautiful pages of the Republic Cicero perhaps wrote more for himself than for his readers, as a consolation and alleviation of his own troubled heart which had burned so ardently for fame and been so bitterly disappointed in its hopes. He wrote his whole book not only for others but for himself, to establish a justification of his own political career, and far more often certainly than we know from his letters to Atticus he tested himself in the coming years by the standards set up in his book as a law for his own actions. Thus he sought to work upon and influence himself as well as others." [240]

Conceived in this way, Cicero's idea of the *moderator* and *rector* is obviously difficult to connect with any such purpose as that of justifying Pompey's dictatorship, as Eduard Meyer supposes. It has been pointed out in an earlier chapter how severely Cicero criticized Pompey's position as oppressive and subversive of the constitution in the very year 52 [241] to which Meyer believes the justification to refer, and similar criticisms are found everywhere throughout his correspondence in the years 55–52. In view of this, as Heinze says, it is more than questionable whether Cicero could have regarded such an all-powerful position of a single man as a good thing for the state. His own expressions in the year when he commenced writing the *Republic* show that he felt the supremacy of Pompey as an intolerable burden, hard as he exerted himself to accommodate himself to it outwardly. This in itself should suffice to acquit Cicero of the charge of demanding for his republic an officially recognized and permanent principate, since the possibility of abuse and misrule was present before his eyes in the case of Pompey's principate. He had long recognized that ambitious striving for leadership in the state was a grave danger for the republic. In the third oration against Catiline he had traced from it all the civil wars of the preceding generation, and in the *De Officiis* he stigmatizes it as a maximum source of danger. Accordingly, the idea of sanctioning a permanent state leader as a necessity for the commonwealth could hardly have occurred to Cicero. [242]

This conclusion seems confirmed by Cicero's belief that leadership in the state should be informal and unofficial, arising out of the needs of a particular occasion. It is therefore difficult to find in his conceptions the intentional or unintentional basis for an official dictatorship or for such a permanent and institutionally organized principate as was afterwards established by Augustus. This does not mean, however, that strong traces of Cicero's influence are not suggested in some parts of the policy of Augustus, who was a student of Cicero. It was a major feature of the policy of that complex, compromising and profound statesman to give to his position in the state as much of the appearance of informality and unofficial character as possible. Although he maintained control over the machinery of government by holding a variety of more or less inconspicuous offices, he prided himself on the fact that he led the state by influence, in the sense of respect for his personal unofficial leadership rather than by the exercise of official power. It is not possible to say in the case of a man like Augustus that this was a wholly dishonest claim, or that he did not at least to some degree believe in it; moreover, insofar as he did, and sought to realize it in action, Cicero may not unjustly be regarded as unconsciously and unintentionally the spiritual father of the Roman principate. The difficulty was that if Cicero's concept of the *rector* and *moderator* was to be made useful as part of the ordinary machinery of government, it had to be institutionalized. Every concept which is mainly spiritual or moral in its content tends to alter its significance and be perverted from its original intention when it becomes institutionalized. Thus, the principates of Caligula and Nero were completely removed from anything that Cicero had in mind. There is every reason to suppose that Cicero was a clear enough thinker and a sufficiently experienced observer of practical politics to understand that this would be the case, and that he therefore neither recommended nor contemplated any such institution as a permanent component of the Roman constitution.

VI

From this review of the main outlines of Cicero's works on political philosophy it is obvious that his aim was not to devise a program of specific practical remedies for the immediate emergency confronting the Roman state but to discuss without direct reference to that emergency the broader issues presented by the problem of government in general and, in addition, the fundamental principles which, if correctly apprehended, would serve at least to identify the nature and causes of the crisis. He was consciously writing a tract not for the times but, as he hoped, for the ages. In this hope fortune favored him, with the result that, as has been earlier pointed out, most of the basic conceptions and lines of analysis in the political thought of Western civilization down to the end of the nineteenth century follow patterns directly derived from Cicero. Many of his ideas became conventionalized and ossified in the traditions of the schools, many acquired a stiffness and absolutism foreign to the spirit and intention of their author, many were oversimplified by later and less subtle minds, but this very process served to vest some of Cicero's central concepts with a toughness and permanence that enabled them to live through the lapse of Western thought during the primitiveness of the early Middle Ages and afterwards to survive through the changing mental climates of later centuries. It is no small achievement—in fact, it is one of the major successes in the history of thought—that Cicero was thus able to become the father of the natural law philosophy which dominated Western thinking in the field of government and jurisprudence until recent times. For better or for worse, that philosophy in its systematic traditional form lost its hold on the mind of most Western countries and went into eclipse about the middle of the nineteenth century; yet much of what was basic and vital in Cicero's political thought is still living and influential.

In his writings about law and politics Cicero emphasizes six points: first, the idea of law that expresses long-range and abiding conceptions of justice, or right and wrong, which should be the standard and rule of governmental action; second, the conception of governmental power as an office of trust and responsibility, a magistracy to be exercised according to law for the public promotion of justice rather than for the benefit of any group or class, or for the maintenance or extension of the power of the ruler; third, the conception that if governmental power is not to be abused it must be subdivided among a number of organs or agencies which will check and balance each other in a mixed form of government; fourth, that if government is to function properly it must represent an organic growth embodying the traditions, and expressing the continuity, of community life; fifth, that in the last analysis the power to determine the character of government rests in the people, so that every people in the long run has the kind of government that it desires or at least is willing to put up with; and, finally, that the character and nature of government is determined by the human character of the civic body and its leaders, more particularly of the leaders because of the human tendency of imitation.

It is at once apparent that these basic elements of Cicero's political thought are not the neatly dovetailed parts of an abstract academic system and that, superficially at least, some of them seem not entirely consistent with others. It is this characteristic of Cicero's thinking which has brought it under the criticism of modern scholars and philosophers but which at the same time saves it from being doctrinaire and maintains its contact with actuality. In fact, the chief merit of Cicero's thought, like that of Burke, is that in his approach to the problems of politics he never follows an abstract conception so far toward its logical conclusion as to lose sight of the observations of experience which qualify and limit it in practice. The result may be to sacrifice consistency in outward appearance, but at the same time there is preserved the greater advantage of recognizing the element of truth in opposing principles, and so of gaining the opportunity to confine each within its appropriate field of application. This is particularly well illustrated by the way in which Cicero combines the basic propositions summarized in the preceding paragraph. Thus, the doctrine of natural law in its later systematic development tended to take on an air of unreality by assuming the form of a rigid artificial code deduced with remorseless logic from abstract premises without regard for actual laws and existing institutions. Cicero's adoption of the basic idea of natural law, on the other hand, does not prevent him from recognizing that the actual laws and institutions of a particular state represent an organic growth, legitimately influenced by the temper and character of a people and the quality of its leadership over a period of time. Again, his conception of mixed government leaves room for the ultimate supremacy of the people and for the leadership of an eminent individual. Likewise, his emphasis on the importance of laws and institutions is combined with recognition of the necessity and value of the non-institutional element in a nation's life—the spirit and temper of the people, their character as individuals, and above all the personal character and qualifications of their leaders. In other words, the striking quality of Cicero's thought is that there was nothing mechanical or doctrinaire about it—he was not, in Napoleon's phrase, an ideologue. It was the loss of this flexibility and of this respect for realities that caused much of the later thought which was based on his ideas to lose its influence, so that ultimately it was superseded by a different order of ideas.

The challenge which, since the middle of the nineteenth century, has been directed with ever increasing intensity against the Ciceronian tradition in Western political thought has left none of Cicero's basic propositions unassailed. Under the newer views which have been forcing their way to wider acceptance in all the countries of the West, except perhaps the American republic, government is represented not as an agency of impartial justice but as the instrument of a dominant group for making its will effective. Law today is widely conceived not as embodying abiding principles but as expressing the immediate interests of a ruling class. The idea of continuity and organic growth in institutional development is rejected in favor of the view that a complete break with the past is desirable, that an absolutely fresh start should be made in institutional arrangements, and that an entirely new group of rulers from a different social class should supersede the type of leaders to which the state has become accustomed. Checks and balances in government are renounced on the theory that nothing should be allowed to impair or impede the power of government to carry out the will of its masters. Personal leadership is emphasized not from the standpoint of its moral and educational functions but as an embodiment of unified power and supremacy. In the years when Cicero was writing on politics and government, the rudiments of many of the foregoing ideas were to be found in the policies of Julius Caesar, and their expression and ultimate consequences for the Roman state were largely manifested in Caesar's career. It is therefore appropriate to identify and trace the ideas and conceptions that underlay the policies which he initiated and followed.

7

Caesar
the
Instrumentalist

I

Caesar's political conceptions and his theory of government are to be found not in what he wrote but in what he did. Although he was one of the great writers that the world has known—articulate, lucid and a master of style— yet with that indomitable quality of secrecy which was among his most notable traits he never expressed in words or exposed for discussion the wellsprings of his conduct or the principles on which he acted. This characteristic cannot be attributed wholly to policy or caution, for it seems to have resulted from an ingrained and calculating quality of his mind. He did not think in terms of principles, or even of policies, but always of objectives and results. Hence, he adopted any line of conduct that for the moment seemed likely to promote the immediate end he aimed at, and this habit of mind inevitably, and no doubt unconsciously, dictated a view of government and an approach to its problems totally removed from those of a reflective and analytical thinker like Cicero.

Cicero thought of government as a continuing and permanent institution that would go on indefinitely into the future throughout the life of a state. Hence he felt obliged to consider the arrangement of its organs, the direction of its policies and the qualifications of its leaders, which in the long run would best serve the basic interests of the community as well as the material prosperity and moral well-being of its individual members. This broad view necessarily led to the consideration of the immediate problems of government in the light of their effect on established institutions and of the principles which those institutions embodied. From this standpoint, principles and institutions were the touchstone and standard of immediate day-to-day political conduct: current policy must be so shaped as to fit within the long-term institutional framework and conform to long-range principles of action. The entire body of Cicero's political thinking, evinced in his practical statesmanship no less than in his theoretical writings, rests on these assumptions.

The assumptions on which Caesar acted were entirely different. If Cicero can be described as an "institutionalist" because he believed that current policy should always proceed within an institutional framework, Caesar may be called, by a slight modification of the meaning of a current philosophical term, an "instrumentalist." He regarded the machinery of government simply as a tool to accomplish his purposes. No one could observe more closely the niceties of legal and constitutional forms when it served his ends to do so, as during the trial of the Catilinarian conspirators,[1] or when he made the disregard of the tribunes' veto the excuse for beginning the civil war with Pompey.[2] On the other hand, he was equally ready flagrantly to disregard established constitutional principles, as during his consulship when he deprived the senate and his consular colleague of their functions in the government,[3] or when he broke open the treasury in defiance of a tribune's veto during the first part of the civil war.[4] Caesar subordinated institutional arrangements to his immediate purposes, using them so far as they served him and disregarding them otherwise.

Obviously no system could long survive under such conditions, for institutional patterns break down or dissolve when they are followed or departed from arbitrarily. It is on this fundamental premise that the institutionalist and the instrumentalist part company. The institutionalist believes that the long-run advantage of maintaining soundly devised institutional arrangements outweighs any temporary benefits that may accrue from breaking down the institutional system, whereas the instrumentalist sees no reason for permitting the institutional system to stand in the way of some supposed immediate gain. Doubtless the conflict between these two points of view is a perennial one which will continue as long as there are basic differences in human temperament. For that reason, it becomes especially worthwhile to examine in particular instances what advantages, if any, have resulted to a state from the instrumentalist method. Few better examples are to be found than in Caesar's statesmanship and in the effect of the application of his philosophy of government upon Rome and the Roman world.

It has become almost impossible objectively to assess the aims and achievements of Julius Caesar because of the partiality which historians have always accorded him. Estimates and evaluations of Caesar have been almost uniformly eulogistic and never more so than since the middle of the nineteenth century. His overwhelming competence and efficiency in everything he undertook, his exhibition of almost unparalleled skill and ability in so many different lines of thought and action, his extraordinary lucid and forceful capacity for expressing himself, have captivated the imagination of scholars and historians. Moreover, he has had the rare and unusual advantage of being regarded as a hero by both the protagonists and the opponents of democracy—by the former because he stood at the head of the "popular" opposition to the governing aristocracy at Rome, by the latter because he successfully established a personal absolutism.

Against such unanimity of praise few historians have been willing to express dissent or even reasoned criticism, whereas those who have been drawn into the main current of opinion have been led into statements of surprising extravagance. Mommsen says of Caesar that he "worked and created as never any mortal did before or after him." [5] Dean Merivale, author of the standard history of Rome in the Victorian age of England, viewed him as among the greatest names in history, while a recent American scholar has called him "the greatest man the earth has ever produced." [6] Another American historian speaks of him as "a statesman of unparalleled insight, sympathy, and effectiveness." [7] Warde Fowler, a leading Oxford scholar of the last generation, says that Caesar learned to keep his mind fixed on one great end, the reconstitution of the Roman state on a rational and humanitarian basis.[8] Rice Holmes calls him "the greatest man of the world who has ever lived." [9] Perhaps the most remarkable judgment is that of James Anthony Froude, who states that Caesar "fought his battles to establish some tolerable degree of justice in the government of this world; and he succeeded, though he was murdered for it," and goes on to discover "a strange and startling resemblance" between the careers of Caesar and Christ: "Each was maligned as the friend of publicans and sinners; each was betrayed by those whom he had loved and cared for; each was put to death." [10] One of the very few voices raised in opposition is that of Dr. Thomas Arnold, who says of Caesar, "Never did any man occasion so large an amount of human misery with so little provocation." [11]

In the face of the majority of these judgments, an objective appraisal of Caesar's philosophy of government which penetrates below summary generalizations to specific facts is long overdue. From what has been said in earlier chapters about the course of Roman politics during his rise to power it is evident that he was first and foremost a great political tactician. It is accordingly pertinent to inquire into the ends to which his tactics were directed and what contributions they made to the Roman state.

Admirers of Caesar have generally distinguished two stages in his political career: a first stage covering the period down to his departure for Gaul, and therefore covering most of his political life; and a second stage, consisting of the brief, final period when to all intents and purposes he was master of Rome. During the first of these periods, when he was a leading figure in the so-called "popular" party, he is represented as actively promoting the cause of democracy in government, whereas in his final period of absolute rule he is said to have crowned his work of successfully establishing democracy by reorganizing the state to achieve a greater measure of efficiency, justice and humanitarianism. This is the conventional interpretation of Caesar's career which has become standardized in the writings of modern historians. Its accuracy may be tested by drawing appropriate conclusions from the account of his political conduct set forth in earlier chapters.

Caesar's political career may be said to have begun in the year 71 when, with Cicero and others, he assisted in promoting the election of Pompey and Crassus to the consulship. During the next decade he figured as an important leader of the "popular" party, at first largely because of his family connections with Marius, whose memory he was careful to keep alive, and afterwards because of the relations which he formed with leaders of the political underworld like Catiline and his associates. In this period, Caesar's name is not directly connected with any important democratic legislative proposal, despite the fact that he was probably the promoter of the radical land law of Rullus introduced to embarrass Cicero at the commencement of the latter's consulship.[12] Caesar's political activities in these years were mainly carried on in behalf of others, and in the end chiefly for Crassus, whose political manager he became in return for large loans of money. At that time, it was the ambition of Crassus to build up his own power and influence by undermining Pompey during the latter's absence in the East. To this end Caesar's efforts were chiefly directed, and one of the few legislative measures in which his hand can be traced was the proposal to confer on Crassus a military command in Egypt to counterbalance the position of Pompey. It will be recalled that at that time both Crassus and Pompey were professedly leaders of the "popular" party, so that Caesar's activities in the interest of Crassus had the effect of dividing that party and thus playing temporarily into the hands of the senate. The situation was aggravated after Pompey's return, when Crassus and Caesar lent their aid to the intrigues which were intended to stiffen the senate's resistance to Pompey.

In the face of this record it can hardly be maintained that during the first period of his career Caesar's efforts were directed to strengthening any truly democratic tendencies in the Roman government or to the promotion of any measures which can properly be described as democratic reforms. Rather, they took the form of playing a game of power politics and using influence with the "popular" party for that end. They were concerned with intensifying the struggle for power between the great rival leaders and building up one against the other in the struggle for supremacy. By these means Caesar maneuvered himself into a position where both Pompey and Crassus felt that his help was indispensable, and he was thus enabled to bring about his own election to the consulship and to form the triumvirate.

During his consulship, Caesar's chief accomplishment was to deprive the senate of its constitutional position and reduce it to practical nullity in the government. So long as the senate continued to exercise its traditional functions, it operated inevitably as a check on the accumulation of powers in the hands of aspirants for supremacy. By the elimination of the senate, those aspirants were left free to pursue their aims by controlling the tribal assembly through bribery, intimidation and mob management. In other words, a way was opened for more effective use of that assembly as an instrument to achieve personal ambitions. This result may be called "democratic" if democracy is identified, as many historians identify it, with a suppression of the powers of the senate, but all that it amounted to under the conditions then existing at Rome was to make the people a tool of the manipulators of power politics. During Caesar's consulship he employed that tool solely for the purpose of obtaining personal advantages for himself and his partners in the triumvirate and not for the enactment of any measures of constructive reform designed to improve the condition of the people. When he prepared to leave Rome at the expiration of his year of office, he built up the power of Clodius and his mob to control the assembly during his absence. Clodius carried through two important pieces of legislation: one legalized the political ward clubs and thereby tightened the control of the mob over political action; the other extended and liberalized the grain dole. Although Caesar was known to be the power behind Clodius, he did not appear publicly as a sponsor of either of these so-called democratic measures, and how little he really believed in them is shown by the fact that when he ultimately attained supreme power he promptly brought about their repeal.[13]

The effect, and almost certainly the conscious objective, of Caesar's tactics down to the time of his departure for Gaul was to create a condition of affairs in which the Roman constitution would be paralyzed, so that government could proceed only by vesting extraordinary powers in the hands of an individual. Not only could the senate, intimidated, cowed and divided by intrigue, give no general direction to the government or cope with the gangs of mob leaders like Clodius, but it was reduced to the necessity of seeking the support of other gang chieftains and abetting the rule of force in the streets. Under these circumstances, orderly government could obviously not go on, and there was more and more demand for the irregular interference of powerful individual leadership, so that the public mind was prepared for acquiescence in personal rule. Pompey, however, was neither ready nor willing completely to break down the established conventions of political action, with the result that the existing disorder continued. At the same time, his rapprochement with the senate, which at last determined to resist Caesar, made conflict inevitable, and the civil war broke out. It is usually said that Caesar's action in establishing his own personal supremacy at the close of that war was necessary and salutary as the only way of ending a condition of governmental confusion which had become intolerable, but what does not seem to be so generally recognized is that that very confusion was largely the result of Caesar's own tactics, pursued deliberately and consistently over a period of years. One of the arts in which he was most successful in statesmanship, as in military strategy, was to create conditions which he could most effectively turn to his own use.

It is appropriate at this point to inquire how Caesar's career up to that time has come to be so generally regarded as democratic in intention or tendency, and in what sense, if at all, it can properly be so judged. During this period one of his chief objectives, as stated, was to destroy the place of the senate in the constitution. Since the power of the senate may be viewed as the undemocratic element in the Roman government, it is easy to assume that whatever tended to undermine that power can be identified with democracy. Before this assumption can be accepted, however, it seems necessary to ask certain further questions. What part did Caesar conceive it appro-

priate for the people to play in government and what was his attitude toward the popular element in the Roman constitution? Was
his desire to destroy the senate accompanied by a desire to transfer
its power to the people? Does his course of conduct indicate that he
wished governmental policies to be determined by the deliberate
will of the people expressed after consultation and debate?

It is clear that in his opposition to the senate, both before and
during his consulship, Caesar relied heavily on the support of the
tribal assembly. It is also clear, however, that he did not treat the
assembly as a deliberative body or seek to influence its decisions by
argument or rational persuasion. Instead, he sought always to control
it, to make himself master of it, by agitation, intimidation, force,
street fighting and gangster rule. Here again, his instrumentalist
attitude is exhibited. He wished to accomplish certain objectives, and
for that purpose he had to make use of the assembly: it was a tool
for his ends, and he therefore resorted to the methods which would
make the tool most immediately effective. It doubtless never occurred to him to consider the effect of these tactics on the processes
of self-government, for all that he was interested in was the immediate result. His tactics stimulated the Roman people to act chiefly
from the twin motives of excitement and fear, and such motives are
hardly compatible with self-government in any proper sense or consistent with its permanence. When these motives did not seem sufficient to achieve his objectives, he appealed to the cupidity and self-
interest of those who desired to be supported at the expense of the
state: hence his land laws and the enlargement of the grain dole by
Clodius. In short, Caesar always encouraged and accustomed the
voters to act from the baser motives of human nature because that
seemed the quickest and cheapest method of attaining his ends. In
the words of Montesquieu, "These leading men of the republic [sc.
the triumvirs] sought to make the people disgusted with its own
power and by rendering the inconveniences of republican government as difficult as possible in order to make themselves essential." [14]
Thus, having destroyed senatorial government, he made democratic
government in any proper sense likewise impossible, leaving only
the alternative of the rule of a single individual. If his final triumph
is therefore to be regarded, as many historians have regarded it, as

the triumph of democracy, it can only be on the assumption that democracy is by its very nature self-defeating, that, as Mommsen believed, and doubtless honestly, and as perhaps Caesar also believed, democracy and absolute monarchy are the same thing.[15]

II

It is the accepted view that after Caesar had achieved the mastery of the Roman state he set about using his power to improve conditions and to restore governmental effectiveness in promoting the public welfare. His conception of his task is generally represented as a combination of absolutism and democracy—an absolutism administered in the interest of the people. Thus it is said that Caesar "saw the value of absolute command in ordering a disunited state, and the value of implicit obedience as a discipline; at every turn he learnt that he had the requisite force within him to make men obey him willingly. . . . And so it was that when the last year of his government arrived, his political insight was clearer than ever, and his capacity for enforcing his will was ten times greater than it had been." [16] At the same time, it is said that "in the last six years of his life we find in him an unparalleled combination of hard work and strong will on the one hand, and of high aims and true humanity on the other. . . ." [17] Caesar is also alleged to have been a true friend of the people and to have "fought his battles to establish some tolerable degree of justice." [18] The correctness of these appraisals may be tested by examining, first, the measures adopted by Caesar in what may be called the field of social and civic reform, and afterwards, his reforms in the organization and operation of the machinery of government.

Most of Caesar's reform measures of an economic and social character were introduced after his return to Rome from his campaign in Egypt and the East.[19] We are informed of a number of measures of this kind, but unfortunately our knowledge of their details is scanty and incomplete. It is clear, however, that they did not add up into any such connected or systematic body of reforming policy as was represented, for example, by the economic reforms of Solon or even those of Gaius Gracchus. Instead, they were fragmentary, disconnected and obviously the outcome of momentary improvisation. An example of such makeshift legislation was the rent law,[20] which Caesar put into effect to quell the agitation of Dolabella on the eve of the African campaign. It has sometimes been said that the reason for the unsystematic and disconnected character of Caesar's legislation was the briefness of his final dictatorship, which covered only thirty-two months between his return from the East and his death. Yet a shorter space of time has sufficed in other instances to lay down the outlines of more coherent and better coordinated programs. The truth, as might be expected, is that Caesar was no more systematic in his legislation than in other directions. He was a great improviser, ingenious to invent something that would serve the immediate needs of the moment, and quite ready and willing the next moment to turn in an entirely different direction. Nevertheless, there is a quality of fancifulness and lack of realism about some of his legislation which suggests that he was acting in an unfamiliar and uncongenial sphere.

In spite of his sense of efficiency, or perhaps because of his overwhelming self-confidence, Caesar seems to have been a victim of the delusion that a social or economic result may be attained by simply adopting a law or governmental regulation which orders that it shall come about. That assumption seems to underlie most of his economic and sumptuary legislation. Thus, one of his laws appears to have been designed to drain off the pauper population of Rome and distribute it through Italy by enacting that Italian stock farmers must employ at least one free laborer for every two slaves.[21] The burdens and dangers of landholding in a revolutionary period had apparently made agricultural pursuits unattractive and thus depressed the price of farmland. Caesar accordingly sought to create by law an artificial demand for land by requiring that persons with capital must invest a fixed proportion of it (possibly two-thirds) in landed property. At the same time, he forbade by another law the mortgaging of landed estates beyond a statutory percentage of their market value.[22] To force money into circulation and maintain prices, he limited the amount of cash that a man might keep uninvested to a comparatively small maximum—roughly the equivalent of a few thousand dollars.[23] There is nothing to indicate that these economic regulations produced their intended results, or indeed any results whatever. They must have been practically impossible to enforce, and, insofar as sporadic and occasional attempts may have been made to enforce them, the result can only have been to oppress particular individuals and increase the economic insecurity and confusion of the times.

In the field of sumptuary legislation Caesar again acted differently from what might have been expected. Fond of luxury as he was himself, and completely cynical about the traditional simplicities and austerities of old Roman manners, he nevertheless made a show of reviving and strengthening the archaic sumptuary laws of the preceding century which were designed to prevent luxury and expense in dress and diet.[24] He is said to have enforced these laws rigorously, "placing officers about the markets to seize and bring to him provender exposed for sale contrary to his regulations; and sometimes sending his lictors and soldiers to carry away from a dining-room any such victuals as had escaped the notice of the market-searchers, even when they were upon the table."[25] Caesar can certainly have had no thought that the prevailing luxury of high Roman life could be destroyed by these means, and there is no evidence that he wished to destroy it. The object of his sumptuary laws can therefore only have been to curry favor with the proletariat by imposing conspicuous restrictions on the well-to-do, and at the same time to provide himself with opportunities to harass and intimidate particular members of the upper class so that that class as a whole would have a pervading sense of his power over them. One of Caesar's most remarkable measures imposed a strict limitation on freedom of foreign travel by providing that no citizen between the ages of twenty and forty should be absent from Italy for more than three years unless he was a soldier or officer in the army. The measure also provided that no son of a senator might go abroad at all unless he was on the staff of a magistrate or general in a civil or military capacity.[26] Clearly, Caesar did not want wealthy Romans, particularly of the senatorial class, to have free access to the provinces or the opportunity to make connections with important provincials unless they were to be subject to his control.

Another department of Caesar's program was a spectacular

scheme of public works. Almost none of these was actually carried out, and the grandiose scale on which they were conceived raises a possible doubt as to how seriously they were intended. "Italy was to be the scene of colossal undertakings. A great road was to be driven through the Apennine range, giving Rome more direct communication with the Adriatic. The lake Fucinus was to be drained, and the Pomptine marshes as well. In connexion with the latter work a new channel was to be dug for the Tiber, discharging into the sea at Terracina." [27] Outside Italy a ship canal was to be cut through the Isthmus of Corinth in Greece. None of these projects was ever carried beyond the planning stage, but the scale on which the plans were projected doubtless immensely enhanced Caesar's prestige, added luster to his rule and created enthusiasm and support for his personal power.

In the field of provincial administration, Caesar's record is also disappointing. Here he had an opportunity to deal with a subject with which he was probably better acquainted than any other Roman and where there existed gross abuses with which he was thoroughly familiar. Yet the only step that he took was in a backward direction. Not only did he repeal Pompey's salutary "law of the five-year interval," [28] which had done something to prevent provincial governorships from being the prizes of election contests, but he enacted a new law of his own which "limited governorships in consular provinces to two years, in praetorian provinces to one. . . . As the Empire was to demonstrate, what the provinces needed was government by men who were adequately paid and allowed to remain in provinces after they had acquired a knowledge of them." [29] A one-year governor was almost certain to try to reap the largest possible profit in the brief time available to him. Here, however, as at so many other points, Caesar seems to have been guided mainly by what he felt to be his own personal interests. He knew only too well from his own experience what massive power could be welded together during a long governorship of an important province, and he apparently did not intend that any rival should be in a position to follow the example he himself had set. Hence short terms were to be the order of his regime. That Caesar had any very high standards of provincial administration in respect of honesty or decent treatment of the provincials seems difficult to believe in the light of some of his appointments to governorships. Not only did he use these officers to reward loyal partisans without regard to integrity or fitness, but he was not above letting them pay themselves off at the expense of the provinces. In the latter respect, he was no worse than many of his contemporaries, but it is idle to represent him as a high-minded reformer of provincial abuses.

All in all, the most successful and beneficent of Caesar's economic measures was his great program of colonizing Romans abroad, and that he was able in large measure to carry out. The program had its origin in an immediate practical necessity of a very pressing kind, namely, the need to provide some sort of reward or bounty for the disbanded soldiers of his legions. Attention has been drawn to the enormous donations which he felt obliged to distribute to his veterans at the time of his triumph,[30] and obviously a method which required such vast sums of cash and bullion could not be employed indefinitely. Caesar had built up an army so large that it had become too expensive to support, and a reduction was imperative. Although at the time of his death he still had thirty-five legions under arms,[31] he had disbanded nine others during the two preceding years.[32] The cheapest way to provide for these disbanded soldiers was to give them land. This was the origin of Caesar's colonization program, which in a number of respects exhibited great ingenuity and novelty of conception and had most valuable results.

Caesar began by finding land for some of his veterans in Italy. How he obtained it is uncertain, but some of it may have been confiscated from prominent partisans of Pompey, although, as pointed out, Caesar does not seem to have carried out any thoroughgoing program of expropriation. Other lands were probably bought either with Caesar's own cash or with state revenues. Italy, however, could obviously not supply enough land. Moreover, he considered it highly dangerous to settle discharged soldiers in compact masses for fear of their becoming centers of mutiny and sedition, and he therefore decided to intermingle them with a civilian population. These two problems—the shortage of land in Italy and the wish to intermingle soldier colonists with civilians—were responsible for the nature of Caesar's colonial program as it was developed. He decided to found colonies abroad and to send out as colonists civilians as well as soldiers.

The policy of colonizing Romans in the provinces had first been sponsored by Gaius Gracchus, but it had been received so unfavorably that it had been largely responsible for his downfall. Caesar's program was projected on a far grander scale, and its theater extended across the Mediterranean world, from Spain, Gaul and Africa to Asia Minor.

The necessity for providing civilian settlers gave Caesar an opportunity to accomplish another objective, namely, that of thinning out and reducing the pauper population of Rome. He seems to have drafted and exported eighty thousand of these sturdy idlers without ceremony to the new settlements.[33] Obviously, most colonists of this kind were not fitted for agricultural labor, and they were accordingly sent to urban settlements where they could work at handicrafts or in mercantile establishments. Some of the settlements were almost entirely of this character, as for example Corinth, which received few if any soldiers; others, which were dominantly agricultural, like certain of those in Gaul, Spain and Africa, received chiefly veteran colonists, and there the proportion of civilian proletarians was correspondingly reduced.

This large-scale redistribution of populations was a measure that was congenial to Caesar's mind and temper and to his executive inclination. In the long run, it constituted, apart from his conquest of Gaul, his most lasting and valuable achievement. Its ultimate effect in reducing the cost to the state of maintaining the pauper population of Rome does not seem to have been large, but it contributed immeasurably to Romanizing the western Mediterranean provinces. By planting communities of Romans as centers from which Roman speech, habits, tastes and law would ultimately radiate, it began for the first time, on a large scale, the work which in the end dictated the civilization and character of these parts of the earth for succeeding centuries.

It has been said that Caesar conceived and inaugurated a melting-pot philosophy for the Roman empire[34] and that, by spreading his colonies through the provinces, he was really seeking less to Romanize them than to imitate the policy of Alexander and break down the distinction between the Romans and their subject peoples. Proof of this supposed policy has also been seen in the liberality with which he conferred the boon of Roman citizenship. While only a general, he had stretched his prerogative by granting citizenship to individuals and groups when it was a means of gaining political or military support or financial aid. During his dictatorship he continued the same practice more unreservedly, extending the favor to groups or classes whom he wish to conciliate to his cause, for example, professional teachers, medical practitioners, and technical specialists, most of whom were Greek of the pure or half-blood, or members of Oriental nations.[35] His most lavish act of this kind was his wholesale grant of citizenship in 49 B.C. to the entire population of Cisalpine Gaul, where he had spent his winters during his Gallic governorship and had won wide popularity in the rapidly growing frontier communities which were being built up by the enterprise of Roman capitalists and Romanized Italians.[36] By this one stroke he is said to have increased the Roman citizen body by 50 percent.[37]

However, the policy of liberally extending Roman citizenship, although it diluted and cheapened civic privileges, does not necessarily indicate a deliberate intent to level down the position of Rome in the empire, for Caesar may have followed it simply as an easy way of winning provincial support and enlarging the area for recruiting legionary soldiers, who were still supposed to be Roman citizens. Mommsen, on the other hand, finds evidence of such an intent in certain bronze tablets discovered near the old city of Heraclea in southern Italy and containing an inscription generally referred to as the *"lex Julia* concerning municipalities."[38] Because its provisions include regulations special to Rome, he concluded that Caesar had formulated a deep design to make Rome merely one of the municipalities of the empire and to put Rome and Italy on a par with the provinces.[39] Warde Fowler, who adopts this view, summarizes the plan as follows: "Rome herself was to be henceforward in the eye of the law only a municipal town, the first of all in dignity, but not in power. She was to resign her place as mistress, and to be no more than a convenient centre for the conduct of the business of the Empire . . . no one city was henceforth to dominate the rest."[40]

Certainly this conclusion is a broad one to draw from the evidence. As Professor Reid has said, "it is to be feared that few men in the world would be able to catch an idea so profound, intimated in a manner so trivial." [41] Accordingly Mommsen's interpretation has long been suspect, and general acceptance has more recently been accorded to Herzog's view that the legal provisions preserved in the table of Heraclea are parts of separate and distinct enactments, and not a single code at all.[42] The significant thing about the evidence preserved in the Heraclean tables is only that Caesar at some time promulgated a law enacting general rules applicable to municipalities and colonies with respect to such matters as qualifications for office in their local governments. In this sense it may be said that he prescribed a model charter for particular kinds of communities, but it is far from certain for precisely what type of communities the charter was intended.[43]

In any event, two points seem clear. First, if Caesar in fact drafted or enacted any general charter provisions applicable to a certain class of municipality or colony, he also issued special and separate charters for particular settlements, and one such charter has actually been preserved.[44] Second, the provisions of the model charter itself were clearly not democratic. The charter "adopted the conservative principle already in vogue in older Roman municipalities of using a city council of a hundred ex-magistrates as *decuriones* in whose hands lay the power of making all city ordinances. Democrat though he claimed to be Caesar did not think it proper to employ the general town-meeting for this purpose. The executive and judicial power was held by a board of four men elected annually, the elective power remaining in the whole democratic assembly of citizens." [45]

In these various municipal arrangements, therefore, it seems impossible to discover a systematic plan or any broad conceptions of policy—certainly not a deliberate program of breaking down the distinction between Romans and provincials. All that the evidence permits is to say that Caesar did a number of specific things which show a disregard and contempt for the special position of Romans without necessarily intending to place provincials on a level with them. Here, as elsewhere, his policy was not systematic but sporadic, for he never permitted established distinctions and rights to stand in the way of his doing a particular thing that for one reason or another he wished to do.

In a sense this judgment must be passed on Caesar's legislation as a whole, which is an aggregate of disconnected expedients rather than the application of definite principles, or the systematic pursuit of particular goals. Historians, however, have never tired of attempting to trace in the fragmentary laws a pattern and clue to large ultimate conceptions toward which it is supposed that he was working. One of the most recent and eloquent of these attempts has been contributed by the late Lord Tweedsmuir, himself a writer and statesman of distinction, who frankly confesses that he became fascinated with Caesar through the writings of Mommsen and his school, and who states his own conception of Caesar's ultimate goals in the following paragraph:

Julius conceived of a world-empire of which Rome should be the shrine and the heart, but without predominance. That empire would be an oecumene, a unity of civilization, its citizenship would be extended to all found worthy, and Roman law made its common law. A standing army, which should also be a school of citizenship, and a centralized bureaucracy would provide order and just government. The forms of the Roman city-state might to some degree be preserved as antiquarian curiosities, but Julius had the contempt of the realistic mind for shells from which the life had departed. He stood not for Rome or Italy, but for a new imperial culture, which would draw what was best not only from the Latin tradition, but from Greece, from the East, even from the wilder lands of the West and North. At the head of this economy must be one man, a monarch by whatever name he might be called, sole chief of the army and of the bureaucracy, the ultimate fount of power.[46]

If these results followed ultimately in the wake of Caesar's career, and if particular measures that he adopted appear to point in the direction of some of them, it nevertheless seems more than doubtful in the light of the record that he consciously envisaged such a goal or followed any definite program for attaining it. Although a few of his measures were bold and ambitious, for example, his colonization policy and the plan of public works that was never carried out, most of them were expedients dictated by the necessity of the moment and not of a character to promise any real cure for the economic or political ills of the Roman world.[47] In the main they were stabs in the dark, haphazard, scrappy, and largely trivial. The really significant things that Caesar accomplished were nearly all in the direction of breaking down the established institutions of Roman government and building up his own personal power in their place.

III

Contemporaries who observed how Caesar was gathering power into his own hands after the end of the civil war waited with curiosity and anticipation to see whether he intended to effect a stable and permanent reorganization of the government of Rome, and, if so, what institutional form it would assume. Cicero in particular was reluctant to give up the hope that Caesar would restore the republic.[48] Writing not long after the battle of Munda, in September, 46, he said: "He who has the chief power appears to me to be daily moving insensibly toward just views and natural equity; and our cause itself is such that . . . the republic, which cannot lie prostrate forever, is necessarily recovering life and being restored to a sound condition." [49] A few weeks later he took advantage of Caesar's pardon of a distinguished Pompeian, Marcellus, the consul of the year 51, to make one of his rare appearances in the senate and address a bold plea to Caesar to reestablish the constitution.

. . . This, then, is the part which is left for you, this is the task that remains, the course of action which must be followed—to reconstitute the republic. . . . Posterity already has many things at which it may marvel, now it also expects from you something that it may praise. Certainly future generations will stand in amazement when they hear and read of your military campaigns . . . your innumerable battles, your incredible victories, your monuments, your munificent donations, your triumphs. But unless this state is now once again firmly and securely stabilized by your wise counsels and institutions your name will float long at large on the winds of history, but secure abode and fixed dwelling it will not have.[50]

In these bold words, Cicero the institutionalist challenged Caesar the instrumentalist to become the restorer or founder of stable institutions. It remained for Caesar to disclose whether he cared to assume the task.

Up to this time Caesar had given little indication that he intended to abolish or even make any formal alteration in the historic institutions of the republic. In accomplishing his purposes theretofore, he had used and manipulated those institutions, but in doing so had employed them in such novel and unprecedented ways and had so obviously diverted them from their traditional functions as to throw the operation of the constitution into complete confusion. The nature and extent of that confusion, which was so great as to nullify practically all the institutional arrangements of Roman government, can be understood only by reviewing the course which he adopted toward the republican magistracies, the assemblies and the senate.

Nominally and legally Caesar exercised his power as the holder of certain of the republican magistracies. What was novel and extraordinary about his position was that he held simultaneously a multiplicity of those offices that were never intended to be combined at one and the same time in the hands of a single individual. Thus, in the year 48, while consul and absent in Egypt, he had himself named dictator, and in the following year, on his return from the East, his dictatorship was renewed and he was made consul at the same time.[51] After the battle of Thapsus, his dictatorship was extended to ten years, he was again named consul, and was made sole censor, under the title of "guardian of manners and morals," for three years.[52] After Munda the dictatorship was conferred on him for life.[53] He had also been vested permanently with tribunician power, carrying with it a veto on the acts of all the other magistrates and of the senate. He was made consul for the year 46 without a colleague.[54] Moreover, he was assigned a seat in the senate beside the consuls, together with the right, if there were any other consul, to speak first.[55] He had long been chief pontiff and now was made a member of the college of augurs and of the other priestly colleges.[56] After Munda he seems to have been granted permanently the proconsular imperium, with the right to command all the armies of the state, and was offered, though he declined it, the consulship for ten years.[57] With all these offices combined in the same hand, the checks and balances of the constitution were utterly destroyed. It was almost as if in the American Republic the same man were simultaneously President, Chief Justice, chairman of all the committees of the Senate and the House, Chief of Staff, and Archbishop of a state-church. No one had ever contemplated the possibility of such a combination of miscellaneous and inconsistent offices; on the other hand, the combination was not prohibited by any specific provision of the constitution.

Although the legality of Caesar's power was based on his tenure of these various offices, with characteristic inconsistency he pursued a policy of belittling the republican magistracies in general and of bringing them into contempt insofar as he did not hold them himself. In the year 47, and for the first nine months of 45, there were neither praetors nor aediles nor quaestors, and their functions were transferred to, and exercised by, deputies whom he appointed by virtue of his wide general powers.[58] He also lessened the dignity and importance of those offices by greatly increasing their number. For example, in the period between his return from the East and his departure for the African campaign he raised the number of praetors to ten.[59] After his return from Munda and prior to the elections for the year 44, he increased the number of praetors to sixteen, the number of aediles to six, and the number quaestors to forty.[60] For the consular office and dignity he showed special disdain. Not only, as stated, did he decline the ten-year consulship which was offered him after Munda, but he signalized the lack of importance which he attached to it by leaving the office unfilled or only partially filled for considerable periods of time. Thus, in 47 b.c. there were no consuls until late in the year, and in 46, and for the greater part of 45, there was no consul but Caesar himself, who held the dictatorship at the same time. At the end of 45, he decided to fill the consulships with two of his retainers, and when one of these died near the end of the year, he named another of his favorites, who served only a few hours.[61]

Not only did Caesar absorb the powers of all the highest magistrates, including the judicial functions of the praetors when it suited his purpose to preside in court, but he took personal charge of the public revenues. The latter he treated as his private property, and it is not surprising that Cicero sarcastically referred to the Roman provinces as "Caesar's estates." [62]

Caesar's attitude toward the assemblies, the democratic part of the constitution, was no less high-handed. He had long known how to control the tribal assembly by the methods which he and Clodius had so successfully devised, and there was little if any chance that they would refuse to ratify whatever he proposed, so that he could use them for his purposes whenever he needed without interfering with their power. The situation with respect to the *comitia centuriata* was different. To control that body was much more difficult, as experience had shown, and Caesar had to employ a different expedient and a summary one—nothing less than to take the electoral power out of their hands. Accordingly, after Pharsalus, Caesar was given, either by decree of the senate or by a law of the tribal assembly, the right to fill by appointment all except the plebeian magistracies.[63] He exercised this power on his return from the East by naming consuls for the few remaining months of the year 47 and by appointing himself consul for the next year; after Munda, his power to nominate to the magistracies was renewed and was at that time also extended to the tribunes.[64] These constantly recurring changes in the method of filling the magistracies wrought such confusion that the only thing which was clear was that the holders of those offices were all the creatures of Caesar's will.

The senate and the senatorial class Caesar sought constantly to degrade and rob of power and importance. However, in so doing he found himself faced with a dilemma which he does not seem to have been quite willing to resolve, and in consequence his policy in that direction is marked by vacillation. On the one hand, he clearly could not afford to have the senate continue as a powerful institution and organ of government; on the other, he seems definitely to have felt that he needed the support and assistance of at least a large segment of the senatorial class, not only for the sake of appearances and to minimize opposition but also because in that class alone could he find a sufficient number of competent, experienced and trustworthy administrators. Without the sincere and patriotic cooperation of a substantial part of the nobility he could not hope successfully to carry on his government, which was in constant danger of succumbing to inefficiency and violence.[65]

Apparently Caesar had little confidence in most of his associates, who were of doubtful character, and whenever his back was turned "there was disorder in Rome fomented by his own partisans. In spite of all their faults and vices, the republican nobility still had almost a monopoly of official experience and training for public affairs. . . . Without them it was a difficult, if not an impossible, task to govern the Roman world." [66] This accounts, at least in part, for Caesar's policy of clemency, as well as for his persistent and continuing effort to win the support of prominent and reputable senators.

Yet, although Caesar might need the aid of individual senators in considerable numbers and might trust them to the extent of appointing them to high offices, it was another thing to trust the senatorial class as a group or the senate as an organized body. His acts show that he recognized, as did de Tocqueville centuries afterward, that an aristocracy is the surest and most certain bulwark against personal absolutism; that "of all societies in the world those which will always have the greatest difficulty in escaping . . . absolute government will be precisely those in which an aristocracy no longer exists." [67] Accordingly, Caesar was confronted with the delicate and difficult task of winning and retaining the support of influential senators and at the same time degrading and debasing the order to which they belonged and abolishing the power of the institution from which their importance stemmed. The difficulties inherent in such a task account for some of the inconsistencies in Caesar's policy, which in the end contributed in no small part to his own destruction.

On his return from the Eastern campaign, Caesar began to dilute the membership of the senate with men from among his own partisans, who were not of the type from which senators had hitherto usually been chosen. The numerous vacancies in the senate he filled by promoting obscure knights, who had helped him financially, and even some army centurions whom he wished to reward.[68] On his return from Africa he carried the process further by adding men who had been condemned by the courts and others who were under the stigma of the censors for infamy.[69] After his victory at Munda had further confirmed and consolidated his supremacy, he fully disclosed his policy by re-forming the senate in a drastic way. He increased its membership to the enormous total of nine hundred and thereby completely destroyed its usefulness as a governing council and rendered it quite unworkable as a deliberative body. Among the vast numbers of new members were common soldiers, freedmen and even newly enfranchised Gauls from beyond the Alps.[70] The shock to Roman public opinion seems to have been serious. Satirical placards were posted on walls, reading "In the interest of the public: it is forbidden to show any new Senator the way to the Senate-house." [71] Songs and lampoons were circulated, particularly about the Gallic senators.[72] In short, Caesar turned the senate into a farce, but, in choosing the method he did to humiliate and degrade it, he courted the danger of making himself ridiculous at the same time.[73]

With the senate reduced almost to a nullity as a governing body, Caesar seems personally to have assumed its prerogatives and even proceeded to draw up and promulgate decrees in its name. This practice is described in a letter of Cicero's in which he writes:

When I am at Rome and in the thick of the forum, decrees of the senate are written out in the house of . . . my friend. Indeed, if it comes into his head, I am listed as one of those who signed the enrollment as a witness, and I get news of the arrival in Armenia or Syria of decrees said to have been adopted on my motion before any mention has been made of the matter. . . . I assure you I have already had letters from kings at the ends of the earth thanking me for having voted to confer the royal title on them when as a matter of fact I was not only ignorant of their having been given any such title, but even of their very existence.[74]

While the senate was thus to all intents and purposes extinguished as an organ of government, it seems to have been Caesar's idea to convert senatorial membership into something like a badge of social status or distinction, as it was to become in the last age of the empire four centuries later, for the purpose of founding on this basis a new nobility or aristocracy which would owe its origin to his own pleasure. Another reform with which he toyed was "the creation of new patrician houses, a plan, it would seem, for reviving the old nobility of birth, in place of that worn-out nobility of state-service, which had come to an end with the extinction of its functions under his own sway." [75] However, at the same time that he was thus contemplating a new type of social distinction, Caesar proceeded, with characteristic inconsistency and a kind of amused impishness, to undermine established class distinctions in Roman society. "Worse was it that knights fought as gladiators; even a senator is said to have wanted to do the same, but the dictator drew the line at this. He had however already gone far enough in encouraging men of good position to disgrace themselves . . . as tending to level all in common servitude to the autocrat." [76]

IV

It should now be clear that the government which Caesar provided for Rome during the years of his supremacy represented an attempt to administer a complete personal autocracy behind the façade of institutions devised to function in an altogether different way. The natural result was that the actual exercise of authority and administrative supervision proceeded through informal channels which were uninstitutionalized and fluid, extending downward from Caesar through such personal friends and dependents as he cared to employ from time to time for different purposes. More often than not, these men held no constitutionally or legally recognized governmental position. In this way, actual government, on the one hand, and legal institutions, on the other, grew apart, and the former tended to become highly informal and responsive to the temporary fluctuations of Caesar's personal will. In Mommsen's words: "Caesar was able to carry personal government to an extent which puny men can scarcely conceive . . . [avoiding] so far as was at all possible, any delegation of his functions. Where it was inevitable, as especially when during his frequent absences from Rome . . . the person destined for this purpose was significantly enough . . . a confidant without officially recognized jurisdiction." [77]

Obviously if Caesar wished to exercise power in this way, he could not afford to institutionalize it. The essence of institutional arrangements is that insofar as they exist they impose regularity and therefore restraints on the conduct of government and on the methods of administering it. Since he seems clearly to have wished to be free to use his power through any channels or instruments and in any way that from time to time seemed best to him, he had no intention of restricting his freedom of action either by institutionalizing his own position, and thereby defining it within limits, or by building up any institutionalized system of organs through which his supremacy would have to operate. In this sense, as Mommsen points out, under the type of monarchy which Caesar was administering "there could hardly be room for a constitution at all." [78] Instead, his purposes were more satisfactorily served by the confusion resulting from the mixture of his informal government with the remains of the republican constitution still nominally functioning, since in this fluid and more or less unorganized state of affairs he retained greater flexibility for the exercise of his own personal power. In any event, with his strongly instrumentalist cast of mind, he saw little utility in institutions, which he viewed as abstractions, names, or forms having no concrete or physical substance. [79]

For these reasons, there seems less relevance than might otherwise attach to much of the discussion that has gone on as to the ultimate form of organization which Caesar intended for the Roman state. It has been widely debated, for example, whether he meant to establish a monarchy and, if so, of what type. [80] For all practical purposes, he was already a monarch in the fullest sense, and the only question which remains open is how, if at all, he intended to regularize or institutionalize his monarchical position. To this question the answer seems to be that he apparently did not intend to do so at all. Accordingly, there is much truth in the verdict expressed by Professor Adcock, "the assertion that he had formed any clear plan for the future of the Roman State goes beyond the evidence and is not made necessary by his character." [81]

Although Caesar regarded institutional arrangements as unimportant because lacking reality, he seems to have felt it all the more necessary to emphasize and enhance the visible reality of his own actual power and to confirm and establish it in ways that would appeal directly to the senses and emotions of the Roman world. As one of the world's great masters of popular psychology, he seems to have felt that, having gone as far as he had in achieving for himself a position of supremacy, he was compelled to go still further in strengthening that position by public recognition. In this sense he was driven forward by the impulse of his own accomplishments. Here, as elsewhere, however, his native caution and habit of calculation governed his course, so that once again he proceeded gradually and step by step.

In addition to the powers and offices conferred upon him after Munda, there were others of a different and more extraordinary nature which are summarized by the historian Appian as follows: "All kinds of honors were devised for his gratification . . . sacrifices, games, statues in all the temples and public places. . . . He was proclaimed the Father of his Country . . . and his person was declared sacrosanct and inviolable. It was decreed that he should transact business on a throne of ivory and gold; that he should perform his sacerdotal functions always in triumphal costume . . . that every five years the priests and Vestal virgins should offer up public prayers for his safety; and that the magistrates immediately upon inauguration should take an oath not to oppose any of Caesar's decrees." [82] Further details are supplied in other accounts. For example, an ivory figure of Caesar was to be paraded along with the figures of the gods in the processions at the games. His statue was to be set up in the Capitol beside those representing the seven legendary kings of Rome,[83] and at the same time his effigy began to appear on coins which had hitherto carried only that of a god and never before a representation of a living man.[84]

The obvious inference to be drawn from these circumstances is that Caesar was preparing the way for his deification or something like it, yet many historians have found difficulty in attributing such an objective to a man of his bold and rationalistic spirit. Those who choose to regard him as remaining cool and detached in the face of the extravagant adulation accorded him consider that he submitted cynically to honors which he must have valued at their true worth but which he did not feel it safe to decline. It is suggested that the "readiness to offer to Caesar divine honours does not mean that he claimed them." [85] His "ceaseless clear-headed activity," it is said, "disposes of the legend of him as the pathological study in diseased greatness which Shakespeare has read out of his Plutarch." [86] The evidence, however, is too plain and cumulative to be disregarded, and a reasonable explanation of Caesar's conduct in the light of his character is available without adopting either the view that he had become pathological or Mommsen's conception that the principle of monarchy leads by necessary logical sequence up to its realization in a god-king.[87] Thus, Professor Frank says:

Caesar, like Alexander the Great, observing that in all Oriental nations autocracy had succeeded only where the ruler based his power upon the theory of divine rights, had deliberately chosen to accustom the Roman people gradually to acknowledge the superhuman character of their ruler. In Persia as in Egypt the king was more than man. He was a descendant of gods, a spokesman of gods, or himself a divinity, whose utterances could not be gainsaid. Alexander, comprehending the fact that his reforms and his great plans for unifying Greece were hindered on every hand by treaties, laws and constitutions, and that he might over-ride these only if he could accustom the Greeks to the idea that his decrees, emanating from a superhuman source, were final, had deliber-ately spread the story of his descent from Zeus Ammon. Julius Caesar, who was a close student of the career of Alexander, who knew Asiatic and Egyptian customs from personal observation, seems to have adopted a similar policy. . . . Caesar's plan, difficult to comprehend in the light of modern customs, was after all very reasonable in the society of that day. Rome was filled with Orientals who were accustomed to the theory of divine royalty. The mob at least would only too readily adopt the idea and would be all the more devoted to the ruler for his elevation.[88]

In an earlier chapter it was noted that Caesar's mind seems first to have turned toward such ideas during his sojourn in Egypt in the course of his early association with Cleopatra, and it was there suggested that to some extent, at least, he was actually convinced of the genuineness of his supernatural pretensions by the spectacu-lar success of his career.[89] It is one of the paradoxes of his complex nature that mysticism and practical rationalism were both combined in it, so that it should not be regarded as unnatural that he indulged the former when he saw that it might promote his practical ends. If due weight be given to all these considerations, it is impossible to disregard the strong evidence that during the last years of his life Caesar was by gradual steps promoting his deification.

The first open step which he took in this direction was on his return to Rome after Thapsus, when he dedicated a magnificent new temple to Venus Genetrix, the mother of the Julian family and therefore his own ancestress, and at the same time the legendary mother of the people of Rome. "The new state-cult, celebrated with a magnificence that no one could forget, was far more than a simple claim to divine ancestry such as many a noble Roman of the day might have set forth with equal justice. It was a formal declaration of Caesar's position as the representative of the state, the favored son of the goddess who was the mother of all the Romans." [90] This "served as a legitimization of his rule much as the Libyan oracle's declaration of Alexander as the son of Zeus served to establish Alexander's position." [91] It is not without significance that inside the new temple beside the cult-statue of the goddess, a masterpiece by one of the great artists of the Hellenistic world,[92] Caesar placed an image of Cleopatra.[93] This act suggests that the conception of the new position which he wished to assume he had brought with him from Egypt.[94]

It is in the light of the dedication of this temple and the establishment of the cult of Venus Genetrix that the subsequent honors which Caesar received after Munda are to be interpreted. When he accepted the formal title of "Father of his Country" and stamped it on his coins, he assumed a position by the side of Romulus, the founder of the city, who was worshiped as a god. He emphasized that position by placing his own statue in the temple of Romulus, "where a bust of a mere human being had no right to appear." [95] He further signalized his position as the divine representative of the state by permitting his statue to be set up in the Capitol, the center of the Roman state worship, beside the seven ancient kings. In allowing his image to be paraded at the games among the statues of the gods, he made it difficult if not impossible to distinguish his own mortal effigy from the divinity of the gods whom it accompanied.[96] Although historians have been at pains to point out that all these honors may be construed as falling short of actual deification, their tendency in that direction is unequivocal.

The next step that Caesar took was equally unequivocal. Sometime near the end of the year 45, the senate decreed a temple to "Caesar and his Clemency" and instituted a permanent priest or *flamen* of the "divine Julius" (*divus Julius*). It has been suggested that the temple was not dedicated to Caesar personally but only to the abstraction of his special quality of clemency,[97] but there is no room for doubt about the priest.[98] The only Roman deities who had their special priests were Jupiter, Mars and Romulus, so that the appointment of a special priest of Caesar placed him in a peculiar position of preeminence in the Roman state religion. The word *divus* applied to Caesar also seems conclusive. "The word . . . at that time, as we know from its use in earlier writers and from the comments of ancient scholars, had nothing of the meaning of man made into god which it eventually acquired after it had been applied for generations to . . . emperors [deified after death]. It was used by the poets almost interchangeably with the more common *deus*."[99] It meant quite simply "god." The divine honors thus conferred on Caesar naturally produced disgust among traditionally minded Romans, and, if Cicero is to be believed, Caesar's divinity was not always received with favor even by the Roman populace. "The procession was odious," he writes, after attending the games. "The people were splendid not to applaud the statue of Victory because of its impious neighbor [Caesar's image]."[100]

It seems evident that enough Romans were unimpressed by the device of deification to make it worthwhile for Caesar to seek a different and additional psychological basis for his supremacy. For those Romans who could not stomach the idea of an Oriental godking, Caesar resorted to a different kind of religious sanction for his power, more in keeping with Roman traditions and Western habits of thought. This was the use to which he turned the oath. The importance of the oath was deeply rooted in Rome's legal and constitutional tradition. Invoking as it did the intervention of supernatural power to enforce the performance of the promise or promises to which it was annexed,[101] it vested those promises with a religious sanction which remained an essential feature of Roman jurisprudence from the early period of Rome's history when her civil law and religious code were identical, and in the developed law of

Rome "the importance of the oath was overwhelming." [102] No group of Roman citizens was so sensitive to this importance as the conservative traditionalists who were most likely to object to Caesar's pretensions, and he therefore apparently sought to employ the oath in three ways to overcome their possible resistance.

In the first place, public officials on assuming office were required to take an oath that they would not oppose any of his decrees.[103] In this way, the sanctions of religion were invoked to avert and prevent official resistance to his acts; they were invested, as it were, with divine protection in advance. Secondly, in the formula used for official oaths there was added to Jove and the household gods of the Roman people the guardian spirit or "destiny" of Caesar himself.[104] In the Oriental monarchies it had become customary to swear by the "destiny" of the king,[105] and this conception of the "destiny" of an individual was comparable to the old Roman notion of the "genius" or guardian spirit who attended a man throughout life. The new form of oath thus had the effect of including Caesar's attendant spirit in the foremost rank of the deities of the state, thus suggesting his own divinity by implication; at the same time, it compelled the officials who were required to take this oath to recognize and acquiesce in such a claim to divinity. The new oath had another effect which Caesar almost certainly intended. It had long been the custom for the clients and members of the household of a Roman family to swear by the "genius" or attendant spirit of its master. By requiring such an oath of the officials of the Roman state, and possibly of all others who had to take an oath in connection with political or other public acts, Caesar obviously sought to create the impression that they were his clients and stood in the same relation to him as the subordinate members of a household to the master of the house [106]—a relationship which was again protected by solemn religious sanctions not unlike the fealty which a liege man swore to his lord in the days of mediaeval feudalism.

Finally, Caesar sought to confirm his supremacy by a third use of the oath. Suetonius speaks of an oath by which "all bound themselves to protect and preserve the safety of one man," [107] and Appian refers to an oath by which "all were pledged to guard Caesar and Caesar's body with all their strength, and all were devoted to

perdition who should not avenge him against any conspiracy." [108]
It has often been assumed that these passages refer to some special
oath taken only by the senate under circumstances and for reasons
otherwise unaccounted for,[109] but a different explanation seems more
probable. Near the end of Caesar's life, perhaps as late as the beginning of the year 44,[110] there was specially conferred on him "tribunician sacrosanctity." As stated above, he had already enjoyed for some
time tribunician power, which invested him with the prerogatives of
the tribunate while not actually holding the office, but apparently
sacrosanctity was separately conferred at a later date. Now tribunician sacrosanctity rested traditionally in fact, and subsequently in
theory, on an oath taken by the Roman plebs to protect the tribunes,
maintain their inviolability and avenge any injury done to them. As
Livy says, "Commentators deny that any person is sacrosanct by
virtue of this law, but that he who harms any of them is deemed to
be devoted [to Jupiter]; . . . that the tribunes were sacred and inviolable by virtue of the ancient oath sworn by the people when they
first created that office." [111] Accordingly, when we are informed of
the tribunician sacrosanctity conferred on Caesar and also learn that
at the same time there was an oath whereby all swore to guard
Caesar, it is hard not to connect the two circumstances and draw the
necessary conclusion that Caesar intended to confirm his sacrosanctity
by the oath thus described and make the entire Roman citizen body
swear to hold his person inviolable. This view has been taken by several recent historians who have also suggested a connection between
the oath of sacrosanctity and the oath by Caesar's "genius" above
referred to.

According to this view, "Caesar attempted to bind to himself
in a kind of superclientele all the senators and citizens alike. The
step was not taken until the last months, perhaps the last weeks, of
Caesar's life. . . . There probably was not time before Caesar's death
to administer the oath universally, but the senators had certainly
taken it. . . . By this oath, actually taken or to be taken by all the
Romans, Caesar was accepted as the patron or rather the *pater* of the
whole state and the old relation of *fides* [religiously sanctioned loy-
alty], the tie that bound patron and client or father and son, united
him with all the citizens." [112] From a slightly different standpoint,

what Caesar was attempting to do was analogous to the action of William the Conqueror when he made all the landowners of England swear personal fealty to him by the oath on Salisbury Plain in 1086.[113]

If this view is correct, and there is every reason to suppose that it is, there is obvious consistency between Caesar's policy in exacting a general oath to his person and the policy which he pursued in promoting his deification. In both instances he sought to identify himself personally, as no man had been identified before, with the Roman state itself. In the one case he did so, first, by representing himself as the descendant of Venus, the divine ancestress of all Romans, and, afterwards, by associating himself with the gods who were specially and peculiarly the gods of the state—Jupiter, Mars and particularly Romulus, the deified founder. In the other case, he sought to compel recognition of himself, through the instrumentality of the oath, as the patron or master of a household which included the whole Roman people. It is remarkable how closely and logically these various strands of policy mesh together from the standpoint of aiming at a single psychological impression that "Caesarism meant the identification of the Roman people with Caesar." [114]

In his efforts to find additional psychological fortification for his power, the question of the title by which to describe his supreme position seems also to have engaged Caesar's serious attention. To minds saturated in the common sense of the nineteenth century such a question may appear trivial, but it seems clear that, to a man who sought so obviously to rest his power on psychological foundations, words and names necessarily assumed a large importance. This was especially true because the office by virtue of which he nominally ruled was the dictatorship, which he knew had an evil and unsavory connotation, as well as ill-omened historical associations. Like dictators of recent times, he was anxious to clothe his position with a name that would be free from constitutional associations and would mark his supremacy as a complete break with the past.

On many of the coins on which Caesar's effigy is stamped he is described as "imperator," the Latin word from which the modern title "emperor" derives. The designation was familiar in Roman military usage and was applied to a commander-in-chief of an army who had won a notable victory and who was customarily saluted as "imperator" by his troops until he crossed the *pomerium,* or civil boundary of the city, for the purpose of celebrating his triumph.[115] With characteristic disregard of constitutional niceties, Caesar had not hesitated to go back and forth freely across the *pomerium* in advance of the celebration of his triumphs.[116] He had borne the title for years at a stretch—longer than it had ever been borne by any Roman before—from the commencement of the civil war to his first triumph in June, 46, and afterwards from his salutation in Spain in February, 45, until his triumph after Munda in the following October. "Thus during four-fifths of his period of supremacy Caesar was an imperator in the ordinary sense of a victorious general who was awaiting a triumph." [117] This long-continued use of the title caused it to become associated characteristically with Caesar, as is shown by the inscriptions on his coins. Mommsen accordingly advanced the view that "imperator" was the title by which Caesar wished his supreme position to be specifically designated. "The new name of Imperator," he says, ". . . appears in every respect the appropriate formal expression for the new monarchy; just because it is new, and no definite outward occasion for its introduction is apparent. The new wine might not be put into old bottles; here is a new name for the new thing." [118]

This view has been sharply challenged by recent scholars, who point out that Caesar cannot be proved even to have used the title except during periods when he would have been allowed to do so by traditional military usage. These scholars argue, therefore, that there is no ground for supposing that he intended it as in any sense a new or characteristic designation of his supremacy.[119] The premise of this argument may be accepted, and yet the conclusion does not necessarily follow. Certainly Caesar so managed to have the title associated with his name, whether in accordance with tradition or not, in a way that had never been associated with any other Roman. Thus it came perforce and as a matter of habit to be one of the peculiar emblems of Caesar's power—a new designation, as Mommsen puts it, for a new thing. However, the title was only a symbol of the military aspect of his rule, and it implied all too clearly that by military force he was exercising functions which at Rome had always been reserved for the civil authority. Accordingly, although Caesar emphasized the title "imperator" by displaying it on his coins, he does not seem to have been quite content with it as providing the unique and peculiar designation of his power.

There is abundant evidence that during the last months of his life Caesar was weighing arguments for and against another and far more momentous title, one which did not have the unhappy recent connotations of dictatorship. This was nothing less than the title of "king," which had been borne by Romulus, the founder of Rome, and by the other ancient legendary rulers of the city with whom he had already shown his wish to be associated by the placing of his statue in the Capitol. More than one historical account has stated that the proposal to make Caesar king was contrived and initiated by his enemies in order to make him unpopular and to stimulate an uprising against him,[120] but an early writer suggests that he himself sent up a trial balloon by threatening any who should talk of making him king.[121] However that may be, Caesar seems to have indulged in loose talk on the subject, which may well have influenced his enemies no less than his friends. Cicero reports that Caesar used to quote with approval the verses of Euripides' *Phoinissai* to the effect that if wrong can ever be right, wrong for a throne's sake would be most right.[122] Certainly, from an Oriental standpoint, the title of king was entirely consistent with the divinity of his personal supremacy for which he had now won recognition; [123] but he seems to have underestimated the strength of the traditional Roman antagonism to kingship, which he apparently thought was a prejudice that was long outmoded. Nevertheless, his attitude remained ambiguous for some time, and he preferred temporarily to let the forces for and against his assuming the royal title try themselves out.

The accounts which have survived of the early and momentous months of the year 44 tell little of the suppressed excitement which must have pervaded them. Sometime in January, a statue of Caesar which had been erected on the rostra was found to have been crowned by unknown hands with a royal diadem. When two of the tribunes removed the crown, Caesar apparently became incensed. Subsequently, when he was riding into Rome from Alba Longa, some bystanders along the road hailed him as king, whereupon he replied that he was not a king, but Caesar. However, when the same two tribunes prosecuted these men, he no longer restrained his anger and showed his irritation publicly by saying that these tribunes were conspiring against the stability of the government. "He added that they were deserving of death, but that it would be sufficient if they were deprived of their office and expelled from the Senate. Thus he confirmed the suspicion that he desired the title . . . for the cause of their punishment was their zeal against the title of king. . . . By not waiting for the expiration of their office he sharpened the public indignation." [124]

A few weeks later, in the middle of February, occurred the famous incident at the Lupercalian festival. Caesar was presiding in his triumphal costume and seated on his gold-and-ivory throne when Mark Antony, now restored to the dictator's favor and his colleague in the consulship, approached him and sought to place a golden diadem on his head, saluting him as king and saying, "This the people give to you through me." [125] Caesar seemingly refused, and drew aside to avoid it, and was applauded by the people with great shouts. Again Antony pressed it, and again he declined its acceptance. And so the dispute between them went on, with Antony's solicitations receiving but little encouragement from the shouts of a few friends, and with Caesar's refusal accompanied by the general applause of the people.[126] In the end Caesar announced that Jupiter alone was king of the Romans, and "sent the diadem to be placed on his statue in the Capitol: but he was not angry and caused a record to be inscribed in the public archives that he had refused to accept the kingship when conferred on him by the Roman people through their consul." [127]

It is certainly not possible to attribute Mark Antony's action to Caesar's enemies, for no Roman in public life at the time was more closely in his confidence. It was accordingly suspected that what had been done was by prearrangement between them and that Caesar desired the royal title, but wished to be compelled to assume it.[128] Apparently Caesar was sending up another trial balloon through Antony and found from the popular response that kingship at Rome was still beyond the bounds of possibility. In doing so, he acted ill-advisedly, and if there be an excuse, it must be found, if at all, in Mr. Heitland's explanation: "While we may admit that Caesar's head was somewhat turned by his present elevation, it is perhaps to the loneliness of his position that we should primarily attribute these ill-judged proceedings." [129] In any event, he saw that if he desired to be king he would have to adopt a different course to attain the title. Unfortunately for him, he had already so fatally unmasked his ambition that he had in fact brought about his own downfall. As Cicero afterwards proclaimed to Mark Antony, "It was you, you, I say, who slew him at the Lupercalia." [130]

V

The total impression left by Caesar's years of power is that, like his predecessors in the democratic movements at Rome since the age of the Gracchi, he devoted far more attention to enhancing and confirming his personal position than to satisfying the real needs of the people or achieving social or political betterment by constructive reforms. In this respect he was very much the heir of his first father-in-law, Cinna. After his culminating victory at Munda, although he seems to have gone forward with the task of carrying out his great colonial program and also continued to busy himself with plans for his projected public works, his attention was mainly concentrated on such measures for confirming and implementing his personal supremacy as have just been reviewed. The bent and temper of Caesar's mind were clearly not congenial to broad ideas of economic or social welfare. Moreover, with his instrumentalist fixation on practical objectives and on an immediate job to be done, he took little interest in projects less concrete and specific than the physical movement of populations or the displacement of masses of earth and stone. Accordingly, as he reached the point where not much remained to assure and confirm his personal possession of absolute power, he was confronted with the need to decide whether his colonization and public works programs were sufficiently important to engage his entire future attention, and he apparently concluded that they were not, and that he should use the power of the Roman state, now at his complete disposal, for some other and more impressive and spectacular achievement. He determined to employ it for the purpose of embarking on a new course of military conquest.

It is not unnatural that Caesar came to this decision. For nearly fifteen years his life had been lived almost continuously in the field, engaged at first in providing a military basis for his power and afterwards in winning a supreme position by military means. Not only had he become habituated to the life and excitements of the camp, but he had found in warfare the occupation to which his talents were superbly suited. Military activity is adapted, as is practically no other form of enterprise, to the instrumentalist type of mind: it supplies a clean-cut and clearly defined immediate objective, the overthrow of the enemy, with which competing considerations must not be allowed to interfere, and it calls only for the contrivance and execution, by strategy and administrative efficiency, of the means necessary to attain that object. This was the kind of task and problem that Caesar had found particularly congenial, and it is hardly surprising that he preferred the pursuit of military objectives to the vague and uncertain tasks of civilian politics, which constantly involve the assessment and adjustment of intangible competing values.

Caesar's decision to use for military rather than civil ends the supremacy he had obtained sheds light not only on his temperament and the innate bent of his mind but also on the view he must have taken of his political position. There seems reason to believe that he had serious doubts about his ability to give satisfaction as a civil ruler and to maintain by political means a durable supremacy. He must have known that he had attained power largely by creating, on the part of many different individuals and groups, expectations of all sorts which it would be utterly beyond his ability to satisfy. More than any other man, he had fomented dissensions in the state over a long period, and he must now have recognized his powerlessness to provide a solution for them. As he looked into the future, he doubtless anticipated that if he should stay in Rome and seek to govern as a civil ruler, he would be bound to incur the active hostility of large and important elements of the community. Even if he could overcome any actual outbreak by military force, he preferred to avoid the necessity of facing such a possibility. It seems to be almost a law of history that political power which is gained by predominantly military means is regarded by its holders as requiring to be maintained by the continued exercise of force either at home or abroad. From this standpoint, foreign war is simply an alternative to civil war. Even if it can be concluded that there was no real danger at this time of an outbreak of civil war against Caesar, it is possible to understand how the thought of such an alternative reinforced his temperamental preference to resume the career of conquest in which he had found so much satisfaction and success.

The course of Caesar's rise to power makes clear that he was not restrained by the traditional Roman conception that war should be initiated only to repel actual or threatened aggression, and his conduct in Gaul had been an example, almost the first in Roman history, of a frank and outright war of conquest. There is therefore little reason for surprise that in the then existing posture of his affairs he had no difficulty in finding an enemy against which to direct the military force of Rome. This was Parthia. A war against the Parthians could be depended on to have a certain popularity, for the disastrous and humiliating defeat suffered by Crassus ten years before in his own aggressive campaign against Parthia still rankled in the mind of Romans and could be made to supply an excuse for a war of revenge.[131] If an additional excuse were needed, it could be alleged that Parthian aid had recently been given to one of Pompey's former lieutenants who was still in arms on the Syrian border and whom Caesar's governor of that province had been unable to subdue.[132] It is not certain that news of this incident could have reached Rome in time to have affected Caesar's decision,[133] and the seriousness of any impending danger from a Parthian attack seems highly doubtful in view of the fact that no such attack was made during the confusion in Roman affairs which followed Caesar's death a few months later. In any event, sometime near the end of the year 45 Caesar determined to organize a vast military expedition against the Parthian empire.

A number of other reasons may have made the idea of a Parthian war attractive to Caesar. For one thing, Parthia was now the only part of the known civilized world that still remained out-

side the orbit of Roman power: the rest was already tributary and
was pouring revenue into the treasury. Caesar's need for money
knew few if any bounds, and at least one historian, therefore, has
seen financial considerations as a major reason for the Parthian
project.[134] Business and economic activity in Italy and throughout
the Roman world seem to have been in a state of torpor during
Caesar's rule, and it was going to be difficult for him to obtain the
great sums needed for his colonial and public works projects. An
easy way out of this difficulty would be to tap once again the fabulous
resources of the East. As the historian Dio Cassius wrote, Caesar
was always a money-getter, that it was his maxim that power was
got and kept through men and money, and that these two produced
each other by reciprocal action; for armies were recruited and supported by money and money was got by armies; and if either of
them were lacking the other would fail at the same time.[135] Undoubtedly, the conquest of Parthia was an attractive way of filling
Caesar's coffers.

The Parthian campaign had the further attraction of taking
him back again to the East and immersing him once more in an
atmosphere which he had found so congenial. He must have come
to recognize by now that the prosaic and practical environment of
Roman traditions not only did not afford the full scope that he
sought for his feeling of divinity but imposed a hampering influence
on the display and enjoyment of his supremacy. A great Eastern
campaign would give him the sense of following once more in the
footsteps of Alexander, and the magnitude and brilliancy of the
enterprise would invite recognition of his heaven-sanctioned absolutism among peoples accustomed to worship the divinity of a great
royal conqueror. "Perhaps he also hoped by means of a brilliant
campaign in the East to justify a marriage with Cleopatra, which
would in turn secure the annexation of Egypt and the legitimization
of the new Julian dynasty whose throne would then remain in
Alexandria or Troy until its claims had been accepted by the
West." [136] Rumors that he was indulging in such dreams were widely
circulated at Rome,[137] and it is difficult to explain them unless they
originated in the talk of his intimates.

A strange air of grandiose charlatanism pervades the last months of Caesar's life. He "made promises of all sorts, possible and impossible, to everyone who came near him, and he no longer even attempted to stop the wholesale pillage of public money which his friends were conducting under his very eyes. The dictatorship was degenerating into a senile and purposeless opportunism." [138] Ferrero continues:

. . . The wildest dreams were bandied about in the streets of Rome and over the Italian country side. Caesar, with his colonies and his Parthian War, would bring back the age of gold; the tyranny of the rich and powerful was drawing to its close, and a newer and better government was at hand. The memories of the great popular revolution became so lively in men's minds that a certain Erophilus, a native of Magna Graecia, a veterinary surgeon by profession and no doubt more or less weak in the head, passed himself off as the grandson of Marius and immediately became the hero of the hour. Associations of workmen, colonies of veterans and even municipalities chose him as their patron, and he actually formed a sort of court around him and dared to treat Caesar and the aristocracy on terms of equality. Afraid to embroil himself with the people, Caesar did not dare to remove him; and the utmost he would do was to turn him out of the metropolis. [139]

Throughout the early months of the year 44 military preparations were going forward on a vast scale. [140] Caesar took particular pains in arranging the personnel of the government for the period of his expected absence. Mark Antony, his colleague in the consulship, was to be in charge during the year 44, but Caesar designated Antony's old rival Dolabella as consul to fill out his own unexpired term. For the year 43 two of his generals, Hirtius and Pansa, were named consuls, and, for the year 42, Decimus Junius Brutus and Lucius Munatius Plancus. Other prominent followers were awarded provincial governorships from which money could be made. Farther Spain was assigned to Gaius Asinius Pollio and Nearer Spain and Narbonese Gaul to his old favorite Marcus Aemilius Lepidus. Gaius Trebonius was given Asia, and Plancus and Decimus Brutus were appointed to Celtic Gaul and Cisalpine Gaul, respectively, pending their succession to the consulship. [141] With his principal supporters thus provided for and his army awaiting him at Apollonia on the Greek coast, all seemed in readiness for his departure for the East.

It was precisely at this time, however, that the question of his title and of whether he proposed to become king was being actively agitated. Although the incident at the Lupercalia which occurred on February the fifteenth had resulted in a fiasco, the question of the royal title had come to be associated in a peculiar way with the project of the Parthian war, and Caesar would not let the matter drop. Some months earlier, the keepers of the sacred Sibylline books, the traditional oracles of the Roman state, had searched them for prophecies bearing on the Parthian expedition, and it was rumored that they had found a prediction that the Parthians could be conquered only if the Romans marched against them under the command of a king. Whether by intention or not, this rumor received widespread publicity. Caesar could thus represent himself as confronted by a dilemma. He could hardly, at this stage, forego his campaign, but "if he disregarded the interpretation of the Sibylline books, its publication would arouse the superstitions of the people and perhaps of the soldiers. Ten years before, Crassus had set out against Parthia; he had left Rome under the solemn imprecations of a tribune, and he and his army had met with disaster." [142] If Caesar can be regarded as really believing this argument of a modern historian, he may well have taken a further step and convinced himself that he was under an obligation to make himself king. Unfortunately, he seemed to have foreclosed that possibility by his weakness in the face of public disapproval at the Lupercalia, but his ingenuity was as fertile as ever, and he appears to have thought that he had discovered a solution.

This solution was a product of his conviction that Rome, and probably Italy, would not tolerate a king. An autocrat might be endured to be rid of civil war, but the prejudice against the name of "king" remained ineradicable.[143] This attitude of the Roman people may have been incomprehensible to Caesar, for he had a contempt for mere names and words divorced from facts or results, but in this instance he bowed to the prejudice and determined not to recede from his renunciation at the Lupercalia. However, he was right in thinking that the prejudice was not shared in the provinces, particularly those of the East. On the contrary, those countries had been accustomed from time immemorial to the name and rule of

kings, and of sacred divine kings; in fact, they expected their ruler
to be a divine king. Caesar's solution was therefore this: he would
not assume or bear the title of king in Rome, but he would satisfy
the Sibylline oracle and set himself right with the gods by marching
against the Parthians as king not of Rome or of Italy but of the
provinces.[144] Accordingly he summoned the senate for the 15th,
or Ides, of March to ratify this solution and vote "that he should be
declared king of all the provinces out of Italy, and might wear
a diadem in any other place but Italy, by sea or land."[145] Kingship
in title as well as in fact was at last to be his.

The historic meeting of the Roman senate on the Ides of March
of the year 44 was held in a hall attached to the portico of Pompey's
theater in the Campus Martius.[146] Caesar was late in arriving, and
the assembled senators were in the portico to greet him as he stepped
down from his sedan chair. They followed him into the hall, and
a crowd gathered around him when he took his seat. The entreaties
of an importunate petitioner irritated him, and he started to rise.
Suddenly one of the senators in the group around him struck him
and pulled his toga from his shoulders, while another stabbed him
in the neck. "What are you doing, villain?" he cried out, and
then the whole group attacked him. Wherever he turned he was
confronted with daggers and was driven about like a wild animal
cornered by enemies. He made no further resistance but wrapped
his gown over his head and fell mortally wounded at the base of
Pompey's statue, which was spattered with his blood.[147] So passed
Caesar from the stage of Roman history.

VI

The widest of gulfs separates the philosophy of politics as ex-
pounded by Cicero from the art of politics as practiced by Caesar.
Ceasar's main contribution to an understanding of government
consists in his having provided a crucial case history or laboratory
study of the process of attaining personal power and of using it
when attained. To Caesar the art of government meant the promotion of any measure, however inconsistent with his previous or even
present professions, that promised to advance the next step in his

plans; his only long-range objective which can be definitely identified was the enhancement of his power. For this he indulged in a lifetime of double talk, professing the slogans of democracy, while debasing and destroying the powers of the electorate, and insisting on constitutional technicalities, while persistently undermining the constitution. In the end, his prescription for government turned out to be a surprisingly simple one: to reduce its mechanism to the simplest and most primitive of all institutional forms, personal absolutism, and to employ it for one of the simplest and most primitive of all purposes, foreign conquest.

Caesar was undoubtedly a great genius, but if his genius is to be properly appreciated it must be understood for what it was. It consisted in an ability to achieve entirely unexpected and stupendous results by phenomenal skill in adapting means to ends, by an uncanny assessment of situations and possibilities, by an amazing willingness to take chances, by an almost unparalleled combination of audacity and subtlety, by superb self-confidence and never-failing faith in fortune and good luck. He was utterly without the inhibitions which restrain ordinary men by consideration for their fellows and by reluctance to risk bringing disaster on others. These were the qualities of his genius, and however much it may be admired, it must not be regarded as including other qualities merely because they happen to be admirable. Despite his extraordinary ingenuity and boldness, Caesar had little originality. He produced all his effects, both political and military, by devices which had been employed and developed by others; he owed his success to the ways in which he combined them, to the scale on which he employed them, to the decisiveness with which he executed them, and above all to his mastery of timing and surprise. He invented no new system of army reforms like Marius or of political strategy like Gaius Gracchus. The most original of his political methods were his revival of street fighting and gang organization to control the action of the tribal assembly, his assumption of numerous and inconsistent offices at the same time (in which he had been anticipated by Pompey), and, finally, his bold and total disregard of all constitutional restraints.

Genius is generally assumed by its admirers to be constructive. Because Caesar was undoubtedly a great genius, it has been taken for granted that his career produced great constructive results. Nevertheless, such results are difficult to identify. In the field of government, for example, he built nothing but a simple uninstitutionalized personal absolutism, with no deeper or more lasting foundations than his own remarkable personality. His lifelong profession of democratic objectives brought no increase of popular control over the measures or processes of government, but rather the reverse. He effected no social or economic reorganization of the state. When his work was done, the gap between rich and poor was as wide as ever, or perhaps wider; the cities of the empire were still filled with a poverty-stricken proletariat and with the luxurious mansions of the rich. The only substantial change he effected was a change in faces: some were now rich who had once been poor, and some were poor who had once been rich. This is not to say that important forces were not released and great changes set in motion by his career. His overthrow of established patterns of social action provided opportunities for many new men to rise to importance who would not otherwise have done so. His ceaseless campaigning back and forth across Europe, Asia and Africa, his colonizing schemes and distributions of land pried men loose from their hereditary homes and created a new mobility of populations which stimulated the strong and adventurous to go forth to seek new fortunes. The most important consequences of his work, aside from those that resulted from the conquest of Gaul, were those which inevitably follow from any period of combined confusion and expansion—a reshuffling of opportunities and material rewards, a shift in the balance of interests and social values, and a widespread release of human energies resulting from the intensification of the struggle for wealth and survival. These results are hardly of a kind that can be regarded as planned objectives. Rather they were the incidental consequences of Caesar's methods and designs, the natural outcome of social and political confusion. Confusion was in fact the chief legacy that Caesar left to the Roman world. Viewed in its proper light, his work was not that of a builder, but rather of a great destroyer.

From the standpoint of Rome's political development, Caesar's greatest and almost only important contribution was the destruction of the republic. Most modern scholars and historians since Mommsen have regarded his achievement with such approval that it has stamped upon Caesar's work the judgment of constructive accomplishment of the highest order. Implicit in this judgment, and underlying it expressly or tacitly, are generally to be found one or both of two more fundamental assumptions or conclusions: first, that the republican government of Rome had so deteriorated that in the interest of human welfare and social justice it needed to be destroyed; secondly, that it had become so weak and unstable that it was bound to fall in any event, and that whoever put an end to it was therefore performing a great public service.

The view that the republican government of Rome had so deteriorated that it needed to be wiped out and superseded by the personal absolutism of Caesar for the sake of social justice is commonly based on two grounds: first, the succession of bloody and destructive civil wars which marked the last century of the republic, and, second, the corruption and extortion of so many of the republican governors in the provinces. Civil tumults had put an end to the Gracchi; then, after thirty years, had come the war with the Italian allies, followed almost immediately by the reign of terror under Marius and the civil war of his successors with Sulla; later came the uprising of Lepidus and the slave revolt under Spartacus; afterwards, the conspiracy of Catiline; and finally, fifteen years later, the civil war between Caesar and Pompey. The devastation caused by all these upheavals except the last had been chiefly confined to Italy and had done little damage in the provinces, yet during this period the latter are said to have suffered without intermission from the cruelty and rapacity of republican governors. Both the constant recurrence of civil strife and the prevalence of oppression in the provinces are traced to the same supposed cause, the greed and corruption of the Roman aristocracy who controlled the senate and through the senate the republican government. It is therefore alleged to have been necessary to wrest the government from their grasp. "[T]he defenders of the worn-out system must be resisted and defeated. They were deaf to appeals of either reason or humanity. In the penetrating insight and iron resolve of Julius Caesar, there was found, at last, a power of destruction equal to the task . . ." [148] Other writers have expressed the same thought in different ways. For example, Heitland says: "Rome as the corrupt mistress of a subject world had come to an end. Some one master, corrupt or not corrupt, was to rule the vast empire as an empire, with an eye to its well-being as a whole, were it only for his own interest. . . . Order and public prosperity rested on the control of the one strong master . . . and whoever put down senatorial misrule must become an autocrat, whether he wished it or not." [149] "A later generation might idealize the republican system and ignore the corruption and iniquities that made it utterly intolerable in Caesar's time." [150] For the time being, as Mommsen puts it, "Caesar's work was necessary and salutary . . . because . . . absolute military monarchy was the copestone logically necessary and the least of evils." [151]

It may properly be asked whether this is not too simple a diagnosis and prescription for what was obviously a highly complex malady. History hardly supports the generalization that personal absolutism affords at all times and under all circumstances a sure remedy for civil disorder; there is ample evidence for maintaining the contrary, including the career of Caesar himself, which ended by plunging the Roman world into the worst and most devastating of all the civil wars that marked Rome's century of revolution. Nor can the senatorial government of Rome be fairly charged with sole or even main responsibility for the succession of civic upheavals between the rise of the Gracchi and the supremacy of Caesar. Most of the so-called "popular" measures which the senate opposed during that period were neither sound economically nor socially justifiable. This was true of the programs of the Gracchi themselves, of Saturninus and Glaucia, of Sulpicius, Marius and Cinna; and, if force was frequently resorted to, it was because force could be met only with force. The senate may perhaps be blamed for not discovering a sound and constructive solution for the great evils that undoubtedly existed, but it must be remembered that the "popular" leaders, including Caesar himself, succeeded no better in discovering a solution, and that in the end the problem of the Roman and Italian proletariat was solved, if solution it can be called, by simply forgetting it and acquiescing in the conditions which had originally been thought to constitute the problem. Doubtless the senate was wrong in resisting the demand of the Italians for enfranchisement, but in that instance it was acting in entire accord with the "popular" party and deserves credit for ending the crisis by a timely and sensible compromise. In the main, what the senate stood out against was imperialist aggression abroad and the unsound domestic policy which ultimately triumphed under popular pressure—that of making the proletariat of the city of Rome state pensioners at the expense of the inhabitants of the provinces. At the same time, the senate exerted itself to maintain law and order against the attempts of irresponsible and unworthy intriguers, like Lepidus and Catiline, to seize the government by force for selfish personal ends. Certainly it is hard to suppose that these plots, had they been successful, could have benefited the Roman lower classes or promoted social welfare in any useful way, and it is therefore hard to see how the senate can be blamed for opposing them.

The senate has also been blamed for using unconstitutional means in its opposition to so-called "popular" measures. This hardly affords a justification for Caesar, who disregarded the constitution at every turn when it served his purpose; but even so, that charge against the senate rests on grounds that cannot be regarded as substantial. The first of these is the condemnation of the Catilinarian conspirators, but this charge assumes that in a case of constitutional doubtfulness it is wrong to construe the constitution in such a way as to permit the state to defend itself against treason. The second ground is the opposition of a substantial part of the senatorial class to the restoration of the tribunes' power in 70 B.C. Aside from the fact that the senate made no effort to resist the restoration when it was finally carried by popular vote, the argument assumes that the powers of the tribunes as asserted by the Gracchi and the "popular" leaders who followed them were an essential and unalterable feature of the Roman constitution. Certainly experience had shown that those powers were not only capable of grave abuse but had persistently been employed to promote public disorder in the interest of unsound and inequitable policies. Under these circumstances it can hardly be treated as culpable for the senate to oppose the restoration of powers which had been employed for such purposes.

Although senatorial government cannot justly be made responsible for the civil disorders of the Roman state in the era between the Gracchi and Caesar, this does not, of course, mean that the senate did not include in that period a large proportion of unworthy, greedy and corrupt members who, when appointed to provincial governorships, followed the bent of their natures and scandalously oppressed the subject or allied communities committed to their charge. However, provincial corruption was no monopoly of the senatorial or conservative group, and the "popular" party can lay claim to a list of men of equal infamy, including Catiline, Pompey's henchman Gabinius, Caesar's father-in-law Piso and his retainer Vatinius. Similarly, Caesar's personal absolutism cannot be credited with the purpose or effect of purifying provincial administration or eliminating corrupt administrators; on the contrary, Caesar was responsible for the appointment of some of the worst governors in Roman history, Cassius Longinus in Spain and the historian Sallust in Africa.

It is hardly more than wishful thinking to conclude that corrupt provincial administration was a result of Roman republican government and could be corrected by the substitution of Caesar's absolutism. Historical observation no more supports the conclusion that honest provincial administration is to be expected from personal absolutism than it supports the conclusion that personal absolutism affords a guarantee against civil disorder. For several centuries before the worldwide expansion of the Roman republic there had been ample opportunity to observe the nature of provincial administration under the absolute rule of the Hellenistic monarchs, and, by way of comparison, a modern commentator by no means unfavorable to Caesar concludes that, when compared with the Hellenistic monarchies, the Roman system of the radiation of power from a republican city-state had proved a great success.[152] The history of the Roman republic for the century and a half following the war with Hannibal disproves the assertion that a city-state could not successfully govern an empire. Rome had done so with greater fairness and justice on the whole than the task had ever been performed before. If, a generation after Caesar, a still better system was finally to be founded by Augustus, under different circumstances and as a result of different necessities, this affords no ground for concluding that the personal absolutism of Julius Caesar was needed as a means of obtaining fairer and juster government for the provinces. The conclusive answer to such an argument is that it did not in fact do so.

If Caesar's destruction of the Roman republic cannot then be regarded as a great constructive achievement because of the iniquity and depravity of senatorial government, there remains the view that it must be so considered because the republic in any event was on the verge of collapsing and therefore needed to be overturned to make way for a stronger and more efficient governmental structure. On this view, to use Niebuhr's words, "Rome could no longer exist as a republic," [153] and Caesar's great service consisted in bringing about the inevitable without delay. This view has the merit, from the standpoint of Caesar's accomplishment, of throwing into the background the question of what new type of government he proposed to substitute and of emphasizing only the fact of impending collapse. However, it is obvious that the two questions cannot be kept altogether separate and that the reasons for regarding the collapse as inevitable must be studied to determine whether Caesar's destructive surgery was a sound remedy for the disease. This requires a brief review of the factors, most of which have already been discussed, which created friction and caused obstructions in the operation of the republican constitution and which in retrospect may be thought to justify Niebuhr's view that Rome could no longer exist as a republic.

If Cicero's premise is sound, that the senate was the mainspring of the republican mechanism although ultimate power resided in the people, the senate's attitude and course in one important respect must be held at least indirectly responsible for many of the ills of the Roman state from the time of the Gracchi down to Caesar's consulship in the year 59. This judgment does not relate to the senate's course with respect to domestic legislation or foreign policy, which in the main was sound and statesmanlike, but to the narrow and extreme social and political exclusiveness of the senatorial class toward the Roman knights or businessmen and the middle class generally. These non-senatorial families included most of the energetic members of the community, and the attitude of the senate consequently undermined senatorial government and strengthened the opposition to its leadership in two vital respects. First, it created a vigorous and aggressive concentration of opposition to the senate's policies on the part of the group at Rome which had the energy and initiative to rise in the world; second, it deprived the senate of the support for sound and cautious policies which the middle class of Rome and Italy could normally have been expected to supply. Senatorial opposition to middle-class participation in politics was one of the causes [154] which reduced the Roman electorate, the ultimate repository of political power, to the city mob of tumultuous artisans, freedmen's sons and state-supported paupers who could be swayed by the illusory promises of demagogues and organized for purposes of agitation and disorder.

During the first phase of the revolution, which lasted from the Gracchi to Sulla, the knights, bitter against the exclusiveness of the senate, made common cause, largely against their best interests, with the demagogues and the mob. From this alliance resulted not only a great deal of the opposition to sound senatorial policies during that period but also in great degree the bloody and ferocious civil upheavals with which the era was filled. The savage cautery of Sulla forever put an end to the alliance between the knights and the mob, and never after Sulla did the knights as a compact group support the agitation of demagogues. Thereafter they lapsed into apathy, and in the face of the continued exclusiveness of the nobility, the most ambitious and energetic members of the Roman community withdrew from politics, exerted themselves from time to time only to promote their private financial objectives, and as a group lost interest in and felt no loyalty toward a constitution under which they could not hope to influence policy. At the same time, the exclusion of the Italian middle classes from the assemblies on all save rare occasions left the Roman government after Sulla's time almost exclusively to the senatorial aristocracy and the mob, which stood face to face with no intervening buffer and with the power of the state divided between them. This was the condition of affairs during the twenty years from the abdication of Sulla to the first consulship of Caesar.

In those years, the senate and the electorate came to an unstable but mutually satisfactory *modus vivendi*. Against senatorial opposition the electorate asserted its position of supremacy by restoring the power of the tribunes, and the senate, yielding tactful recognition to its master, was content to rule by discreet management of the mob. This meant ward organization, personal intrigue and manipulation, and wholesale bribery, but both sides seem to have obtained in the main what they wanted. The danger of disturbance was from a different direction. The prevailing political apathy and indifference among the orderly elements of the community, combined with the general conduct of politics by manipulation and intrigue, induced bolder spirits to try their luck and trespass beyond the limits of conventionally accepted political methods. This explains the abortive plot of Autronius in 65 [155] and the conspiracy of Catiline two years later. In both these instances the reaction of the senate was remarkably sluggish and tardy; it seemed as if the responsible governing body of the state was reluctant to resist the seizure of the government by brute force. For this reluctance there were two obvious causes: first, the not discreditable aversion of a generation which had passed through a dreadful civil war to repeat the experience; second, the reluctance and timidity of men who had seen power pass from Sulla to Marius and from Cinna to Sulla in a short span of months to risk their position by opposing a potential ruler of Rome. There can be no doubt that across these years the memory of the horrors of civil war cast an evil shadow and that most senators of that time wished above all to be safe and to make the most of their existing position and opportunities by standing well with whoever might be the ruling power. However, in the course of the affair of Catiline, first Cicero and then Cato were able to kindle a burning fire of resolution and public spirit, and for the moment senators in sufficient numbers forgot to intrigue and temporize and took a bold and forthright stand for the preservation of the constitution. Cicero was not wrong in regarding his consulate as the high point of the last age of the republic. Almost immediately, however, the long shadow of Pompey fell across the senators' resolution and caused another period of hesitation.

It is customary to say that the collapse of the Roman republic was made inevitable by the so-called "great," or "extraordinary," military commands of which the career of Pompey affords the outstanding example. Through historical accident, the progressive stages of the Roman revolution occurred while a series of great defensive foreign wars was being conducted. Those wars, which required military exertions on an unprecedented scale, and which lasted with occasional intervals over forty years, gave new weight and importance to the military element in the state. The part which both Marius and Sulla were able to play in the revolutionary agitations of Roman politics was largely the result of their military position as commanders of the legions which gave them more or less permanent influence over great numbers of soldiers and veterans.

The dictatorship of Sulla halted civil strife for a generation but did not make more than a passing interruption in the succession of foreign wars. In the end, the Roman empire was held together through the military successes of four exceptional generals—Quintus Caceilius Metellus Pius, Crassus, Lucullus and Pompey. This was the period that witnessed the emergence of the so-called "great" or "extraordinary" commands, which are often said to have doomed the republic. Of these great commands, there were, properly speaking, only two in this era of the republic, and both were conferred on Pompey, the first for the suppression of the pirates and the second for the termination of the Mithridatic war. Metellus, Crassus and Lucullus commanded their armies like Roman generals of the era before Marius, by appointment, and under the direction, of the senate.

The Gabinian law of 68 and the Manilian law of the following year, both enacted in favor of Pompey, first created by vote of the people a military command to last for an extended period of years. There can be no doubt that such commands, and particularly their origin in popular vote, set a dangerous precedent. They pointed the way toward a more or less permanent military head of the state, independent of the regular governing body, the senate, who could, with the votes and support of a large body of veterans, maintain his position and achieve his purposes after the conclusion of his campaigns. The possibility of attaining such a post, with the power, prestige and material rewards which it promised, offered an additional incentive for electoral corruption and manipulation. It is important to note, however, that, after his first two extraordinary commands, Pompey made no attempt to use his position for the purpose of assuming a supreme place in the government. On the contrary, as explained in an earlier chapter,[156] he disbanded his troops and submitted his proceedings for ratification to the senate in the traditional manner. The latter body, without doubt keenly aware of the very great importance of maintaining its civilian control over military commanders, adopted an attitude of resistance to Pompey that was not only captious but, under the circumstances, distinctly unwise. The point which needs to be emphasized here, however, is that the senate was for the time being victorious. It was able to assert its supremacy over a general who had held an "extraordinary" command and achieved extraordinary military success. Pompey was effectively defeated until Caesar came to his rescue and showed him how the normal processes of the constitution could be subverted.

It was Caesar's consulship of the year 59 which from every point of view marks the turning point, the great divide, in the later history of the republic. Before that time there is little ground for maintaining that the Roman constitution had ceased to function, or that the republic was necessarily bound to fall. It was Caesar who, in his first consulship, created the conditions which are relied on by historians to show that the fall of the republic was inevitable. Caesar did this, first, by using his power as consul to dispense with meetings of the senate and, second, by governing with the support of the votes of the tribal assembly, guided and controlled by the mob of Clodius. No consul had ever done such things before, yet they had always been within the range of political and constitutional possibility. The Roman constitution had continued to function until the appearance of Caesar because of the respect for time-honored traditional usage and constitutional practice, because no Roman politician before had ever been willing to employ the powers of the consulship to bypass the senate and govern by direct popular action, and because no Roman consul had ever undertaken to control the action of the people by mob violence.

The consuls before Caesar had always undertaken to govern with the cooperation, if not always as ministers, of the senate. When the tribal assembly had been mobilized against the senate, it had always been by a tribune, not by a consul. Caesar in effect converted the consulship into a kind of tribunate, reenforced with the added powers of the consul over convoking the senate in session, and as a result he demonstrated how the senate could be excluded from the government. The senate, however, as has continually been pointed out, was the mainspring of the republican machine; with the senate eliminated, government was in the hands of the mob and of whoever could control the mob. It was this kind of republican government, introduced by Caesar himself, which could not function permanently, and whose fall was inevitable.

Similarly, it was Caesar's ingenuity that prevented the senate from regaining the power of which he had deprived it during his consulship. This he accomplished in two ways: first, by obtaining the election of subservient consuls for the following year, thereby leaving control of the mob, and therefore of the government, in the hands of his henchman Clodius; second, by rehabilitating Pompey and putting him in a position to employ the prestige and exert the influence which he enjoyed as the heritage of his "extraordinary" commands. So long as the senate had retained its traditional weight in the government, it had been able more than to counterbalance the influence of the holder of a great command; but, with the senate paralyzed, Pompey's stature immeasurably increased and afforded for the time being a cloak of prestige for the doings of Clodius. Meanwhile, Caesar clinched the situation by obtaining an "extraordinary" command for himself through initiating a war of conquest. The senate was thus caught between the two great military rivals for power, on the one hand, and the sovereign Roman mob, driven hither and yon by rival gangs, on the other. In these conditions its independence was reduced to a nullity. Under these circumstances it is not remarkable that the senate's morale, such as it was, went to pieces. A large number of the members sought only to save their skins and fortunes in the face of impending catastrophe, while bolder spirits saw no alternative but to try the desperate game of playing the rival dynasts one against the other. Such was republican government in the years between the conference of Lucca and the outbreak of the civil war, and obviously the collapse of such a government was predetermined. What needs to be remembered, however, is that this government which was doomed to fall was no longer the republican government as it had existed before Caesar's consulship: it was the government which eventuated from that consulship.

Accordingly, if Caesar's ultimate destruction of the republic is to be justified as a great constructive achievement because the fall of the republic was inevitable, we must not fail to note that the inevitability thus relied on to justify his achievement was largely of his own making. This is but another, though strikingly significant, instance of Caesar's ability to create the conditions of which he could take advantage. It may be that he destroyed the republic because it was doomed to fall; but it was doomed to fall because he had made its continuance impossible.

It goes without saying that Caesar could not have created conditions which doomed the republic if certain underlying factors had not been present which offered him his opportunity. A mind less fertile would almost certainly have failed to apprehend these factors or to discover the possibilities which they afforded. Before Caesar's consulate there was nothing which made it inherently impossible that senatorial government as it then existed might not have continued to function for many years, perhaps indefinitely, until someone else with a character and mind like Caesar's should make his appearance on the stage of Roman politics. For all its weaknesses, it was the senate that had suppressed Catiline and checkmated Pompey. The balance between senate and electorate, described above, was doubtless unstable and insecure but might have long maintained itself. This instability and insecurity were the result of causes which Caesar apprehended and knew how to exploit for his purposes. He had the insight to divine the true roots of the instability of the republic, and he was therefore able to overturn it.

The basic causes of the instability of the republican government were two, and Cicero no less clearly than Caesar diagnosed them both. The first is what Cicero so frequently harps on as loss of personal character, or lack of character, on the part of the members of the senate and of the electorate as well. On the part of the senate, the lack of personal character in too many members of the governing body had imperceptibly evolved from an origin that was by no means entirely bad in itself, namely, the spirit of exclusiveness of the senatorial class. Such a spirit on the part of a class traditionally endowed with superior opportunities for culture, sound taste and proper behavior, and at the same time traditionally vested with responsibility for public service and the welfare of others, far from being evil may nurture and perpetuate a sense of values as well as preserve and develop the fruits of civilized living. Such a spirit becomes a vicious influence when, as too often happens, the privileged order loses its sense of responsibility and insists on exclusiveness primarily for the purpose of monopolizing material advantages and enjoyments, and when it rejects the cooperation of able individuals born outside the charmed circle out of fear of having to share with them the emoluments of power. This is what happened to the senatorial class at Rome. The perversion of the aristocratic spirit caused a large number of senators to look on their political opportunities not as a challenge to service but as a source of profit, which led them not only to corrupt others but to allow themselves to be corrupted in the complacent assurance that they were thereby only collecting what was their due.

This irresponsible acquisitive spirit among the Roman senatorial nobility was intensified by two more or less accidental circumstances peculiar to the era of the revolution: first, the vast expansion of the Roman dominion as a result of the foreign wars of this period, and, second, the ferocity of the civil wars of the age of Marius and Sulla. The great foreign wars opened up unprecedented opportunities for exploitation and personal enrichment by political officeholding, which were too attractive for the weak human nature of many aristocrats to resist, and the standards of political behavior among the nobility sank lower as the prizes of political success mounted in value. At the same time, the experiences of the civil wars hardened men's hearts and consciences, as they had never been hardened before in any period of Roman history, to the violation of the ordinary decencies of human conduct. Wholesale murder, confiscation, theft, enrichment by betrayal of enemies, friends and relatives—these were for a time the order of the day. Men who had passed through such scenes were enured to practice, or at least to tolerate, self-seeking by methods which transgressed the normally permissible standards of conduct.

All this produced a profound cynicism on the part of Rome's governing class; or, if not cynicism, it at least produced a pervasive apathy toward, and toleration of, aggressive methods of self-aggrandizement which in earlier times would not have been allowable. Hence the remarkable sluggishness and inertia of the senate toward Lepidus, Verres, Autronius and Catiline; hence the difficulty which Cicero and Cato experienced in kindling any sense of alarm or any spirit of indignation against attacks on the constitution. The Roman senators as a class should have been vitally interested in preserving the constitution, which was the source of their influence and importance; but habituation to irregular and unlawful efforts to attain power, together with the desire of individual members of the aristocracy to maintain or enhance their wealth and position by private bargains and compromises, constantly tended to paralyze the senate as an effective governing body. Thus its morale and power to resist was weakened for Caesar to play upon. First, he shocked and intimidated the senate by excluding it from the government during his consulship and thereby frightened the timid with fear of losing their emoluments. Then he picked off and purchased the members who were willing to make deals with him at Lucca. When the senators finally awoke to what they had done to themselves and rallied around Pompey, it was too late. It was thus in large measure a failure of human character which, as Cicero perceived, finally brought about the end of senatorial government.

This failure of character on the part of the senate was accompanied, as Cicero also saw, by failure of character in the electorate. Cicero attributed this to imitation and placed all the blame on the nobility, but there were other causes besides. For several generations a substantial part of the Roman populace had not been able or willing to support themselves by their own labor, and since the time of Gaius Gracchus they had insisted on substantial food doles from the state. At first the senate fought this policy, but finally succumbed to the inevitable, and the grain dole became, as it ever afterwards remained, an unchallenged fixture in the Roman governmental system. The Roman populace, with its livelihood thus assured, ceased almost entirely to be interested in agitation for economic reform; its attitude toward politics became one of apathy, matching on a different level the apathy of the senate. One emotion, however, remained strong among the people and could always be counted on to furnish a certain amount of support for whoever appealed to it— a mood of resentment, jealousy and envy toward the senate, the envy of the class-conscious poor against the rich. In Caesar's time this envy was no longer a highly combustible political reagent, for in the main it was damped down by the sedative of the grain dole; but enough of it nonetheless remained to afford a source of excitement when discreetly inflamed. The Roman populace was content on the whole to play the political game for the same stakes as the senators, that is, for what they could get out of it. Generally, this took the form of bribes for their votes, measured by what the market would bear. In this way was achieved the rough adjustment or working arrangement by which the senate and electorate got on together and governed in unstable concert until Caesar took a firm hand in politics.

In the apathy of the voters and their unwillingness to participate in political action except for direct gain Caesar perceived an opportunity to introduce a new method, or rather restore an old one, for controlling the action of the assemblies, and particularly the tribal assembly. That was the method of rioting, street fighting and intimidation by gangs of thugs. It was cheaper than bribery and was also far more sure. Voters who could only be induced to come to the polls by the prospect of a bribe could be depended on to stay away if their attendance were at the risk of serious personal injury or even of their lives, and thus the voting body could be reduced to the few who would vote the way the master of the mob desired. This method of controlling the voting body by intimidation and violence had been tried and found successful during the agitations of the period before Sulla, but its obvious part in bringing on the horrors of the civil wars of Sulla's time had made senatorial leaders of the subsequent period reluctant to resort to it, and it had fallen into disuse for a generation. Caesar's revival of it had the effect of clearing the tribal assemblies of all except his followers, so long as he had the aid of the mob of Clodius. Meeting in the Forum as these bodies did, and requiring no quorum, it was easy to pack the narrow space with swordsmen and carry a measure by the few voters in attendance.

Caesar's example was contagious, and after the conference of Lucca, when his strategy was to foment discord between Pompey and the senate, he could safely rely on popular government to founder in the clash of rival gangs whose collisions turned the assemblies into a shambles. The effect of a decade of use of these methods was to confirm the populace of Rome in a distaste for the risks of participating in politics from which they never afterwards recovered. Peace-loving citizens henceforth preferred to stay at home and leave the forum to the rioting of unruly mobs.

Caesar's way of managing the electorate, like his way of managing the senate, was thus to play upon and use for his purposes the weaknesses of both. Their failure of character, of stamina, of public spirit, and of disinterested concern for the welfare of the community, the appetite of individuals for gain, or their apathy toward their public responsibilities, all were instruments he used in his rise to power. In short, he built upon the failure of Roman character as one of the foundations of his supremacy. Equally aware of the failure of Roman character, Cicero took an entirely different attitude toward the problem than did Caesar. However hopeless the task appeared to be, he concerned himself with suggestions for improvement by way of education, reform of social customs, dissemination of moral ideas and ideals. To the practical instrumentalist mind of Caesar such concern doubtless seemed fanciful and Utopian. He took the world as he found it and accepted Roman character as it was; his only interest was in discovering and making use of those traits which were available for his purposes. In so doing, he accentuated and helped to cultivate the vices of which he took advantage. He whetted the senators' lust for corrupt gain by the bribes he distributed and the opportunities he bestowed for unjust enrichment; he increased the timidity, apathy and subservience of the citizen body by driving it from the assemblies with armed force. No single individual ever did so much to lower and demoralize the tone and atmosphere of Roman public life.

If the first of the two underlying causes of the instability of the republic was the deterioration or failure of Roman character, the second was a related but broader one which was likewise diagnosed by Cicero—the disappearance of what he calls "concord" in the state.

This is a matter of living interest today in considering the plight of many of the nation-states of Western civilization, and in this connection it has elicited some wise remarks from Señor Ortega y Gasset in his little book of reflections on Cicero's *Republic*.[157] Señor Ortega observes that by "concord" Cicero does not mean mere agreement with respect to current subjects of controversy, or willingness to compromise about them, but a common underlying belief or faith in the institutions of the state and in the principles which they embody. Such faith can coexist with serious differences and contentions about matters of day-to-day policy, but it provides a substratum of common purpose and fellowship which makes the peaceful and satisfactory solution of those controversies possible. Without a substratum of such common faith the differences and disputes which inevitably arise in the course of current determinations of policy create a constant danger of disrupting the state to its foundations. The presence of this kind of faith operates to deter the parties to a controversy from going too far and from resorting to methods of conflict incompatible with the continued functioning of the state's institutions; its absence removes all restraints and encourages resort to methods that make orderly government impossible. Señor Ortega develops this thought as follows:

> . . . *Concord implies a firm and common belief regarding the exercise of supreme power.* . . . A belief must be distinguished from an accepted idea, a scientific truth, for instance. Ideas are open to discussion; they convince by virtue of reason; whereas a belief can neither be challenged nor, strictly speaking, defended. While we hold a belief, it constitutes the very reality in which we live and move and have our being. . . . Concord, that kind of concord which forms the foundation of stable society, presupposes that the community holds a firm and common, unquestionable and practically unquestioned belief, as to the exercise of supreme power. . . . For a society without such a belief has little chance of obtaining stability. Ideas, even great ones, may be improvised; not so beliefs. Beliefs, to be sure, begin as ideas. But in the process of slowly pervading the minds of the multitude they lose the character of ideas and establish themselves as "unquestionable realities." A belief, moreover, in a matter so intricate and stirring as the problem of rule cannot exist of itself. It must derive from more fundamental beliefs concerning human life and the reality of the universe. . . . Political una-

nimity implies more than an agreement on politics. However secondary political questions by themselves may be, they can be resolved only if agreement prevails in nonpolitical matters. . . . Man . . . will be lost in the arbitrary and boundless fancies of his mind if he is not able to contrast them with something truly and inescapably real. . . . When this reality, the one and only power that checks and disciplines man from within, vanishes because belief in it is slackening, the social domain falls prey to passions. The ensuing vacuum is filled by the gas of emotion. Everyone proclaims what best suits his interest, his whims, his intellectual manias.[158]

But if dissent affects the basic layers of common belief on which the solidarity of the social body lastly rests, then the state becomes a house divided, society dis-sociates. . . . And such precisely was the turn events were taking in the lifetime of Cicero's generation. What he beheld was not merely a struggle, if an uncommonly violent one, *within* the human setting that from time immemorial had been the Roman commonwealth, but the total destruction of that community. The state of mind accompanying such a situation has little to do with the motives underlying surface disagreements. These the citizen fights out with zest, nay with gusto. His adversary is not his deadly foe; friendship endures beneath hostility. . . . Above the contending parties there persist in full validity certain common circumstances to which they both can resort. These are dogmas about life and the universe, moral norms, legal principles, rules regulating the very forms of the struggle. Thus both sides feel that in their fight they are securely held and equally protected by one familiar world. While they fight, state and society stand firm around them.

But when all this has crumbled, when the state lies in ruins, when laws, norms, ideas have gone down with it, when parties find no common ground on which to meet—then a man may feel that he witnesses "the decay and dissolution of the whole universe—*si omnis hic mundus intereat et concidat.*[159]

What Señor Ortega, interpreting the thought of Cicero, here seems to say is that faith is necessary to the stability and permanence of a state—a widespread common faith in its constitution and institutions and, over and above these, in the basic way of life, the habits, customs, ideals and standards of values which they embody. Doubtless Señor Ortega expresses this thought somewhat too absolutely and dogmatically, for at all times and in every age the kind of faith of which he speaks is never all-pervasive and universally present throughout a community; it is a matter of degree. A state can tolerate absence of such faith on the part of a minority or minorities up to a certain point, but no further; it becomes unstable and its institutions are in danger of being overthrown when this kind of faith is no longer dominantly present among the elements which have the operation of those institutions in their keeping. This was a fundamental malady in the last age of the Roman republic, where there was a pervasive lack of vital faith and conviction in Rome's historic institutions among a large part of the senatorial class and of the electorate generally.

This absence of faith was an aspect of that apathy which has already been mentioned; it was in part a result of it, in part a cause. Naturally men of the senatorial class who had emerged from the civil wars of Sulla's time with no object but to be safe, and meanwhile to lay their hands on everything they could, had no vital faith in the republic. That faith was also lacking in an electorate whose principal interest in politics was to sell their votes and who justified themselves by thinking that their leaders were equally selfish, base and corrupt. In this way, apathy was a cause of failure of faith; in another way, it was a consequence and result.

Among the Roman upper class, one of the principal reasons for failure of faith was the emancipation of so many members of that class from the traditional Roman sense of values, or indeed from any sense of values whatever. This was quite generally the result of the abandonment of old habits which no longer accorded with conditions of life in a new age. Among the intellectually inclined it followed from exposure to the winds of conflicting doctrines that blew in every direction from the Greek world. Those intellectual influences had a powerful solvent effect: the skepticism of Carneades dissolved faith of every kind, whereas Epicureanism and Stoicism exalted the interests of the individual above the claims of community life. Doubtless only a minority of the Roman upper class were directly affected by these intellectual influences, but indirectly they created the mental atmosphere of the age. Roman senators who had never studied philosophy imbibed a sense of liberation and felt that it was old-fashioned and unmodish to display too strong an attachment to the ways and institutions of their fathers. Men who were steeped in their sort of sophistication lacked the will to resist an innovating movement of any kind that had accumulated force behind it and seemed likely to succeed.

Among the populace of the city of Rome who constituted the electorate in the age of Caesar lack of faith in Rome's institutions was partly a matter of their way of life and partly of their ethnic heritage. The Roman populace was by now largely made up of the descendants of freedmen, people of almost every nation and creed— Africans, Gauls and Spaniards, but in the main Eastern Greeks, Syrians, Jews and Egyptians who had no part or inheritance in the traditional institutions of Rome, no pride in them and no under- standing of them. Yet even among the lower-class population of Roman or Italian ancestry there was little evidence of such pride or understanding. For a number of generations the Roman populace, whether of native or foreign origin, had lived under circumstances as different as possible from those which had prevailed in the early republic. Then, the Roman people had consisted of hard-working farmers, who made their living by cultivating their small plots of land, who had a strong sense of private property, who were made aware by their daily circumstances of their participation in respon- sibility for the successful conduct of public affairs, and who brushed shoulder to shoulder with leaders who were farmers like themselves and lived in the main the same kind of life. Under such conditions the institutions of the republican state were accepted by the citizen body as part of the order of nature, part of the reality of their daily lives. They were features of the familiar world which stood fast around the individual and the family, and supplied mental and spiritual security in times of war and civic dissension.

All this was completely changed by the great revolution of life and manners which had been going on ever since the war with Hannibal when Rome had become involved in the affairs of the Mediterranean world. Now the Roman people were in the main an urban proletariat living huddled together in the crowded streets and alleys of a great city, looking for their livelihood not to their own efforts but to the bounty of government, feeling no responsi- bility to contribute to the common concerns of the state, and completely divorced physically and emotionally from their leaders, the senatorial nobility, whom they regarded with a mixture of cynicism, listless suspicion and jaundiced envy. Such a population had entirely lost touch with their political traditions; they had no understanding of the institutions of the republic and felt no loyalty toward them. They were ready to accept passively any change which could be made attractive to their desire for novelty, excitement and possible personal advantage.

With his bold insight into popular psychology, Caesar sensed the pervasive lack of loyalty to the republic among his contemporaries; he understood, as no other Roman except possibly his father-in-law Cinna had yet dared to understand, that he could attack its institutions with impunity and success. He accordingly did so and found, as he doubtless expected to find, that he met with only slight resistance and that the unstable fabric crumbled before him. All the barriers were absent which would have been supplied by a deep-seated faith in Rome's traditional institutions and by the emotional texture of loyalties and repugnancies, inhibitions and ideals which would have been present among a people characterized by true "concord" in the Ciceronian sense. For a long time it was a necessary element of Caesar's strategy to dissolve and disintegrate still further such concord and faith and loyalty to the constitution as still existed. He did so in every possible way, by appealing to the greed, ambition and spirit of self-aggrandizement of prominent individuals and to the desire of enterprising members of the middle classes to rise through his personal favor in defiance of established norms of conduct and orderly institutional arrangements. In this respect, again, Caesar's influence was that of a solvent, a destroyer. He destroyed not only the republic but the psychological basis of social unity on which the stability of a state necessarily depends. He promoted a kind of political chaos and centrifugality which could only be held together by his own strong hand.

When Caesar at last found himself in a position of unchallenged and unchallengeable personal supremacy, he had the insight and foresight to perceive that, if his government was to be more than a transient episode, it must rest on a more permanent and secure basis than military force exerted over cowed and indifferent subjects.

The evidence indicates that he sought to discover and establish some such basis; it also indicates that apparently the only one he was able to find that was consistent with the position he wished to hold and with his conception of the capacities of ordinary human nature was the deification of his own person as a god-king. This seems to provide the sole intelligible explanation of certain aspects of his policy after he had made good his supremacy by arms. Apparently he conceived that the faith in the republic which had so long served as the emotional substratum of Roman unity, and which had gradually waned until he had been able to destroy it, could be supplanted by a new emotional basis of unity in the form of the common and universal worship of his own godhead by his subjects. Such a common religious faith, if it could be achieved or imposed, would on this theory provide the bond of unity essential to the fundamental "concord" of the state; it would supply a new psychological basis for the new kind of personal government which he proposed to substitute for Rome's historic institutions.

A dispassionate description of this objective of Caesar's would be to say that he sought a basis for the psychological unity of the state in a form of mysticism. More than one civilization has lived for a time under the spell of a craving for miracle, mystery and authority. Caesar, who was an incomparable opportunist, seems to have been convinced by his own extraordinary career that he was living in such a time. He accordingly sought to substitute a new mystical basis of authority for the traditional sanctions of the old republic, but in so doing he both overestimated his own capacities and underestimated the cynicism and realism of the Latin mind. As one scholar has observed, the "world-spirit" which Caesar and some of his modern admirers believed that he embodied was too much a reflection from the languorous eyelashes of Cleopatra,[160] and so many Romans certainly regarded it. At the same time, many of the emotions which respond most sympathetically to mysticism and rebel most strongly against rational considerations always require the protection of cool rationalism for their survival; and this Caesar, intoxicated by his own grandeur and perhaps also by Cleopatra's influence, failed in the end to observe.

Caesar thus failed to provide a basis of "concord" for his new government of Rome, and because of this failure he did not establish anything that was lasting. His achievement must therefore be regarded, as already stated, as simply that of a great destroyer, the destroyer of much that was noble and valuable and of little that was contemptible and mean, for most of the contemptible and mean he preserved and perpetuated in his own new system of government. At the moment of his death he had built nothing, founded nothing, although he had created conditions which required the ultimate emergence of a new basis of political stability in the future. Thus he marks an end, not a beginning. As Mazzini wrote: "Caesar did fulfill a mission, but it was an unconscious one. . . . It was the same that was fulfilled at a later period by the conquering barbarians. . . . [He] did not . . . *initiate* . . . [he] concluded, an era."[161]

Caesar's failure to provide a new faith in his new government, a basis of psychological acceptance for his rule, a new kind of "concord" to supplant the old faith in the republic, was the measure of his ultimate failure in statesmanship and the fundamental reason for his downfall. He had nothing to put in the place of what he destroyed: he merely created a vacuum which it remained for the future to fill. Meanwhile, the only faith which remained at all, though reduced to a dying spark, was a modicum of faith in the republic which still persisted among some of the more tough-minded and resolute members of the nobility and was fanned into a momentary flame of resistance by the un-Roman acts and policies of Caesar in the last months of his life. For a moment the spirit of Cato came alive again and was able to destroy Caesar at the height of his power by inspiring the conspiracy which brought about his assassination.

NOTES

CHAPTER 6

1. Long, II, 254.
2. Cicero, *Leg.*, I, ii, 5.
3. C. T. Cruttwell, *A History of Roman Literature* (New York, 1878), 103–104.
4. *Id.* at 88.
5. *Supra,* pp. 138–140.
6. This conclusion is based on the reference to the death of Clodius as a recent event. Cicero, *Leg.*, II, xvii, 42.
7. Cicero, *Fam.*, IX, ii, 5.
8. E. G. Sihler, *Cicero of Arpinum* (New York, 1933), 293.
9. *Id.* at 432. See also Cicero, *Att.*, XVI, 11.
10. Cicero, *Rep.*, I, xxii, 36.
11. R. L. Conway, *Makers of Europe* (Cambridge, Mass., 1931), 30.
12. See generally, T. Zielinski, *Cicero im Wandel der Jahrhunderte* (Leipzig, 1908), 99–118.
13. *Supra,* pp. 116–119.
14. Cicero, *Rep.*, I, i, 1.
15. *Id.* at I, iii, 4.
16. *Id.* at I, v. 9.
17. *Id.* at I, vi, 10.
18. *Id.* at I, vi, 10–11.
19. *Id.* at I, xvii, 27.
20. Cicero, *Off.*, III, v, 25.
21. Cicero, *Rep.*, I, ii, 2.
22. Cicero, *Q.F.*, I, 1.
23. Cicero, *Rep.*, I, xxv, 39.
24. *Id.* at I, xxxii, 49.
25. *Id.* at III, xxxiii, 45.
26. *Id.* at I, xxv, 39.
27. *Id.* at I, xxxii, 49.

28. Cf. Aristotle, *Politics*, III, 6.

29. C. H. McIlwain, *The Growth of Political Thought in the West* (New York, 1932), 116.

30. J. J. Parker, "Liberty and Law: The Role of Law in a Free Society," *American Bar Association Journal*, XXXVI, 523 at 524 (1950).

31. Cicero, *Rep.*, I, xxxv, 55.

32. Cicero, *Oratio Pro A. Cluentio Habito*, ch. 53.

33. Cicero, *Rep.*, III, xxxi, 43.

34. Cicero, *Leg.*, III, i, 3.

35. *Id.* at III, v, 12.

36. *Ibid.*

37. Cicero, *Rep.*, I, xxvi, 42.

38. *Ibid.*

39. *Id.* at I, xxvi, 41.

40. Plato, *Statesman*, 301–303.

41. Aristotle, *Politics*, III, 7.

42. E. S. Shuckburgh, transl., *The Histories of Polybius* (London, 1889), VI, 7.

43. *Id.* at VI, 8–10.

44. Cicero, *Rep.*, I, xxviii, 44.

45. *Id.* at I, xlii, 65.

46. *Id.* at I, xliv, 68.

47. *Id.* at I, xxix, 45.

48. *Id.* at II, xxv, 45.

49. *Id.* at III, xxxi, 43.

50. Cicero, *Off.*, II, vii, 23.

51. Cicero, *Rep.*, II, xxiii, 43.

52. *Id.* at II, xxviii, 50.

53. *Id.* at II, xxvi, 48.

54. Cicero, *Fam.*, IX, 16.

55. Cicero, *Rep.*, III, xxxv, 47.

56. Cicero, *Off.*, III, vi, 32.

57. *Id.* at I, xxii, 76.

58. *Id.* at II, xii, 43.

59. Cicero, *Rep.*, I, xxxiv, 51.

60. *Id.* at I, xlii, 65.

61. *Id.* at III, xxxiii, 45.

62. *Id.* at I, xlii, 65.

63. Plato, *Republic*, III, 562–563.

64. Cicero, *Rep.*, I, xliv, 68.

65. *Id.* at II, xxii, 41.

66. *Id.* at II, xxxiii, 57.

67. *Id.* at I, xlv, 69.

68. *Id.* at I, xlvi, 70.
69. *Id.* at II, i, 2.
70. E. Coke, *Seventh Report,* 4a.
71. Cicero, *Rep.,* I, xix, 31.
72. *Id.* at I, xix, 32.
73. *Id.* at I, viii, 13.
74. *Id.* at II, i, 3.
75. *Id.* at II, xxix, 51.
76. *Id.* at II, xxv, 46.
77. *Ibid.*
78. *Id.* at II, xxix, 51.
79. By "Fathers" Cicero means the patrician senators.
80. Cicero, *Rep.,* II, xxxii, 56.
81. *Id.* at II, xxxiii, 57, 58.
82. *Id.* at II, xxxiv, 59.
83. *Id.* at II, xliii, 69.
84. Cicero, *Oratio Pro P. Sestio,* ch. 48.
85. Cicero, *Rep.,* II, xxii, 39.
86. *Id.* at II, xxii, 40.
87. *Id.* at VI, i, 1.
88. *Id.* at I, xxvii, 43.
89. *Id.* at I, xxxiv, 53.
90. Cicero, *Leg.,* III, vi, 15–16.
91. *Id.* at III, vii, 17.
92. *Id.* at III, viii, 19–ix, 22.
93. *Id.* at III, x, 23–25.
94. *Id.* at III, xi, 26.
95. Cicero, *Rep.,* I, xxxi, 47.
96. *Id.* at IV, viii, 8.
97. C. W. Keyes, "Original Elements in Cicero's Ideal Constitution," *American Journal of Philology,* XLII, 309 at 321 (1921).
98. Cicero, *Rep.,* II, xliii, 69.
99. *Id.* at I, xix, 32.
100. Cicero, *Off.,* III, vi, 26.
101. *Supra,* pp. 116–118.
102. Cicero, *Oratio Pro. P. Sestio,* ch. 45.
103. *Id.* at ch. 46.
104. *Id.* at ch. 47.
105. Cicero, *Off.,* I, xxv, 85–87.
106. Cicero, *Rep.,* II, xxxii, 56.
107. Cicero, *Oratio Pro P. Sestio,* ch. 65.
108. Cicero, *Leg.,* III, xii, 28.
109. How, "Cicero's Ideal in His *De Republica*," *The Journal of Roman Studies,* XX, 24 at 31 (1930).

110. Cicero, *Leg.,* III, xii, 26.
111. *Id.* at III, iii, 6.
112. How, *loc. cit. supra,* note 109 at 33.
113. *Ibid.*
114. Cicero, *Leg.,* III, xii, 27.
115. Cicero, *Oratio Pro P. Sestio,* ch. 65.
116. How, *loc. cit. supra,* note 109 at 33.
117. Sihler, *supra,* note 8 at 294.
118. *Supra,* pp. 117–118, 281.
119. Cicero, *Leg.,* III, xii, xiii, 29.
120. *Id.* at III, xiv, 32.
121. *Id.* at III, xiii, 30–xiv, 31.
122. *Id.* at III, xiii, 30.
123. Cicero, *Rep.,* I, xxxi, 47.
124. *Id.* at V, i, 2.
125. *Ibid.*
126. Cicero, *Leg.,* III, xiii, 29.
127. W. Windelband, *A History of Philosophy* (J. H. Tufts, transl., New York, 1901), 165.
128. Cicero, *Rep.,* II, xliv, 70.
129. *Id.* at III, ix, 16.
130. *Id.* at III, xv, 24.
131. *Id.* at III, xviii, 28.
132. *Id.* at III, xiii, 23.
133. *Id.* at III, viii, 13.
134. For these schools, see Windelband, *supra,* note 127 at 103.
135. Cicero, *Rep.,* III, viii, 13.
136. *Id.* at III, x, 17. This law of 169 B.C. limited women's rights of inheritance.
137. *Id.* at III, xi, 18.
138. *Ibid.*
139. *Ibid.*
140. Cicero, *Leg.,* I, v, 17.
141. *Id.* at I, x, 28.
142. *Id.* at I, x, 30.
143. *Id.* at I, vii, 22–23.
144. *Id.* at I, viii, 24.
145. *Id.* at I, viii, 25.
146. J. F. Dulles, "Thoughts on Soviet Foreign Policy and What to Do About It," *Life Magazine,* XX, 119–120 (June 10, 1946).
147. G. H. Sabine and S. B. Smith, transl., *On the Commonwealth* (Columbus, 1929), Introduction.
148. Windelband, *supra,* note 127 at 172.
149. *Id.* at 169.

150. *Id.* at 176.
151. Cicero, *Off.*, I, iv, 14.
152. Cicero, *Leg.*, I, xiii, 35.
153. *Id.* at I, xv, 43.
154. Cicero, *Rep.*, I, xxv, 39.
155. Cicero, *Off.*, I, xliv, 158.
156. *Id.* at II, iv, 15.
157. Cicero, *Leg.*, I, xii, 33.
158. *Id.* at I, vi, 19.
159. *Id.* at I, xviii, 48.
160. Cicero, *Off.*, I, iv, 11.
161. See *id.* at I, iv, 14.
162. Cicero, *Leg.*, I, vi, 18–19.
163. *Supra*, p. 293.
164. Cicero, *Leg.*, I, x, 28.
165. *Id.* at I, xvii, 47.
166. *Id.* at I, vi, 19.
167. *Id.* at I, v, 17.
168. *Id.* at II, iv, 10.
169. *Id.* at I, xv, 42.
170. *Id.* at I, xvi, 43–45.
171. *Id.* at I, xiv, 40–41.
172. *Id.* at II, vi, 14.
173. Cicero, *Rep.*, V, iv, 6.
174. Cicero, *Off.*, III, xvii, 69.
175. Cicero, *Leg.*, II, v, 11.
176. *Id.* at III, i, 2.
177. These were agrarian and grain laws of 99 and 100 B.C.
178. The grain law of 91 B.C.
179. Cicero, *Leg.*, II, v, 11–14.
180. *Supra*, p. 111.
181. Cicero, *Leg.*, III, iv, 11.
182. *Id.* at III, xix, 44.
183. Cicero, *Off.*, II, xii, 42.
184. *Id.* at I, v, 15.
185. *Id.* at I, vii, 20.
186. *Id.* at III, v, 23.
187. *Id.* at III, vi, 28.
188. *Id.* at I, v, 15.
189. *Id.* at I, vii, 23.
190. *Id.* at III, v, 21.
191. *Id.* at II, xxi, 73.
192. *Id.* at II, xxiv, 85.
193. *Ibid.*

194. *Id.* at II, xxii, 78.
195. *Id.* at II, xxii, 79–xxiii, 80.
196. *Id.* at II, xxiii, 83–84.
197. *Id.* at II, xxiv, 84.
198. *Id.* at II, xxi, 74.
199. Cicero, *Leg.*, II, viii, 19.
200. *Id.* at II, x, 26.
201. Cicero, *Rep.*, IV, x, 11–12.
202. Cicero, *Leg.*, I, xii, 33.
203. *Id.* at I, xi, 32.
204. Cicero, *Off.*, III, vi, 27–28.
205. *Id.* at III, xi, 47.
206. Cicero, *Rep.*, III, xxiv, 35.
207. Cicero, *Off.*, I, xi, 34–35.
208. *Id.* at I, xxiii, 80.
209. *Id.* at I, xii, 38.
210. *Id.* at I, xi, 35.
211. *Id.* at II, viii, 26–27.
212. Cicero, *Rep.*, III, xxix, 41
213. Cicero, *Off.*, II, viii, 27.
214. Cicero, *Rep.*, IV, vii, 7.
215. Cicero, *Off.*, III, xxii, 87–88.
216. *Id.* at III, viii, 36.
217. *Supra,* p. 310.
218. Cicero, *Leg.*, I, xi, 31, 32.
219. *Id.* at I, xi, 32.
220. Cicero, *Rep.*, IV, iii, 3.
221. *Id.* at V, i, 1.
222. *Id.* at IV, *passim.*
223. Cicero, *Q.F.*, III, 5, 1.
224. E. Meyer, *Caesars Monarchie und das Principat des Pompeius* (Stuttgart, 1919), 182 *et seq.*
225. R. Reitzenstein, "Die Idee des Principats bei Cicero und Augustus," *Nachrichten von der Königlichen Gesellschaft der Wissenschaft zu Göttingen* (Berlin, 1918), 399–436.
226. *Id.* at 414.
227. R. Heinze, "Cicero's 'Staat' als Politische Tendenzschrift," *Hermes,* LIX, 73–94 (1924).
228. See Cicero, *Oratio Pro C. Rabirio,* ch. 9.
229. Heinze, *loc. cit, supra,* note 227 at 75.
230. Cicero, *Rep.*, V, vi, 8.
231. *Id.* at VI, i, 1.
232. *Id.* at II, xlii, 69.
233. *Id.* at V, iv, 6.

234. *Id.* at VI.
235. Heinze, *loc. cit. supra,* note 227 at 91–93.
236. *Supra,* p. 276.
237. Cicero, *Rep.,* II, xxix, 51.
238. *Id.* at II, xxv, 46.
239. *Id.* at II, xxix, 51.
240. Heinze, *loc. cit. supra,* note 227 at 94.
241. *Supra,* p. 159.
242. Heinze, *loc. cit. supra,* note 227 at 80–81. Cf. also Cicero, *Att.,* VIII, 11, 1, where Cicero, after quoting a passage from the *Republic* in which he sketches the ideal character of the *rector* and *moderator,* goes on to say that such a conception never occurred to Pompey, least of all in the contest of 49 B.C. "Absolute power is what he and Caesar have sought; their aim has not been to secure the happiness and honor of the community." *Ibid.*

CHAPTER 7

1. *Supra,* pp. 57–58.
2. *Supra,* p. 187.
3. *Supra,* p. 75.
4. *Supra,* p. 203.
5. Mommsen, IV, 665.
6. See C. Merivale, *The Romans Under the Empire* (London, 1890), I, v; III, 10; E. L. White, *Why Rome Fell* (New York, 1927), 136.
7. T. Frank, *Roman Imperialism* (New York, 1914), 334.
8. W. Warde Fowler, *Julius Caesar* (New York, 1892), 242.
9. T. Rice Holmes, *Caesar's Conquest of Gaul* (London, 1899), xii.
10. J. A. Froude, *Caesar* (New York, n.d.), 549–550.
11. T. Arnold, *History of the Later Roman Commonwealth* (London, 1845), II, 110. See also *id.* at I, 542.
12. *Supra,* p. 51.
13. *Supra,* p. 236.
14. Montesquieu, *Considerations sur les Causes de la Grandeur des Romains et de Leur Decadence* (Edinburgh, 1751), ch. 13.
15. Mommsen, IV, 256.
16. Warde Fowler, *supra,* note 8 at 242.
17. *Id.* at 243.
18. Froude, *supra,* note 10 at 549.
19. *Supra,* p. 229.
20. *Supra, Ibid.*
21. Heitland, III, 341.
22. *Id.* at III, 324.
23. *Id.* at III, 293.
24. See Heitland, II, 202.

25. Suetonius, *Julius,* ch. 43.
26. *Id.* at ch. 42.
27. Heitland, III, 357.
28. *Supra,* p. 162.
29. *Cambridge Ancient History,* IX, 698.
30. *Supra,* p. 235.
31. *Cambridge Ancient History,* IX, 707.
32. *Id.* at 710.
33. Suetonius, *Julius,* ch. 42.
34. T. Frank, *A History of Rome* (New York, 1923), 312.
35. Heitland, III, 358.
36. L. R. Taylor, *Party Politics in the Age of Caesar* (Berkeley, 1949), 47.
37. *Id.* at 173.
38. E. von Herzog, *Geschichte und System der Römischen Staatsverfassung* (Leipzig, 1887), II, 2–3, note.
39. Mommsen, IV, 650–651.
40. Warde Fowler, *supra,* note 8 at 356.
41. J. S. Reid, *The Municipalities of the Roman Empire* (Cambridge, 1913), 132.
42. Herzog, *supra,* note 38 at II, 2–3, note.
43. Reid, *supra,* note 38 at 133.
44. E. G. Hardy, *Three Spanish Charters* (Oxford, 1912), ch. lxxvi of text.
45. Frank, *supra,* note 34 at 306.
46. J. Buchan, *Augustus* (Boston, 1937), 97.
47. Cf. Heitland, III, 358.
48. J. L. Strachan-Davidson, *Cicero and the Fall of the Roman Republic* (New York, 1894), 355.
49. Cicero, *Fam.,* VI, 10.
50. Cicero, *Pro M. Marcello,* ch. 9.
51. Long, V, 237, 306–307.
52. Heitland, III, 334–335.
53. Long, V, 368.
54. Heitland, III, 335.
55. Long, V, 368.
56. Heitland, III, 335.
57. *Id.* at III, 352–353.
58. *Id.* at III, 350.
59. *Id.* at III, 325.
60. *Id.* at III, 354–355, 362.
61. Cicero, *Fam.,* VII, 30.
62. *Id.* at IX, 7.
63. Heitland, III, 322.
64. *Id.* at III, 325, 327.

65. R. Syme, *The Roman Revolution* (Oxford, 1960), 50.

66. F. B. Marsh, *The Founding of the Roman Empire* (Austin, Tex., 1922), 152–153.

67. A. de Tocqueville, *L'Ancien Régime et la Révolution* (Paris, 1856), 16.

68. Heitland, III, 325.

69. *Id.* at 344.

70. Long, V, 420.

71. *Ibid.*

72. *Ibid.,* note.

73. *Ibid.*

74. Cicero, *Fam.,* IX, 15. Presumably "my friend" in this passage refers to Caesar, but otherwise probably to his agent Balbus. Cf. Chapter 1, note 46, *supra.*

75. Warde Fowler, *supra,* note 8 at 365–366.

76. Heitland, III, 337.

77. Mommsen, IV, 570–572.

78. *Id.* at 567.

79. Suetonius, *Julius,* ch. 77.

80. Warde Fowler, *supra,* note 8 at 336; Syme, *supra,* note 65 at 54–56.

81. *Cambridge Ancient History,* IX, 724.

82. Appian, *Bell. Civ.,* II, 106.

83. Heitland, III, 353.

84. L. R. Taylor, *The Divinity of the Roman Emperor* (Middletown, Conn., 1931), 66.

85. *Cambridge Ancient History,* IX, 722.

86. *Id.* at IX, 733.

87. T. Mommsen, *Römisches Staatsrecht,* II, 755 (Leipzig, 1887): "Da die förmliche Monarchie nach logischer Consequenz endweder von der sacralen Seite auf den König Eigenthümer hinführt."

88. Frank, *supra,* note 34 at 309–310.

89. *Supra,* p. 224.

90. Taylor, *supra,* note 84 at 63–64.

91. *Id.* at 74.

92. R. Lanciani, *The Ruins and Excavations of Ancient Rome* (Boston, 1897), 300.

93. Appian, *Bell. Civ.,* II, 102.

94. Taylor, *supra,* note 84 at 73–74.

95. Frank, *supra,* note 34 at 308.

96. *Cambridge Ancient History,* IX, 721.

97. *Id.* at 719.

98. Suetonius, *Julius,* ch. 76.

99. Taylor, *supra,* note 84 at 69.

100. Cicero, *Att.,* XIII, 44.

101. See W. G. Sumner, *Folkways* (Boston, 1907), 640.

102. H. C. Lea, *Superstition and Force* (Philadelphia, 1878), 21.

103. Appian, *Bell. Civ.*, II, 106.

104. Mommsen, IV, 564.

105. Taylor, *supra*, note 84 at 67, n. 24.

106. *Id.* at 10–11, 67.

107. Suetonius, *Julius*, ch. 84.

108. Appian, *Bell. Civ.*, II, 145.

109. *Cambridge Ancient History*, IX, 730.

110. *Id.* at 729.

111. Livy, III, 55.

112. Taylor, *supra*, note 36 at 174–175.

113. F. W. Maitland, *The Constitutional History of England* (Cambridge, 1908), 161.

114. Taylor, *supra*, note 36 at 163.

115. D. McFayden, *The History of the Title Imperator Under the Roman Empire* (Chicago, 1920), 2.

116. *Cambridge Ancient History*, IX, 728.

117. McFayden, *supra*, note 115 at 16.

118. Mommsen, IV, 561.

119. McFayden, *supra*, note 115 at 15–27; *Cambridge Ancient History*, IX, 728.

120. Dio Cassius, XLIV, 9.

121. Appian, *Bell. Civ.*, II, 108.

122. Cicero, *Off.*, III, xxi, 21, also quoted in Suetonius, *Julius*, ch. 30. The passage in the *Phoinissai* is at lines 524–525:
"εἴπερ γὰρ ἀδικεῖν χρή, τυραννίδος πέρι
κάλλιστον ἀδικεῖν."

123. Taylor, *supra*, note 36 at 175.

124. Appian, *Bell. Civ.*, II, 108.

125. Dio Cassius, XLIV, 11.

126. Plutarch, "Antony," *Lives*, V, 166.

127. Dio Cassius, XLIV, 11.

128. *Ibid.*

129. Heitland, III, 354.

130. Cicero, *Orationum Philippicarum Liber Tertiusdecimus*, ch. 19.

131. *Supra*, pp. 151–152.

132. See N. C. Debevoise, *A Political History of Parthia* (Chicago, 1938), 106–107.

133. Cicero, *Att.*, XIV, 9.

134. Ferrero, II, 282.

135. Dio Cassius, XLII, 49.

136. Frank, *supra*, note 7 at 343.

137. Suetonius, *Julius*, ch. 79; Ferrero, II, 300.

138. Ferrero, II, 298.

139. *Id.* at 301–302.

140. Debevoise, *supra*, note 132 at 106–107.

141. Long, V, 430–431.

142. *Cambridge Ancient History*, IX, 737.

143. *Id.* at 723.

144. *Id.* at 737–738.

145. Plutarch, "Caesar," *Lives*, IV, 321.

146. S. B. Platner, *The Topography and Monuments of Ancient Rome* (Boston, 1911), 375.

147. Long, V, 448.

148. R. S. Conway, *Makers of Modern Europe* (Cambridge, Mass., 1931), 10.

149. Heitland, III, 343, 350, 367.

150. *Id., A Short History of the Roman Republic* (Cambridge, 1911), 472.

151. Mommsen, IV, 557–558.

152. *Cambridge Ancient History*, IX, 723.

153. B. G. Niebuhr, *The History of Rome* (L. Schmitz, transl., London, 1844), II, 89.

154. Of course, the absence of any idea or mechanism of representative government was another and most important cause.

155. See Heitland, III, 72.

156. *Supra*, Chapter 1.

157. J. Ortega y Gasset, *Concord and Liberty* (H. Weyl, transl., New York, 1946).

158. *Id.* at 18–20.

159. *Id.* at 16–17.

160. E. G. Sihler, *Testimonium Animae* (New York, 1908), 380.

161. J. Mazzini, "On Caesarism," *Macmillan's Magazine*, XII, 259 at 264–265 (1865).